PELICAN BOOKS

STEERING THE ECONOMY

Samuel Brittan, after taking first class honours in Economics at Jesus College, Cambridge, started his career with the *Financial Times*. He was economics editor of the *Observer* from 1961 to 1964. He spent some time as an adviser at the Department of Economic Affairs, and then returned to the *Financial Times* as economics editor in 1966. His book, *The Treasury Under the Tories* (the first version of the present volume), was published in Pelicans in 1964. Mr Brittan has also written *Left or Right: The Bogus Dilemma* (1968) and *The Price of Economic Freedom: A Guide to Flexible Rates* (1970)

D1077898

To the Memory of my Mother

CONTENTS

Introduction to the revised Pelican edition   11

Part 1: THE TREASURY IN CONTEXT

1. *The Changing Whitehall Background*   23
Training and recruitment: pay and the career structure:
specialists and all-rounders: economists: the Civil Service
Department: Whitehall at work: Treasury characteristics:
ministers and officials: regularizing the 'irregulars': the
secrecy obsession: the crucial issues

2. *The Organization of Economic Policy*   67
Some Permanent Secretaries: the departmental structure:
Treasury organization: money and sterling: the role of the
Bank: international financial bodies: economists and fore-
casters: economic advisers: other institutions

3. *The Control of the Public Purse*   101
The basis of control: the five-year programmes: forward projection in practice: the size of the public sector: allocation
and efficiency: the distribution of income: appendix–the
nationalized industries

4. *The Budget and Monetary Policy*   128
The Budget: the tax structure: the fiscal balance: the money
supply

Part 2: ECONOMIC MANAGEMENT IN PRACTICE
Calendar of Events   171

5. *Achievements and Missed Opportunities:
from Dalton and Cripps to the 1959 Election*   179
Three Labour Chancellors: controls without a plan:
Labour's first wage freeze: Korean rearmament: the 1949

7

CONTENTS

devaluation: 'Butskellism': expansion under Butler: the Robot plan: the 1955 error: the economics of Stockton-on-Tees: Thorneycrofts I and II: a change of priorities: the PM's position: shelving the issues: kissing the rod

6. *The Reappraisal of the 1960s:*
   the Selwyn Lloyd Era, 1960–62   227
   The traumas of 1960: the effect of Selwyn Lloyd: the Treasury and the Common Market: the Brighton revolution: the new look for state industries: the search for regulators: the 1961 sterling crisis: the growth-rate controversy: an unfortunate Budget: reflation postponed: the departure of Selwyn Lloyd

7. *An Unfinished Experiment:*
   the Maudling Period, 1962–4   270
   Making haste slowly: does Nature move in leaps?: Mr Maudling's reflation: the £800m. deficit: an abortive Statement of Intent: Tory modernization

8. *Three Traumatic Years: the Labour Government,*
   1964 to the 1967 Devaluation   291
   Labour's economic philosophy: the initial phase: the collapse of confidence: the attack on the capital account: uncreative tensions: a Statement of Intent: the DEA's work: the first false dawn: the selective employment tax: blown off course: the July measures: the second false dawn: home-based expansion: a regional payroll subsidy: the beginning of the end: physical intervention–a last attempt: 'The centre cannot hold': the devaluation timetable: 'The pound in your pocket'

9. *The Approach to the 1970s*   367
   The argument about exchange rates: policy in a new era: the Washington gold agreement: the Basle sterling area arrangements: further traumas: the 1969 Budget: the nadir: the news of 12 June 1969: the mark saga: the Fund studies reform: the pre-election Budget: dawn, true or false?

CONTENTS

Part 3: ANALYSIS AND CONCLUSIONS

10. *The Lessons of Experience*   419

Welfare, reserves and living standards: 'underlying' performance: misplaced fundamentalism: the balance of payments: overseas spending: Britain's competitive position: sterling's international role: was policy destabilizing?: the pattern of stop–go: a constraint on growth?: demand and wages

11. *Concluding Thoughts*   468

The machinery of government: unemployment and inflation: automatic pilots: taxation: The EEC: a misguided orientation.

Index   495

INTRODUCTION TO THE
REVISED PELICAN EDITION

> ... every attempt
> Is a wholly new start, and a different kind of failure
> Because one has only learnt to get the better of words
> For the thing one no longer has to say, or the way in which
> One is no longer disposed to say it.
>
> T. S. ELIOT, *East Coker*

THE first version of this book was published as a Pelican entitled *The Treasury Under the Tories*, in 1964. A second, much revised and expanded edition was published in hardback form under the title *Steering the Economy: The Role of the Treasury* by Secker & Warburg in 1969. The present Pelican edition is the third and, I sincerely hope, last version of the enterprise.

All versions have had in common an attempt to explain aspects of the work of the Treasury, to discuss some recent historical events for the light they shed on the formation of policy, and to see what can be learned for the future conduct of affairs. The underlying assumption is that, although there are no simple 'lessons' to be derived from history, the discussion of political and economic problems is more rewarding if it can roam over a larger world of events than the point instant of the present. In so doing I hope to have provided something of a guide to the processes of economic management as they have developed in Britain.

The present version will have to be the last, because, apart from anything else, it will be impossible to go on adding further historical material without hopelessly overloading the volume. As it is, I have had to leave out in this edition the analytical summary of the Treasury's economic forecasting methods and the chapter on 'Indicative

Planning' (as well as the bibliography) in the hardback edition to make way for new sections in Chapter 4 on the fiscal balance and the money supply. (It will be interesting to see which version stands the test of time better.) The period now covered, from the early 1950s to the beginning of the 1970s, does have a natural unity. It begins with the aftermath of the first post-war devaluation and the Korean war, when the transition to a peacetime economy was at last complete. It ends at the opening of the 1970s after the second devaluation had been made effective, but when people were beginning to ask whether a repeat performance of the saga was about to begin. The Treasury too was once more 'under the Tories'. But the emergence of serious inflation as a problem in its own right, apart from its implications for the balance of payments, suggested that we might be entering a new phase.

The changes in content made since the first 1964 edition are too extensive to be listed here. But it might be worth mentioning a few of the changes since the second 1969 edition, which appeared under the present title *Steering the Economy*. The most obvious is that, instead of having to clutch at a few straws in the wind, I have been able to supply a complete Chapter 9 on events from the 1967 devaluation to the aftermath of the 1970 election. Chapter 11 'Concluding Thoughts' is largely new. This is not a summary of my policy views, and will be no use as a short-cut method of assimilating the book. It is, instead, more of a personal essay on some current problems and liable to date more quickly than the rest of the work. Some clarifications (especially in the devaluation chronology) have also been made in Chapter 8, which deals with the 1964–7 period, and in the analysis of Chapter 10 on 'The Lessons of Experience'.

Otherwise the main changes since the 1969 hardback edition have been in Part I dealing with the Treasury, Whitehall and the concepts of economic management. This is in many ways the most important part of the book, containing information not easily available elsewhere. If this volume is referred to at all by future historians, it will be for Part I. I have less hesitation than might be expected in making this point as a great deal of effort has been put into improving and updating the material by some of the most brilliant of the younger Treasury officials. They have done this with the utmost cheerfulness in the midst of many other duties, with the consent of their superiors, and in the full knowledge that their material was likely to be inextricably mixed with comments and interpretations of which they could not possibly approve, even in their capacity as personal friends.

*

I cannot pretend that if I were starting the whole enterprise today with the views I now hold, it would have taken exactly the same form, or even that I would have had the courage to attempt it at all. But as the book is meant to be of some current use to readers, I have had no misgivings in bringing the judgements, as well as the factual statements, up-to-date wherever possible.

A fairly large number of the judgements of the 1964 *Treasury Under the Tories* have been confirmed by events: others have been radically revised. I am naturally inclined to emphasize the former category, but am hardly the most impartial judge, and must leave it to any readers who may happen to have seen both volumes to make their own assessment.

The Treasury Under the Tories was regarded by some reviewers as strongly critical of the Treasury. But what I find most interesting, looking back on it now, is the extent to which it shared the Treasury outlook of the time. An obvious example was the concentration on fiscal rather than monetary policy, but this was not the most fundamental criticism of the earlier work. Monetary and fiscal policy are both *instruments* for regulating demand, and my main interest in all editions has been less in the instruments than the way they are used – a question which is all too rarely discussed in the more technical British literature on economic policy. My real main concern has been, not how to change demand by £*x*m., but *why* £*x*m. has been chosen rather than £*y*m., whether the choice has been correctly made, and what were the political and economic pressures which have made ministers intervene at certain times rather than others.

Much more important than any possible underestimation of monetary policy in earlier editions is that I no longer believe that – irrespective of the instruments used – the Treasury and other monetary authorities have the power to determine the exact degree of full employment and capacity utilization (or 'pressure of demand' as it is usually known) in the longer term. For a time they can push up economic activity on the lines explained in Part I of this book. But the ultimate effect of 'expansionist' demand policies is on the price level rather than on output and employment.

How long does it take for the long run to arrive? This will vary according to circumstances. If inflation has been proceeding at a moderate and fairly stable rate, as it was up to the middle 1960s, the 'temporary' effects on output and employment of demand-boosting policies can last a number of years before they are exhausted as a result of increased inflationary expectations. But at times when people are highly conscious of any signs of price acceleration, as they are at present, any temporary boost to output will be over much more quickly.

There is also an asymmetry between upward and downward movements of demand. Although expansionary demand policies may not be able to boost production for long, deflationary ones can easily cause prolonged stagnation. For, in the face of strong trade-union and other resistance to reductions in the growth of nominal wages and prices, deflationary measures first hit output and employment; and the effect on price movements is smaller and takes a long time to make itself felt. This 'new old' view of the working of the economic system was of course explained by Keynes long ago, in connection with the return to gold in the 1920s, and the Keynes of that period is probably much more relevant to current problems than the Keynes of the 1930s on which British post-war economics has been so largely based.

The difficulty of making quick downward adjustments in costs and prices, or their rate of increase, without adversely affecting output and employment, is the heart of the case for flexible exchange rates. Everything that was said on this subject in earlier editions has been reinforced by subsequent events. So too have the criticisms of the jerky and de-stabilizing character of much of British internal policy resulting from the balance of payments preoccupation of the authorities.

The 'new old' view of the effects of demand management, to which I have now moved, does not in fact rule out attempts to run the economy for a well-chosen period of, say, four or five years at a higher pressure than would be sustainable in the longer run. In the USA there may have been in the Kennedy–Johnson period a case for pushing unemployment below the 'natural' level in prevailing labour market conditions, to provide a breathing space and incentive for structural reform, or to improve the opportunities for Negroes and teenagers. In the UK a period of steadily rising demand, at slightly above trend levels, might in the early and middle 1960s, before the inflationary explosion of the end of the decade, have speeded up the underlying growth rate via its effects on expectations and business investment. Because of the devotion to an arbitrary exchange rate the experiment never had a chance, and we shall never know whether it could have worked.

My real policy error in 1964 was in the institutional sphere. I believed that the setting-up of the NEDC 'indicative-planning' machinery, and the nominal en-dorsement of the 4 per cent growth target, could have exercised valuable back-door pressures on official policy. On the contrary, the whole 'planning' movement was a bad tactical mistake which actively delayed the basic re-appraisal of the exchange rate and of other priorities desired by its adherents. The moral I would emphasize is that it is better for critics and reformers to argue for their beliefs directly and avoid getting caught up in fashionable causes of doubtful validity.

*

To prevent the volume from bursting its bindings completely, it has been necessary as in past editions to limit the field. The book is principally concerned with the Treasury's role as economic helmsman and makes no attempt to provide more than an outline guide to all the many other functions which that department has at different times undertaken. The chapter on the public sector concentrates on the determination of the broad totals of expenditure. A detailed analysis of the way in which the public sector is run and a discussion of how the taxpayer could get better value for money would require a separate book of a different kind.

The passage about which I feel most strongly at the time of going to press is, however, that entitled 'The Secrecy Obsession' starting on p. 60. But perhaps I can also draw attention to dissatisfaction with the Treasury definition of public expenditure expressed on pp. 111–17. I have risked a new definition of my own and have gone briefly into the logic of the present political debate on 'government spending versus tax cuts'. The discussion is taken up again in the concluding chapter.

An important omission is the lack of discussion of the international economic environment, which is a necessary complement to the studies here, but could not have been included without enlarging it to intolerable length. A good account and discussion of recent international financial events is to be found in Davidson and Weil's *The Gold War*[1], and there is an extended analysis of the issues in

1. Secker & Warburg, 1970.

Fred Hirsch's *Money International*.[2] Readers interested in the earlier history of the Treasury are recommended to read H. G. Roseveare's recent book[3] on the subject, which would form an excellent prelude.

Finally, it would be as well to warn readers new to the subject that they may find the later parts of both Chapters 3 and 4, Chapter 10 (after the initial section) and perhaps a few pages in the middle of Chapter 11, heavier going than the rest of the book, and they may prefer to leave them until last.

*

In the course of preparing three editions I have received so much kindness and help from so many people that full acknowledgement would require an essay to itself.

I must start with Sir Gordon Newton and the Hon. David Astor, editors of the *Financial Times* and the *Observer* respectively, not only for the generous time and facilities they have placed at my disposal, but also for the opportunity of watching the evolution of economic policy from such excellent observation posts.

The Treasury itself went out of its way to give me all the information it properly could. My thanks are particularly due to Sir William Armstrong and Sir Douglas Allen, Permanent Secretaries over the period of composition, who arranged this assistance and also the Treasury Information Division. Among the other officials who came to my aid special mention should be made of Robin Butler and David Walker, who bore the main burden of my detailed requests for information and cheerfully went out of their way to help whenever they legitimately could. All the assistance given by them, and everyone else occupying official positions, was confined to Part I of the book and was within the limits imposed by the bar against their dis-

2. Allen Lane The Penguin Press, 1969.

3. *The Treasury: The Evolution of a British Institution*, Allen Lane The Penguin Press, 1969.

cussing their advice to, or relations with, ministers. Even in Part I it formed part of my source material only; and the responsibility for statements of fact and for surmises, as well as for opinions expressed, is entirely my own.

I shall also always be grateful to Lord George-Brown, Sir Eric Roll and Sir Donald MacDougall, who were then respectively First Secretary, Permanent Secretary and Director General at the Department of Economic Affairs, for the opportunity to observe the working of policy-making in a practical way during my period as a temporary Civil Servant from November 1964 to January 1966. The section of the historical narrative covering that period is based entirely on published sources; and I hope readers will forgive the frequency of my references to them.

Among the many others who have most generously given me time, help and advice in one or more editions, I should mention Leon Brittan, Alan Day, M. H. Fisher, Charles Goodhart, David Hancock, David Henderson, Patrick Hutber, Peter Jay, Nigel Lawson and A. Shepherd.

The National Institute of Economic Social Research gave me a great deal of help with the statistical material. Mr George Fane, formerly of the Institute, carried out some computations. Mr Michael Artis, the editor of the Institute's *Economic Review*, and my colleague William Keegan kindly allowed me to read typescript copies of their chapters for the *1970 Annual Register*. The *Financial Times* library and the library of the Institute of Public Administration provided me with indispensable references. Miss Gritta Weil of the *Observer* also gave me important assistance.

I am grateful to *PEP*, *Crossbow*, the *Banker* and the *Journal of Common Market Studies* for allowing me to adapt some paragraphs in articles or pamphlets prepared for them. I must also thank Faber & Faber for permission to reproduce two quotations from T. S. Eliot's *Four Quartets*, and to Mr George Bull for permission to reproduce a quotation from his Penguin translation of *The Prince*.

Above all I must thank Mrs Anne Shotts who has now deciphered and typed so much manuscript that she almost ranks as co-author. Miss Anne Melson and Miss Janet Pearson were earlier pioneers in the field.

As the exact date of composition matters a great deal in a work of this kind, it is worth pointing out that the great bulk of the present revision was completed and sent to the publishers at the very beginning of 1970, but that some of the more topical sections were finished later on in the same year.

Part 1

THE TREASURY IN CONTEXT

Here is an infallible rule: a prince who is not himself wise cannot be well advised, unless he happens to put himself in the hands of one individual who looks after all his affairs and is an extremely shrewd man. In this case, he may well be given good advice, but he would not last long because the man who governs for him would soon deprive him of his state. But when seeking advice of more than one person a prince who is not himself wise will never get unanimity in his councils or be able to reconcile their views. Each councillor will consult his own interests; and the prince will not know how to correct or understand them. Things cannot be otherwise, since men will always do badly by you unless they are forced to be virtuous. So the conclusion is that good advice, whomever it comes from, depends on the shrewdness of the prince who seeks it, and not the shrewdness of the prince on good advice.

Machiavelli, *The Prince*
(Penguin edition, translated by George Bull)

I

THE CHANGING WHITEHALL
BACKGROUND

Training and recruitment: pay and the career structure:
specialists and all-rounders: economists: the Civil Service
Department: Whitehall at work: Treasury characteristics:
ministers and officials: regularizing the 'irregulars': the
secrecy obsession: the crucial issues

THE best introduction to the work of the Treasury is to
glance at the Civil Service of which it is part.

The Fulton Committee, which reported in 1968, began
its description with the words 'Civil Servants work in support of Ministers in their public and parliamentary duties.'[1]
This statement is deliberately open-ended. The work involves preparing programmes and advising on policy, drafting regulations or Parliamentary Answers and producing
briefs for ministerial speeches and conferences. There are
motorways to be planned, weapons systems to be designed,
and contracts to be placed. There are the less glamorous
jobs, such as collecting tax and running employment exchanges, which provide the public with its main impression
of the Civil Service at work.

These examples could be multiplied over many pages.
There is, however, an important distinction to be made at
the outset. The Fulton Committee remarked: 'Operating
policies embedded in existing legislation and implementing
policy decisions take up most of the time of most Civil
Servants.' While perfectly correct for the majority of
government departments, this is much less true of the
Treasury, most of whose work is concerned with policy of
one kind or another. The boundary line between the two
kinds of activity is, of course, a vague one. A Treasury

1. *The Civil Service*, Paras. 27 and 28, Cmnd 3638, 1968.

official who recommends a change in credit restrictions to prevent consumer spending from diverging from the Chancellor's intentions is indeed suggesting new measures; but, from another point of view, he is trying to enforce an existing policy. The expression 'economic management' indicates how blurred the distinction is.

Nevertheless, compared with other ministries the Treasury is clearly at the policy-making end of the spectrum. This characteristic became even more pronounced with the 1968 decision to hive off the responsibility for running the Civil Service onto a new department. For this reason, the emphasis in the following pages is more on the central policy-making function of the Civil Service than on managerial responsibility or contacts with the public

The total size of the non-industrial Home Civil Service (excluding the Post Office) amounted to about 480,000 in 1970. The Treasury accounted for a very small fraction of this number; its total staff is likely to fluctuate around 1,000, depending on the precise allocation of functions between economic departments. By contrast the Ministry of Defence had 110,000 and the Health and Social Security Department had a staff of 70,000 members. The Inland Revenue had about 70,000, the Department of Employment well over 30,000, the Ministry of Public Building, the Customs and Excise, and the Home Office had in the neighbourhood of 20,000 each, while even the Ministry of Transport had about 8,000. The smallness of the Treasury staff reflects, of course, its central policy-making functions and its relative lack of responsibility for detailed administration and casework. The number of officials in 'administrative' and 'economist' grades, on whom responsibility for policy largely falls, comes to around 200.

The Fulton Committee reporting in 1968 severely criticized the division of the Civil Service into a great many classes, both vertically between levels, and horizontally between different areas of work. The three main non-specialist grades were known as Administrative, Executive, and Clerical. This was a rather confusing nomenclature, as much of the real administration was done by Executive Officers, while Administrative Civil Servants were responsible for advising ministers on policy.

It is clearly impossible to run an organization such as the Civil Service on a basis of spurious equality; and however much names are altered there always will be a group of people occupying higher-level posts whose identity will be perfectly obvious to those around them. There were, however, cogent arguments against the particular system of classes which grew up in the Civil Service.

To begin with there were far too many different 'classes'. There were in 1968 47 general-service classes, whose members were distributed over the Civil Service, and over 1,400 classes confined to particular departments. In many cases, particularly in the scientific and technical grades, it was extremely difficult to say what the exact difference was between them. Perhaps the worst single result of the system was that they encouraged restrictive practices. Certain posts were regarded as reserved for certain classes, and staff associations fought tenaciously for the preservation of their particular territories. Accountants, for example, were prevented from working on financial forecasting and control, or O and M operations, because those functions were the preserve of other classes.[2]

Another defect was 'parallel hierarchies', with Administrators reporting to Administrators, scientists to scientists, and economists to economists. This made it very difficult to put one man in charge of a project and allocate responsibility according to the needs of the job in hand. Even more serious, it assumed that jobs fell neatly into rigid categories, instead of calling for varying combinations of skills for which the right individual should be found irrespective of label.

Within particular classes promotion was normally based on the criterion that a man must be fit to carry out *all* the jobs which might be assigned to his class at the higher level.

2. Fulton Report, Para. 209.

Such a system of promotion handicaps those who might have something important to contribute in a narrower range of activities, while it benefits the man who is competent over the whole range but not necessarily very inspired in any part of it. An earlier inquiry, the Priestley Royal Commission of 1955, summarized rather well the qualities required in an Administrative class Civil Servant as the capacity 'in an unusual degree' to 'master and marshal detail in many different fields at different times, to interpret effectively the ideas and policies of others, and to operate a complex administrative machine. It is rare to find these qualities in balanced proportion in one individual.' It is probably a mistake to insist on seeking the combination.

The Fulton Committee recommended a unified system and with the higher posts open to all, irrespective of the route by which they had come. The abolition of all classes was accepted by the government and it was hoped to make a beginning by merging the Administrative, Executive and Clerical classes early in 1971. But it would be wrong to suppose that the mere replacement of one hierarchical system by another, however improved, will automatically remove the defects endemic to large organizations, in which it is always difficult to tailor jobs to individuals. Although the 'job evaluation' so warmly recommended by Fulton is a step in the right direction, it will not solve the problem in many of the higher posts, where both qualities required and the merits of particular individuals are likely to be matters of keen controversy.

Fulton indeed missed one obvious reform, which would probably make more practical difference than the abolition of classes. This would be to unify the Home and the Overseas Civil Services. The case for unification is particularly strong now that the commercial and economic aspects of diplomatic work are so heavily emphasized. Under present arrangements these tasks are bound to seem chores which few diplomats can carry out with first-hand knowledge. Equally, officials in home departments too often have to speculate, with no real background understanding, about the overseas implications of British policies. Such a unification would widen the horizon of both branches and would have a genuine effect on *social* class barriers in the one area of Whitehall where they still exist. The very ferocity with which the proposal is so often resisted shows how near the bone it reaches.

TRAINING AND RECRUITMENT

The Administrative class of the Home Civil Service was always only a tiny fraction of the total, and numbered nearly 3,000 in 1970. As there is bound to be an élite group, its characteristics are worth examining even though the name is to disappear.

Contrary to the impression conveyed by the word 'class', about 40 per cent of the Administrators were promoted from the Executive grades. Of the post-war entrants who came direct from university, about a third probably attended grammar schools, a third came from direct-grant schools and a third from public schools. A survey suggested that about four fifths were first-generation university students. The graduate recruits did, however, have an overwhelmingly Oxbridge character. In 1968–9 some 60 per cent of successful graduates came from Oxford or Cambridge. This was a big drop compared with an 85 per cent average in 1957–62, but still a remarkably high proportion when one considers the relative numbers at different universities.

A sample of 1956 entrants were interviewed for the Fulton Committee ten years later, when they were nearly all Principals in their early 30s.[3] Some thirty-five answered the questionnaire, including a few who had left the Service. The replies showed that only four out of thirty-five belonged to a London club. (The proportion would almost certainly

3. Memorandum, No. 2, 'Profile of a Profession', in *The Civil Service*, Vol. 3, (2), HMSO, 1968.

be higher among their seniors.) Eighteen were regular church-goers. Over half voted Labour at the 1966 election, and only a fifth Conservative. But it is unlikely that these young officials were immune to general political fashions; and it is probable that in earlier or later years the proportions would have been different, although not entirely reversed.

According to the survey, a number had family backgrounds which they felt were below the social class to which they felt they now belonged. As 'at work they often dealt with people of a higher social class than themselves', they regarded themselves as unattached to any particular group. The author of this study, Dr Richard Chapman, concluded that this was both pleasant and an advantage in their work. But the fact that about a third tried to avoid the subject, or were embarrassed by it, suggests that the situation was neither quite as happy nor as simple as that.

Why the provincial universities should do so badly is something of a mystery. It is difficult to imagine that the older universities, which cater for a very small proportion of the undergraduate population, are as good at skimming off the cream as the recruitment figures imply. The recruitment authorities are themselves worried by the trend, which can hardly be explained away by any social bias at the entrance interview. Redbrick competitors fared much worse than Oxbridge ones in the purely written qualifying examination. The Civil Service Commissioners have emphasized that 'the idea of a public service career is neither part of their family background nor a tradition in their universities'. This is borne out by the statistics. Not only is their success ratio dismal, but, far more significant, the number of Redbrick candidates is very small indeed in relation to their share in the university population.

Until about 1965 the Civil Service Commissioners used to complain that they were not getting enough candidates of the right quality; but the position later became a little easier, and by 1967 they were in fact able to recruit as many Assistant Principals as they needed. There were in the middle and late 1960s about 100 vacancies each year in the Administrative class and about nine times as many candidates. Following the Fulton recommendations, the Civil Service now hopes to increase the graduate intake in the non-specialist groups to reach a total of about 200 a year.

Among subjects studied at university by successful entrants classics no longer has the preponderance it once had. Its place seems largely to have been taken by history, which has accounted in recent years for about a third of all entrants. Not merely does economics account for a small proportion (including the Oxford PPE course), but even if one adds in the mathematical and scientific subjects the number whose degree course involved an ability to use figures intelligently, or even an aptitude for rigorous conceptual thinking, is relatively small.

The Fulton Committee made the very reasonable point that two sorts of expertise are required in a successful Civil Servant: practical knowledge of the government machine, and knowledge of the subject with which he is dealing. For too long all the emphasis was on the first requirement at the expense of the second. There is a real need to provide for people who will be dealing with complicated economic or social problems a theoretical framework on which they can hang their observations, but which they will not adopt uncritically. The theories of social science may not be up to much, but the home-made theorizing of 'practical men' on the same topics is even less adequate. Whitehall rightly rejected the Fulton Committee's idea of preference for 'relevant' undergraduate degrees. The way to provide this framework is by appropriate training after entry. It is impressive how much more quickly people can learn subjects outside school or university, when occupational pressures are substituted for the pedantries of teachers and examiners.

PAY AND THE CAREER STRUCTURE

The number and titles of the grades in the new Civil Service structure have not been decided at the time of going to press. It is therefore best to stick to the traditional titles for posts at various levels. The nature of the work will not change all that quickly; and for quite a time to come the old names will continue to mean more, even in Whitehall, than the new.

A new graduate recruit into the Administrative Civil Service normally started in a training grade, known as Assistant Principal, in which he might have stayed for about seven years. Some time in his late 20s he would become a Principal. Later on, at around the age of 40, he might have expected to become an Assistant Secretary, often the deputy head of a large division, or the head of a smaller one. (He might, if he were in the Treasury, for example, have been responsible for watching the finances of the nationalized transport industries and steel, with five Principals underneath him.) Most recruits into the Administrative class would have been expected to reach such a rank.

From then on age was less important and promotion depended on the normal combination of luck, merit and ability to please. The next grade was that known as Under Secretary, often the head of quite a large division. The occupant might be responsible for a whole area, for example Treasury policy towards all public enterprises. About half of those who reached this rank might have been expected to move on to the rank of Deputy Secretary or Permanent Secretary.

One change decided on early in 1970 was to abolish the Assistant Principal grade and substitute a broader training grade for both the enlarged graduate entry and the ablest non-graduates. After two to four years in the training grade a special fast stream is to be selected for a second training grade for early promotion, with prospects similar to Assistant Principal in the old régime.

As far as pay is concerned the level hitherto known as Assistant Secretary marks the parting of the ways. Up to this level, pay and conditions are intended to be broadly comparable to equivalent jobs outside. For the record, an Assistant Secretary's salary ranged from £4,045 to £5,200 per annum in early 1970, while a Principal's was in the £2,599 to £3,596 bracket. But such figures date quickly. The more important point is that they are brought into line every few years with what are regarded as equivalent business scales.

The levels corresponding to Assistant Secretary and above have been known as the Higher Civil Service. Fulton labelled the top grades of Under-Secretary and above 'The Senior Policy and Managerial Group'.

A Standing Advisory Committee on the Pay of the Higher Civil Service was in operation for a long time. Its Ninth report of 1969 recommended substantial increases at these levels. It suggested £6,750 for an Under-Secretary, £9,000 for a Deputy Secretary and £14,000 for a Permanent Secretary, and differential payment of £15,000 for the Heads of the Treasury and Civil Service Departments and Cabinet Secretary. The government accepted the recommendations and announced a policy of implementing them in stages. The increases were based on 'minimum standards of comparability' with 'the most senior positions beneath the Boards of large companies'. But there was no breach in the traditional doctrine that higher Civil Servants could not hope to match the financial rewards of top executives at boardroom level. A brilliant career in Whitehall is never likely to be the road to a fortune (at least while the person concerned remains in the public service); but the exact compromise to be drawn between what Professor Paul Samuelson has called 'good clean money' and 'bad dirty power'[4] is likely to remain con-

4. *Problems of the American Economy*, University of Athlone Press, 1962.

31

troversial and shift in different directions from time to time.

The unhappiest aspect of the hierarchy just described is the fifteen or twenty years which the ablest young men have had to endure before they could hope for promotion to Assistant Secretary level, and exert any real influence. This, probably more than pay as such, deterred some of the more adventurous and enterprising graduates and helps to account for the sense of frustration at being given too little responsibility noted by Fulton among the younger men. During the war the usual formalities were waived, and many officials were promoted while still very young, but the Civil Service too quickly lapsed back into a rigid seniority system.

Some 80 per cent of the young men and women who joined the Service as Assistant Principals in 1956 were still there ten years later. But seventeen out of twenty-eight who answered a question on the subject in the Fulton survey said they would consider leaving, and eight had actually applied for other jobs. Many taking part in the survey reported in 1966 that their work made only moderate demands on their ability. Of those who said it made great demands nearly all attributed these mainly to the time factor.

The Fulton Committee did indeed condemn the excessive emphasis on seniority in the middle and lower levels and recommended that the really able 'should be appointed to the equivalent of Assistant Secretary, and parallel ranks at an earlier age'. Unfortunately, the recommendation about faster promotion was vague in the extreme. There is a real risk that the bulk of the post-Fulton effort and energy may go into working out the intricacies of a unified set of grades, and thereby even increase the emphasis on seniority.

The traditional method of training Civil Service Administrators was 'learning on the job'. Whitehall was becoming increasingly dissatisfied with this approach long before Fulton. The real change of heart, especially in relation to economic studies, came with the opening of a

Centre for Administrative Studies in Regent's Park in 1963. This Centre, which inaugurated formal courses for Assistant Principals in economics and related subjects, was absorbed in 1970 into the new Civil Service College, set up on Fulton's recommendation. Unlike the Centre, which relied on temporary lecturers, the College is based on an established staff. It has taken over some of the training hitherto provided by individual departments and is providing residential seminars for senior officials. Its first Principal is Mr Eugene Grebenik, formerly professor of social studies at Leeds University. The former Civil Defence College at Sunningdale is already in use as the first residential centre. A building in London continues to be used as a non-residential teaching establishment; and a third residential centre is to be set up in Edinburgh. The College is to undertake research as well as teach. It may ultimately be open to selected students from outside the Civil Service.

The whole subject of Civil Service training is now under review. But even before the formal opening of the College, the amount of formal training had grown considerably. By 1969–70 Assistant Principals received a two-week numeracy course in their first year. This was followed in their third year by a twelve-week course in organization, staff management and the machinery of government. In their fifth year they all went on a much longer twenty-eight-week course. This covered aspects of economics, statistics and operational research most likely to be useful in government. At suitable stages the concepts were applied to areas such as the balance of payments, economic forecasting and growth. Short sections on the organization of industry (including visits to business firms) and on social administration were also included. Twenty-two of the twenty-eight weeks were common to all those attending. These were followed by alternative six-week courses of a more specialized kind, selected in the light of the work to which particular individuals were likely to be posted. In the initial year of the experiment the options were: project appraisal and control, international economics, industrial growth, environmental planning and administration. Two examination papers in economics and one in statistics were set.

Nobody would claim that those attending the economic courses became economists (nor would a first degree have accomplished this). But it did give those with the right basic aptitude an opportunity to become economically literate. On this side at least the training compared favourably with that available to Civil Service recruits in most other countries, including France.

The most important difference between the British and French systems of training Civil Servants is no longer in the amount of formal instruction, but on the practical side. During his first year at the École Nationale an aspirant to the French Civil Service is sent to assist one of the Prefects who represent the central government in a provincial centre. The psychological motive for sending him is not disguised. 'It is to give the student a complete break from all past associations and ideas, to force the metropolitan man to live in the provinces, and to bring him into contact with those parts of French society which, once started on his career, he will have no further chance to contact or explore.'[5] Yet in this area Fulton is surprisingly vague, simply saying that 'as many as possible' of the young entrants should spend a spell at places where they can meet individual members of the public, and should gain experience of work outside the Service. A different point rightly emphasized by Fulton is that the lack of familiarity with foreign languages is an increasing handicap in the Home Civil Service, but again there are no specific recommendations.

There was indeed a move in the mid 1960s to promote short-term interchange with industry for people at Principal level on two-year secondments. The Civil Service did, however, find it extremely difficult to spare good people for

5. Brian Chapman, *The Profession of Government*, Allen & Unwin, 1962, pp. 115–16. An account of the French, Swedish and American Civil Services is contained in an Appendix to Fulton.

such assignments. Fulton naturally advocated that this interchange should be increased; but this would only touch the surface of the problem. It is not healthy that practically all senior posts should be held by people whose whole career since their early 20s has been in Whitehall, and that it should be almost impossible to seek the best man for a particular post, irrespective of background. The infusion of new blood in the Second World War was generally regarded as a healthy experience; and several of the wartime 'late entrants' eventually rose to Permanent Secretary. The staleness which many students noted in the Civil Service in the 1950s was partly the result of the 'return to normal' as the war years receded.

The pendulum began to swing back in 1964 with a plan for late entry of Principals, under which about a dozen people per annum have been recruited in recent years. A scheme was also introduced for the late entry of Assistant Secretaries, but by the end of the decade it had produced perhaps half a dozen appointments in all. This was probably due to the very restrictive conditions, which allowed such appointments to be made only if the specific qualifications were not obtainable inside the Service.

Such restrictive practices – which officials would be quick to condemn in their briefs if found in the private sector – ought to have no place in a full-employment economy; and the Fulton Report advocated more outside recruitment at a senior level, although again it did not make specific suggestions. There is still food for thought in Professor Brian Chapman's suggestion that senior posts above Assistant Secretary level should be advertised as a matter of routine. This need not conflict with a career Civil Service, in the sense that all recruits who came up to a reasonable standard could still expect to stay on until retiring age; and the value of departmental experience would probably be sufficiently great to ensure that a good two thirds of the senior positions went to career Civil Servants. In any business organization most senior posts are filled from below, but existing staff have no exclusive prerogative; and there is nothing to prevent an approach being made to particularly attractive outsiders. This would seem a reasonable model for large organizations in both the public and private sector.

As a *quid pro quo* to make such changes acceptable there should be a faster promotion among career Civil Servants at all levels, which is in any case desirable on other grounds. A corollary is that a good many officials would reach their ceiling at an earlier age than in the past; and there would then be absolutely no reason why they should have to stay until retiring age. In a reformed Civil Service a good many officials would want to leave earlier, both in the category just mentioned, and among the highfliers who reached the top at an early age and wished to move to fresh pastures. One of the biggest barriers to mobility has been pension arrangements. This may be lessened by the new provisions for the preservation of pension rights for officials who leave before retirement age.

SPECIALISTS AND ALL-ROUNDERS

The Fulton Committee's denunciation of the philosophy of the 'amateur' (or 'generalist' or 'all-rounder') aroused a good deal of understandable resentment among the Civil Service. First of all it passed over too lightly the change of sentiment and practice which had already begun by the beginning of the 1960s. Secondly, it swallowed, without any pinch of salt whatever, the fashionable slogans about professionals versus amateurs. Of course more ideas and more expertise would always have been beneficial in Whitehall, but they are not necessarily the same thing as formal professional qualifications. The organized professions, such as law and medicine, with their rigid demarcations, examinations and entrenched conservatism, have not always, to put it mildly, been forces of enlightenment. Some of the worst Whitehall appointments have gone to officials with admirable paper qualifications and relevant experience who would have scored very highly in any Fulton-type appraisal.

Having said all this, it must be admitted that Fulton found some severe shortcomings in the level of expertise. This applied in particular to the frequency with which officials were removed from one job to another, often among entirely unrelated activities. The sample of Administrators (other than Assistant Principals) interviewed had spent on average 3·2 years in their last completed jobs. For Principals (who had to write many of the working papers) it was as little as 2·5. The result was that no sooner had someone really learned his job than he was getting ready to move to a new task. The average time-span of dealing with a problem was larger than the time spent by the Administrator in his post, and the knowledge of imminent transfer undoubtedly discouraged too large an involvement in background research (for example in investigating how other countries were tackling similar problems).

A specific example given in the Management Consultant Group's Report (which appears as Volume II of Fulton) was that of a Principal reviewing the investment programme of a nationalized industry. In the first annual cycle he was himself learning the elementary facts. The following year he could deal more confidently with the subject, but by then he would be under consideration for a move – 'just at the time when he would have acquired sufficient familiarity with the routine to permit him to enquire more deeply into such factors as the structure of industry, its standards of operating efficiency, its management and to apply analytical techniques.'[6] There is no real inconsistency between advocating a reduction of artificial organizational barriers between the Home and Overseas Civil Services, or between the Civil Service and the outside world, and wanting to keep people longer in particular posts.

6. Paragraph 69.

ECONOMISTS

Quite apart from the improvement in training of Administrative Civil Servants there was in the course of the 1960s an explosive increase in the employment of professional economists. When Sir Alec Cairncross took over as the government's Economic Adviser in 1961 there were about a dozen. By 1964 there were twenty-five, including six Economic Assistants; and the numbers had shot up to well over 150 by 1970.

Up to 1964 almost all Whitehall economists worked in the Treasury, and the remainder were mostly on secondment from that department. The real criticism to be made before 1964 concerned the absence of economists in other ministries that dealt more directly with the real world. For most of the preceding decades, departments such as the Board of Trade, the Ministry of Labour, the Revenue Departments, and the Ministries of Transport, Housing, and Aviation did not have a single economist professionally employed as such. The excessive concentration of analytical power on the problems of economic steering at the expense of industrial and social issues in the 1950s and early 60s provoked a predictable reaction in the other direction. Table 1 shows where the subsequent expansion was concentrated. (It includes 'Economic Assistants' but excludes 'Cadet Economists'.)

Few would argue that the distribution was optimal even then. The particular shape of the distribution shown in the table reflects in large measure the accident of the particular departments through which Mrs Barbara Castle passed (Overseas Development, Transport, and Employment and Productivity). It is possible that some or all of the economists at the Former Overseas Development Ministry will become the nucleus of a Foreign Office economic division.

A new Economist class, offering some of its members a permanent career, was established in 1965; but about 70 per cent of its members continued to be academics on temporary or contract appointment. At the beginning of the 1970s there were still some unresolved problems about the organization of Whitehall economists. One of them was their relation to statisticians, hitherto an entirely separate class, but often employed in related and overlapping work.

TABLE I

THE NUMBER OF ECONOMISTS IN
THE CIVIL SERVICE IN SPRING 1970

Treasury	50
Ministry of Transport*	39
Ministry of Technology†	27
Board of Trade†	27
Ministry of Overseas Development‡	23
Housing and Local Government*	7
Department of Employment and Productivity	6
Health and Social Security	4
Scottish and Welsh Departments	4
Foreign and Commonwealth Office‡	3
Ministry of Defence	2
Home Office	1
Civil Service Department	1
Cabinet Office	1
Inland Revenue	1

*, †, ‡ indicate departmental mergers in October 1970.

A great deal of the analysis of the current situation and of short-term prospects, which was performed in the Treasury by economists, was carried out by statisticians in the Board of Trade. There was a case for unifying the occupational groups – not to force all economists to be professional statisticians or vice versa, but to recognize the existence of a whole spectrum of different aptitudes, abilities and interests in this broad area, which could not be chopped into two convenient halves.

For the normal Civil Service Administrator, the Fulton idea is that he should have an area of special knowledge where he can have a fruitful dialogue with the professionals and make use of their contributions, without pretending to be one himself. This is surely a reasonable goal; in the economic sphere it has for some time been formulated in terms of Civil Servants being 'economically literate'. More generally, the types of special knowledge required are likely to be based on spheres of activity within departments. Work was still going on in 1970 on a detailed scheme, but the Fulton idea of a broad division into two spheres, economic-financial and social, looks (fortunately) unlikely to survive.

THE CIVIL SERVICE DEPARTMENT

The supervision of a rapidly changing Civil Service is going to be a formidable undertaking; and in 1968 the government accepted Fulton's recommendation that it should be taken away from the Treasury and given to a new Civil Service Department. The Civil Service Commission has become part of this department, while retaining complete independence on individual selection on which it is not responsible to ministers.

This was not as revolutionary as it sounded, as the former Pay and Management Sections of the Treasury, which were responsible for this work, had already become a distinct section of the Treasury under their own Permanent Secretary. There were also some arguments against a complete separation. As Chapter 3 will show, the best way of obtaining value for money in public expenditure is not by the scrutiny of the candle-ends, but by ensuring that departments are efficiently organized and use the most up-to-date techniques of financial appraisal. The public sector divisions of the Treasury may be less effective in this direction if they are separated from those concerned with the staffing and efficiency of departments. Another danger is that a purely Civil Service Department, which does not offer the prospect of early transfer to a Treasury division, may not seem a very attractive career for a really able Civil Servant.

The supporters of the new Ministry inside Whitehall would turn the last argument on its head. They maintain that for far too long 'establishment' work, including the old Pay and Management sides of the Treasury, was treated as a Cinderella activity, and that the glamour of a new Ministry with its attendant publicity was required to give the work a new impetus. The Cinderella-nature of the Management side of the Civil Service was not merely a matter of bad organizational planning in the abstract. The Principals in the Fulton inquiry felt keenly about the insensitivity and heavy-handedness of staff relations. One of them learned of a posting only by accidentally overhearing a telephone conversation of his Assistant Secretary in the office. 'Bad man-management' was far and away at the top of the list of features that the Principals disliked about the Civil Service. The Treasury's former Management side had a bad reputation here. Some of this unpopularity spilled over to the other side of the Treasury, and there was a widespread belief that it was unwise for any officials to become *persona non grata* with the Treasury as a whole, because of its role in Civil Service promotion. There were thus strong arguments for making a fresh start.

WHITEHALL AT WORK

The Civil Service Department will have a long haul ahead if it tries to change the unique working atmosphere which exists in the policy levels of Whitehall. As the Fulton Management Consultancy Group pointed out, this atmosphere results from the constitutional fusion of the politician and the state machine, which does not exist in most Continental countries. The Parliamentary Question and 'the minister's case' are always in the background. There is also the scrutiny of the Gladstonian Public Accounts Committee (discussed in Chapter 3), as well as of other Parliamentary bodies. Public accountability brings with it a constant awareness of public involvement even in many of the smallest of decisions and the likelihood of disproportionate publicity for the smallest of errors. Inevitably therefore records are kept in detail, decisions are taken at a higher level than on the surface appears to be necessary and negotiations and discussions leading to them are fully documented.[7]

The closeness of Civil Servants to ministers also leads to a degree of political consciousness far removed from the popular picture of super-bureaucrats above the battle.

These aspects are sometimes summarized as *the duty to 'protect' one's minister* in a governmental rather than party sense. (This is a fine distinction. Defending a minister from opposition attacks in the House of Commons is governmental; a constituency speech is 'party political', except if it is 'in the national interest' to prevent him going wrong on some point dear to the department.) A former Treasury Permanent Secretary, Lord Bridges, explained that some minister would get the praise and blame for all that Civil Servants did. This 'absence of responsibility' was perhaps 'responsible for the Civil Servant's highly developed sense of caution'. Lord Bridges also mentioned the official's 'vigilance in defence of his Minister. For this reason he was at times too unwilling to admit anything which looked like a defect and he wished to be certain that a decision made in a particular case would not be used as a lever for other concessions which might embarrass his Minister.' Lord Bridges regarded these faults as occupational maladies, like housemaid's knee.[8]

These pressures are aggravated by a tendency to emphasize procedures rather than policies and to develop a crisis mentality, grappling with an issue only when it becomes urgent. When officials negotiate with a foreign power on business groups at home, they are affected by similar influences. 'The important thing', in the words of one critical study, 'is to avoid concluding an agreement

7. Paragraph 23.
8. *Portrait of a Profession*, Cambridge, 1953.

which will lead to extensive criticism, rather than to register an outstanding success.' Such negotiations are characterized by a relative lack of personal involvement on the part of the Civil Servants participating. There are no direct bonuses for success or penalties for failure.[9]

Another characteristic of Whitehall work is the *proliferation of inter-departmental committees* and *ad hoc* working groups. Some 33 per cent of Administrators interviewed by the Fulton group spent a quarter *or more* of their time on such committee work. The philosophy that governs these committees was once labelled by Sir Burke Trend (who became Secretary to the Cabinet in 1962) as the *disposition to seek agreement*.[10] There is a working rule that every department affected, however remotely, by any change of policy should be consulted and an attempt made to 'carry it' before ideas are put to ministers.

One characteristic of Whitehall was labelled by Lord Bridges the *departmental point of view*. Out of each department's store of knowledge and experience, Lord Bridges wrote, a 'practical philosophy' took shape. Every Civil Servant going to a new job 'finds himself entrusted with this sort of inheritance'. The good official would 'improve' and 'mould' his inheritance, but 'it is something he will ignore at his peril'. It will take more than Fulton to sweep such philosophies away – not that it would be wholly desirable to do so.

Not surprisingly, an air of civilized scepticism is to be found in many parts of Whitehall. It is still regarded as inappropriate to show excessive enthusiasm for a new idea; and the words 'there is nothing new under the sun' seem to be written on the walls in invisible ink. It is unfortunate that many of the supposedly new ideas with which officials have had to cope have appeared to justify this scepticism up to the hilt. For 'scepticism' of the Whitehall variety is a

9. *The Administrators*, Fabian Tract 355, June 1964.
10. *International Bulletin of Social Sciences*, Vol. VIII, No. 2, UNESCO, 1955, p. 242.

very different animal from the Cartesian doubt of the philosophers, which questions old-established assumptions as a prelude to a new synthesis. British official scepticism is more often directed towards new, reforming ideas than towards accepted beliefs and is not necessarily a prelude to anything at all. The Fulton Committee was obviously unhappy about some of these well-known features of Whitehall life; but its search for reform was inhibited by its narrow – and narrowly interpreted – terms of reference.

The committee pointed out that 'O and M' staff were rarely above Executive Officer grade themselves, and this made it difficult for them to work at higher levels. Partly as a result they tended to focus on methods rather than organization, and hesitated to ask whether a job needed to be done at all. Fulton did recommend more 'accountable management'. In other words specific individuals, rather than committees, should be responsible for performance, which should be measured wherever possible. One now popular solution is to hive off operational or managerial activities – such as aircraft contracts or the paying out of social benefits – to independent agencies not under day-to-day Parliamentary and ministerial control. The nationalized industries might be a tentative model here; and the Post Office has already been set free in this way. The aim would be to have, as in Sweden, much smaller ministries, concerned more with policy than with detailed execution.

An interesting suggestion of Fulton's which Whitehall has been spending a long time considering, was that most departments should have a Senior Policy Adviser of at least Deputy Secretary rank with direct access to the minister. He would usually be a career Civil Servant with special knowledge of a particular field, although occasionally he might be brought in from outside. His main job would be to look beyond day-to-day issues, 'prepare for the future', and make sure that the research of his staff was not overlooked in current policy.

This proposal certainly points in the right direction. It was argued earlier in this chapter that it was a mistake to seek in one man the complete combination of qualities traditionally required in a good Civil Servant. At Permanent Secretary level, moreover, the sheer range of duties is too much for one man, however diverse his talents. Fulton lists four functions: advice to the minister; acting as managing director of the operations of his department; responsibility for its staff and organization; and personal responsibility as Accounting Officer for all departmental expenditure. Some regrouping is highly desirable, although it is likely to be strongly resisted in Whitehall where the mystique of the 'Permanent Secretary' is high.

One can, however, have reservations about the implied identification of the Policy Adviser with crystal-gazing and long-term research, which could easily be a recipe for impotence. In this respect it is all too reminiscent of the kind of thinking that led to the division of the long and the short term after 1964, between the Department of Economic Affairs and the Treasury. The trouble with the vogue for research and statistical investigation is that it can too easily be exploited by politicians or officials who want to avoid making difficult policy choices. It can in this form become just a modern version of the time-honoured expedient of setting up a committee. As Fulton conceded, the best division of labour at the top will have to be worked out experimentally, taking into account the personalities involved, including that of the minister himself.

The Treasury itself has long had a policy adviser of the kind suggested by Fulton in the shape of the chief economic adviser. The set-up has not, however, been ideal. The Treasury has a relatively small organization, but deals with urgent and important questions of national policy. In this particular case a suitably qualified Permanent Secretary should himself be the chief policy adviser. The job of running the organization, keeping the staff happy and advising on promotion ought perhaps to devolve on to another senior official, exclusively concerned with such matters.

TREASURY CHARACTERISTICS

Some of the characteristics which distinguish the Treasury from the rest of the Civil Service have been touched upon in the preceding pages. But it is extremely difficult to convey the distinguishing qualities of this institution without either crude caricature or unconvincing apologetics. Even those who have studied or worked closely with the Treasury for many years find it difficult to form definite conclusions, or even to verbalize adequately their impressions; and readers who persevere to the end of this volume will find no attempt at a total judgement on the department.

It is as well to bear the physical surroundings in mind. Until the war the Treasury was housed in a distinguished building more appropriate to its importance than to its traditions of frugality. This was William Kent's 'Treasury', built in 1737. It faces on to Whitehall, just on the left-hand side as one comes out of Downing Street. The rooms are lofty and elegant; the state rooms for ministers were once the best in Whitehall, and even the garrets used to be spacious by Whitehall standards. The Board Room, where the early Georges used to meet the Treasury Lords and where later Chancellors presided in lonely majesty, has been described as 'a model for all board rooms in proportions and furniture'.[11]

The older members of the Treasury look back nostalgically on Kent's building, which they had to leave after a wartime air-raid. Although its reconstruction has now been completed as part of the Downing Street scheme, it is no longer big enough for the present Treasury staff (which, small though it is, has multiplied many times over since the war). The old 'Treasury' now houses the Cabinet

11. A. J. D. Winnifrith, *Country Life*, 14 November 1957. This is a fascinating article, attractively illustrated.

Secretariat, whose members can walk through a passage to No. 10 Downing Street without once venturing out into the open air.

The Treasury itself now occupies a singularly charmless 1908 building known as the New Public Offices; one irreverent inmate now retired called it the mausoleum, but its most common title is simply the Great George Street Front. The exterior of the Great George Street Front has been described as a gentlemanly copy of the Italian style, which looks as though it had been designed by Inigo Jones when suffering from indigestion. The interior resembles a municipal hospital. One end of the building, containing the Ministry of Housing, faces Whitehall. The other end, overlooking St James's Park, has been used by a variety of departments and was given over in 1964–9 to the now de-funct Department of Economic Affairs. The Treasury is between the two in the long stretch looking out onto Great George Street and Parliament Square.

In assigning new entrants, Whitehall works on the as-sumption that the Treasury requires a high standard of intellectual sophistication. In pre-war days no one was appointed to the Treasury as his first post, but some came earlier to it than others. Today suitability is judged by performance in the entry competition. Senior Treasury officials have a better chance than most of their colleagues of being sent out to run another department as Permanent or Deputy Secretary. In 1968, of twenty-four posts of Per-manent Secretary rank which were outside the Treasury or Cabinet Office, ten were held by men with ten or more years' Treasury service (a qualification also enjoyed by the Cabinet Secretary himself).

The most highly regarded younger Treasury officials tend to circulate between the Treasury itself (where they will have done spells of duty in the private offices of ministers and senior officials) and the very small staff who make up the Cabinet Office and the Prime Minister's own band of personal secretaries. Mr Harold Wilson made efforts to reduce the Treasury role in the staffing of both of these other offices; and it is not yet clear whether the new Civil Service Department will continue to be part of the inner circle. Nevertheless, there is every sign that this nucleus which in a very real sense has been the centre of the government machine, will continue in being. The close personal contacts involved do have some use in short-circuiting a great deal of cumbersome and archaic protocol.

Despite these contacts, and a few personal friendships, Treasury officials do not see a great deal of each other socially in their own homes. A few senior officials, especially on the overseas side, have to attend a large number of official lunches and cocktail parties, mostly to meet foreign visitors and embassy representatives. But these officials are very much in a minority. A handful of the more senior Treasury men do come together for more informal and private dinner discussions at one or two dining groups, such as the Political Economy Club and the Tuesday Club, where they are joined by a few selected academics and business figures and one or two very senior financial journalists.

More important nowadays are the links with the independent National Institute of Economic and Social Research. The contacts here are of a different kind, and perhaps not quite so near summit level. Clearly the Treasury and the National Institute will not always have identical views either on the economic situation or on the appropriate policies, but the occasional well-publicized disagreements give a false impression. The whole argument is conducted like an eighteenth-century battle, with the commanders on each side on the friendliest of terms. Both sides use forecasting techniques first developed in the Economic Section of the Treasury, and interchange of staff is frequent. Indeed the National Institute's widely quoted quarterly *Review* emerged as a direct result of the desire of Sir Robert Hall, the government's economic adviser from 1947 to 1961, to have an independent check on the Treasury's forecasts. Allowing for all disagreements and frictions, the Treasury economists and the National Institute have more in common with each other than with any other group of laymen or economists in the whole of the country.

Another organization with which many Treasury men have connections is Nuffield College, Oxford, which specializes in politics, economics and social studies. The Warden, D. N. Chester, used to be editor of a journal, *Public Administration*, to which many Civil Servants contribute, and its Fellows have included men such as Sir Donald MacDougall, now Head of the Government Economic Service. Ministers and officials frequently come to dine at Nuffield, and Mr Heath, Mr Maudling, and Mr Callaghan have all been Visiting Fellows.

Members of the Treasury, like members of any large organization, discuss some of their thorniest problems at informal and unrecorded meetings; but these are to prepare the ground for more formal sessions and for papers to be submitted to the Chancellor or to Cabinet Committees. Such papers try to harmonize conflicting views as far as possible, before submission to ministers; and where different opinions have to be stated, no names are mentioned (with the possible exception of some of the senior economic advisers).

Papers for ministers are usually set out in a fairly simple, standardized form. If the subject is at all complex, there will often be a summary at the beginning, the adequacy of which may sometimes be open to question. Alternatively, the main paper will be kept short, and much of the information and analysis relegated to an appendix. Decisions are usually taken around the long thin table in the Chancellor's room. Nearly all such meetings are with high-level officials. In the Foreign Office the expert on a particular region is present as a matter of course at highly secret meetings and personally interrogated by the Foreign Secretary. Most recent Chancellors, by contrast, have not met the real specialists who have actually written the papers discussed around their table.

One special Treasury characteristic is that it *normally*

deals with the outside world through other Departments, which act as its eyes, ears and arms. If Treasury economists want to find out how business is feeling they must inquire through the regional officers of the departments responsible for industry, or through NEDC. If they want to make a suggestion to the coal industry they must go through the minister responsible. Even chairmen of nationalized industries have been known to complain that they can only approach the Treasury through intermediate ministries. Treasury officials are more likely (although the chances are not great) to visit Paris, Washington or Brussels in the course of their official duties than Newcastle, Liverpool or Glasgow. The Permanent Secretary and his immediate deputies might now and then see the leaders of the CBI, TUC or one or two very large firms; and there are more frequent encounters at business lunches and dinners. But most Treasury officials below this level see very little of industry or the City in the course of their professional duties.

As the Treasury is responsible for economy in government spending *it feels bound to set a parsimonious example in its own activities.* The normal office amenities enjoyed by executives in any medium-sized commercial firm are often lacking. Principals writing papers on high state policy have no proper secretarial assistance, apart from the use of a common typing-pool, and even have to correct their own carbons. The remarks in the Fulton Report (Appendix I) about the neglect of 'working environment' apply with considerable force to the Treasury. Anyone who has worked in the building will confirm Fulton's remarks about the shabby impression of many offices,[12] and the absurdity of senior officials 'keeping their personal towels and soap in a drawer of their desk and walking the corridor with them'.

More serious perhaps is a psychological atmosphere in which long hours of work, and a pressure of duties which give no adequate time for reflection, are seen as positive

12. A stricture that applies with even greater force to journalism.

virtues. When Mr Roy Jenkins became Chancellor he had the greatest difficulty in dissuading officials from working far into every evening as a matter of course. In this respect Treasury practice reflects in extreme form more general conditions in the Administrative ranks of the Civil Service. One of the complaints that emerged most strongly from the Fulton survey of Principals was excessive working hours, coupled with long journeys to and from work. Most of those interviewed were normally in the office from 9.45 a.m. to 7 p.m. and took home about five hours' work per week. But weeks of 55 hours in the office were not unusual; Private Secretaries expected to work a 60-hour week; and one Principal had worked 75 hours in Downing Street during the Rhodesian crisis. Many complained that they had little leisure time and that their circle of friends and interests had contracted. One wrote that the work was 'not a job but a way of life. It demands most of one's time and energy and this pressure is kept up so that one can see people becoming paler editions of themselves.' How far these rather worrying aspects reflect the disadvantages of metropolitan life for any ambitious young professional or businessman who cannot afford a house near his work, and how far they are a reflection on Whitehall, must be left for the reader to determine.

As far as the Treasury itself is concerned, its weaknesses arise directly from its virtues. One of them springs from the fact that it is a small organization of highly intelligent and sensitive individuals. As in most such organizations, members tend to be intensely loyal to each other and they will not query too deeply reports or recommendations which emanate from among their number, but have an instinctive reluctance to take seriously contributions from outside.

Added to this is a certain primness. Ministers below the rank of Chancellor are made to feel that they must show great diligence at the less attractive chores before they can be taken seriously. The Treasury insisted far longer than other departments on the constitutional fiction that it had no policies of its own, but was simply there to advise ministers. It takes the doctrine that everything is secret until it is publicly announced much more seriously than other departments or overseas governments with whom it may be negotiating, as a result of which the British case has too often been allowed to go by default (and British journalists have had to find out about it from overseas governments). Not surprisingly the Treasury's public relations have been appalling – perhaps an endearing fault in the second half of the twentieth century.

MINISTERS AND OFFICIALS

The relationship between ministers and Civil Servants, and the relative influences of the two groups on policy, is extremely difficult to state without distortion; and it is a topic that Fulton avoided as far as possible. The view that Civil Servants are pliant mind-readers, executing policies which they have had no say in making, has always been absurd. The opposite view, that senior officials blatantly urge one single course of action on minister after minister, is equally false, if stated in this crude form. The usual procedure, in the words of Sir Burke Trend, is to indicate 'both the range of possible decisions open to ministers and the probable consequences of adopting any one of these rather than any other'. An American observer, Professor Samuelson, remarks that 'it is all done in oh-so-subtle and pleasant a way as to make the minister feel that he is enjoying Hegelian freedom – that delicious freedom which represents the cheerful recognition of necessity'.[13]

The position, of course, varies with the personalities, and also with the departments involved. The Treasury deals in issues which are both more technical and more abstract than those of any other department. In this situation the dice are loaded against the conventional type of politician; and it is almost inevitable, as Lord Woolton remarked, that 'the Civil

13. *Problems of the American Economy.*

Servants in the Treasury should have a very large, if not dominant say'.[14]

One should not in this context overestimate the extent to which permanent Civil Servants are influenced by conscious views on policy. Like most other human beings, permanent officials want to get to the top in their jobs, and dislike avoidable complications and unpleasantness. They know they are judged not by their policy views, but by their ability to do a series of practical tasks, such as drafting reports on which committee members can agree, chairing difficult meetings, and above all else in getting documents 'cleared' quickly with all the many interested parties.

Much of this work is far more high-grade than the description would suggest, and calls for considerable finesse. Nevertheless, it is hardly surprising that shrewdness in matters of policy is only one of the qualities – and in itself neither sufficient nor necessary – required in a good Civil Servant. The sheer process of getting something out and agreed (or clearly disagreed) exerts a great pressure for orthodoxy and following precedent. The most valued man of all – as in other walks of life – is the one who can cope with a sudden flap.

One trouble is that officials at the top are too busy to think imaginatively about policy and are in fact dependent on policy papers originating in the middle or lower reaches of their departments. Yet all these lower officials are bound by the framework laid down from above. The net result is that policies change infrequently and slowly, and usually in response to, rather than in anticipation of, external disturbances. It is through institutional pressures of this kind, rather than ideological commitment, that characteristic Whitehall attitudes emerge.

Civil Servants are understandably irritated by any tendency to exaggerate their influence on government decisions. They are conscious of the futility of a head-on clash with strongly held political beliefs and prejudices, and are con-

14. Lord Woolton, *Memoirs*, Cassell, 1959.

scious of the many occasions in which their advice has been rejected. On peripheral matters, such as self-balancing changes in taxes and social-service charges, politicians are usually able to push through reforms which they think will please their supporters. On the major issues they may ignore the analysis presented to them and refuse to choose between alternatives. They may also prevaricate, or add verbal glosses; but the one thing they are rarely able to do, without expert assistance, is to question the analysis on which advice to them is based. Still less are they able to offer an intellectually credible alternative of their own. In the years preceding the 1967 devaluation, politicians interfered enough to prevent the Treasury policies from being carried out logically and consistently, but were not able to produce a substitute policy of their own.

It should be noted at this point that on many questions concerning foreign exchange markets and international finance the Treasury has itself often been dependent on the Bank of England's expertise, and has stood in the same relation to it as ministers normally do to departmental officials. Whereas the Treasury maintains the polite fiction of having no view other than the Chancellor's, this is not true of the Bank even in theory. In the last resort it has to obey his will; but, despite nationalization, it is an independent self-perpetuating entity with a distinctive viewpoint of its own. On issues like devaluation or exchange control it does not pretend to be impartial. It is professionally against them both.

The Bank of England has fewer inhibitions than Treasury officials about making its views public. The Governor's speeches occasionally criticize government policy with little attempt at concealment and frequently take sides in arguments over public policy. It is normally a good thing to bring policy arguments into the open instead of confining them to a closed circle. But the reason why the Governor of the Bank of England should have special privileges in this respect, denied to, say, the Permanent Secretaries of the Treasury and Department of Trade, has never been convincingly explained. The other unfortunate element is that ministers often feel it imprudent to answer the Governor, fearing that a criticism of the Bank of England would damage sterling; it probably would.

The appointment of ministers, especially Chancellors, who are at home in the arguments of their departments is, on balance, helpful. My own view is that there is no longer a place for a Chancellor who does not have a feeling for economic management. (The vague expression 'feeling' has been deliberately used, to signify something more than the normal front-bench politician can bring to the subject, but not necessarily amounting to academic or professional qualifications.)

Such appointments do not, however, solve all problems. A politician's life is utterly different from that of an academic specialist or official adviser; and he is unlikely to have the time or be in the mood for really rigorous study and analysis once he is in charge of a department. Considerable harm has resulted in some recent years from politicians in the highest positions who held exaggerated ideas of their own economic understanding.

REGULARIZING THE 'IRREGULARS'

It was against this background that the recruitment of a few special advisers, to be appointed directly by ministers, was widely recommended in the mid 60s and endorsed by the Fulton Committee in 1968. A small number of such appointments had in fact been made by Conservative ministers when they returned to office after 1951, but they did not become a pronounced feature of the Whitehall scene until Labour was elected in 1964. The experiment was continued by the Conservatives, when they returned to office in 1970, but with the emphasis more on business administrators than on academics.

It was probably Mr George Brown who first coined the

term 'irregular' for such appointees. In practice the distinction between 'regular' and 'irregular' was blurred at the edges. Some temporary Civil Servants recommended to incoming ministers might equally have been recruited by departments on purely professional grounds. Moreover, as time goes on, some irregulars become established, whether technically or in spirit.

One argument for the irregular is that, as he does not owe his appointment to the Civil Service heads and his place in the hierarchy is less closely defined, he ought to be in a better position to question accepted departmental attitudes at the vital stage before policy alternatives are presented to ministers. Outside critics, especially where the subject is technical rather than crudely political, have little opportunity of influencing policy in a specific way. Not having seen the confidential minutes of all meetings and not knowing the stage which departmental thinking has reached, they have little chance of making headway against a minister's official advisers. They can only hope to make an impact if they are taken into a department as antibodies and participate in the real discussions where a policy is made. (Many of the established Civil Servants who were originally most opposed to the new recruits came to regard them as a stimulating influence.)

The whole concept of irregular advisers, who were specially prominent in the economic field, came under a cloud as a result of the Wilson government's disappointing economic performance in its first few years of office. The argument about who was really to blame is never likely to be resolved, although the narrative in Chapter 8 should be of relevance. Whatever one's views on this historical episode, the very nature of much Civil Service work puts the irregular at a disadvantage. The scarcest commodity in Whitehall is information, and like all scarce commodities it is not freely exchanged. It is quite wrong to think that someone in another department (or even always in one's own) will give freely of his knowledge. Therefore those best able to find out what is really going on are off to a head start; and these are usually the established professionals.

Despite their pre-Fulton title, 'Administrative' Civil Servants in the central policy-making departments such as the Treasury are not, on the whole, responsible for the detailed execution of policy. For this they are dependent on the men-on-the-ground in departments such as the Inland Revenue, Customs and Excise, Department of Trade or Department of Social Security (or, in a different category, the Bank of England). The really successful policy-making Civil Servant is the one with the knack of getting these less glamorous departments to produce ideas of their own, or to envisage in outline schemes which fit the long-established working habits of these departments. Such qualities may be regarded as aspects of the more obvious, but all-important, knack of knowing what buttons to press to make things happen in Whitehall. Clearly these qualities are by their nature more likely to be found among regular Civil Servants.

While irregulars inevitably run with leaden boots in any race against professionals, the Labour government unnecessarily increased their handicaps in 1964 by putting the majority of them in newly created departments outside the traditional centres of power. Nearly all the industrial advisers seconded from leading management positions went initially to the Department of Economic Affairs, and afterwards to Technology. The Conservatives have tried the difficult compromise of basing the irregulars on the Civil Service Department and Cabinet Office. The results will take time to judge.

Another difficulty about using irregulars profitably is that they are on the whole a phenomenon of newly elected governments (or very occasionally new ministers). This timing is a misfortune, for irregulars come in when they and their ministers are very inexperienced. They would be more useful several years later when ministers have become part of the machine and their ideas have dried up. But that is just when lines of policy have already been established, when ministers have discovered the wavelengths on which career Civil Servants work, and least feel the need for outside stimulation.

The really questionable assumption once made by reformist literature (including the first Pelican edition of this book[15]) was that it would be desirable to strengthen the influence of politicians against officials. It really is doubtful if the day-to-day horizons and public relations obsessions of most ministers in any administration are any more worthy of reinforcement than the intellectual conservatism of senior officials. Indeed in some ways the greatest criticism of conventional Civil Servants is that they let ministers pursue too many ill-considered ideas, and do not sufficiently push forward unpalatable truths. Yet at the same time ministers are terribly in the hands of the Civil Servants for the analysis of problems, and the enumeration of practical policy alternatives. Such is the inwardness of the system that both these statements can be simultaneously true. Perhaps at the root of it all is the view of the Civil Servant as a Court eunuch who has his own special kind of influence but must not presume to argue with his ministerial overlord on equal terms.

The insulating mechanism is strengthened by the fact that a large number of the briefs put up to ministers are not advice on matters of policy at all, but defensive briefs for use in speeches, meetings, negotiations and even social occasions where ministers may come under fire. The job of any Civil Servant, regular or irregular, in writing such briefs is, like that of a barrister, to put up the best case he can for the client, whether he believes it himself or not – and with imagination it is possible to put up a good brief for almost any policy under the sun. The constant exposure of ministers to briefs of this kind encourages self-delusion, both on the strength of their case and on the degree of expert support it commands.

15. Published in 1964 under the title of *The Treasury Under the Tories 1951–64.*

Despite all these weaknesses, temporary personal advisers appointed by ministers are on balance desirable as the only practicable way of bringing fresh air into Whitehall in quantities or packages which have not been selected by the Civil Service itself.

Fulton recommended that 'irregular' appointments should be 'regularized' on the clear assumption that they are temporary and that the person concerned has no expectation of remaining when there is a change of minister. This is reasonable enough; but with the recent rate of ministerial turnover it may well be difficult to get good people to interrupt existing careers to take up such appointments. Fulton, however, made the wrong concession to traditional opinion in dismissing the idea that ministers should be served by a small personal *cabinet* on the French model. The virtue of such *cabinets*, which Fulton did not discuss at all, was that they would contain a mixture of regular and temporary officials, in proportions which would vary with the personality of the minister. Such *cabinets*, apart from providing useful policy forums for the minister, could widen the horizons of both types of official. The real knowledge about what is wrong with existing policies or institutions, and the most practical way of changing them, is often to be found not among outside academics but among the Young Turks within departments. Ministerial *cabinets* might provide them with an outlet for their energies (even if the selection were in the nature of a lottery) which they lack under a strictly hierarchical system. More generally, they would provide some, admittedly limited, way of promoting younger officials to policy-making positions and of avoiding the dead hand of the seniority system.

A permanent Civil Servant who became too closely identified with the *cabinet* of one minister might, it is true, find himself in an embarrassing position after a marked change of personality or political direction in his department. But such difficulties are not insuperable. There are posts, both in his own and in other departments, which would be less politically sensitive, to which he could be transferred. More fundamentally, an ambitious and energetic official who wants to by-pass some of the rungs in the normal career ladder and take personal policy initiatives cannot expect to enjoy the opportunities without running the risks.[16]

THE SECRECY OBSESSION

One Whitehall characteristic not so far discussed, but far and away the most unattractive, is the *obsession with secrecy*. This is partly due to the Official Secrets Act, which makes it a criminal offence for a Civil Servant to communicate any note, document, or information to any unauthorized person. But it is also rooted in the doctrine that ministers alone are responsible for policy and that the advice given to them is on a par with the secrets of the confessional.

For many years the economic forecasts which lay behind the Budget and other acts of economic intervention were closely guarded secrets. Mr Roy Jenkins's decision to publish in the 1968 Financial Statement a carefully abbreviated version was rightly hailed as a major step forward. So was his decision in 1969 to publish three-to-five-year projections of public expenditure which would be rolled forward every year. But what appeared was only the tip of the iceberg. Much of the analysis, argument and differences of view which lay behind the figures presented were concealed; and so was the continuing re-examination of the outlook that goes on between Budgets.

It is sometimes argued that certain economic predictions – for example, ones that indicate a worsening of the balance of payments – would affect foreign confidence adversely. But if Britain is heading for a payments deficit there will be no dearth of gloomy private forecasts for holders of

16. A somewhat fuller discussion of the lessons of the post-1964 irregulars can be found in my chapter of that title in *Policy-making in Britain* (edited by Richard Rose), Macmillan, 1969.

sterling to read. By keeping silent, Treasury officials may keep British MPs in the dark. They will not reassure those who matter in New York, Paris, Frankfurt, Zurich or the City of London. Even if they do succeed in glossing over the facts for a while, the public is likely to lose rather than gain from any increase in the ability of ministers to postpone decisions. Another objection is that a realistic prediction might differ from the government's professed aims. Forecast wage increases might be higher than ministers have publicly stated to be desirable. The fallacy behind such arguments is the belief that silence about a disagreeable prospect will help change it.

The Fulton Committee agreed that 'the administrative process is surrounded by too much secrecy'. It drew attention to the Swedish system under which the files of any administrative office are open to the Press and public unless declared secret on grounds of military security, good international relations or protection of individuals. Before policy is formulated in Sweden, a committee of inquiry is normally set up and its results published. This model could clearly not apply to some matters, for example a decision on Bank Rate. But the spirit behind the two systems is very different.

Here again Fulton suggested another inquiry. This presumably took place within the Civil Service Department and led to the publication in June 1969 of a thoroughly perverse and unsatisfactory White Paper, entitled 'Information and the Public Interest'. In a highly objectionable passage (Paragraphs 31–5) the White Paper defended the very wide scope of the Official Secrets Act – one unparalleled in other major Western countries – by pointing out that there 'could be no prosecution without the consent of the Attorney General'. It described this provision as a 'valuable and effective safeguard' against prosecutions not really necessary to protect 'national security or some other major public interest'.

The fact that this justification could be offered – and

attracted so little comment – was a sad reflection on the decline of belief in the rule of law and the elementary principles of a free society. A bad, and potentially totalitarian, law is justified by offering the protection of a particular individual – a member of the government and party politician. One can think of individuals who have held this post on whose protection one would not like to have relied. But this is not the real point. For the whole defence is a negation of the principle of a government of laws rather than of men.

In the most practical everyday terms there cannot be the slightest doubt that the existence of the Official Secrets Act affects the whole atmosphere of work in Whitehall. Anyone who doubts this should ask any acquaintance in a major policy-making ministry. Every new entrant goes through the ritual of signing the Act; and there is a horror among most officials of inadvertently mentioning some harmless fact or figure – even one whose disclosure would be helpful to his department – for fear that it may not already have been disclosed in an official statement or publication. There is no parallel between this and the normal requirements of commercial security imposed in private organizations – without threat of criminal prosecution – to which the White Paper refers. It was only when an official was sacked from the Department of Health and Social Security for criticizing under a pseudonym the administration of supplementary benefits, that it became known that the rules on the application of these benefits were then an Official Secret.[17]

The obsession with secrecy is harmful not only because it lowers the standard of public discussion, and prevents the real arguments which move Whitehall from being brought out into the open. Even more important is the creation of an inquisition atmosphere in the Civil Service

17. On this remarkable episode see 'Robert Odams RIP' by Robin Page, *Spectator*, 10 January 1970, and *Policy for Poverty*, I.E.A., 1970, pp. 34 and 82.

itself. Peter Jenkins once explained in the *Guardian* that when a newspaper reporter happens to hit the mark a 'leak procedure' is usually set in motion in which all officials with access to the information are interrogated directly, or through their superiors, on 'When did you last see your father?' lines. This practice has applied particularly to the central economic policy departments; and in periods of pathological ministerial preoccupation with security these have been an almost weekly occurrence. What makes the whole procedure particularly intolerable is that leaks often originate from ministers, or others in a relatively invulnerable position; and the leak procedure has all the appearance of a search for scapegoats.

The result is a working atmosphere in which a disproportionate amount of time is spent making sure one's door is locked, that nothing is left on one's desk, and that there is nothing in the wastepaper basket which a literal-minded security officer will not report as an offence. Despite frequent admonitions not to over-classify papers, the habit is endemic, at least in the economic policy departments. Very often a 'secret' classification on a paper is no more than a way of drawing attention to its importance; and a draft with no security marking has little chance of being taken seriously. It becomes more important to keep one's thoughts on policy confidential than to get them right.

Here is one of the main roots of the monastic isolation so often alleged of departments such as the Treasury. Whatever abstract encouragement may be given to the idea of the exchange of ideas with outsiders is more than offset by the need to avoid suspicion of 'having said too much'. This is best done by minimizing contacts. Such a system puts a premium on the type of official who is happy never to discuss his work once he has left the office, who makes a rigid division between his professional and personal life and whose intellectual interests are totally divorced from his main work. The system encourages not versatility, but compartmentalization, which is something different. An example was the period *after* the 1967 devaluation, when public ignorance and suspicion of government economic strategy was at its height; and where officials who could have helped to improve understanding were reduced to silence, lest they be accused of leaking some trivial piece of Whitehall guesswork.

In some areas of policy (of which the Budget is only the most notorious example) secrecy limits the exchange of information not only with the outside world but within departments. To safeguard security the smallest possible number of Civil Servants, whether regular or irregular, are brought in on many of the really key decisions; and a large number of officials, whose own work might have had a useful contribution to make to the discussion, are presented with a *fait accompli* arrived at during high-level huddles.

THE CRUCIAL ISSUES

Some of the grosser absurdities could be removed by the exercise of a sense of proportion and a sense of humour, and less devotion to the conspiracy theory of history by political leaders. Nevertheless, any major move towards more open government would soon come up against three constitutional conventions: the anonymity of Civil Servants, ministerial responsibility, and collective Cabinet responsibility. It is arguable that all three need drastic modification.

The importance of official advice to ministers remaining in all circumstances confidential is more often asserted than convincingly justified. Very often it is just an accident whether an outside committee, which publishes its report, or an inter-departmental committee, which does not, is appointed to advise a minister. The traditional argument for confidential reports was that officials could only give of their best if they could speak frankly and without fear of public attack. It is equally arguable that the quality of advice would improve if officials had more often to defend it against expert outside criticism, whether in Parliamentary Committees or more generally. Indeed some Civil Servants would positively welcome a chance to explain work which is so often buried from view, bowdlerized in ministerial statements or subject to ill-informed public criticism. The spirited counter-attack by some of the Treasury economic forecasters during the Select Committee Enquiry of 1966–7 was a foretaste of what could happen.

There must obviously be some limits to open government; it is not suggested that the Budget Committee should sit in public. But it is very doubtful if the right dividing line is between factual analysis and the policy advice which flows from it. Attempts to publish pieces of Whitehall analysis, with all hint of policy recommendation carefully removed, usually bear a castrated and intellectually impoverished look.

The real obstacle to more open processes often comes from ministers, anxious to preserve the myth that all policy originates with them, and that they alone can explain in public what their departments are doing. This myth becomes every day more difficult to maintain. With the proliferation of international and national economic organizations, officials are having to appear in public (or semi-public) more and more; and it becomes increasingly apparent that what they say is a mixture of their own professional analysis and the need to put the best face on ministerial policy. The old relationship between ministers and officials is disintegrating, but new principles of public accountability have still to be invented.

The most deeply rooted obstacle of all to more open government is probably the third convention: that of a plural executive, operating on the principle of collective responsibility. This convention also lies, incidentally, behind the excessive role of inter-departmental committees, and the difficulty of making one man clearly responsible for a project. For just as no minister has jurisdiction over any other minister, no official in one department can overrule an official in another; and in the last resort unresolved differences have to go right up to the Cabinet, or one of its Committees. If a greater amount of the analysis and advice coming to ministers were published, it would soon become apparent – as it does in the USA – that more than one view exists inside the government and that some ministers have in the end prevailed over others.

It is no accident that the Fulton Report was most disappointing in just those areas where reform would challenge hallowed principles and practices of the political system. These principles are not nearly as ancient as is often made out; and it is mainly since the First or sometimes even Second World War that they have hardened into dogmas. Not only do constitutional doctrines require re-examination. The same applies to some of the concepts of traditional politics, such as the stage battle between government and opposition, the belief clusters of the two main parties, and even the party system itself. To take the argument any further here would be to wander too far from the main subject of the book.[18] But it is in these directions, rather than the Civil Service as such, that reforming energies could now be much more profitably challenged. For it would be sad if this field were left to extremists or fanatics who correctly sense that something is wrong, but whose remedies would prove worse than the disease.

18. These subjects are analysed in my book *Left or Right: the Bogus Dilemma*, Secker & Warburg, 1968.

2

THE ORGANIZATION OF ECONOMIC POLICY

Some Permanent Secretaries: the departmental structure: Treasury organization: money and sterling: the role of the Bank: international financial bodies: economists and forecasters: economic advisers: other institutions

THE first job of all finance ministries all over the world is to raise money to finance government spending. Although the British Treasury is far too sophisticated to proclaim so *simpliste* a doctrine, it is, like all other finance ministries, still very much concerned to restrain government spending and combat tax proposals that threaten the revenue. Anyone trying to predict the Treasury's behaviour will do well to bear this in mind before plunging too deeply into the more sophisticated doctrines which the department proclaims and which also influence its activities.

One preliminary difficulty in outlining the work of the Treasury is that, because of its great age, it is one of the few Whitehall departments whose functions are not defined by statute. As a result, its powers and responsibilities have always been the subject of confusion and argument.

SOME PERMANENT SECRETARIES

For a large part of the twentieth century the Treasury's responsibility for running the Civil Service was a main preoccupation of its Permanent Secretaries and affected its whole ethos.[1] This was far and away the principal interest of Sir Warren Fisher, an unusual figure who was Permanent Secretary to the Treasury from 1919 to 1939. His main

1. For the historical background see Henry Roseveare, *The Treasury*, Allen Lane The Penguin Press, 1969.

object in life was a unified and, in practice, self-regulating Civil Service; and he would on occasion send out circulars about the four Crown Services, the Army, Navy, Air Force and the Civil Service. In Sir Horace Hamilton's authoritative biographical article[2] on Fisher there is not one reference to the great depression, the gold standard, the general strike, reparations or any of the other main financial problems of the inter-war years. These were tackled by others.

Fisher was followed by Sir Horace Wilson, the government's Chief Industrial Adviser, who became Chamberlain's *éminence grise* on foreign policy. He reigned from 1939 to 1942, when the Treasury was at its wartime ebb, and was succeeded by Sir Richard Hopkins, who was actually an authority on finance. Hopkins had the usual Civil Service reserve towards all great projects, but it was a deeper and more personal scepticism than the professional mask worn by most of his colleagues. Between the wars Hopkins had been the fountain-head of the Treasury view that nothing could be done through government spending to relieve unemployment. Yet this hardened empiricist, as Sir Roy Harrod calls him,[3] was also a highly individual and unpredictable character. During the war he came under the spell of Keynes and threw all his influence behind that great economist's ideas. Nor was his respect born of fear; for Hopkins was perhaps the only man in public life who was ever able to stalemate Keynes in an argument on a subject of Keynes's choosing.[4]

Hopkins was followed in 1945 by Sir Edward (later Lord) Bridges, who held office until 1956. Bridges was the last Permanent Secretary to preside over both financial and economic policy and the management of the Civil Service.

2. 'Sir Warren Fisher and Public Service', *Institute of Public Administration*, 1951.
3. Sir Roy Harrod, *The Life of John Maynard Keynes*, Macmillan, 1951, p. 529.
4. ibid., pp. 420–2.

In most other ways, too, he was the last great figure of the old school. He was the son of Robert Bridges, the poet, and deeply interested in all the arts. He carried his broad humanist principles into his official work, and his lectures, extolling 'the principle of the intelligent layman', provided, because of their very frankness and clarity, an inexhaustible quarry of quotations for radical critics.

By this time the Treasury work had expanded so much that the Permanent Secretary could not hope to be equally at home in all its aspects. Bridges never claimed to be an authority on economic policy. He had spent the seven years before his Treasury appointment as Secretary to the Cabinet; and his heart probably lay in the more personal work of looking after the Civil Service. Bridges's period in office, which spanned the first post-war decade, was nevertheless an extraordinarily eventful one. The most important changes, from the point of view of the Treasury's own responsibilities, occurred in 1947. For it was as recently as this that the Treasury was made the chief economic ministry.

The Treasury had long had responsibility for money and credit. These functions arose naturally from its relations with the Bank of England, and its responsibility for government borrowing. But responsibility for questions such as production, exports, wages, manpower and the co-ordination of economic policy between departments was, in the war and early post-war years, the job of a separate coordinating minister outside the Treasury. Responsibility for the balance of payments was divided uneasily between the Chancellor and the coordinating minister. Until 1947 the coordinating job was done by the Lord President of the Council, Herbert Morrison. In that year his economic responsibilities were taken over by Sir Stafford Cripps, who was appointed Minister of Economic Affairs. Sir Stafford had hardly been in his job for six weeks when the Chancellor of the Exchequer, Dr Dalton, resigned over a minor and innocuous Budget leak. When Cripps succeeded him as Chancellor he took with him his economic responsibilities and his personal staff.

There was, of course, more to the move than the personality of Cripps. The Labour government after some disastrous experiences in its first two years of office was moving rapidly away from the idea of detailed regulation of particular industries. Critics remarked that the Economic Survey of 1950 marked the end of all attempts to plan the economy. Whether this was so or not depends entirely on the meaning attached to the word 'plan' – an old verbal dispute perennially topical.

The post-war Labour government's latter-day doctrine was, in fact, stated quite explicitly by Sir Stafford Cripps in 1950. In his Budget speech of that year he pointed out that it was not always sensible to decide from the centre all the details of production. Such day-to-day decisions must obviously be made by individual undertakings within the broad framework of national policy. 'Indeed the Budget itself can be described as the most important control and the most important instrument for influencing economic policy that is available to the Government.' The idea, which was based on the doctrines of Keynes, was that when there was too much unemployment, or unused industrial capacity, the Chancellor reduced taxes or allowed government spending to rise. In this way more goods were bought and jobs created. If, on the other hand, the Chancellor wanted to restrict business activity – because a boom was getting out of hand or the reserves were running out – he raised taxes and tried to contain government spending. In other words the government regulated businessmen and consumers by acting on their pockets rather than by direct controls. Thus was born what later came to be called the Butskellite doctrine which, despite frequent changes of political fashion, has, with varying accretions, governed economic policy ever since.[5] With the end of rationing in the early 1950s,

5. Although it has recently come under increasing challenge from the 'monetarist' school. This is discussed in the Introduction and in Chapter 4.

and the abolition of most of the remaining physical controls by the then Conservative government, the Treasury became still more important as the only remaining department with effective economic sanctions.

The next main change came after the retirement of Bridges in 1956, when it was at last recognized that no single man could carry the whole responsibility of the Head of the Treasury. The Permanent Secretary's function was accordingly split into two parts. One Joint Permanent Secretary, Sir Roger Makins, was put in charge of economic and financial policy, and another, Sir Norman Brook (later Lord Normanbrook), became Head of the Home Civil Service. For the following six years Brook combined his Treasury post with his old job of Cabinet Secretary, which he had held since 1947. It was not until the 1962 reorganization that the three separate jobs of Cabinet Secretary, Head of the Civil Service, and Head of the economic and financial side of the Treasury, were finally disentangled and given to three different people.

The choice of Sir Roger Makins (now Lord Sheffield), until then Ambassador in Washington, as the Treasury's economic chief was a bold gamble that did not quite work. The country's economic problems were too complex for anyone, however intelligent, with a mainly Foreign Office background to assimilate overnight.

Sir Frank Lee, who succeeded Makins at the beginning of 1960 and who had previously been Permanent Secretary to the Board of Trade, was the first post-war Head of the Treasury to be familiar with current economic controversies. Basically he was a man of affairs who was at home with industrial leaders as well as politicians and Civil Servants. He was himself succeeded in 1962 by Sir William Armstrong, who was dramatically promoted at the age of forty-seven from the rank of Third Secretary. Armstrong had probably a better grasp of the then prevailing framework of modern economic policy than any previous Permanent Secretary. When he moved on in 1968 to become Head of the Home Civil Service he was succeeded by Sir Douglas Allen, who had actually read economics and statistics at the London School of Economics and had been concerned with these subjects for most of his career as a Civil Service administrator, the first Treasury Permanent Secretary to have had such qualifications. Allen had until 1968 been Permanent Secretary to the Department of Economic Affairs but most of his professional life had been spent at the Treasury.

Although both 'new men' in the C. P. Snow sense, rather than old-style mandarins, there were interesting differences between Armstrong's and Allen's method of working. Armstrong was on the whole content to let official committees and groups take their course, exerting his very real influence by careful hints to the participants, and in his confidential conversations with ministers. Allen on the other hand is more inclined to take a definite line and exert his influence through the machine.

THE DEPARTMENTAL STRUCTURE

The Treasury has, of course, never been the only ministry with economic functions – although it is the only one with effective power over the level of employment and business activity. The organization of the economic ministries has varied, often with dazzling rapidity, according to the whims, personality problems, and public relations requirements of different governments. Nevertheless, the jobs to be done have remained very similar for long periods at a time.

The basic functions, falling primarily to other departments, include commercial policy, industrial and incomes policy, relations with the trade unions, social service payments, regional policy, responsibility for local government, housing, public building and works, power, and transport policy. In the spring of 1970 the departments concerned were known as the Board of Trade, Department of Employment and Productivity, the Department of Health and Social Security, and the Ministries of Technology, Housing, Transport, and Overseas Development. After the reorganization of autumn 1970 the Board of Trade was combined with the Ministry of Technology to form a single 'Department of Trade and Industry'. Housing, Transport, and Public Building and Works were also merged to form the 'Department of the Environment', and Overseas Development merged with the Foreign and Commonwealth Office.

One institution responsible for a great deal of the analysis of economic and social trends is the Central Statistical Office. Its importance is sometimes forgotten, partly because it is not headed by a minister. It is attached to the Cabinet Office (and is thus ultimately under the Prime Minister, who in Mr Wilson's case took a very active interest in its affairs). The CSO is also sometimes overlooked because it does not give advice on policy. In fact the CSO, apart from its general responsibility for developing and coordinating official statistics, has been specifically responsible for preparing and publishing the figures for the national income, the balance of payments and the factors influencing the money supply. The appropriate presentation of the material, especially in the last two areas, requires a keen feeling for what is relevant to policy decisions. The CSO does a good deal of interpretation for official committees; and it may often be a matter of chance whether a particular piece of analysis, on which important decisions depend, is done by statisticians in the CSO or economists in a ministry dealing with economic affairs.

The Treasury's role in this medley arises from its control over the government purse-strings and from its responsibility for demand management and the balance of payments. It has also had varying degrees of responsibility for other aspects of economic coordination. A second central coordinating ministry, known as the Department of Economic Affairs, was set up in 1964, with special responsibility for the longer term and the more 'physical' aspects of planning, but was wound up in 1969, and its major economic interests transferred to the Treasury.

The insoluble problem of organization is that all areas of

economic policy are, or ought to be, interrelated. But the number of tasks involved, even of a central coordinating kind, are more than one minister can handle. To represent Britain in international financial discussions, to follow the intricate course of wage negotiations and attend to the regional balance, while at the same time thinking of government spending and taxes, is simply not possible for one man except in the most superficial way; and the nature of these activities does not make delegation easy. There is no final solution and any given demarcation will be impermanent and unsatisfactory.

These tensions are not entirely overcome by the network of inter-departmental committees. There has since the war normally been one principal Cabinet economic policy committee which has at various times been presided over by the Prime Minister, the Chancellor and (when the post existed) the Secretary of State for Economic Affairs. Its name has varied slightly over the years and in 1970 was known as the Steering Committee on Economic Policy (SEP) and was chaired by the Prime Minister. It has usually been a fairly large committee, containing all the principal economic ministers, and two or three others. There is, in accordance with the normal rule, a similar committee at official level – attended in this instance by Permanent Secretaries. There are also numerous special committees on subjects ranging from incomes policy to environmental planning, some of which have an independent existence, and others which are subordinate to the main economic policy committee.

The Cabinet's main economic committee is much too large and unwieldy to discuss major or sensitive topics, such as the Budget or devaluation; and its energies have tended to be consumed either in generalized discussions or in limited and non-strategic issues, such as state aid for shipbuilding. The key issues of economic strategy are very much the personal province of the Chancellor, who has, of course, to carry the Prime Minister with him.

TABLE 2

THE SHIFTING BALANCE OF POWER

May 1947	Central Economic Planning established; responsible first to Morrison and then to Cripps.
November 1947	CEPS moved with Cripps to Treasury.
November 1953	Economic Section of the Cabinet Office transferred to the Treasury.
December 1958	Planning Staff dissolved. Work given to other Treasury divisions.
February 1962	National Economic Development Council established.
October 1964	Labour government establishes Department of Economic Affairs, Ministry of Technology and Overseas Development Ministry.
April 1968	Responsibility for Incomes Policy transferred to Ministry of Labour – renamed Department of Employment and Productivity.
November 1968	Civil Service Department takes over Treasury's Civil Service responsibilities.
October 1969	DEA abolished. 'Macro-economic' functions go to Treasury and industrial ones to expanded Ministry of Technology.
October 1970	Department of Trade and Industry and 'central policy review staff' established.

TREASURY ORGANIZATION

In view of the Treasury's wide ramifications it is hardly surprising that it should possess a number of lesser ministers of a higher rank than the normal junior minister. The oldest of these posts, that of Financial Secretary, has existed since the eighteenth century. The holder has certain well-established duties; for example the Financial Statement, which appears at the time of the Budget, is issued in his name. But his traditional responsibilities for supervising public expenditure were taken over by the Chief Secretary, a superior post created in 1961. The Chief Secretary actually sat in the Cabinet until the 1964 election, and was again placed there by Mr Wilson in 1968–70. There has sometimes been a fourth minister at the Treasury, who until 1964 carried the title of Economic Secretary. This was allowed to lapse in the first few years of the Labour government, but then revived in 1968 under the title of Minister of State. The allocation of duties between the various subsidiary ministers at the Treasury has been as fluid as their titles.

The best way to cope with the transfer of responsibilities within and between departments, with each breath of the political wind, is to put the emphasis on continuing functions rather than on changing office labels. The Treasury has since the beginning of 1970 been divided into three main 'groups':

1. *Finance:* This group is concerned, not with taxation, but with government borrowing and lending, the balance of payments and foreign exchange. It is therefore also in charge of international financial negotiations.

2. *Public Sector:* This all-important group discharges the Treasury's central role of controlling the spending of the central government and other public bodies.

3. *The National Economy Group:* This was set up under the Armstrong reorganization of 1962, but dissolved when the DEA was set up late in 1964 and re-established early in 1970. The work of strengthening the Treasury's economic side had thus to be taken up again after an interval of over five years. It is now concerned with demand management, medium-term strategy and other economic topics, such as incomes and prices, on which the Treasury has to form a view.

Following the report of the Fulton Committee, this list of functions no longer includes the management of the Civil Service, which has been transferred to a new Department. But the Treasury is bound to take a continued interest in Civil Service pay and numbers as part of its responsibility for the regulation of government spending. The subject is also important from the point of view of incomes policy. (It is not merely Civil Servants, strictly defined, who are relevant here. The whole of the civilian public services, excluding nationalized industries, employed over four million people, with a pay bill which well exceeded £4,000m. in 1968–9 – over a fifth of the national total.

The inclusion of the nationalized industries would bring the proportions, both for pay and manpower, up to a quarter.)

But the central government's authority varies enormously from one public service to another. It is in complete charge of the employers' side on Civil Service and Forces pay. It can influence the Health Service and the Police through the Health Department and the Home Office. On the other hand, its responsibilities for teachers' pay are notoriously muddled and controversial. In the case of local authority staff the government has no power at all; but, as it foots so much of the bill, it does quietly insist on its right to whisper a word of advice. Its authority over the nationalized industries is also notoriously indirect and controversial.

MONEY AND STERLING

The Finance group is an appropriate place to start a tour of the Treasury in view of its responsibility for the management of sterling. In 1962 the sections of the Treasury dealing with home and overseas finance were brought together. Thus the responsibilities of the group cover not only overseas financial negotiations and the balance of payments, but domestic monetary policy, debt management, National Savings and a host of other subjects related to government borrowing and lending. No economics minister who does

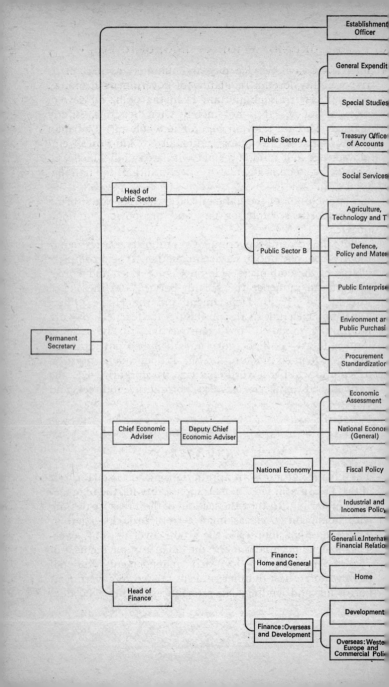

Permanent Secretary

- Establishment Officer
- Head of Public Sector
  - Public Sector A
    - General Expendit
    - Special Studies
    - Treasury Office of Accounts
    - Social Services
  - Public Sector B
    - Agriculture, Technology and T
    - Defence, Policy and Mater
    - Public Enterprise
    - Environment an Public Purchasi
    - Procurement Standardization
- Chief Economic Adviser
  - Deputy Chief Economic Adviser
    - Economic Assessment
    - National Econor (General)
- National Economy
  - Fiscal Policy
  - Industrial and Incomes Policy
- Head of Finance
  - Finance: Home and General
    - General i.e.Internat Financial Relatio
    - Home
  - Finance: Overseas and Development
    - Development
    - Overseas: Weste Europe and Commercial Poli

not have direct and personal control over the Treasury divisions concerned can really live up to his title.

The Finance group had unfortunately to fight for a long time with one hand tied behind its back. For a very long time almost the only way it was able to influence the balance of payments was by depressing home demand, which in turn depressed imports. A little 'help' was provided in the mid-60s by the short-lived import surcharge and by the restrictions on overseas investment, but not until 1967 did a major relief come from devaluation.

The Finance group also provides the Treasury's main links with the Bank of England, which has been another professional reason for the group's reputed conservatism. Many of the key decisions on subjects, such as whether to change Bank Rate, alter gilt-edged market policy or borrow from overseas Central Banks are made at highly confidential meetings between a small number of senior Bank of England and Treasury officials. More of the real business is done in conversation and less is put down on paper here than anywhere else in Whitehall. The Treasury has no direct contacts with the financial markets. Its operations are conducted for it by the Bank of England in both the foreign exchange and the domestic money market. The Bank itself still claims to have the initiative on Bank Rate changes, which are announced in the Governor's name 'with the approval of the Chancellor'. No other member of the Cabinet, apart from the Chancellor (and the Prime Minister, who has to give final assent), has any say at all in the matter.

The Finance side of the Treasury is in many ways in an unenviable position, falling professionally between two stools. As one of its jobs is to convey the Bank of England's views to Whitehall, it is inevitably imbued with some of the Bank's approach; and as it is professionally concerned with

Figure 1. HM Treasury organization chart, spring 1970

the welfare of sterling, it cannot adopt the detached attitude to reserve movements advocated by some economists. On the other hand, although it helps to prepare the balance-of-payments statistics, it has no direct contact with the traders and speculators who actually buy and sell pounds. This detachment of the Treasury from the foreign exchange market is not part of the inevitable order of things. Before the war two expert Treasury officials, Sir David Waley and Sir Frederick Phillips, played a considerable role in market management.

From about 1964–5 onwards, the Finance side of the Treasury began to recapture some of the initiative from the Bank of England on the overseas side. This was partly because the troubles of the pound could no longer be accommodated by short-term credits from other central banks, but required frequent recourse to the IMF – which dealt directly with the Treasury – as well as political understandings between governments. In addition, the growing momentum of international liquidity negotiations, concerned with new forms of 'paper gold' to augment world reserves, called for skills in which the Treasury was as well endowed as the Bank. These negotiations imbued the heads of the Finance side of the Treasury with strong feelings in favour of a new international paper asset and against an increase in the gold price. Finance group officials also began in the late 1960s to make serious economic assessments of subjects such as export credit, and inward and outward investment. Many of these arose out of exchange control for which the Treasury had by 1970 not only the ultimate responsibility but also the main initiative. Assessments have been increasingly concerned with the effect of various proposals on the efficient allocation of resources, and not just on the balance of payments itself.

On the home side the revival of interest in the money supply stemmed mainly more from the Treasury's Finance group. Until the 1960s it had been the custom to leave the

initiative on monetary policy mainly to the Bank. As Lord
Bridges rather abjectly put it to Radcliffe in 1958: 'The
high officials of the Bank of England have long and intense
training and experience in their particular field. . . . On
the other hand, officers of the Treasury are laymen.'[6] The
Radcliffe Report in one sense delayed the Treasury's venture into this territory by the way it played down monetary
policy in its conclusions. In another sense, however, it
provided an opportunity through the impetus it gave to the
publication of a mass of monetary statistics; and the
Treasury and the CSO played a leading part in devising a
framework for classification for this, initially bewildering,
new material.

The next stage came with the arrival of a handful of
people with an interest in monetary economics. A. H.
Lovell, himself an LSE graduate, returned from India as an
Assistant Secretary in 1965 in charge of the relevant home
finance division and was assisted by Geoffrey Bell, then a
lone pioneer of the 'new quantity theory' of money in the
economic section. At a later stage, Robert Armstrong –
who had previously been secretary to Radcliffe – became the
Under Secretary in charge of the relevant division; Frank
Cassell also arrived on the economic side and Andrew
Edwards joined as a very active Principal. L. Berman
played a key role in the CSO. These officials were concerned with the flow of funds throughout the economy,
but they also took the lead against a sceptical Bank of
England in the revival of interest in the behaviour of the
aggregate money supply and were working out figures for
Domestic Credit Expansion at the beginning of 1969, just
before the Letter of Intent to the IMF came to be written.

The monetary officials have had to contend with a curious
coalition of doubters among economists still attached to
post-war Keynesian doctrines and Bank of England repre-

6. 'Committee on the Working of the Monetary System', *Evidence*,
Vol. III, 1959, p. 47.

sentatives, concerned for the management of the gilt-edged market. It was some time before officials in the monetary division had a major influence on economic policy, but their chance came with the disappointing reaction to devaluation in 1968, when a strict fiscal policy had been undermined by lax control of the money supply.

Nevertheless, the basic imbalance between the Treasury's Finance group and the Bank, due to the latter's involvement in the market place, will not be easy to remove. An additional difficulty is that Finance group officials, especially on the overseas side, are so concerned with immediate and short-term problems, such as financing the next IMF repayment, or diplomatic matters such as reacting to moves by other governments, or preparing briefs for international meetings, that there is too little time to look beyond the current year's problems. Although their situation is not identical, there may be some lesson to be learned from the public sector group whose work now revolves around medium-term management.

A great institutional advantage possessed by the Bank – which enjoys an independent income from the interest on the securities held by its Banking Department – is that it is more generously staffed than the Treasury. The Bank will normally be able to devote more personnel to a subject, who will be supported with better clerical and other assistance than the Treasury. Bank of England officials frequently travel abroad to gather information and talk to their opposite numbers. In a recent year no less than 60 different countries were visited. Such regular journeys have no counterpart in the Treasury. The latter used to have a number of permanent overseas missions, but in 1970 had, apart from an important delegation in Washington jointly staffed with the Bank, only individuals in Paris and Kuala Lumpur.

THE ROLE OF THE BANK

The Bank of England has for centuries had a greater say in many important matters than Her Majesty's ministers. It regards itself as at one and the same time the Chancellor's instrument in the City, and the spokesman for the City in government circles. Unfortunately there can often be a conflict between the two roles. This may have nothing to do with the political colour of the government of the day, but may for example reflect the tension between the Bank's interest in safeguarding the balance of payments – which may at times, under a pegged exchange rate, require control over overseas investment – and its role as a defender of the City, which naturally favours the freest possible movement of capital. There is a strong case for having a separate body which can argue uninhibitedly the case for the City, leaving the Bank to concentrate on its monetary role. (A City Liaison Committee was in fact set up in the mid 60s to brief Sir Kenneth Keith, the City representative on NEDC, and this could possibly form the nucleus of such a representative group.)

Although the Bank of England is concerned to show that it is not a government department (which is somewhat anomalous, for its role is almost entirely governmental), there has been a big change in recent years in its relations with Whitehall. In the days of Montagu Norman (who reigned from 1920 to 1944) the Governor of the Bank would normally go alone to see the Chancellor and no Treasury officials could be present. Since the publication of the highly critical Radcliffe Report on the Monetary System in 1959, the Bank has gradually been drawn more tightly into the Whitehall committee network. For many purposes the Bank is coming to behave more like a government department, but like all government departments has some information that it keeps to itself. An important remaining difference is that, unlike a Permanent Secretary, the Governor of the Bank of England has the advantage of being able to express his views in public as well as private, but unlike a minister he enjoys security of tenure for at least his five-year-period of office.

The gulf in ethos between the two institutions narrowed considerably in the 1960s. The anti-intellectualism of the Montagu Norman and the early post-war periods diminished considerably. By 1970 the three executive directors concerned with policy were of an academic rather than central banking background, and the Chief Cashier was an official with some economic training. The Bank also began to try in the 1960s to attract graduates, with promotion prospects more nearly comparable to the Civil Service than existed in the past, and a formal economic section was established in 1970. It is, however, wrong to over-dramatize the changes. On a typical committee there is still likely to be a contrast between the Bank of England representative, who may well have come straight from public school and had a thoroughly practical training, and the Treasury representative with a background of Oxbridge and the Ministerial Private Office. The secondment in 1966 of a Treasury Principal to spend six months in the Bank studying City institutions was a new departure compared with the complete barrier to the interchange of staff which had hitherto prevailed. Two further Treasury Principals were sent on a similar tour in the subsequent three years and – on this very modest scale – the principle is now well established. In addition one or two Bank of England men are now normally found working in the Treasury for up to two years in areas such as the interpretation of external monetary movements.

The last exponent of the Montagu Norman tradition among Bank Governors was Mr Cameron (now Lord) Cobbold, who was Governor from 1949 until 1961 and had been first an adviser to Norman and then executive director under him. The Earl of Cromer, who succeeded Cobbold, was less secretive in his approach than his predecessors, and keener to improve the Bank's economic and statistical services, following the Radcliffe strictures. But being a merchant banker by background he was more dependent on expert advice on some central banking matters; and his greater public frankness was indeed an element in the clash of personalities which developed with the Wilson government. Less well known is the fact that Lord Cromer had previously clashed with Mr Maudling when the latter was Chancellor. In the Conservative leadership contest of 1965, Lord Cromer's preference for Mr Heath was made known to a number of Tory MPs; and this probably had some influence on the 'sound money' men, which could well have made a difference, considering that the contest was decided by fifteen votes.

Sir Leslie O'Brien, who succeeded Lord Cromer in 1966 after a period as Deputy Governor, had been a professional central banker all his life. Coming straight into the Bank from Wandsworth School he did not arouse the same hostile feeling among Labour ministers as Cromer, even when the views he was expressing were identical. Although O'Brien developed quite a taste for public speaking and seemed almost to enjoy provoking Labour backbenchers, he accepted more unreservedly than most earlier Governors that the government was in charge of financial policy; and he was far more at home in the Whitehall machine than any of his predecessors.

Two of the Bank of England's functions are especially important for policy-making. These are managing the foreign exchange market and running the market in government securities. Just as its responsibility for restraining government spending is a better clue to how the Treasury will behave a great deal of the time than any more sophisticated theory, so these two concerns of the Bank are at the bottom of most of its policy attitudes.

The Bank is more interested in whether foreigners are buying or selling pounds, and will be less easily reassured by theoretical calculations about the balance of payments than the Treasury. As the Bank is interested in foreigners holding pounds, it is instinctively anti-devaluation. It dislikes exchange controls nearly as much, partly because it believes that they weaken the attraction of London as a financial centre.

At home the Bank of England is more concerned than the economic side of the Treasury with the size of the *government borrowing requirement*. For the smaller the borrowing requirement the less the Bank has to borrow net for the government in the gilt-edged market; and in addition, a low borrowing requirement is believed to be good for confidence in sterling. Although the Bank will advocate higher taxes to keep government borrowing down, this is seen only as the lesser evil. Successive Governors have felt passionately about the evils of government spending and have devoted more of their public exhortations to this than to any other single subject. Unfortunately they have been generous with broad doctrine and sparing of detailed prescription.

Like all unchallenged monopolies, the Bank's position as the sole source of advice and expertise in the foreign exchange gilt-edged and money markets is unhealthy. Despite its undeniable technical competence, the Bank's actions have by no means always exhibited the unquestionable wisdom taken for granted by its City and political admirers. There was, for example, the contrast between the enormous support it gave to the forward market in the three years up to November 1967, when there was always a good chance that the no-devaluation gamble would come unstuck, and the subsequent complete departure from the forward market, when the parity was less unrealistic than it had been for a long time. In addition it was not at all obvious why, after devaluation, the Bank started dealings at the top end of the $2·38–$2·42 range, at which holders of sterling would be aware that the rate could only go downwards. Nor has the Bank's role in the loss of reserves on the Friday before the 1967 devaluation, when the foreign exchange market remained open after Mr Callaghan's non-committal answer in the House of Commons, been entirely clarified; and it is not easy to overlook the suggestion of a failure of morale in one or two parts of the institution in the months immediately following devaluation. These past controversies are mentioned simply to show that these are issues on which more than one opinion is possible.

INTERNATIONAL FINANCIAL BODIES

After this unavoidable digression it is time to return to the organization of British financial policy. At most international financial discussions the UK is represented by mixed Treasury–Bank delegations. The most important bodies to mention in a brief survey are the *International Monetary Fund, the Group of Ten, OECD's Working Party Three* and the *Bank for International Settlements*. The IMF is the nearest equivalent to a world central bank, but is still a long way short of that objective. It has been responsible since the War for medium-term credit for countries in payments difficulties. Its biggest success to date has been the launching on 1 January 1970 of *Special Drawing Rights (SDRs)* – man-made reserve assets, which form part of 'owned reserves', side by side with gold and dollars. The initial distribution for all member countries is $3,500m. in 1970 to be followed by $3,000m. in each of the years 1971, and 1972. The Fund's Articles of Agreement (originating in the Bretton Woods Conference of 1944) also provide a framework of rules for exchange rate, gold and balance-of-payments policies, which have in fact been surprisingly well observed by the main Western countries. The IMF staff and Managing Director have no supra-national powers, but have acquired considerable influence as a result of their expertise and full-time involvement. Major decisions are by weighted voting, and in practice require near-unanimity among the main industrial countries.

The meetings of the Fund's Executive Board in Washington tend to be fairly formal occasions. More intimate discussions have been held with the IMF staff in connection with Britain's drawings from the Fund. International financial agreements are often worked out in the first place by the Group of Ten. This is a sub-group of the principal members of the Fund, originally formed in 1962 to provide it with extra resources under the *General Arrangements to Borrow* (*GAB*). Its members are the USA, Canada, UK, Sweden, Germany, France, Italy, the Netherlands, Belgium, and Japan. This Group has been in charge of talks on 'world liquidity' and was responsible for the SDR scheme, which was provisionally drafted in 1967, under Mr Callaghan's chairmanship.

As soon as the Group's meetings are over, the same countries, normally represented by the same delegates – with the addition of Switzerland and the omission of Belgium – reassemble the following day, under the title of 'Working Party Three' (WP3). This is a sub-committee of the Organization for Economic Cooperation and Development (OECD) comprising twenty-two Western nations, with headquarters in Paris. WP3's main role is to try to exercise 'multilateral surveillance' over members' policies, particularly in demand management and the balance of payments; and it attempts to combine full employment, steady growth and balance-of-payments equilibrium on an international scale. It will characteristically put pressure on creditor countries, such as Germany in the 1960s, to give higher priority to expansion, and on deficit countries to keep demand and costs on a tighter rein. Lacking supranational powers, WP3's success has depended on a close network of confidential links among the high officials concerned, who have come to know each other very well over the years.

The background briefs for WP3 are provided by OECD's economic staff, among whom British economists have played a notable and distinguished role. Its economic side is known jocularly in Paris as 'The British Treasury in exile'; but there has never been any suggestion that it is more sparing of the UK than of any other country in its strictures.

The Bank for International Settlements (BIS) is responsible for the monthly meetings of Central Bank Governors at Basle. The BIS was formed in 1930 in connection with the German reparations problem. It is now mainly an instrument of the European central bankers, although the US Federal Reserve is also associated with its work. The Basle meetings are best known for the network of automatic short-term credits, developed from 1961 onwards, which member banks make available to each other. These are from three to six months, but in practice renewable, compared to the IMF's three to five years. They usually take the form of 'swaps' under which other central banks will agree, for instance, to provide their own currencies to the Bank of England in exchange for sterling, if the British reserves are under pressure. Other important central banking matters are discussed at Basle, including policy towards gold markets. Unlike those of the other organizations so far discussed, BIS meetings are confined strictly to central bankers. The Governors attending like to boast that no Treasury official has ever been present; and the insistence of the Under Secretary of the US Treasury, Fred Deming, on going to Basle in December 1967 to meet delegates (outside the formal sessions) called forth a volume of wrath that no mere policy issue would have been capable of arousing.

Perhaps this is a good place to point out that the expression 'gnomes' has no definite meaning, even as a colloquialism. It is sometimes used to refer vaguely to the above series of organizations and meetings, without attempting to distinguish between them, and sometimes to private individuals (by no means all bankers or foreigners) whose feeling about currencies influence movements of funds between countries. The identification of 'gnomes' with Switzerland had its origin in the 1950s when the market in 'transferable sterling' (a particular variety of inconvertible sterling long since defunct) had its main centre in Zurich. Swiss banks still play a role in looking after the accounts of many international clients, but they are only one of many elements in the international flow of short-term funds. Nothing was more misguided, for example, than the procession of television reporters in the 1960s to interview Swiss private bankers on their views about the British economy – views which were in fact mostly derived from the British press. The creditors who impose conditions are not private bankers at all but the IMF – and sometimes Working Party Three, acting on behalf of the Group of Ten. Central bank credits arranged at Basle carry no conditions; but undoubtedly the assembled Governors 'convey views' to each other, which are passed back to governments.

Although not directly concerned with the UK's own economic health, no list of international financial organizations can be complete without mentioning the *International Bank for Reconstruction and Development* (usually known as the *IBRD* or just *World Bank*), which is concerned with lending to developing countries. The World Bank has a 'soft loan' affiliate known as the *International Development Association* (*IDA*) on which a growing share of the aid burden has been falling. In 1964, Britain's own aid programme was transferred from the Treasury to a newly formed Overseas Development Ministry (ODM). If, as is likely, the ODM is eventually absorbed into the Foreign Office, where it may become the nucleus of an economic section, responsibility for aid is likely to go with it. But the Treasury is still the most influential voice in deciding how much aid Britain can afford to give. Moreover, the Treasury and Bank still appoint the British Governors and Executive Directors of the World Bank.

ECONOMISTS AND FORECASTERS

Officials throughout the Treasury are, of course, handling economics all the time, whether they know it or not (like Molière's M. Jourdain, who discovered that he had been speaking prose all his life). The professional economists have, however, certain distinguishing characteristics. As a result of the reorganization following the reabsorption of the DEA in 1969, the former 'Economic Section' disappeared as a unit of organization – although the time-honoured title is likely to remain in colloquial use. The latest arrangements are a compromise between the ideas of keeping the economists together in a separate body and 'bedding them down' in the operating divisions. A handful work in the Public Sector and Finance groups, but the majority work in the National Economy group.

All the economists now belong to the 'Treasury Economic Service' and come professionally under the head of the Government Economic Service and Chief Economic Adviser to the Treasury, who since 1969 has been Sir Donald MacDougall. Whether these two very important jobs will always be combined in one person remains to be seen, as will the way in which Treasury economists will combine their responsibility to their professional head with their responsibility to the administrative chiefs of their operating divisions. The National Economy Group itself comes under the Head and Deputy Head of the Treasury Economic Service and a Third Secretary. Treasury economists hold regular meetings, and when there were only a handful of them, they tended to develop strong feelings of corporate loyalty. It will be interesting to see how much of this remains now that they have grown in number and now that the post-war Keynesian consensus has given way to renewed theoretical controversy.

The National Economy group consisted at the beginning of 1970 of the following divisions – each individually, very small:

Economic Assessment. This is concerned with short and medium-term forecasting and related research.

National Economy (General). This covers a wide field of economics outside the strict forecasting field. Members may be called upon to provide advice on almost any subject, ranging from a proposed tax reform to general questions of economic strategy. This division is also concerned with economic briefing both within the government, and for speeches and official publicity.

Industrial and Incomes Policy. This, as its name suggests, is concerned with general industrial problems such as investment incentives, monopolies and mergers, the movement of prices and incomes and consultation with the two sides of industry through NEDC. In many of these areas the prime responsibility lies with other departments – especially, in the case of incomes policies, the DEP. This Treasury division has the very necessary function of trying to see that wider economic considerations are not overlooked in the pursuit by departments of their pet enthusiasms.

Fiscal Policy. This is concerned with coordinating work on the Budget and other packages of economic measures. Its functions will be discussed extensively in Chapter 4.

Professional economists are often employed on what Sir Alec Cairncross has called 'odd jobs like writing speeches, attending international conferences, coping with economic advisers, and trying to recruit more economic advisers'.[7] Without eternal vigilance these not entirely uncongenial tasks will take up a great deal of the available time. But the job which, rightly or wrongly, has become in Cairncross's words 'the most important role' of professional economists is that of forecasting. It is the one area where professional economists rather than career Civil Servants have, ever since Cripps, taken the lead in advising ministers. Current data on production, employment, exports, and other variables are assessed as they come in, and are collected

7. 'The Work of an Economic Adviser', *Public Administration*, spring 1968.

together in the Treasury monthly economic report, which has been published since 1967. Special minutes may, of course, be written for much more limited circulation, if new data suggest the possible need for a change in policy, or if they are likely to prove politically sensitive.

These spot assessments are essentially subordinate to the short-term and medium-term forecasts, which occupy a much more fundamental role. The short-term forecasts are carried out three times a year in February, June and October by Treasury economists together with officials of other economic ministries, the Bank of England, and Central Statistical Office. All short-term forecasts try to give a picture of how the national income will move ahead quarter by quarter; the February one will try to predict in detail the behaviour of the economy for a two-year period from the end of the previous year to the end of the following year. Each *National Income Forecast* (*NIF*) is accompanied by a *World Trade* and by a UK *Balance-of-Payments Forecast*. The Finance divisions play a special role in the balance-of-payments assessment. On world trade and British exports the Treasury has to lean heavily on background papers prepared by the Board of Trade, although it also takes account of the Bank of England's view of prospects in different parts of the world. The June and October forecasts have often, as in 1961, 1965, 1966 and 1968, led to deflationary packages more important than the Budget itself. There is, in fact, no longer anything particularly unusual about measures which amount to a Budget in all but name at any time of the year.

The medium-term projections normally go up to about five years ahead and are completed in early summer, although fresh projections may be made at any time in response to special requests. The short-term assessments are really forecasts of business cycle movements on the assumption of no change in policy. The medium-term assessments, on the other hand, assume that the level of economic activity will be determined by government policy, and they are better described as projections than forecasts. Their outcome depends mainly on the assumptions made about the underlying growth of productivity and of the working population. These give the growth of productive capacity. To translate this into the growth of output, a view must also be taken about how close to capacity the economy can be operated, bearing in mind the likely balance-of-payments situation and other constraints. The next stage is to subdivide this output into broad categories. A certain amount has to be set aside for the probable growth of investment and for the prospective change (if any) in the current balance of payments. The remainder is available for consumption, whether public or private.

These medium-term assessments began in an experimental way in the late 1950s, and started in earnest in the early 1960s; their main use at first was to help the Treasury form a view of the growth of public expenditure the nation could afford without major tax increases. With the emergence of the large payments deficits of the mid 1960s and the associated international debt repayment problems, attention was also focused on the 'underlying balance of payments', i.e. what the trend of balance of payments was likely to be over a period sufficiently distant to assume that good and bad years would offset each other. The same problem can be posed in a different way by asking what the implications are for domestic economic policy (mainly demand and incomes policy) of giving overriding priority to a particular payments objective.

In 1962–4 the National Economic Development Office carried out rival medium-term assessments of its own. These contained an element of 'targetry'. In other words both the productivity and balance-of-payments projections were made at or above the upper end of the likely range, to act as a spur. The element of targetry was at first continued when medium-term assessments passed to the Department of Economic Affairs, but was banished from the exercise after the National Plan was abandoned in the 1966 crisis, well before the work moved back to the Treasury.

The DEA did develop considerably the technique of medium-term projection; in particular it evolved a computerized model, in which the consequences of alternative assumptions about the key variables could be rapidly calculated – a procedure showing how very far removed the whole exercise is from anything to do with prophecy. The model also shed light on the effects on the main industrial sectors of alternative growth rates of the GDP and its main components. One of the main tasks of the re-united forecasting team – for which W. A. B. Hopkin has special responsibility – is to see what can be done to bring together the methods used for the medium-term and short-term forecasts. It will also attempt to make assessments for intermediate periods – of say three years — in which the senior levels of the Treasury have become particularly interested and which, as will be seen, are important for public expenditure control.

ECONOMIC ADVISERS

Although several of the most senior Treasury officials have a say in economic decisions, the leading role in assessing the implication of the forecasts is naturally taken by the Chief Economic Adviser. From 1947 to 1961 this role was occupied by Sir Robert Hall, who was succeeded in 1961 by Sir Alec Cairncross, who in turn was replaced by Sir Donald MacDougall early in 1969. All three tended to be middle-of-the-road economists, sympathetic to the problems of their official colleagues and not inclined to thrust 'politically unacceptable views' on ministers.

A good many Civil Servants found Hall somewhat inarticulate, while Cairncross was just the opposite, with a quick reply to every point raised. On the other hand Hall's advice was often of a personal kind rather than a collective Economic Section view. At his best Hall had an almost feminine intuition for the way the economy was moving. His influence probably suffered from the departure in 1953 of Sir Edwin (now Lord) Plowden, an incisive practical operator who worked very closely with him. While Hall was mainly interested in the broad problems of economic management, Cairncross was at heart more of a 'micro-economist' and was extremely curious about the forces affecting individual firms and industries. Such interests could, however, have only a limited outlet in a central management department such as the Treasury. He did, however, become known for his keen scrutiny of even minor details and his unwillingness to take any figures at their face value.

MacDougall's distinguishing characteristics include a great curiosity, which shows itself in a constant stream of questions. Unlike many other leading economists, he has a perfectly genuine interest in other people's opinion and even more in any facts they can give him. As an economist he has a passion for quantification and calculation. If this occasionally led him astray in his earlier work, it was because of his courage in documenting thoroughly and at length views which were just as strongly held by many of his colleagues. His experience in government service is exceptionally long and varied, stretching from Lord Cherwell's statistical unit in the War to NEDC in 1962–4 and the DEA in 1964–8, of both of which he was economic director.

An important bridge-building role between the forecasters and the policy-makers, which is seldom appreciated in the outside world, has been held by a handful of career economists at Deputy Director level or a little below. Indeed many of the guiding ideas of economic policy, which will be discussed in the chapter on the Budget and again in the historical section, originated among such people. Five names singled out for special mention for 'standing and originality' by Sir Alec Cairncross are Christopher Dow, later in charge of economics at OECD, Bryan Hopkin, Fred Atkinson (who in 1969 became Controller of Economics and Statistics at 'Mintech'), Wynne Godley (who in 1970 became the Director of the Department of Applied

Economics in Cambridge) and the late Jack Downie.[8] A senior economist in an international body once remarked privately that when such key career economists came to the conclusion that the pre-1967 exchange rate could no longer be maintained, devaluation became inevitable.

The Economic Service's influence is normally used to stress 'real' forces rather than monetary or confidence aspects. It will be more concerned with the movement of output and employment than with the government borrowing requirement, and again, more concerned with the basic balance on current and capital account than with month-to-month movements of 'hot' money in and out of the reserves. But it would be idle to hide the impression of defensiveness given by the central core of Treasury economists after the revival of interest in the money supply and the growing scepticism about 'fine tuning' from about the end of the 1960s. In assessing this, it is important not to be blown overboard by what might be passing fashions; and indeed it was natural that in a period of severe payments strain some of the initiative should pass to the Finance group.

Nevertheless, the approach to policy via economic forecasts and fiscal adjustments, pioneered in the Treasury and National Institute, was by the late 1960s no longer in the vanguard of applied economics. Those concerned brought about a revolution in national affairs by successfully asserting the government's responsibility for the level of economic activity, and developing the concepts and statistical techniques required to give an operational meaning to Keynes's theoretical insights. Whatever faults are found with their methods, this achievement will always stand to their credit. But as Cobden said about the Corn Law League in another era, the men who brought about one revolution would not be the ones to fight in the next.[9]

Until 1964 the Treasury's principal economic adviser

8. 'Economists in Government', *Lloyds Bank Review*, January 1970.
9. Morley's *Life of Cobden*, Macmillan, 1908, Vol. II, p. 64. The reference was to Parliamentary reform.

was the only government economist of any real seniority. With Labour's return to office the position changed overnight. Mr Callaghan brought into the Treasury Mr Robert Neild on a full-time basis, and Professor Nicholas Kaldor as a part-time adviser with special reference to taxation. Dr Thomas (now Lord) Balogh, a personal *confidant* of Mr Wilson was installed at the Cabinet Office. Sir Donald MacDougall in his DEA days was another top adviser outside the Treasury hierarchy. In 1967 Mr Anthony Crosland appointed Mr Wilfred Beckerman Economic Adviser to the Board of Trade; and when Robert Neild left the Treasury he was replaced by Mr Michael Posner and Mr Kenneth Berrill. Thus there came into existence a very informal group who – together with Cairncross – were known as 'the Economic Advisers' to whom difficult questions could be referred for collective consideration. (These assignments could also be used to keep the advisers from becoming too closely involved in current policy.)

As Labour's term of office wore on, nearly all these advisers left or became part-time, or succeeded to an established Whitehall position. But it seemed unlikely that any *new* government of any political complexion would go back to the system of a single Civil-Service-appointed senior adviser. When the Conservatives returned to office in 1970 they did however make the initial mistake of putting all the new economic appointees in posts outside the Treasury.

OTHER INSTITUTIONS

One branch of economic management that has wandered into and out of the Treasury is incomes policy. The Treasury had overriding control until 1964 when the responsibility was transferred to the DEA, where it stayed until 1968, when it went to the Ministry of Labour (which had always been responsible for much of the detailed implementation) under its rechristened name of Department of Employment and Productivity. This was a disastrous mistake. For whenever the conciliation-oriented Ministry of Labour has been allowed to rule the roost, whether under Lord Monckton in the 1950s or under Mrs Barbara Castle at the end of the 1960s, the result has been an anti-incomes policy. In other words, public sector and even private sector wages have gone up faster than economic forces dictated, owing to the desire of the ministry to buy off trouble, and its basic sympathy with union leaders (a relationship similar to that of the Bank of England and the City). A growing body of senior Treasury opinion has become more and more convinced with the passing of the years that the conciliation and policy-making aspects of the DEP must be separated in one way or another.

The *National Board for Prices and Incomes* (known confusingly either as NBPI, or just PIB) should be mentioned at this stage. Set up under the chairmanship of Mr Aubrey Jones in 1965, this was responsible for examining cases and problems referred to it by government departments. Some of its reports were notable for the emphasis on productivity; and the better ones amounted – within the limits of the time and resources available – almost to an efficiency audit on the industries concerned. Like all zealous bodies of this kind, its efforts yielded diminishing returns as time passed. In 1970 the Labour government made the mistake of proposing the merger of the PIB – which was concerned with the politically highly charged subject of incomes policy – with the semi-judicial Monopolies Commission. The Conservatives abolished the PIB, but some residual functions were transferred to an *Office of Manpower Economics*.

A somewhat older institution is '*Neddy*', which consists of three branches. There is the *National Economic Council* (*NEDC*), meeting monthly under the chairmanship of the Prime Minister, Chancellor or other senior minister, and attended by ministers, employers, trade unionists, and one or two 'independents'. There are the *Economic Development Committees* (*EDCs* or '*Little Neddies*'), which attempt to improve performance in particular industries on a similar tripartite basis; and there is the *National Economic Development Office* (*NEDO*), which provides independent briefings for the Director General and Council members and supplies staff for the 'Little Neddies'. The whole apparatus was set up in 1962 as part of the Conservative government's experiment in indicative planning. The independent 'Office' was shorn of most of its economic staff when Labour came to power. The government then took over from NEDC the responsibility for working out medium-term national economic projections or 'plans'. The Council itself is likely to continue in being as a meeting place. The future of the independent Office is less assured, although the Council will obviously need a secretariat of some sort. Some pruning is likely of the 'Little Neddies' and also some rationalization of the whole over-extended network of government-industry committees.

3

THE CONTROL OF THE PUBLIC PURSE

The basis of control: the five-year programmes: forward
projection in practice: the size of the public sector: allocation and efficiency: the distribution of income: appendix–
the nationalized industries

DURING nearly all the Treasury's recorded existence the
great majority of its officials were concerned with controlling
government spending, either directly or by virtue of their
responsibilities for pay and management in the Civil
Service. The hiving off of the Civil Service Department in
1968, the amalgamation with part of the Department of
Economic Affairs in 1969, and the increase in the number of
economists have, together with the growth of domestic and
international monetary work, changed the statistical
picture drastically. At the beginning of 1970 there were 61
Treasury administrators in the public sector group, still
more than in any other single group; but there were 44 in
finance, 17 on the national economy side and 18 in private
offices and other miscellaneous work. In addition, there
were over 50 economists.

Nevertheless the public sector group has more contacts
with the rest of Whitehall than any other part of the
Treasury. In most government departments the Treasury
was still regarded at the beginning of the 1970s, as it had
been two centuries before, primarily as the body that held
down their spending. One reform which, if it could be
carried out, would change this image would be the creation
of an American-style 'Bureau of the Budget' – separate
from the Treasury and under another minister – concerned
with the detailed regulation of the public sector. But it
would not be easy to introduce it successfully into a non-

presidential system of government. The experiments in 1961–4, and 1968–70, of having a Chief Secretary in the Cabinet in charge of public expenditure, did not result in a real separation, because both ministers worked in a single unified department of which the Chancellor was head. The small 'central policy review staff' established under Lord Rothschild after the 1970 election was superimposed on the normal machinery of Treasury control.

THE BASIS OF CONTROL

The control traditionally exerted by the Treasury over government spending has, as Sir Ivor Jennings stressed, in the last resort 'no basis save in the authority in the Cabinet of the Chancellor of the Exchequer. If his authority is overborne, the Treasury must comply.'[1] But, subject to this proviso, the Treasury's authority rests on three time-hallowed rules.

The first is the famous *Standing Order 78* of the House of Commons, which dates back to 1713. This prevents any member of the House of Commons from putting forward any Bill, or amendment, which would cost the Treasury money, without the government's consent. The second rule, which was formulated in 1924, but had existed in substance before, is that no memorandum proposing additional expenditure should be circulated to the Cabinet until it has been discussed in draft with the Treasury.

Thirdly, any proposal involving an increase in expenditure or any new service, whether or not involving an increase in the total expenditure of the department concerned, requires Treasury sanction. This principle was first made explicit in 1884. Even when the Treasury has agreed to a new service in the Estimates, its consent has still to be sought separately for each item of expenditure as it is incurred, although a certain amount of delegation now takes place, which is likely to grow.

The Exchequer accounts are audited eight or nine

1. *Cabinet Government* (3rd ed.), Cambridge, 1959, p. 163.

months after the financial year is over by the Comptroller and Auditor General, who is a House of Commons official with a staff of 500 or 600. The Comptroller is responsible for spotting illegal expenditure; but nowadays he is personally mainly concerned with waste and extravagance. His reports are made to the House of Commons' Public Account Committee (PAC), which is chaired by an opposition MP; for a long time, prior to 1964, this was Harold Wilson. The PAC dates back to 1861, and was a formidable body when the House was very economy-minded. Even today it still commands a healthy respect in Whitehall. It is the PAC that has the power to recommend that a Permanent Secretary should have to make good irregular spending out of his own pocket, a penalty last imposed in 1919.

A former Treasury official and Permanent Secretary of the Ministry of Defence, Sir Edward Playfair, has complained with some justice that the PAC 'has a firm grasp of the inessentials and pursues relentlessly issues of minor importance'. He adds: 'It works by public condemnation, under a procedure which guarantees to its victims at least two or three doses of public ignominy for matters which, *mutatis mutandis*, would in industry be written off out of profits with the full approval of the auditors.' Sir Edward has no doubt that the effect of the PAC is to make the Civil Service play safe with innovation.[2] Unfortunately the determination to pursue trivialities and hunt for scapegoats is a strong human characteristic.

The Select Committee on Estimates – now superseded by the 'Committee on Expenditure' – chose topics which seemed worth exploring by its sub-committees. Its reports went more deeply into policy matters than the more Gladstonian PAC. It was the Select Committee, and not the PAC, which carried out the highly critical analysis of Treasury control methods in 1957–8, which sparked off the Plowden Report on public expenditure. It was also a Select Committee Report which led to the appointment of the Fulton Com-

2. 'The Edge of the Maelstrom', *Listener*, 8 February 1968.

mittee on the Civil Service. The Select Committee on the Nationalized Industries, which is modelled on the Estimates Committee, has been, in a series of bipartisan reports, a pacemaker in the cause of a more rational approach to the nationalized industries.

Nothing has been said of the complex rituals by which the annual departmental spending plans are vetted inside Whitehall and then by the House of Commons, as they are already well documented in other volumes.[3] They may still be necessary in one guise or another for constitutional reasons, or as a protection against improper behaviour. But from the point of view of regulating public expenditure they are usually devices for strengthening the lock on the stable door when the horses are already many miles away. The Treasury employs quite different methods in its more serious attempts to exert control.

THE FIVE-YEAR PROGRAMMES

The Treasury's main instrument is a forward programme, covering each of the next five years after the financial year just ended, which is 'rolled forward' every year. The present procedures stem from the well-known report made by Lord Plowden in 1961, as chairman of a small committee containing both officials and businessmen with Whitehall experience. It had long been evident that the conventional financial year, which grew out of the agricultural crop cycle, was a ludicrously short period for expenditure control. To take a simple example: the education bill depends to a large extent on the number of trained teachers in the country

3. For a full account of the processes see *The British Budgetary System* by Sir Herbert Brittain, Macmillan, 1959. Another good source is Lord Bridges's book, *The Treasury*, Allen & Unwin, 1964. The story of the Treasury's struggle over many centuries to establish control over government expenditure, and the role played by the House of Commons in establishing the principles of Gladstonian finance is well told in Henry Roseveare's *The Treasury: The Evolution of a British Institution*, Allen Lane The Penguin Press, 1969.

(assuming that no significant numbers are forced to leave the profession or remain unemployed). It takes about three years to build a teachers' training college and another three years to put a trainee through one. The main effect on the current education bill of the decision to build such a college is not, therefore, felt until six years later.

Well before Plowden, separate four- or five-year spending plans had been in existence in some individual sectors. Mr Selwyn Lloyd had an unpublished defence plan made when he was minister in 1955, and in 1956 Sir David Eccles launched a five-year plan for technical education. The novelty of the Plowden approach was that it went beyond the piecemeal scrutiny of individual sectors. All the different expenditure plans were added and considered together, against a forecast of the probable growth of the national income. The first of these comprehensive surveys was made in 1961. The early Plowden exercises were, however, forecasts rather than operational instruments. The innovation in 1965 was that a definite Cabinet decision was made on 'how much the country could afford' and how the resources available should be allocated.[4]

The first survey to be made public was the Conservative government exercise of 1963, in response to an election challenge. Another survey was published by Mr Callaghan in early 1966 in the aftermath of the National Plan exercise. But it was only at the end of 1969 that the Treasury began to publish such surveys on a regular annual basis, beginning with a White Paper *Public Expenditure 1968–9 to 1973–4*. The Treasury maintains that Year 3 of a projection is the first at which there is scope for substantial change without disruption. This doctrine is most appropriate to 'physical' expenditure on goods and services. Faster changes can and are made in a large category of transfer payments such as social-service charges, family allowances or housing subsidies, especially by incoming governments after elections. The figures in the White Paper for Years 4 and 5

4. *Public Expenditure: Planning and Control*, HMSO 1966, Cmnd 2915.

show 'provisional allocations on which firm decisions have still to be taken by the government'. Against these projections is a rough forecast of future economic growth, framed – in 1969 at least – in deliberately cautious terms.

Such White Papers are the one type of long-term economic programme which actually represents official decisions as distinct from desires; and it is arguable that they represent the real National Plan, to the extent that there is one. The biggest innovation of 1969 was that the Treasury published for the first time figures for the 'buoyancy of the revenue', assuming existing tax rates, on the same constant price basis as expenditure. Unfortunately, revenue estimates were not published for the last two years on which, according to the Treasury's own doctrine, the public debate was supposed to centre.

The basic survey of future public sector spending intentions is known as *PESC* because it comes from the interdepartmental *Public Expenditure Survey Committee*, which reports in early summer. Each survey starts out with the cost of continuing the policies contained in the previous year's forward projections, adjusted for any decisions taken in the intervening period. The cost of the PESC survey is then set against an estimate of the probable growth of the economy over the same period. The best available guesses have to be made about the other main claims on these resources, including consumption, the trade balance and private investment, assuming the continuation of existing government policies. If the total claims on resources add up to more than is likely to be available, then ministers have to order cuts in public expenditure, or reconcile themselves to an increase in tax rates over the next few years, or face some combination of the two.

A variety of devices has been tried to adjust the programmes to the permissible total laid down by the government. An innovation introduced in 1965 was to divide departmental spending programmes into 'basic' programmes, relating to policies already agreed, and 'additional' programmes, to be considered if extra resources were available. By the later 1960s more sophisticated system was in operation. The starting point was the PESC projection of the cost of existing policies and plans. There were further columns costing possible changes put forward by the spending departments themselves, the departments in conjunction with the Treasury, and the Treasury alone. Needless to say, most of the suggested changes in the last categories were reductions. The resulting documents gave ministers, if they were prepared to use it in the right way, a variety of options, both for the total size and for the composition of future public expenditure. The table on page 108 shows the public expenditure decisions taken after the 1969 PESC projection for the first three relatively 'firm' years of the programme. The Conservative government did shift the figures, for the third year, but the form of the exercise is unlikely to change very quickly.

In 1965 the public sector's programmes were considered by a group of senior ministers, none of whom had large departmental responsibilities for any particular block of expenditure, with the Chancellor in the chair. Such a committee had been recommended in an unpublished section of the Plowden Report, but had not been accepted by the previous government. Unfortunately the Labour government allowed this procedure to lapse and by 1967 there had been a return to a system of bilateral haggling between the Chancellor and each Departmental minister, with the final decisions being taken in full Cabinet, or in a large Cabinet Committee with spending ministers present. The semi-public Cabinet wrangle over the emergency reduction in spending programmes, which took place after devaluation in January 1968, was an extreme example of this method in operation. The method has advantages for a Chancellor who is able to play off one minister against another, especially if he has the Prime Minister behind him. But it makes a rational discussion of priorities very difficult and there is much to be said for the

TABLE 3

PUBLIC EXPENDITURE BY PROGRAMME: 1968-9 TO 1971-2

	1968–69 provisional outturn £m.	1969–70 estimate £m.	1970–71 estimate £m.	1971–72 estimate £m.	Average annual percentage increase
At 1969 Survey prices					
Defence and external relations					
1. Defence Budget	2,292	2,252	2,211	2,161	−1·9
2. Other military defence	146	85	66	28	−42·4
3. Overseas aid (i)	206	224	234	251	6·8
4. Other overseas services	128	127	124	125	−0·8
Commerce and industry					
5. Technological services	190	205	226	207	2·9
6. Other assistance to employment and industry	857	954	925	937	3·0
7. Research Councils, etc.	90	98	105	111	7·2
8. Agriculture, fisheries and forestry	361	421	432	442	7·0
Environmental services					
9. Roads and public lighting	610	629	691	758	7·5
10. Transport	251	242	244	247	−0·5
11. Housing	1,095	1,073	1,141	1,202	3·2
12. Local environmental services	693	742	769	797	4·8
13. Law and order	558	595	635	673	6·4
14. Arts	16	18	20	22	11·2
Social services					
15. Education	2,232	2,300	2,381	2,499	3·8
16. Health and welfare	1,790	1,853	1,920	2,002	3·8
17. Social security *	3,295	3,545	3,738	3,820	5·1
Other services					
18. Financial administration	219	225	220	212	−1·1
19. Common services	164	186	205	223	10·8
20. Miscellaneous services	57	65	80	95	18·5
21. Northern Ireland	403	426	443	451	3·8
22. Nationalized industries etc., capital expenditure	1,510	1,439	1,474	1,436	−1·7
23. Debt interest	2,051	2,050	2,050	2,025	−0·4
24. Relative price effect and other adjustments	381	303	345	521	
25. Contingency reserve	—	—	75	175	
At 1969–70 outturn prices					
Total	19,595	20,057	20,754	21,420	3·0

* At outturn prices. Source: *Public Expenditure, 1968–9 to 1973–4*

Plowden concept of an independent committee of non-departmental ministers.

FORWARD PROJECTION IN PRACTICE

The chronic weakness of the public expenditure surveys of the 1960s was their tendency to under-estimate future costs. The 1963 survey showed public expenditure rising by an annual average of 4·1 per cent in real terms. When the survey was rolled forward a further year in the summer of 1964 a figure well in excess of 4 per cent emerged – either as a result of new programmes adopted in the intervening twelve months, or as a result of the recosting of the earlier programmes. On the top of this were added the social benefits decided upon by the Labour government in October 1964 in its first days of office. The new government announced in February 1965 a new $4\frac{1}{4}$ per cent annual average limit for the growth of public expenditure for the five-year period 1964–5 to 1969–70. Not only was this geared to unrealistic National Plan target rates of growth for the whole economy, but public expenditure failed to stay even within the announced guidelines. After the announcement of the $4\frac{1}{4}$ per cent ceiling, emergency cuts were announced on no less than five occasions – July 1965, July 1966, July 1967, November 1967 and January 1968. It was only in 1968–9 that the growth of public expenditure really came under control with an increase of only 1·6 per cent in real terms; and it was expected to rise by an average of 3 per cent in the following three years under the Labour government's original plans.

It would be wrong to suppose from this very recent success that the tendency to understate the growth of public expenditure has vanished. There are formidable technical snags in the whole exercise. There are for example complications resulting from changes in classification. Investment grants count as expenditure, while similar sums given as investment allowances count as offsets against revenue.

The system was changed from allowances to grants in 1967 and is to be switched to early depreciation under the Conservative government. These reclassifications can be allowed for in government calculations of percentage rates of increase (although they are one further reason, apart from the others to be mentioned shortly, why the Treasury definition of public expenditure is pretty meaningless if expressed as a proportion of the GNP).

There is also a snag in forward projections at constant prices. This arises from the fact that there is little scope for measurable productivity increases in many public sector activities – of which defence and educational expenditure are conspicuous examples. For this reason, even if public expenditure increases no faster than output when both are measured at *base year* prices, the *share* of public expenditure in the total will increase on the basis of *current* prices. The most recent PESC exercises have therefore continued a relative price adjustment, which is essentially a mark-up on future public expenditure to allow for this effect.

One of the biggest technical problems is how to translate authorizations made for control purposes – e.g. school building starts – into figures which can be checked against what has actually happened. Some Treasury studies have found as many as half a dozen figures given for the costs of certain forward plans for different purposes, none of which could be checked against the outcome. Work is being done to establish a unified set of definitions which can be used for control, economic forecasting and for monitoring against actual results.

There are other intrinsic uncertainties which no technical refinements can overcome. There exist, for example, whole areas such as the agricultural subsidies, or (at one time) the railway deficit, where commitments are to some extent open-ended, and where the concept of a long-term financial allocation makes little sense. Even outside these special areas the central government does not have complete control. The Supply Estimates presented to Parliament cover rather less than half of all public expenditure. The local authorities account for more than a quarter of the total. Although their capital expenditure can be controlled through loan sanctions they have a good deal of independence in their current expenditures.

One of the few really unfortunate aspects of the 1969 White Paper is that it made no overt allowance for increases in the real value of social-security benefits, which it was government policy to provide, on the grounds that these needed to be decided only a few months in advance. This gave a built-in under-estimate to the social-security component. An allowance for such increases was buried in the 'contingency reserve' which, probably for this reason, reached £500m. for 1973–4.

One unresolved problem, not of classification but of actual policy, is the part that public expenditure should play in demand management. No good way has yet been found of varying public expenditure at short notice without disrupting programmes wastefully. The ideal of a specific margin of postponable projects within the public sector programme, which can be accelerated or retarded at short notice, has still to be achieved.

THE SIZE OF THE PUBLIC SECTOR

How large should public spending be? The instinctive answer of many on the left is 'As large as we can get away with' and on the right 'As little as we can manage'. Indeed the hard core residue of left–right differences seems to turn on this question. It is one that a reasonable person should refuse to answer.

To begin with a distinction must be made between state expenditure on goods and services (labelled 'expenditure on resources' in the 1969 White Paper), and transfer payments. The latter covers a vast variety of cash payments, from investment grants and housing subsidies, to pensions and family allowances. Public expenditure on goods and services, however desirable, leaves people with less to spend out of their pockets. Transfer payments are intrinsically less paternalistic (especially when like pensions, and unlike housing subsidies or investment grants, they are not tied to specific purchases). For they do not reduce the amount available for personal consumption and private investment, although they do redistribute it.

At least three entirely separate questions are involved in any judgement of public sector spending: (1) Which goods and services do we wish to purchase collectively rather than privately? (2) Having made this decision, how much do we wish to spend on collective provision? and (3) By how much and to whom do we want to make net transfers of purchasing power?

The concept of a 'public good' is of help in answering the first question. In the case of a pure public good one person's enjoyment does not diminish the amount available for others; and if it is provided at all it is impossible to limit access by a charging system. Pure public goods would include national defence or clean air. An example of a pure private good would be a refrigerator or a meal. In between the two extremes there is a big intermediate category such as medical services or education or slum clearance, which are not pure public goods, but which have semi-public aspects. The demolition of slums has large 'spill-over' effects on the general appearance of a city, which all can enjoy. Except for a few motorways it would be difficult to organize a charging system for new roads; and until a certain degree of utilization is reached, one person's enjoyment does not detract from another's.[5]

There is no necessary connection between views on the range of services which ought to be supplied collectively and the amount that ought to be spent on them once this

5. For an excellent discussion of private and public goods see Charles L. Schultze, 'The Politics and Economics of Public Spending', *Brookings Institute*, Washington, 1968.

decision has been made. It is possible to believe that insufficient is spent on the vast range of goods and services for which the state has a near monopoly, but that some of these services should in an affluent society be treated as private goods and left to individuals of average incomes and above to provide from their own resources. There might be less public squalor if the state, by contracting out of some of these activities, were able to spend more on genuine public goods such as parks, well-designed city centres and good civic buildings.

In discussing transfer payments, it is important to distinguish between gross and net payments. There is a large two-way flow among many citizens who pay tax and receive pensions or allowances. The more 'selective' the benefits the less that needs to be spent to return with one hand what is taken with the other.

Intelligent discussion of public expenditure is made no easier by the large number of different figures of its total size. Different definitions are suitable for different purposes; and even non-partisan estimates are liable to range from about 20 per cent of the Gross National Product to well over 50 per cent. A few of the more important definitions are given below; but each one has many alternative variants.

1. As an *employer of labour* the public sector accounts for well over 25 per cent of the nation's manpower and over 60 per cent of those with full-time higher education. This is an important index for those interested in individual freedom. As John Stuart Mill put it:

If the roads, the railways, the banks, the insurance offices, the great joint-stock companies, the universities, and the public charities, were all of them branches of the government; if, in addition, the municipal corporations and local boards, with all that now devolves on them, became departments of the central administration; if the employés of all these different enterprises were appointed and paid by the government, and looked to the government for every rise in life; not all the freedom of the press and popular constitution of the legislature would make this or any other country free otherwise than in name.[6]

Another measure of public power – although not a definition of the public sector – is purchases from the private sector by government departments, local authorities and nationalized industries. These were running in 1970 at about £5,000m. or about 12 per cent of total output. These purchases were over and above the output produced by the 25 per cent of the working force in public employment.

My own judgement would be that we have not yet passed the danger point for liberty, although we are pretty close to it especially in the sphere of employment for those with higher education. A fuller analysis of the problem would have to pay careful attention, on Mill's lines, to the degree of independence of government of other parts of the public sector such as the nationalized industries and local authorities.

2. Another fundamental figure is the *current and capital expenditure of central and local government on goods and services at factor cost*. Such expenditure[7] was running at the beginning of the 1970s, at about 25 per cent of the GNP. It is the best measure of the proportion of the national income devoted to collective rather than private purchases. For what is left over after this expenditure is available for personal spending and for commercially directed investment (nationalized industries' capital expenditure is included, at least in principle, in the latter), and for any net export surplus. Even this category, however, is blurred at the edges. Health service charges can be treated as an offset, reducing the total figures, in line with the present official convention – or they can be treated as a tax and the expen-

6. *On Liberty*, Dent edition, p. 165.
7. It is nowhere clearly labelled as a single category in the published statistics but has to be compiled by the user for himself from different tables in the *National Income Blue Book* and *Financial Statement*.

diture shown gross. There are even greater headaches about local authority housing, for which rents are charged, but not at market levels.

3. For purposes of economic forecasting and analysis, discussed in the next chapter, *current* public sector expenditure on goods and services at factor cost is treated as a separate item. This has been running at about 20 per cent of the GNP. It is of little intrinsic interest, but frequently used in international comparisons.

4. A special purpose definition is *Supply Expenditure,* which is simply that portion of central government spending which has to be voted annually by the House of Commons. This has been running just under 30 per cent of the GNP. To it is sometimes added expenditure on *Consolidated Fund Standing Services* (mostly net interest payments on the National Debt), to give the total of *Consolidated Fund expenditure,* which has to be financed from central government revenue. This total, which appears in the Financial Statement produced on Budget Day and is often reproduced in the press afterwards, has been running at just over 31 per cent of the GNP.

The above definitions exclude, however, pensions financed from National Insurance contributions, rate-financed local authority spending and a great many other important items. They are therefore of little interest apart from their role in the Parliamentary ritual.

5. The *Treasury definition* of public expenditure is a very wide one covering the whole of the current and capital expenditure of central and local government on goods and services and transfers; the gross outgoings of the National Insurance funds; and the capital spending of the nationalized industries. It is clearly the most comprehensive of the definitions and is quite independent of Parliamentary formalities. Defined in this way public expenditure amounted in 1970 to some 52–3 per cent of the GNP, and had risen from about 43 per cent in both 1959 and 1964.

While this wide definition is a useful indicator of the

flows of spending, which in some sense pass through public hands, it gives a grossly inflated idea of the state's pre-emption of income; and the Treasury and CSO have played into the hands of the more unthinking anti-public-expenditure lobby by focusing so much attention upon it. Ministers themselves have confused the issue by sometimes using this definition and at other times much narrower ones in their own Parliamentary Answers.

It is certainly true that transfer payments, such as pensions or family allowances, have to be financed by deductions from earnings, just as much as state expenditure on goods and services. But the Treasury definition overstates the burden on the citizen by leaving out sources of revenue other than taxes, of which the most important are the gross trading surpluses of the nationalized industries and the next most important, local authority rents. *Surely the definition of public expenditure in which most people are interested is that which determines what they have to pay in taxes, rates, national insurance contributions and other such deductions from their incomes*; and this ought to become 'the' definition (although it certainly is not at present), unless expressly stated to the contrary.

A tentative calculation along the lines suggested is shown in Table 4 for 1968–9 which comes to £15,700m. or some 42½ per cent of the GNP. The purist might object that this total will vary according to the public sector borrowing requirement, the permissible amount of which may change according to the economic situation. Nevertheless a given public sector programme really is a smaller burden where the public sector can safely run a substantial borrowing requirement than when it cannot. The fact that the suggested definition is identically equivalent to whatever is regarded as the effective tax burden is a virtue. For this is what the political debate is about, and it might as well be focused on the right set of figures. But even an improved definition will not prevent us from falling into the tax-cutting traps discussed in the concluding chapter.

TABLE 4

SUGGESTED NEW DEFINITION OF PUBLIC
EXPENDITURE FIGURES FOR 1968–9, £M.

Public Expenditure, Treasury definition		19,150
Deduct		
1. Public sector trading surpluses	1,500	
2. Rents received	900	
3. Interest and dividend receipts	250	
4. Import Deposits	350	
5. Miscellaneous	150	
6. Net borrowing requirement	300	
Total Deductions		3,450
Total Public Expenditure to be financed from rates, taxes and National Insurance contributions		**15,700**

Source: *National Income and Expenditure, 1969,* and *Financial Statement, 1969–70* (figures rounded)

ALLOCATION AND EFFICIENCY

The forecasting and measuring of public spending are only a part of the total task. At least as important are the decisions about how much to spend for different purposes and how to gain the maximum return for each pound spent. New intellectual tools have been developed, mainly in the USA, for this purpose, which go under various names of which the best known is *Planning, Programming and Budgeting,* or *PPB*. This involves allocating spending according to functions, such as 'strategic nuclear defence' or 'income maintenance' rather than by a department agency or piece of equipment. The reallocation of expenditure on such lines is one of the purposes of an 'output Budget'. If taken seriously it means going beyond the old political clichés of miles of roads, or thousands of houses built, and asking what has been achieved per pound spent to reduce transport congestion or relieve overcrowding. Instead of bargaining with a department about whether it should have another £xm. to do a little more of the same, a resolute PPB approach would ask what need the programme was fulfilling and whether it could be better filled in some completely different way, whether in another part of the public sector or in the private one.

Clearly such 'zero-based' reviews cannot be an annual occurrence in all programmes without paralysing activity. Nevertheless all types of public spending ought to come under this type of scrutiny at some time or another. 'PPB' is, of course, a form of common sense, but of a kind that is not at all common, and which it is particularly difficult to build into the government machine. A full discussion of these subjects would take one too far away from the overall economic steering which is the subject of this book. This, however, is not the only limitation. Although PPB techniques have penetrated quite far into defence, they have still not made more than marginal and experimental inroads into civil spending. It will moreover immediately strike the reader of recent Treasury White Papers that most of the really top-grade analysis has been devoted to assessing the effects of public expenditure on total *demand*, as an aspect of economic management. The detailed allocation of resources within the public sector has not yet received nearly as sophisticated an attention.

The Conservatives made it clear in their pre-election plans of 1970 that if they were elected they would set up a central policy staff to help the Cabinet decide its spending priorities. This is now situated in the Cabinet Office. Of much more interest than its location will be its behaviour. The crucial test is whether it will concentrate on the much-needed analytical probes, or whether it will just be an instrument of Prime Ministerial power.

The Plowden Report of 1961 was supposed to mark the official abandonment of the last vestiges of the candle-ends

doctrine. Once the expenditure ceilings have been established it is in principle up to each spending minister to subdivide his allocation. This should leave the Treasury with
what Peter Jay called the rational job of 'refereeing the
annual survey and policing its implementation'[8] while
the departments no longer have to haggle over candle-ends.

It would be wrong to suppose that this principle has yet
been carried to very great lengths. Reallocations of expenditure within departments still have to be approved by
the Treasury (in accordance with the principles set out on
p. 102) and the amount of delegation varies from item to
item. There is still a considerable amount of fussy detail,
and small arguments over individual items continue to
occur at the time of the annual Estimates, which are still an
important ritual. The five-year forward programmes have
not eliminated the game recently described by an anony-
mous official, in accordance with which his department
submitted an Estimate 'carefully calculated to include an
allowance which it knows will be pared down in arguments
with the Treasury'. Some ten per cent of the agreed Estimate is then held over for 'contingencies' and 'eventually
parcelled out among the sections with the unwritten understanding that they must spend it before the end of the
financial year. Otherwise the department might be accused
of overestimating at the next auction and might find its
next estimate more savagely pruned than the year before.'[9]

It is tempting to suggest eliminating such nonsense by
fixing an overall limit for each spending authority, within
which more spent on one service will mean less on some
other one. Those in charge can then, if they are competent,
be left to subdivide their expenditure so that no marginal
shift from one area to another will increase the total 'return'.
The trouble with such a system is that the initial allocation
between departments is itself open to argument. Each

8. 'Planning Public Spending', *The Times*, 6 July 1967.
9. 'The Estimates Game in the Civil Service', letter to the *Guardian*,
18 April 1968.

department will always be able to put up a strong case for more at the expense of other departments; and no central watchdog body will be able to form a sensible judgement of the relative merits of rival claims, unless it takes a close interest in the composition as well as the total of the spending programmes. Public expenditure can thus neither be entirely allocated from the top downwards, nor built up from the bottom upwards, but must in practice be regulated by a mixture of both methods.

The amount of delegation of spending decisions that is desirable is clearly dependent on the 'quality of management' within each department, which was stressed so heavily by both the Plowden and the Fulton Committees. A consequence of their work is that the talents required to run an organization, or control a programme, are gradually becoming more important in the Civil Service and that the ability to write good briefs for ministers is ceasing to be the one main avenue to advancement. The amalgamation of the Administrative and Executive grades should help to increase the status of the managerial functions. There is, however, bound to be some overlap of interest and responsibility between the Treasury and the Civil Service Department, both of which ought to share an interest in departmental efficiency.

The area of expenditure where cost control is chronically weakest is the whole complex concerned with weapons, missiles, aircraft, space and atomic energy. There are genuine difficulties in estimating costs of new and highly complex projects understood only by a few experts. There are also powerful commercial lobbies at work in this area; and considerations of supposed national prestige, or the magic word 'technology', are often invoked to justify misallocation of taxpayers' money to projects which are not commercially worth while.

THE DISTRIBUTION OF INCOME

No discussion of public spending can disregard the way in which the whole issue has been confused at a political level by different views about the distribution of income. This has been explained by Brian Barry in a most important and insufficiently discussed book.[10] Under a British-type progressive tax system, the higher the total tax burden the more 'equal' is the post-tax distribution of income. If the standard rate of income tax is 1s. higher, the relative position of those with high earnings declines relative to the rest of the population. This is superficial as it leaves out tax avoidance, capital values and the peculiarities of taxes on higher salaries. But there is enough in the point to make egalitarians press for a high level of state spending, even if they are not collectivists. Non-egalitarians on the other hand – in practice the middle classes and better-paid workers – feel bound to press for lower state spending even if they would otherwise be enthusiastic about a high level of public services.

By a careful study of the incidence of total public spending on different family circumstances, it would be possible to construct a system of direct and indirect taxes which would be distributionally neutral. In other words if it were raised or lowered by x per cent, the allocation of post-tax income between economic classes would remain unchanged. On top of this there could be a second 'transfer fund' which would pay out cash benefits at the bottom end and impose some form of progressive levy on income or capital at the upper end. The second fund need not be self-balancing and could be fed from the first. But there would be a presumption that any increase in the rate of growth of public spending on goods and services would be paid out of the first fund and that any reduction in such spending would accrue to this fund for the purpose of tax cuts. In

10. *Political Argument*, Routledge & Kegan Paul, 1965, pp. 156–7.

this way the argument about equality and income distribution could be entirely separated from that over public versus private spending.

The Treasury would dislike this suggestion because of its devotion to a single 'Consolidated Fund' for central government revenue. The main obstacle, however, lies neither here nor in the administrative complications. The fact is that the last thing politicians want is a published fund, which makes it clear how much is redistributed from whom to whom. The net recipients would want still more and the net losers would be bitterly resentful at making the transfer. Both left and right feel it safer to blur the question of redistribution in a debate conducted on the basis of 'schools, houses, and pensions' versus 'tax cuts and incentives'.

APPENDIX:
THE NATIONALIZED INDUSTRIES

The Treasury does not attempt to control the spending of the nationalized industries in the same way as the rest of the public sector. The nationalized industries have been moving towards a more commercial orientation, and the Treasury sees its relations with them as that of bankers to clients. The first attempt at a coherent financial policy was the White Paper on the *Financial Obligations of the Nationalized Industries* of 1961 (Cmnd 1337), which laid down financial objectives for the industries to achieve over five years. The idea was that the industries should make a reasonable rate of return on the capital employed and thus also make some contribution to their own capital needs. (The background to the 1961 White Paper is discussed on p. 245.)

Although this new approach enabled the nationalized industries to raise their prices, which had been held back to too low a level for political reasons, and probably also helped to improve the standard of management, it was still defective. The sensible use of a rate of return is to decide whether to undertake a new project. It has no relevance to existing assets. A businessman may find himself with a factory he would never have built had he foreseen the return; but having made his original mistake it is worth his while keeping it open so long as there is any excess of receipts over running costs, and it is socially desirable that he should do

TABLE 5

NATIONALIZED INDUSTRIES: FINANCIAL OBJECTIVES, SPRING 1970*

Industry	Objective	Period Covered
Post Office Corporation		
i. Postal Services	To achieve a surplus equal to 2% of total expenditure.	1968/69–1972/73
ii. Telecommunications	8½% net †	1968/69–1972/73
iii. National Data Processing Service	8% net †	1968/69–1971/72
National Coal Board	To earn revenue sufficient for meeting all current outgoings.	1969/70–1970/71
Electricity Council and Boards (England and Wales)	7% net †	1969/70–1973/74
Gas Council and Boards	7% net †	1969/70–1973/74
British Overseas Airways Corp.	12½% net †	1966/67–1969/70
British European Airways Corp.	8% net † (subject to review)	1968/69–1971/72
British Railways Board British Transport Docks Board British Waterways Board Transport Holding Company National Freight Corporation National Bus Company	Each of these bodies has the statutory obligation to secure that the combined revenues of the authority and of its subsidiaries taken together meet their combined current costs, taking one year with another.	

* Targets for the National Bus Company, British Airports Authority and British Steel Corporation were still under discussion.

† Income before interest but after depreciation at historic cost, expressed as a percentage of average net assets.

so. The setting of a blanket rate of return on both new and old assets only makes for confusion.

A second White Paper published in November 1967, entitled *Nationalized Industries: A Review of Economic and Financial Objectives* (Cmnd 3437), was a big improvement. Its starting point was that nationalized industries were expected to use discounted cash flow[11] techniques for all major investment proposals, which were then expected to yield at least 8 per cent. This figure was raised in 1969 to 10 per cent. Particularly risky projects were naturally expected to show a higher prospective rate of return.

The guiding principle behind the 'test discount rate' was that the rate of return anticipated on a new investment in the public and private sector should be comparable. An 8–10 per cent rate was regarded as consistent with the average return expected on low risk prospects in the private sector, bearing in mind the effects of Corporation Tax, investment grants and other differences between the two sectors. In the period after the 1967 White Paper, the private sector tended to raise its sights to the upper end of the range; and this was the main reason why the Treasury shifted its rate to 10 per cent. Another reason was that, as part of its effort to contain public expenditure, it was looking for a method of eliminating marginal projects. The effect of the change was expected to be modest; the more highly capital intensive methods became less attractive, and there was some slight rephasing of programmes.

The rate of return achieved on a new project is not fixed in heaven, but will vary according to the pricing policy of the industry concerned. The real innovation of the second White Paper was to suggest that prices should be related to marginal costs, both in the short and the long run. (This

11. The rate of return on a discounted cash flow basis is that rate of discount of the future which would make the present value of all expected future revenue equal the present value of expected future costs. It would be the natural method of approach for anyone approaching the subject unencumbered with accounting conventions.

means, roughly, that the Coal Board would produce coal up to the point at which the price realized just covered the cost of the last extra ton produced.)

The combination of a pricing rule and a rate of return for a new investment together determine the earnings of a nationalized industry at any particular time. But the White Paper did not have the courage of its own logic and still retained the old financial objectives expressed as rates of return on existing assets. These were regarded as 'a very flexible instrument'; a sensible use of them might be as management checks to make sure that the agreed policies were being carried out. One suspects, however much this is denied, that they were also there as a safeguard to ensure that the new policies, even if they were applied correctly, did not lead to lower earnings and greater calls on the Treasury for finance.

This Treasury concern with the calls for cash is even more apparent in the qualifications with which it surrounded the marginal cost rule. This was to be waived whenever there was any danger of revenue not covering the total accounting costs of a service. (A rational private industrialist, operating on the principle of letting bygones be bygones, would be prepared to make and sell products so long as his marginal revenue – which approximates in sufficiently competitive conditions to the price received – exceeded his *short-run* marginal costs. He would deal with any failure to cover long-run marginal costs by not replacing the assets in question as they ran down.) A firm decision by the Treasury to stick to its own marginal-cost rule might be more logical than the occasional lump-sum writing down of assets which it allowed, for instance, in the case of the railways, the Coal Board and BOAC. Here, and elsewhere, one sees at work the compromise between the Treasury's traditional concern for saving money in the basic cash sense, and its desire as a modern economic ministry to maximize the return on real resources. The compromise can be rationalized by saying (correctly) that sufficient confidence does not yet exist in the new techniques to abandon completely the old yardsticks.

The 1967 White Paper also considered the cases where 'social' costs and benefits diverged markedly from the return to the nationalized concern itself. An example would be a commuter railway where some of the savings from reducing congestion in the streets might not appear in the books of the transport undertaking at all. For such cases cost – benefit studies were recommended which 'are best carried out by the Government Departments concerned, in collaboration with the industries'. To guard against the danger that the social value of employing men in, say, loss-making coal mines or branch lines might be treated quite differently by the Ministries of Technology and Transport, the Treasury has in fact made some central studies in its Management Accounting Unit. This began by examining the results of 20 or 30 cost – benefit studies already made in the public sector with the object of devising standard values for certain social costs and benefits.

At the beginning of the 1960s, the House of Commons Select Committee on the Nationalized Industries recommended that specific subsidies should be paid out of public funds for services which did not pay their way, but which Parliament wished to maintain. This suggestion, which was repeated in 1967–8, would have clearly separated commercial judgements from wider social and economic decisions which ought to be made by the government. Unfortunately even the second White Paper did not accept this principle unequivocally (although it was subsequently accepted for the railways in the Transport Act, and to some extent, for the coal industry).

The alternative idea of taking into account wider public objectives by adjusting downwards the financial targets of the industries concerned has still not vanished from the scene. One can only re-echo the words of Lord Aldington (who as Sir Toby Low chaired the original Select Committee): 'This goes a little way to meeting the problem, but it does not – and I regret this greatly – mark a clear-cut division of responsibility between the Boards and the ministers.'[12]

The biggest obstacles to rational decision-making for the nationalized industries have, however, been the various ventures in prices and incomes policy. These brought new respectability to the old political urge to trim and delay price increases in state industries, especially when elections were pending. The fact is that the Treasury's objectives for the nationalized industries, and prices and incomes policy as interpreted in practice by ministers, have made most uncomfortable bedfellows.

12. 'The Select Committee on Nationalized Industries', *Public Administration*, spring 1962.

4

THE BUDGET AND MONETARY POLICY

The Budget: the tax structure: the fiscal balance: the money supply

THE BUDGET

Mr Harold Macmillan once said that Budget Day was rather like a school speech day (adding that like speech day it was also a bit of a bore). But it is a paradoxical sort of speech day. If the economy is doing very well and factories can hardly keep up with the demand for their goods, the Treasury is likely to see a case, not for any distribution of prizes, but for higher taxes. For the object of a modern Budget is not just to raise money but to regulate the nation's spending. It is when trade is relatively slack that a Chancellor may want to put spending money into people's pockets, if this can be done without jeopardizing the balance of payments. This simple principle of demand management has been a guide and beacon to most Chancellors since Sir Kingsley Wood in 1941.

It has, however, been subject to considerable intellectual challenge since the late 1960s. Four main grounds of challenge might be mentioned here. Firstly scepticism has been expressed about whether governments possess enough knowledge, or are able to act quickly enough, to engage in this kind of 'fine tuning'. Action taken to remedy a recession may have such long time-lags that its main effect could be to intensify the next boom (and vice versa for anti-inflationary action). If this is so the economy will be more stable if governments do not try too hard to stabilize it. Secondly, and on a different plane, there has been increasing debate about whether Budgetary changes have the effects on demand that are claimed for them. This has been allied with a revival of belief in the potency of monetary policy. Thirdly, the size of the Budget surplus or deficit has important long-run effects apart from those connected with demand management, and these aspects are likely to attract growing attention in the 1970s. A fourth and earthier consideration is that the pre-Budget study of the home economy may in many past years have been a pious ritual to justify decisions pre-determined by the balance of payments, or by immediate political worries about unemployment.

This questioning of post-war orthodoxy has been very healthy. But the arguments will not be quickly resolved. Chancellors are most unlikely to give up the attempt to use the Budget as an economic regulator in the foreseeable future. A fairly orthodox account of the Budget as the Treasury sees it will therefore be given in the following pages, to be followed by a discussion of topics such as the fiscal balance and the money supply, which are once more attracting attention.[1] (The reader new to these subjects is warned that the later parts of this chapter are likely to become increasingly heavy going and that he may prefer to defer them until he has looked at the rest of the book.)

When does the Chancellor start thinking about next year's Budget? Most Chancellors begin to worry about it as soon as they have made up their minds about this year's. Inside the Treasury itself a committee in charge of Budget arrangements meets continuously from July to the end of March. This is a high-powered body under the chairmanship of the Permanent Secretary to the Treasury. The chairmen of the Inland Revenue and Customs and Excise are, of course, members, as are the Treasury's most senior economic advisers and the heads of the Finance and Public Sector groups, together with a very small number of

1. To make room for the new material the summary of forecasting methods has had to be omitted. It can be found in the 1969 hardback Secker & Warburg edition.

supporting staff. The Deputy Governor, or an Executive Director, of the Bank of England is also present.

The role of Permanent Secretaries of other departments outside the Treasury became acutely controversial after the establishment of the Department of Economic Affairs in 1964. Problems arose not merely about who should be present, but about how far and at what stage they could report to their own ministers on what had hitherto been regarded as the Chancellor's most cherished personal prerogative. In the end flexible arrangements were devised for bringing in other Permanent Secretaries before the judgement was taken on how much to 'put into' or 'take out of' the economy. Although the details of these consultations are liable to change with political circumstances, the basic machinery has remained remarkably similar for a very long period.

The summer meetings of the Budget committee started some years ago to take stock of the effects of the previous Budget. Their main purpose now is to see if taxes ought to be changed in mid-year. The Chancellor's 'regulator' power to vary purchase tax and other consumer taxes by a tenth in between Budgets is helpful here.

Government departments send in to the Treasury preliminary forecasts of their expenditure for the following financial year but one in February, with two revisions up to May. (This forms part of the 'PESC' exercise described in the previous chapter.) The Inland Revenue and Customs and Excise (jointly known as 'the Revenue Departments') also send in their preliminary revenue forecasts in time for these summer meetings. The Treasury Accountant – who is not a policy-maker, but had up to 1970 been a very senior Executive Officer – is therefore able to work out his first 'Exchequer Prospects Table', outlining revenue and expenditure in the coming year.

In autumn the pace quickens. By early October, figures for public investment – power stations, hospitals, schools, etc. – have been agreed, and in early November the autumn economic forecasts are ready. Their aim is to predict the growth of demand and output in relation to the country's productive capacity, and forecast the balance of payments on the hypothetical assumption that nothing is done in the Budget. This provides the basis of a preliminary assessment of the sort of Budget likely to be required.

In the course of the autumn, papers are also presented on long-term economic objectives. Ideas for changing the tax system, perhaps abolishing some taxes and introducing others, may be brought up in this context by Treasury economists or other officials. These will often be opposed by the Revenue Departments, who may have quite genuine administrative objections. The representatives of the Revenue Departments take little detailed part in the general economic discussions, confining themselves to a remark here and there on the way they think business is moving. They do, however, put up papers in the course of the autumn or early winter on 'the state' of the various taxes. They might point out, for example, that the revenue from beer and tobacco duties, on which Chancellors have relied so heavily in the past, is not likely to grow very quickly in the future owing to changing social habits. They will have their own ideas for replacements which may be different from those of the economists, but are at least as likely to prevail. By 1 December government departments will have sent in firm estimates of their spending, and during the course of the month the Treasury Accountant will have worked out a revised Exchequer Prospects Table. During most of the post-war period the Chancellor's Budget decisions did not depend so much on these calculations as on his general assessment of the way business was going in the country as a whole, and on the balance of payments.

The clue to the Budget judgement is that the Treasury normally does not think in terms of the rate of growth of output itself, but of the 'pressure of demand' on the economy, as measured by unemployment and vacancies. At the beginning of the 1970s it regarded a pressure of demand

TABLE 6

APPROXIMATE BUDGET TIMETABLE

Month	Events	Information	Assessment
July	Budget committee starts.	Summer National Income Forecast. Preliminary 'Exchequer Prospects Table'.	Need for 'summer package'?
October		Public investment figures agreed for following financial year.	Papers on long-term objectives and on 'state' of various taxes. Need for 'autumn Budget' discussed.
November	Chancellor has preliminary talks with officials.	Autumn National Income Forecast.	First assessment of next year's Budget.
December		Revised 'Exchequer Prospects Table'.	
January	Budget committee presents first report. Intensive discussions with Chancellor.	Estimates of expenditure for coming year agreed.	Provisional 'Budget judgement'.
Feb.– Early March	Main outline of Budget agreed. Tax details formulated.	Final National Income Forecast. Up-to-date 'Exchequer Prospects Table'.	Final Budget judgement, e.g. 'remove £200m. from economy'.
March	Finance Bill discussed. Budget speech written. Last-minute changes.		Specific tax changes agreed.
April	Pre-Budget Cabinet. BUDGET.	Financial Statement published on Budget Day.	
May–July	Finance Bill in Commons.		

corresponding to rather above 2 per cent as optimum; anything less it regarded as inflationary, and anything very much more as an unnecessary waste of resources. If the balance-of-payments outlook is satisfactory, the Treasury will not always over-exert itself against politicians who are prepared to allow unemployment to fall a little below the target. Conversely, if the balance of payments has been, or is likely to be, in deficit, the Treasury will give it top priority and not worry overmuch if unemployment looks like slightly exceeding the target level.

According to the doctrines which have reigned in the Economic Service, if balance of payments equilibrium requires an unemployment rate very much higher than 2 per cent, the price is too great to pay and a lower exchange rate is then appropriate. But every expedient will be adopted to avoid drawing this inference as long as possible. Increases in unemployment can be treated as temporary fluctuations; and attempts can be made to buy time by overseas borrowing or rephasing external debt repayments. By the autumn of 1967 all these expedients had already been used up to and beyond any reasonable limits, and there was no alternative to devaluation (short of a policy of permanent trade restrictions). Exchange rates would, of course, be discussed in an even more restricted gathering outside the framework of the Budget committee.

Different measures affect the economy with different time-lags. Income tax changes, which do not even begin to affect the taxpayer until the following July, start slowly and then build up to a larger effect. Taxes on goods take effect immediately, while hire-purchase changes have a large immediate impact, which then tapers off. Thus, to some extent the Chancellor can vary the instrument to obtain the time pattern he wants. But his power to do so is strictly limited. Irrespective of when a measure has its first impact on consumer spending, it will take a while for the effects to work through fully to the industries supplying components and materials, and to importers. There will be a further interval before those whose real incomes are increased or reduced, step up or trim back their own spending in a continuing 'multiplier' sequence. The indirect 'accelerator' effects of changing sales or profits on rates of investment take even longer to make themselves felt. The result is that almost any action taken by the Chancellor has such long time-lags that it is unlikely to have its full impact on the economy until well into the following financial year. This may present a difficult problem if big changes are needed. If the Chancellor wants a quick impact, he will have to reflate or deflate by an amount which may later prove too great. If, on the other hand, he tries to avoid 'overkill' he will have to reconcile himself to slow results.

It will be seen that the Budget decisions are highly dependent on the economic forecasts. The object of these forecasts is not to replace the crystal ball or the tea leaves, but to help the Chancellor steer the economy. If they give him a better idea of how much to reflate or deflate than he would otherwise have, then they have been helpful, even if every individual component is wrong. The trouble is that, even judged by this test, they have too often been a misleading guide. They failed to spot the rapid boom which was developing in 1959, and thus made it possible for Mr Heathcoat Amory to reflate vigorously with a clear conscience. In 1961 and 1962, on the other hand, they led to a serious overestimate of the expansionary forces in the economy and thus contributed to Mr Lloyd's downfall. Later, in 1963–4, they failed to give Mr Maudling a real hint that his 'growth' strategy was likely to lead to anything approaching an £800m. external deficit. (He expected £400m., which he thought he could finance.) Before the 1967 Budget, the forecasts gave Mr Callaghan the impression that he would have at the $2·80 parity, some balance of payments surplus in 1967 and a large one in 1968, all combined with a 3 per cent growth rate. In 1968 the forecasts overrated the impact of the large tax increases on consumption and, partly for that reason, were much too optimistic about the speed with which devaluation would work. By 1969 the influence of the formal forecasts had passed its zenith – although it was still of importance.

The Treasury economists themselves place a considerable width of margin on either side of their central estimates. In 1969 the balance of payments forecast had a margin of error of as much as £300m. on either side. Some officials would have liked to have done away with the central estimates altogether and presented the forecasts in terms of a range – this would also have brought to the surface differences between individuals and departments smothered by a single set of compromise figures. But the technical difficulties of adding together ranges in the many component figures stood in the way up to the beginning of the 1970s. Instead it became customary for the Chief Economic Adviser to give an idea of the range in his covering note to the Chancellor.

By 1970, work was in hand to put the forecasts on a computerized basis; and Professor J. R. Ball of the London Business School had already been consulted on ways of putting existing forecasting methods on a computer programme. Computer models are, of course, no better than the relationships which are fed into them and they do not provide a magic means of dispelling the problems of analysis, forecasting or policy. Their real value is in the opposite direction, as they enable one to examine the consequences of alternative assumptions about key variables such as exports or savings ratios and come out with all the permutations and combinations at short notice. The value of computerized forecasts is however never any better than the view of economic relationships on which the computer equations are based.

It is most important to look at the forecasts in terms of the balance of risks, which is a different concept from the margin of error. The effects of an upward deviation from the central forecast are not always the same as those of downward deviations. The adverse effects of a shortfall on the balance of payments compared with forecast are much greater, when confidence is shaky, than the beneficial effects of an equivalent excess. When the labour market is already too slack and the balance of payments in surplus, the effects of unemployment exceeding the forecast may be more worrying than the effects of a shortfall. There can of course be nightmare, knife-edged situations when almost any marked deviation in either direction will seem alarming.

The extent to which the Budget committee will look reasonably far ahead and take a sophisticated view of the balance of risks will depend on the temperament, outlook and abilities of the Chancellor and the senior officials. The human temptation to concentrate on this year and its problems, and to look only at the 'central estimates' in the forecasts if anything worse seems too frightening, is very strong. The excessive emphasis on secrecy and the consequent exclusion of all but the most senior economists from the Budget committee can load the dice in favour of the short-term and the politically convenient.

In whatever mood he approaches the Budget, by November and December the Chancellor will already have had a few tête-à-tête discussions with his Permanent Secretary and economic advisers, and he will have also discussed with the heads of the Revenue departments some of the specific tax changes under consideration. In January the Chancellor receives his first set of recommendations from the Budget committee; and from then onwards he plays a very active personal part. He will have a few sessions with the whole Budget committee, into which he may bring the other Treasury ministers. The personality of the individual Chancellor has a great deal to do with the individual tax changes chosen. It has some, but much less, effect on the 'Budget judgement' of how much in total to 'give away' or take back in taxation. In January and February better estimates of revenue are supplied. By early February the Chancellor knows the result of his final battles with the spending departments, and the estimates of 'Supply' expenditure.

As more and more information becomes available, the 'Budget judgement' becomes more precise. In the last few weeks of the old year it is likely to be a very simple one such as 'nothing to give away and perhaps a little extra to raise'. Early in the New Year it grows a little firmer, e.g. 'some extra taxation needed'. By mid February the Chancellor will be advised to intervene by a definite amount.

The meaning of such assessments is far from simple. They relate basically to the desired effect on demand (calculated in 'real terms') rather than to Exchequer revenue. Tax increases which are paid largely out of capital or savings, such as increases in Corporation Tax or levies on investment income, are heavily discounted in working out the economic impact of the Budget. The amount of extra revenue raised in the post-devaluation Budget of 1968 was more than £900m., but the actual amount the Chancellor had 'taken out of the economy' was later given as just over £500m.

The meaning of even this last figure is ambiguous. Two calculations have been common. Firstly to help the Chancellor select his package a table is prepared of the effects of a large number of possible measures. This sets out for each measure (a) the impact on revenue in the first year, (b) the impact in a full year, (c) the direct effect on *demand* at factor cost by the first quarter of the next calendar year and (d) the effect on the retail price index. The demand calculation at this stage excludes indirect 'multiplier' and 'accelerator' effects but also excludes the leakage of demand to imports. Secondly the economic forecasters adjust their estimate for *output* up to the end of the forecast period in the light of the package chosen. It was not entirely a coincidence that the two measures gave nearly identical results for both the 1968 and 1969 Budgets, but this happy similarity cannot always be relied upon to obtain.

Any attempt to present the judgement in the more readily understood revenue terms is full of ambiguities, such as whether it is in terms of the impact this year or 'in a full year' (when the tax changes have yielded their full fruit), or which changes are to be regarded as new and which previously foreshadowed. There is, in fact, a case for avoiding the figure of 'how much the Chancellor has taken out' altogether and publishing a 'before' and 'after' set of economic forecasts. In 1968, for example, the Chancellor aimed, by means of a severe Budget, to bring the growth rate down from an estimated $4-4\frac{1}{2}$ per cent per annum to something over 3 per cent, to avoid any risk of devaluation being frustrated by an excessive growth of home demand. He did not entirely succeed in his objective, but the suggested tabulation would at least have made the intended effect of the Budget clear.

At some stage the Chancellor has to bring the Prime Minister into the picture; the exact timing will depend on the particular Premier and his mood, but mid January has been fairly typical. The degree of interference varies, even with the same person at No. 10. Which other ministers, if any, are brought in, also depends on circumstances. Usually the number has been very restricted. It became customary in the mid and late 1960s to bring a handful of the most senior economic ministers into the discussion of the broad economic judgement. Apart from this, Mr Roy Jenkins made a habit of having bilateral talks with various ministers, as a measure of self-protection so that his actions did not come as a complete shock at the pre-Budget Cabinet. Such talks do not cover the specific tax changes, which are kept a closely guarded secret – although the minister concerned will, of course, be consulted on a move affecting his own department (e.g the Secretary of State for Employment and Productivity on the Selective Employment Tax).

During the winter the Chancellor and the other Treasury ministers will receive a host of delegations from organizations with special interests. The motoring organizations will come, for example, about petrol tax and the distillers about whisky duty. Most demands will be shrugged off with the cynical thought that everyone is asking, to quote Lord Amory, 'for a reduction in one or more taxes and duties, or for an increase in one or more items of expenditure – often both at the same time'. But an unobtrusive representation from backbench MPs on the government side who claim to speak for Party opinion will have a larger effect, especially where a concession can be made at small cost to the Revenue. There are also more technical representations – for example, from accountants' organizations on Inland Revenue practice – which receive very serious attention.

The Budget committee's work is in general treated like a military secret – except that Budget security is usually more effective. Each member of the committee can appoint one deputy to serve in his stead, but even this overstates the number in the picture, as some members may share a deputy. Until the pre-Budget printing, early in March, no more than two dozen people are allowed to know what is happening; and even with the inclusion of secretaries and typists, the total number is no more than about forty. Many other officials, of course, have to investigate particular points. The Inland Revenue experts have to do a great deal of work on income tax changes; but they will not know whether anything is being done on purchase tax, car licences or anything else.

An example of the pains taken to secure secrecy can be found in the duty payable on car licence forms, obtainable from local post and tax offices. To avoid giving any hint of the Chancellor's intentions, special sealed bags are sent to these local offices every year with instructions not to open. If there is a change the bags, which contain instructions and posters for public display, are opened on Budget night; if not the dummy bags are sent back unopened.

The main Budget judgement was for a long time made around the middle of February, and the specific tax changes finalized around the beginning of the following month. But in periods of acute difficulty or controversy there has been some tendency to reverse the order and go ahead on the detail, but postpone the overall economic judgement. The options on indirect taxes close earlier than on the rest, since they normally come into effect on Budget Day, and instructions have to be prepared and distributed to collection points all over the country. The Treasury prefers to have decisions taken at least four weeks ahead of the Budget to allow two weeks for printing and two weeks for distribution. By carefully defining a series of options, decisions on certain Customs and Excise duties can be brought up to within two weeks of the Budget, and slightly less if the choice is narrowed to two or three definite varieties. For vehicle licences, on the other hand, the full four weeks are necessary.

Income tax decisions have, according to the rule book, to be taken a week before the Chancellor stands up in the House. But two or three days could perhaps be saved in an emergency, with a great deal of effort and the use of all-night printing. As income tax changes do not come into effect straightaway, the main work involved in a last-minute change of mind is the recalculation of the tax tables and all the many other estimates in the Financial Statement. As the number of tables in the Financial Statement grows every year, and economic forecasts are added to the traditional Budgetary estimates, the number of alterations consequential to any last-minute change of mind increases, as does the risk of error. Whatever the position in the past, it is now genuinely impracticable to alter the Chancellor's measures at the pre-Budget Cabinet.

Some time in March a change comes over the Budget committee. The main economic decisions should by then have been taken. Even if they have not, the Finance Bill, which gives legal effects to the Budget, and is usually published in late April or at the beginning of May, looms larger. The Inland Revenue may have ideas for blocking tax avoidance or improving administration; or there may be detailed anomalies to remove. At this stage the need is more for tax lawyers than for economic advisers. The

Parliamentary Counsel arrive on the scene; most of the Treasury men, including very often the Permanent Secretary and the economic advisers, withdraw. The Chancellor, or another Treasury minister, takes the chair.

The detailed considerations of tax law which occupy the Finance Bill discussions often have little connection with the economic and social considerations which govern the main Budget decisions. A decision in 1968 to take the whole Finance Bill in committee did not, however, work out very well; and the following year a compromise was adopted under which some provisions of a general interest were taken on the floor of the House, while the major part of the Bill, embodying the bulk of the technical detail, was taken in Standing Committee.

The changes in tax law which figure in the Finance Bill are of two kinds. They can arise directly out of the Budget decisions. A new tax, such as the Selective Employment Tax, has to be specified in detail; concessions to particular areas or industries must be sharply demarcated. Alternatively they may arise out of an independent search for anomalies, abuses and unfairnesses (for example in the setting up of trusts for tax avoidance). A case can be made out for an annual Finance Bill confined to the legal implications of the main Budget decisions, and a separate Tax Management Bill which would not have to be an annual event.

The three weeks before the Budget are partly spent on the Budget speech, which is put together by the Chancellor's Principal Private Secretary. The first stage is the preparation of a provisional outline or series of headings for the speech for approval of the Chancellor. Officials in different parts of the Treasury and other departments concerned are then asked for pieces on their own particular subjects.

The personal contribution of the Chancellor will vary a great deal. At the very least he will at this stage give out some ideas of his own to the speech writers, and perhaps mention the odd phrase or sentence that has occurred to him. He will also try hard, in consultation with his advisers, to find a unifying theme to pull together the various bits and pieces. The theme may be genuine; or it may be concocted as a *post hoc* justification after the real decisions had been taken. Some Chancellors, such as Reginald Maudling and Roy Jenkins, write first or second drafts of sections of the speech themselves (although there are, of course, in any Budget speech, impenetrable lists of figures and complicated Inland Revenue points that not even a Keynes would think of drafting for himself). The more conventional kind of politician, on the other hand, finds himself struggling with incomprehensible abstractions and will confine himself to re-writing some passages, striking out others he does not like, asking for pieces to be rewritten by officials and raising queries on each successive draft – there are usually about half a dozen in all.

The final ritual on Budget morning is the check by the Treasury Accountant of all the Chancellor's figures on the 'speaking copy' of his speech. This is no mere formality; the speech has been retyped so many dozens of times that something may easily have gone astray. The Chancellor spends the last few days before Budget day partly in polishing the speech, partly in preparing his answers to post-Budget questions and the text of his television talk, but mainly worrying whether he has done the right thing. Invariably he goes to see the Queen the previous night, bringing with him a short 'Royal summary' of the speech. The full Cabinet itself hears the Budget only the day before the Chancellor announces it to the House.

How important is all the Budget secrecy? It probably matters more for purchase tax, or drink or tobacco duties of the Exchequer, than it does for income tax, profits tax or vehicle licences. In general it might be worth trading a little extra security risk for the benefit of consultations with people who may have useful counsel to give, but cannot now have a genuine discussion with the Chancellor or the Treasury officials until it is too late. It is just when the

Chancellor goes into purdah that he should be most involved in public and private economic arguments. As cautious an ex-Chancellor as Lord Amory thinks 'it is possible to pay too high a price for the assurance of secrecy' and maintains that economic policy should be a 'collective responsibility of the government, not a proprietary product of the Chancellor's mind'.[2]

There might, in fact, be a positive advantage if the so-called 'Budget judgement' about how much to give away or take back in tax were to be discussed publicly by the Chancellor in advance. There could then be argument among experts in which Treasury officials could take part, instead of listening in sphinx-like silence. Moreover, if the discussion is in public – as it is in the USA, where the President has to put tax proposals before Congress – everyone has access to the same information and there is smaller opportunity for making a profit out of privileged knowledge. The truth is that Budget secrecy has become a cult, which the press and the opposition exaggerate beyond any rational point because discussion of 'leaks' has an easier appeal than difficult questions of policy.

THE TAX STRUCTURE

Before embarking on a brief discussion of the balance of the Budget and monetary policy, a short digression on general tax policy might be helpful. In both its traditional role as a revenue raiser, and its modern role as an economic regulator, the Treasury has always been concerned with tax rates. But contrary to popular belief it has had only a limited role in deciding what kind of taxes to levy and how they should be applied.

The explanation of this little-appreciated fact is the independent existence of the Boards of Inland Revenue and Customs and Excise. There has normally been a very small

2. Viscount Amory, 'Preparing the Budget', *Parliamentary Affairs*, autumn 1961, p. 458.

division of the Treasury which combines a coordinating role on tax and budgetary strategy together with other duties. At the time of going to press the division in question was labelled 'Fiscal Policy' (already referred to on p. 92) and contained a handful of officials. Their job was to oversee the practical arrangements for Budgets, Finance Bills and other economic packages, as well as to hold the ring between the two Revenue departments, which might have conflicting views on the desirable development of the tax system.

At the insistence of Mr Roy Jenkins the task of the Fiscal Policy division was broadened to include studies of future strategy, and an Assistant Secretary with Inland Revenue experience was brought in to help. But this was the merest beginning, and the resources at its disposal could not compare with those of the Revenue departments on whose toes it was carefully instructed not to tread. Another interesting innovation in the late 1960s was the formation of a 'balance of payments and taxation working party' jointly staffed by the Treasury, Bank of England and the Revenue departments concerned with the subjects suggested by its name.

One or more of the 'irregular' advisers may happen to be a tax specialist (such as Professor Kaldor or Mr Cockfield); and other advisers, as well as some of the senior officials, may well have ideas on the subject. Events have shown how very difficult it is to steer a middle course between relying on the professionals of the Revenue departments (who suffer from the inevitable limitation of vision of all such institutions) and rushing in with general ideas which have not been fully worked out and are full of practical anomalies.

The two Revenue departments report independently to the Chancellor, a privilege of which they are very jealous. The only advantage the most senior Treasury officials have is that they are personally closer to him. But as the Chancellor cannot be present at more than a tiny proportion of the meetings, the Treasury representative is normally at most *primus inter pares*. The legal separation of powers does not today produce any overt strains among those few Treasury officials who work with the Revenue departments the whole time. But it does make a large difference to most divisions of the Treasury which have only intermittent contact with them. The ordinary middle-ranking Treasury official cannot drop in on an Inland Revenue man for an informal, no-holds-barred discussion as he can with a Treasury colleague; and representatives from the Revenue departments come along to meetings with an agreed party line. There are similarities between the relationships to the Treasury and those of the Bank of England. In both cases geographical separation is an important factor in the situation. A further difficulty in the case of Inland Revenue is that there is a wide gulf between the Secretary's Department, with which the Treasury normally deals, and the Tax Inspectors, who possess the detailed tax experience.

The root of the Revenue departments' opposition to many tax reforms can be traced to a rather limited notion of equity. The Inland Revenue, for example, regards itself as the spokesman of equity against both the simplifiers and economists. At heart its senior officials regard the function of the tax system as being to raise revenue. This view can be reconciled with a very general Keynesian form of economic regulation, which simply aims to increase or lower total purchasing power. It cannot, however, be reconciled at all easily with the use of the tax system in more specific ways – for example to stimulate exports, or to make adjustments in the distribution of income or wealth. The Revenue departments tend to respond to ideas from Treasury and other economists by asking: 'Will the non-fiscal purposes behind the suggestion be generally accepted by those affected; and, if they are accepted today, will they still be accepted tomorrow?'

After the controversies surrounding some of Labour's tax changes in 1964–7, some readers may be inclined to say 'More power to the Inland Revenue's elbow.' But before they do so, they might reflect that the implied assumption behind a great deal of the talk of equity is the unchallenged assumption that the *status quo* is 'fair'. This fairness is after all defined in relation to conventional definitions of income, which may have very little to do with real capacity to pay. As late as 1970 income was being taxed at confiscatory marginal rates, while much wealthier owners of capital, who knew the Estate Duty law, could escape comparatively lightly.

It is tempting to suggest that the Revenue departments should be brought under the jurisdiction of the Treasury, or even merged with it. Yet any complete merger would go counter to the idea of smaller policy-making ministries on the Swedish model, with semi-independent Boards to carry out executive functions, which many institutional reformers would advocate in other sectors. One compromise solution would be to build up a corps of tax experts in the Treasury, who would have worked in the Revenue departments for a period of their lives. The slight move in this direction taken by Mr Jenkins in 1968 has already been mentioned.

A more rational compromise might one day be to hive off the actual tax-assessment and personnel-management functions, which take up so much of the time of the Revenue departments, onto executive agencies, and develop the policy-making and research sides, which could then be brought into the Treasury. It should be remembered, however, that one of the biggest obstacles to well-considered tax reforms is not institutional at all, but the very great difficulty of establishing the economic and social effects of any suggested change. While there is some limited agreement among mainstream economists about the effects of alterations in the total tax bill, there is no such agreement on the effects of changes in the tax structure. The effects of income tax on personal incentives, or of company taxation on prices and profits, remain extremely controversial.

The subject is not made any easier by the tendency of some business spokesmen first to agitate for a particular tax reform, then to have cold feet when a proposal is actually investigated, and finally to campaign for it again after it has been officially rejected. This is not an unfair parody of the history of the argument over the substitution of the value-added form of turnover tax for some forms of existing taxation, which was turned down by the Richardson Committee in 1964, but became topical again around the end of the decade, after it had been adopted by the EEC, and when it was actively supported by Iain Macleod, both as Shadow Chancellor and as Chancellor.

THE FISCAL BALANCE

If Keynesian economics was associated with any one idea among the educated post-war public it was with Budget surpluses and deficits as a way of regulating the economy. Yet it will be recalled from the first section that the Treasury economists' calculation of how much the Chancellor has 'put into' or 'taken out of' the economy does not refer to the Budget accounts at all. The calculation refers entirely to tax measures, plus some allowance for any alteration made in hire purchase regulations or policy on bank advances.

This peculiar feature of the economic arithmetic stems from the fact that the British Budget is practically unique in the world in being concerned exclusively with taxation and not with expenditure. Decisions on government spending are announced to the House on an earlier and separate occasion. We have thus had the astonishing spectacle of Budgets being judged 'neutral', when public expenditure was rising rapidly, simply because the Chancellor had no taxation concessions to give. Even on the revenue side, the figure of how much the Chancellor 'takes out of' or 'puts into' the economy can be very misleading. For it takes account only of new decisions ('discretionary tax changes') and ignores even delayed effects of measures introduced in earlier years – as well, of course, as the long-term effects of a progressive tax structure on the revenue.

The approach of the Treasury economists has a certain

logic. Their basic assumption is that expenditure decisions, and all the built-in features of the tax system, have already been taken into account in the forecasts, and that the Chancellor's April tax decisions are therefore the only new factors in the situation. This, however, is also the trouble. For it makes the whole exercise dangerously dependent on the short-term economic forecasts, and during the heyday of this approach the forecasts seem to have had a reality of their own, superior to that of present facts or decisions; and it became difficult to talk about economic policy outside the forecasting framework.

Quite apart from the risk of forecasting errors, the traditional kind of Treasury economic assessment can hide important changes in the size of the private and the public sector contributions to national savings under the guise of overall demand management. There is a clear need for an index that measures the impact of all government transactions on the economy independently of the forecasts.

The best measure is probably the 'high employment' surplus or deficit which is used by many American economists. This shows not the actual balance of the Budget, but the hypothetical balance which would prevail if the economy were operating at a constant pressure of demand – say that corresponding to $2-2\frac{1}{2}$ per cent unemployment. The purpose of the adjustment is to remove the automatic consequences of changing demand pressures on revenue (and on some items of expenditure too, such as unemployment pay) from the computation. This adjustment is vital if we are to measure the effect of the Budget on the economy, rather than the effect of the economy on the Budget.

Quite apart from the 'high employment correction' there are a great many snags in measuring the economic impact of a Budget by means of the traditional accounts. The central government surplus (formerly referred to as the above-the-line surplus), is misleading for many reasons. For instance it excludes a large amount of government lending to finance the capital expenditure of the nationalized industries, local authorities and other bodies. But the central government's 'borrowing requirement' so beloved by the City and the IMF can be equally misleading. This will go down, for example, if local authorities do more of their own borrowing on the market instead of through the Treasury, even though their total capital expenditure and their ultimate source of finance are unchanged.

A great improvement has been made in recent Financial Statements, which now show the borrowing requirement for the whole public sector – including local authorities and the nationalized industries – on a 'national income' basis. This table was printed particularly prominently in 1969, and the Budget Speech concentrated on it rather than the traditional central government accounts. The real breakthrough came however as a by-product of the Treasury's work on public expenditure projections discussed in the last chapter. The Public Expenditure White Paper of December 1969 contained for the first time forward estimates of revenue as well as expenditure. Largely on the initiative of Wynne Godley, a senior Treasury economist (now head of the Cambridge Department of Applied Economics), expenditure and revenue figures were set off against each other to give a meaningful balance. The figures for 1969–70 are shown in the table (page 150) and the projection for later years in the graph (page 151).

Receipts of all kinds are shown, not only tax but National Insurance contributions, the surpluses of state industries, local rates and other sources of revenue. A table of this kind can be used for many purposes. The net cost of changes in transfer payments such as family allowances, which yield some offsets in higher tax revenue, can be seen at a glance. It enables one to work out readily the burden of public expenditure or taxation according to any definition one likes.

Of more direct interest for demand management are the two balances shown by items 10 and 15 in the table and the two lines on the chart. Item 15, represented by the dotted

TABLE 7

PUBLIC EXPENDITURE AND RECEIPTS: 1969–70, ESTIMATE

£ million at 1969–70 outturn prices

Line		Receipts	Expenditure
	A. Resources		
1	Purchase of resources for current and capital purposes	—	13,311
2	Deduct charges	—	−439
3	Net expenditure on resources	—	12,872
	B. Transfers, taxation,		
4	Grants and subsidies	—	5,171
5	Debt interest*	—	1,670
	Taxes	14,723	
6	Contributions: (a) National Insurance	2,044	—
7	(b) Other	281	—
8	Other receipts	2,648	—
9	Total	19,696	6,841
10	BALANCE OF SECTIONS A and B ('Balance of resources, transfers, taxation, etc.')		−17
	C. Assets		
11	Net purchase of land, existing buildings and financial assets	—	344
12	Taxes on capital and miscellaneous borrowing, etc.	903	—
13	Total	903	344
14	Total Receipts (Lines 9 and 13)	20,599	
	Total Expenditure (Lines 3, 9 and 13) (Public Expenditure)		20,075
15	TOTAL BALANCE	—	542†

* Excluding debt interest paid abroad, which is included in Section A 'Resources'.   † i.e. negative 'borrowing requirement'.

Source: *Public Expenditure 1968–9 to 1973–4*; Cmnd 4234, 1969, Table 1.2

line, is simply the balance between receipts and expenditure for the whole public sector. It is often called the 'public sector borrowing requirement', which in 1969–70 turned out to be a net repayment. (Hence the plus sign.) Item 10, represented by the thick line, is officially entitled 'Balance of Resources, Transfers, Taxation, etc.' Its purpose is to

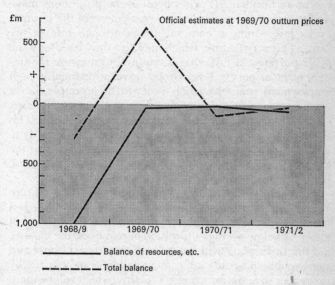

Source: *Public Expenditure 1968/9–1973/4*, Cmnd 4234, 1969 Table 1.2

Figure 2. The 'high employment' Budget

remove from the public sector accounts transactions in existing assets such as purchases of land or buildings, and levies which do not fall directly on income, for example, estate duties. The idea of this adjusted balance is to measure the impact of government transactions on the demand for newly produced goods and services and it would in the Keynesian view be a better guide to the effects of fiscal policy. The 'total balance' would be more relevant to monetary policy because of its effects on official borrowing. The publication of both balances allows the reader to make his own choice for the purpose in hand.

The fact that the balances shown in the graph are adjusted to offset the effects of booms and recessions is to some extent an accident. It arises because the projections make no attempt to guess the year-to-year course of the business cycle, but assume a constant annual growth rate (3 per cent). This very feature, which may be a drawback for some other purposes, is just what is required to measure the impact of fiscal policy. For as 1968–9 was a reasonably high employment year, the whole series in the example shown represented a projection of the 'high employment' Budget on the assumption of no change in existing policies. This was not, however, a way of thinking that came naturally to all Treasury economists, and its future may depend on the extent to which outside commentators insist on bringing the concept into discussion of budgetary policy.

A few snags should be noted. The Public Expenditure White Papers are now to be published every autumn. If a future White Paper projection starts from a base period of above or below average utilization of resources, the balance for the early years will not be high employment ones and some rough-and-ready adjustment will have to be made by the reader to allow for the effects of this (which will be more on revenue than on expenditure). Another point to note is that the projections are on a constant 1969–70 price basis. A confidential assumption has been made of the likely medium-term rate of inflation (then believed to be in the neighbourhood of 3 per cent per annum) to work out the revenue projections; and the resulting estimates have been converted back to a constant price basis. A more important point is that each White Paper is likely to assume (as the 1969 one did) no net tax changes in subsequent Budgets. It will, therefore, need to be adjusted as soon as the Chancellor sits down. It would be a big step forward if the Financial

Statement itself were to contain the balances shown in the table adjusted to a high employment basis.

It is the *change* in the 'high employment' balance rather than its absolute level that measures the impact of a Budget on the economy. For example the 'balance of resources, etc.' was expected to swing from a net deficit of £1,020m. in 1968–9 to one of £17m. in 1969–70, a deflationary swing of nearly £1,000m. – and one much larger than indicated by the £200–250m. which the Chancellor was supposed to have 'taken out of' the economy on the orthodox economic assessment. The fact that the balance of payments in 1969–70 turned out much better than anticipated and home demand was more depressed suggested that there was something to be said for an approach by way of the fiscal balance.

The importance of the absolute level of the public sector balances, as distinct from changes, is more difficult to assess. If a large enough public sector deficit continues year after year, its financing is liable to increase the growth of money supply, unless special precautions are taken to prevent this; and the most extreme Keynesian could hardly deny that the eventual effect would be inflationary. Conversely a long-continued public sector surplus would tend to depress the money supply, unless counteracted by vigorous Bank of England operations.

It is, however, superficial to stop at the monetary and demand management aspects of the public sector balance. The tendency to do this stems from the short-run obsession of British economic thinking. The projected public sector 'balance of resources, etc.' shown in Figure 2 covers capital as well as current transactions and therefore represents a high level of public sector savings. In 1969–70 tax revenues, the surpluses of the nationalized industries, and other current public sector receipts, financed £3,800m. of fixed capital formation and over £600m. of capital transfers to private industry. Let us assume that the national income is already at a high employment level. If the public sector balance is now reduced and the borrowing requirement increased, the public sector would have to bid for savings from companies and industrialists, and real rates of interest would be higher and investment lower. These fundamental effects may be swamped at any one time by Keynesian effects on employment, output and price levels. But if we assume that natural forces or monetary policy keep the economy at the same average degree of capacity utilization then the effects on savings, investment and real interest rates will be the ones that count in the longer term. This does not mean that the public sector surplus should always be as large as possible. For the case for forced savings and tax-subsidized investment is far from cut-and-dried; and it should certainly not be pushed to a limitless extent.

*

As a tailpiece it is worth reproducing in a simplified table the accounts of the *Central Government* alone, as presented to Parliament in the Financial Statement under the National Loan Funds Act of 1968. This split off a new National Loans Fund from the main body of the Budget accounts, known as the 'Consolidated Fund'. The Consolidated Fund shows, on the expenditure side, the 'Supply Services' which have to be voted by Parliament annually for the main parts of the central government's own spending. It also covers *net* interest payments on the National Debt, payments to Northern Ireland and certain other standing charges – these items are collectively known by the un-illuminating title 'Consolidated Fund Standing Services'. On the revenue side the Consolidated Fund covers taxation and some other miscellaneous receipts.

The National Loans Fund is in two parts. The first (not shown in the table) consists of interest received by the government from all sources including other public bodies and, on the other side, interest paid to holders of government securities, the difference being the charge on the Consolidated Fund mentioned above. The second part of the National Loans Fund (shown in the bottom half of the table) consists of net government lending to other public bodies, met partly from the Consoldiated Fund surplus and partly by borrowing. (In 1969–70, it so happened, the net borrowing requirement was negative.) The Budget Accounts are still not strictly comparable to the revenue

TABLE 8

THE CENTRAL GOVERNMENT ACCOUNTS
(£ million)

	Outturn 1967–8	Estimate 1969–70
Consolidated Fund		
Revenue		
Taxation	10,819	14,464
Miscellaneous receipts	413	544
Total	11,232	15,008
Expenditure		
Supply services	9,976	11,800
Payment to NLF to meet National Debt Interest, N. Ireland, etc.	893	751
Total	10,869	12,551
SURPLUS	363	2,457
Loans from the National Loans Fund (net)		
To nationalized industries	1,199	839
To local and harbour authorities	356	540
Other	185	252
Total	1,740	1,631
Less Consolidated Fund Surplus	363	2,457*
NET BORROWING OF NATIONAL LOANS FUND	1,377	−826

* i.e. repayment.
Source: *Financial Statements*

and capital accounts of the private sector; but at least the lending of the central government to other public bodies has now been segregated into a separate account.

In fact neither the Consolidated Fund surplus nor the net borrowing requirement of the NLF is a helpful category for assessing fiscal and monetary policy for the reasons mentioned above; and informed discussion of the subject should be shifting to the 'balance of resources' and 'borrowing requirement' of the whole public sector shown in lines 10 and 15 of Table 7.

THE MONEY SUPPLY

Until the late 1960s, monetary policy occupied a backwater in the British economic scene. This fact had little to do with the historical Lord Keynes, who spent most of his life as a monetary economist, but did stem from the variant of Keynesian economics adopted by the Treasury and much of the British academic world. Official scepticism about monetary policy was canonized in the Radcliffe Report of 1959, which concluded that such policy could not have much useful effect on the level of demand 'unless applied with a vigour which itself creates a major emergency'. This attitude also had its roots in the mechanics of the forecasting process. To a forecaster, a tax reduction or an increase in investment appears to have a direct and measurable effect on the flow of spending. An increase in the money supply has subtler effects, much less easy to trace or measure. It could hardly be a coincidence that most of the forecasting institutions of Western Europe paid little attention to monetary forces. It would be an exaggeration to say that monetary policy was entirely neglected. But to the extent that it was used, the focus of policy was not the total quantity of money, but – at different times – bank advance ceilings and interest rates.

The renewed attention given to monetary policy by a small group of Treasury officials after the mid 60s has been described on page 81. A great deal of effort was devoted to studying the meaning of the new monetary statistics which were the main positive outcome of Radcliffe. Yet the real impact on policy did not come until well into 1968, when, despite a highly restrictive fiscal policy, devaluation was slow to work and consumption rose more than forecast. It seemed to some Treasury administrators that the command over resources, which had been taken out of the economy by the Budget, was simultaneously being released again by a large expansion in the money supply resulting from the Bank of England's support of the gilt-edged market. This was also the view of visiting IMF teams whose views carried more than academic weight. On the initiative of Sir William Armstrong a conference between British and IMF officials was held in October 1968, devoted not to current policy, but to thrashing out the differences of intellectual approach between the two sides. By an interesting coincidence there was a simultaneous failure of fiscal policy in the USA when the 1968 tax increases did not have the expected restraining effect. The Federal Reserve, having previously relaxed because of this increase, had to carry out a vigorous about-turn in 1969.

For several years past, academic studies, particularly associated with Professor Milton Friedman of Chicago and with the Federal Reserve Bank of St Louis, had proclaimed that 'money does matter' or even that 'only money matters'. These writings became fashionable overnight in the policy-making world. The 'monetarist' school was distinguished by the emphasis it put on the quantity of money – a concept subject to endless problems of definition, but which is meant to cover bank deposits plus notes and coins in the hands of the public. It regarded the level of interest rates so emphasized by Radcliffe as misleading, either as an object of policy or as an index of monetary stringency. This was because what mattered for both borrower and lender was not the nominal rate of interest, but the real rate of interest allowing for inflation; and this was a highly subjective and volatile concept dependent on expectations about the future. On this last contention at least, the Chicago writers were entirely justified.

At no time did the British Treasury accept Chicago doctrines lock, stock and barrel. What took place would be described in Whitehall language as a 'shift of emphasis' in their direction. The policy implications of the monetarist school can be summed up in the following four propositions, which are logically independent of each other:

1. Changes in the quantity of money have much more influence on economic activity than was allowed for in economic policy until recently.

2. While changes in the quantity of money have a big effect on total expenditure, fiscal policy has a negligible effect.

3. The quantity of money can be controlled by the central bank.

4. The authorities should aim at a fixed and steady growth in the quantity of money – at, say, 5 per cent per annum – and not attempt to chop and change in accordance with their reading of the economic barometer.

Proposition (4) is an extremely general one related to effects of attempted fine tuning. It is in a sense the *leitmotiv* of this book and will recur both in this section and in most of the following chapters. The main point to make now is the contrast between a neutral *fiscal* policy which calls for a *stable* 'high employment' public sector balance[3] and a neutral *monetary* policy which calls for a continuous increase in the quantity of money.

Proposition (1), that money has an important influence, would now be pretty widely accepted. The mechanism by which the money supply is believed to affect spending is

3. Strictly speaking the balance would have to be a constant proportion of the GNP. But this should make a negligible difference in practice. Even if the public sector deficit were £1,000m. and nominal GNP was growing at 6 per cent the permissible increase would be £60m. per annum at most.

based on the idea that there is a desired ratio of money holdings to total income. If the money supply increases, people will try to reduce their money balances. If they spend it on goods and services, they will increase the national income (it will be a real increase if unemployed resources are put to work and an inflationary increase if prices are driven up). If – as Keynesians consider more likely – they try to switch from money to other forms of wealth by buying securities or other existing assets, nominal interest rates will fall and it will eventually become more profitable to invest in new capital goods, which would again push up the national income.

The usefulness of the money supply either as a predictive instrument or as a policy weapon depends on the stability of the ratio between the national income and the money supply, which is known by the graphic term 'income velocity of circulation'. It is not necessary for velocity to be constant for the money supply to be an important indicator or tool. But there must be some pattern or limit to its variation. Velocity tends to be high when nominal interest rates are high (as money holding is then less attractive). Although the relationship is not a close one, velocity also tends to increase when *real incomes* are rising faster than average. This, plus the interest rate effect, means that velocity tends to rise in the early stages of a boom.

There are also longer-run trends. One difficulty about describing them is that figures on the present ('M_3') definition of the money supply, which includes deposits with the merchant and overseas banks and discount houses, are only available since 1963. On the basis of the older definition which was confined to currency in circulation plus clearing bank deposits, the velocity of circulation varied in the four decades before the First World War within a range of 2 to 3. Between the wars it slowed down and in the depression years it was below $1\frac{2}{3}$. By 1947, it had slowed down still further to about $1\frac{1}{3}$, for the opposite reason that Dr Dalton's cheap money policy flooded the economy with money, the spending of which was restricted by post-war controls. After that, velocity began creeping up again towards the pre-1914 range of 2 to 3. But since 1964 it seems to have flattened out again at just above 3 – on the old definition. On the new definition it varied very little outside the 2·8–2·9 range between 1963 and 1969. The relationship is much less stable on a quarter to quarter basis; and the famous May 1969 article *Economic Trends*,[4]

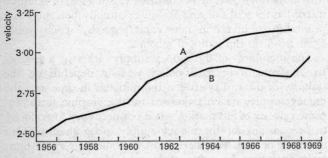

Source: *Money Supply and Domestic Credit*, 'Economic Trends', May 1969

Figure 3. The income-velocity of the circulation of money

which heralded the Treasury's new monetary thinking, contained a Keynesian counter attack in a footnote which pointed out that an offsetting change of 0·1 in the velocity of circulation could undo the effects of a £500m. change in the money supply.

So far, econometric studies have not shown any strong, or reliable, relationship between variations in the growth of the money supply and variations in the growth of national income. Nor has fiscal policy fared significantly better.[5]

4. *Money Supply and Domestic Credit*. The historical information and some of the UK relationships are taken from Professor Alan Walters' *Money in Boom and Slump*, IEA, 1969.

5. See 'Two Aspects of the Monetary Debate', by M. J. Artis and A. R. Nobay, *National Institute Economic Review*, August 1969.

All that one can say in the present state of knowledge is that fiscal policy and the movement of the money supply should reinforce each other and not pull in opposite directions as they did for example in 1955 and 1968. A great deal of new work is now in hand and the apparent position is likely to change with bewildering rapidity as each new econometric study is published.

In the USA the relationship between the money supply and the national income appears more predictable. Nevertheless, Professor Friedman himself has laid more stress on the influence of the money supply on long-run trends in prices and on major cyclical fluctuations. In the small year-to-year fluctuations of the post-war variety he finds that the lag between changes in the money supply and their effect on the economy can vary between three months and eighteen (with six to nine months being typical), and the size of the effect can also vary widely. These considerations lie behind his support of *steady* monetary growth, with no attempt at contracyclical variation except in extreme conditions.[6]

The Treasury's own procedure, as it has evolved up to 1970, is to start off with a conventional economic forecast, which is then translated from constant into actual prices. On this basis a financial forecast is made of the flow of funds between six main sectors – banking, 'other financial', industrial-commercial, personal, public sector and overseas. Transactions in twenty or thirty different types of financial assets are estimated ranging from Treasury Bills and government securities to hire-purchase debt and unit trust assets.[7] These financial forecasts are seen in the first place as a way of checking on the plausibility of the main forecasts; and some people in the Treasury see them mainly

6. The best summary of Friedman's results is in the *Optimum Quantity of Money*, especially Chapter 5, Aldine Publishing Co., Chicago, 1969.

7. A record of flows of this kind, on the latest available figures, is shown in 'Transactions in Financial Assets', an early table in *Financial Statistics*.

in this light. They do, however, also provide a way of forecasting the money supply; and if the results are considered unsatisfactory, alterations in policy can be considered.

It will be seen that the forecast of the money supply is derived from the general economic forecasts. There is a strong case, however, for having two independent and even rival forecasts running together. One would be an orthodox Keynesian forecast and the other a forecast derived from the behaviour of the money supply. If it is true, as the Chicago School maintains, that the main effects of monetary changes appear two or three quarters later, such a forecast could be based on the behaviour of the money supply in the recent past. Further ahead a range of forecasts would have to be given, based on alternative assumptions about the growth of the money supply.

Proposition (2) above, that fiscal policy has a negligible effect, except if it leads to changes in the money stock, appears an extreme monetarist view. But like many extremist positions it raises interesting issues. The key question is pin-pointed by the following question: 'What happens if the government raises taxes by £1,000m. and uses the proceeds to pay off non-bank holders of government debt, thus leaving the money supply unaffected?' Taxpayers then have £1,000m. less in income, but former holders of government debt have £1,000m. instead in cash. The extreme fiscalist would have to argue that government securities are held by people who do not wish to increase their spending relative to their income – for if they did they would already have sold their securities in the market. Consequently they devote their cash receipts, not to buying goods and services, but to the purchase of other securities in the market. This raises security prices and depresses yields until people are prepared to hold a higher proportion of cash in relation to their post-tax incomes. The extreme monetarist would argue that as the cash repayment works its way through the system it will – encouraged by the fall in yields on existing assets – spill over into new investment and consumption until all the £1,000m. is spent. It is a disheartening commentary on the state of economic science that there is nothing resembling a consensus on whether the £1,000m. debt repayment would offset most, some or little of the tax increases in given circumstances.

Some 'practical men', especially central bankers, are tempted to shortcut the controversy by saying that the movement of the money supply is in fact so closely linked with the public sector borrowing requirement that a clear distinction cannot be made between monetary and fiscal policy. In other words they would deny proposition (3) on page 158, that the quantity of money can be controlled by the central bank, and would throw the ball back to the Treasury side of the net.

The UK money supply consists of the domestically owned liabilities of the banking system (the note issue is among the liabilities of the Issue Department of the Bank of England) with the exception of some non-deposit liabilities, such as banks' share capital. An increase in bank lending is an increase in bank assets and therefore creates a corresponding increase on the liabilities side – and therefore in the money supply. It follows that the increase in the money supply in any one period consists of the increase in all bank lending – whether to the private or public sector.[8]

High public sector borrowing therefore tends, other things being equal, to put up the growth of the money supply. But other things are not equal; and both lending to the private sector and the proportion of the public sector borrowing financed from outside the banking system vary widely from year to year. In 1967–8 a record increase of £1,239m. in the money supply coincided with a record peacetime public sector borrowing requirement of £1,957m. If we leave out this extreme year the fit between the public

8. Minus any increase in net deposits by non-residents. The accounting indentities and relevant figures are now exhibited very clearly in the CSO's monthly *Financial Statistics*.

sector deficit and the money supply is far from good as can be seen from the following table for recent years (the substitution of Domestic Credit Expansion for the money supply would do only a little to improve the fit):

TABLE 9

Years	Borrowing Requirement £m.	Increase in Money Supply £m.
1968–9	453	919
1963–4, 64–5, 65–6*	900–1,100	650–1,050
1966–7	1,201	390

* Approximate ranges for these years.

Apart from the British banking system, the public sector can be financed by borrowing from overseas – largely from the IMF and central banks – or by sales to the British public of National Savings, gilt-edged, local authority loans and many other types of official securities. Recourse by the public authorities to the banking system – which for the most part takes the form of Treasury Bills, directly or at one remove – has a double effect, which is not brought out in the strictly accounting approach of *Financial Statistics*. Not only is the money supply directly increased as a result of bank lending to the government, but the resulting increase in holdings of Treasury Bills by the banks can increase their liquidity and thus their ability to lend to the private sector.[9] *Special Deposits* with the Bank of England

9. This presupposes that the banks are content to accept passively the Treasury Bills sold to them by the discount houses and do not actively bid for them in the market. It also assumes that control by the cash ratio is inoperative and that banks do not offset completely the effects of changes in their Treasury Bill portfolios by operations in commercial bills – or alternatively that commercial bills are not allowed to count as part of the liquidity ratio. The whole question of what either does or

were an instrument invented in 1958 to enable the authorities to reduce bank liquidity; but it has been used fairly sparingly and has not been very successful in controlling either the money supply or the movement of bank advances.

Monetarist economists believe that the Bank of England can control the money supply by limiting the supply of Treasury Bills and financing any residual government deficit by selling gilt-edged securities to the public at a price and yield basis determined by the market. The Bank of England on the other hand has tended to be oppressed by the relentless maturing of government securities at a rate averaging £1,500m. per annum, which involves running fast to stay where one is. At least as relevant is the large total of £20,000m. of marketable government securities, which overhang the market. The Bank has maintained strongly that gilt-edged securities cannot be sold on a falling market and has in periods such as 1968 actively bought gilt-edged from the public, even at the cost of inflating the money supply to 'stabilize the market'. As a result of the furore caused by events in 1968, there was a pronounced change of emphasis in the Bank of England's tactics, and sharper falls in gilt-edged prices were permitted than in the past. But the influence of the newer doctrines is still precarious and the battle may have to be fought again each time there is a selling wave in gilt-edged.

A novel concept introduced into economic policy at the time of the May 1969 Letter of Intent was *Domestic Credit Expansion*. British officials first heard from IMF officials at the October 1968 conference about this measure, which was especially associated with the Fund's Economic Counsellor, J. J. Polak.[10] It is based on the fact that an

should determine the lending ability of the banking system (or 'monetary base') has been a subject of great confusion and uncertainty in recent years. The reader is referred to the up-to-date textbooks on banking and monetary theory which may one day appear.

10. See, for instance, his 'Monetary Analysis of Income Formation and Payments Problems', *IMF Staff Papers*, November 1957.

expansion of bank credit to the public or private sector automatically increases money supply in ordinary circumstances. But if there is a payments deficit some of the resulting increase in liabilities will be to foreigners and thus be excluded from the UK money supply.

DCE can be looked at in two ways. It is the total 'credit' extended to the British economy from all sources. This is defined in *Financial Statistics* as the sum of domestic bank lending to the public and private sectors and the overseas financing of the public sector, plus one or two adjustments. Looked at in this way the definition of 'credit', which excludes credit supplied outside the banking system, but includes long-term overseas lending to nationalized industries, seems very arbitrary.[11]

It is much more helpful to look at the liabilities side. This gives an alternative, but equivalent, definition of DCE as the increase of the money supply plus the payments deficit (or minus the surplus). Looked at in this way a DCE limit, such as the £400m. ceiling imposed for 1969–70 under IMF influence, limits the permissible growth of the money supply according to the balance of payments. If this is in surplus, the money supply can grow more than the DCE limit. If this is in deficit it cannot grow as much and, if the deficit is large enough, it may even have to fall.

This link with the balance of payments is both the strength and the weakness of DCE. It means that the growth of the money supply instead of either following a smooth path, or varying in accordance with the needs of domestic stability, has to be governed by balance-of-payments requirements. One must, however, remember that if exchange rates are pegged, domestic policy must in any case be subordinated to the balance of payments to an extent depending on the rigidity of the rate. The amount of deflation will be very much smaller and its impact on production and employment less severe, if it is imposed at the first sign of a deficit instead of waiting until costs, prices and

11. The exact definition is, however, liable to change.

competitive conditions have moved seriously out of line with other countries. A long-term DCE target can thus be seen as a way of making the best of pegged exchange rates – although it would also work well in conjunction with some limited forms of flexibility such as the 'discretionary crawling peg'.

Considerable doubts did, however, develop about DCE in the British Treasury as its implications were closely examined. For DCE purposes the balance of payments surplus included overseas lending to the private sector, on long- and short-term capital account; and officials were naturally reluctant to see the money supply tied too closely to this highly volatile item. Some thought was being given to redefining DCE to relate it to the current balance of payments only. But as this edition was going to press the view that it would be better to go back to the money supply itself seemed equally attractive.

More important than the precise monetary concept used was the growing support in the Treasury for retaining a target figure or range for the annual rate of monetary expansion. There was even some high level support for the Friedmanesque view that this target should not vary much in a normal year.

*

At the end of the day one is left with several different measures of the impact of government financial policy: the orthodox Treasury economists' calculations of the effects of discretionary tax changes and similar packages; the change in the public sector balance (or 'borrowing requirement') preferably on a 'high employment' basis; the growth of the money supply; and Domestic Credit Expansion. Two of the measures mentioned are fiscal and two monetary, but all four are interrelated. In the present and foreseeable state of knowledge, there is no alternative to examining all the alternatives indicated and paying careful attention to any one that seems out of line with the others. The one measure that can be safely disregarded as more misleading than the others is the figure of how much the Chancellor has 'given away' or raised in revenue terms, and which appears so prominently in the post-Budget headlines and, sometimes unfortunately, in the Chancellor's speech itself.

Part 2

ECONOMIC MANAGEMENT IN PRACTICE

Footfalls echo in the memory
Down the passage which we did not take
Towards the door we never opened
Into the rose-garden. My words echo
Thus, in your mind.
                    But to what purpose
Disturbing the dust on a bowl of rose-leaves
I do not know.

T. S. Eliot, *Burnt Norton*

CALENDAR OF EVENTS

This is not a comprehensive record of events or even of Treasury actions. It is simply meant as a selected chronological reference for the narrative in the following pages.

1947	15 November	Autumn Budget. Budget leak; Cripps takes over from Dalton as Chancellor of the Exchequer.
1949	18 September	Devaluation of £ from $4·03 to $2·80.
1950	19 October	Gaitskell succeeds Cripps as Chancellor.
1951	29 January	£4,700m. new rearmament programme announced.
	10 April	Gaitskell's Budget. Tax increases and Health Service charges.
	25 October	Conservatives win General Election. Butler becomes Chancellor.
	7 November	First post-war increase in Bank Rate.
1952	29 January	Import restrictions, capital investment cuts, HP restrictions.
	11 March	Neutral Budget.
1953	14 April	Budget; 6d. off income tax.
1954	6 April	Neutral Budget. New investment allowances.
1955	25 February	Moderate HP controls reintroduced. Bank of England to support market for transferable sterling.
	19 April	Budget; 6d. off income tax, etc.
	26 May	General Election; Conservatives returned with increased majority.
	1 June	Spaak Committee on possible European Customs Union (EEC) set up at Messina.
	26 July	Further HP restrictions; squeeze on bank advances; capital investment cuts by nationalized industries.
	27 October	Autumn Budget; purchase tax increases, etc.

	20 December	Macmillan succeeds Butler as Chancellor.
1956	19 February	More HP controls; investment allowances suspended; cuts in public investment.
	17 April	Neutral Budget.
	29 May	Spaak Committee's report accepted by the Foreign Ministers of the Six.
	26 July	Nasser seizes the Suez Canal.
	1 September	Makins succeeds Bridges as Permanent Secretary to Treasury.
	3 October	British outline plan for a European Free Trade Area announced.
	7 November	End of fighting at Suez.
	11 December	£200m. drawn on IMF and stand-by credit arranged of £440m.
1957	13 January	Macmillan succeeds Eden as Prime Minister; Thorneycroft Chancellor.
	25 March	Treaty of Rome signed.
	9 April	Budget; surtax concession, special tax treatment for overseas companies.
	5 July	Closing of the 'Kuwait Gap'.
	11 August	French measures amounting to a 20 per cent devaluation of the franc.
	12 August	Council on Prices, Productivity, and Incomes appointed under Lord Cohen.
	19 September	Bank Rate raised to 7 per cent; ceiling on public sector capital spending and bank advances.
1958	6 January	Thorneycroft resigns; succeeded by Heathcoat Amory.
	15 April	Budget; small purchase tax reliefs.
	July–October	Gradual relaxation of credit controls and public expenditure limits.
	14 November	France formally rejects proposal for a European Free Trade Area.
	27 December	Convertibility announced for non-resident sterling.
	28 December	Franc devalued.
1959	1 January	EEC's first tariff reductions.
	8 April	Tax relief Budget.
	20 August	Report of Radcliffe Committee on Working of Monetary System.

	8 October	General Election; Conservatives returned with an increased majority.
1960	1 January	Lee succeeds Makins as Permanent Secretary to Treasury.
	21 January	Bank Rate raised to 5 per cent.
	4 April	Neutral Budget.
	28 April	HP restrictions reintroduced, credit squeeze.
	23 June	Bank Rate raised to 6 per cent.
	27 July	Selwyn Lloyd succeeds Amory as Chancellor.
	20 October	London price of gold rises temporarily from $35 to $41 per ounce.
	27 October	Bank Rate reduced to $5\frac{1}{2}$ per cent.
	8 December	Bank Rate reduced to 5 per cent.
1961	19 January	HP restrictions eased.
	5 March	Deutschmark revalued by 5 per cent.
	17 April	Budget; surtax relief, profits tax increase, fuel oil tax.
	1 June	Cairncross succeeds Hall as Economic Adviser to the government.
	1 July	Cromer succeeds Cobbold as Governor of the Bank of England.
	25 July	Crisis measures; Bank Rate raised to 7 per cent; regulator; government expenditure checked; credit squeeze; pay pause, etc.
	4 August	UK granted IMF credit of £714m.
	8 August	TUC and employers invited to join new NEDC.
	10 August	Britain applies to join EEC.
	17 November	OECD, newly formed from OEEC with USA and Canada as full members, agrees on 50 per cent growth target for 1960–70.
	16 November	Electricity Council breaks pay pause.
	21 November	Prime Minister rebukes Electricity Council for break of pay pause.
	13 December	$6,000m. IMF 'Group of Ten' set up.
	18 December	Sir Robert Shone appointed Director General of NEDC.
1962	2 February	2–$2\frac{1}{2}$ per cent 'guiding light' for incomes announced.

	14 March	Orpington by-election; government loses seat to Liberals.
	9 April	Budget; short-term capital gains tax; other minor changes.
	9 May	NEDC to explore implications of 4 per cent growth rate.
	28 May	Sharpest fall on Wall Street since October 1929.
	4 June	Small HP tax relaxations.
	13 July	Maudling succeeds Lloyd as Chancellor.
	26 July	Government to set up National Incomes Commission.
	19 September	Maudling Plan put forward at IMF meeting, opposed by USA.
	1 October	Treasury reorganization; Armstrong succeeds Lee as Permanent Secretary.
	5 November	Increased investment allowances, etc.; purchase tax on cars reduced.
1963	14 January	De Gaulle blocks British membership of EEC.
	6 February	NEDC approves 4 per cent growth rate target.
	3 April	Budget; reliefs for families and depressed regions.
	19 October	Douglas-Home succeeds Macmillan as Prime Minister.
1964	14 April	Budget; £100m. of increased taxation on drink and tobacco.
	28 July	IMF renews $1000m. standby credit to UK for twelve months.
	15 October	Labour Party wins General Election by five seats. Harold Wilson forms government. Creates DEA.
	26 October	Measures to reduce b. of p. deficit, estimated at £800m. for 1964. 15 per cent import surcharge, export rebate, etc.
	8 November	Paris Club places $400m. with IMF for Britain to draw.
	11 November	Callaghan's first Budget: direct and indirect taxation increased. Corporation tax proposed, pensions increased.

	23 November	Bank rate increased to 7 per cent.
	25 November	UK gets $3000m. credits from Central Banks.
	16 December	'Statement of Intent' on Prices and Incomes.
1965	22 February	Import surcharge to be cut to 10 per cent.
	17 March	Aubrey Jones appointed Chairman of PIB. TUC agrees to 3–3½ per cent norm for wage increases.
	6 April	Budget; tax increased by over £200m. Capital gains tax; entertainment allowance abolished, stricter exchange controls.
	12 May	IMF agrees to a further drawing of $1,400m. by UK.
	3 June	Bank Rate cut from 7 to 6 per cent. HP restrictions increased.
	27 July	Measures to improve b. of p.; cuts in government investment, tighter exchange controls, HP restrictions.
	16 September	DEA publishes the 'National Plan'.
	22 September	TUC sets up 'early warning system' for wage claims.
1966	25 January	White Paper on IRC published.
	8 February	Tighter HP restrictions.
	24 February	Prices and Incomes Bill, providing for compulsory early warning.
	24 March	Fred Catherwood appointed Director General of NEDC in succession to Sir Robert Shone.
	31 March	General Election gives Labour overall majority of 97.
	3 May	Budget; Corporation tax at 40 per cent, SET, restraint on overseas investment, 10 per cent import surcharge to end.
	15 May	Seamen's strike begins.
	13 June	New credit arrangements agreed at BIS annual meeting.
	20 July	Crisis measures announced; regulator increase, government spending curb, HP controls tightened, prices and wages freeze, followed by period of severe restraint.

	9 August	Michael Stewart takes over from George Brown as Minister for Economic Affairs.
	10 November	Prime Minister announces discussions with EFTA and EEC on British entry into Common Market.
1967	13 March	Renewal of $1000m. Basle Credits for another year.
	11 April	'Neutral' budget; family allowances raised.
	11 May	UK makes formal application to join EEC.
	5 June	War breaks out between Israel and Arab countries.
	7 June	HP relaxations.
	30 June	Period of severe restraint ends, TUC to vet claims.
	28 August	PM takes over personal responsibility for DEA, Peter Shore becomes Secretary for Economic Affairs.
	29 August	Further HP relaxations.
	11 September	IMF announces agreement on 'Special Drawing Rights'.
	12 November	Britain negotiates $250m. credit through BIS to help finance IMF debts due in December.
	18 November	Britain devalues £ by 14·3 per cent to $2·40 from $2·80. Bank Rate raised to 8 per cent, HP restrictions, defence cuts, standby credits to be sought.
	27 November	De Gaulle announces opposition to UK membership of Common Market.
	29 November	Callaghan resigns as Chancellor; succeeded by Jenkins.
	30 November	Chancellor's Letter of Intent to IMF published.
1968	1 January	President Johnson announces five-point plan to improve US balance of payments.
	5 January	Civil Service changes; Armstrong to succeed Helsby as Head of Civil Service. Allen to become Joint Permanent Secretary at Treasury.
	16 January	Public expenditure curbs announced.

	17 March	Gold Pool ended; two-tier system for gold markets.
	19 March	Budget; tax increases totalling £923m.; purchase tax increases, SET up by 50 per cent, etc.
	31 March	President Johnson announces he will not stand for re-election.
	5 April	Cabinet reshuffle; Barbara Castle becomes Minister for Employment and Productivity.
	9 September	'Basle' arrangements for sterling area announced, backed by $2,000m. standby credits.
	1 November	HP restrictions tightened.
	22 November	End of Bonn Conference on franc–mark crisis. Mr Jenkins announces prior deposits for imports, use of 'Regulator' and tightening of credit squeeze.
1969	15 April	Budget; SET and other tax increases expected to reduce demand by £200m.–£250m.; but much larger turnround in government accounts.
	9 May	New D-mark crisis culminates in 'final, unequivocal and for ever' revaluation denial.
	22 May	Letter of Intent written to IMF in connection with $1,000m. standby credit. £400m. DCE ceiling for 1969-70.
	12 June	Announcement of under-recording of exports together with better figures for visible and invisible trade.
	8 August	French franc devalued by 11 per cent.
	15 September	Good second quarter balance of payments figures followed by publication of £40m. visible trade surplus for August.
	24 September	Closing of German foreign exchange market.
	29 September	Temporary floating rate for mark.
	5 October	Changes in machinery of government, including abolition of DEA.
	24 October	German mark revalued by 9 per cent.

1970   1 January   First $3,500m. allocation of Special Draw-
                     ings Rights. UK receives £171m. Aboli-
                     tion of UK travel restrictions.

      10 February   White Paper 'Britain and the European
                     Communities'; b. of p. cost put at
                     £100–1,000 m. p.a.

      26 March   Final drawing from IMF of 1969 standby;
                     repayment of 1965 drawing advanced from
                     May.

      14 April   Budget; moderate direct-tax cuts aimed
                     to boost demand by ½ per cent, but little
                     change in fiscal balance. Bank Rate re-
                     duced to 7 per cent. Increase of 5 per cent
                     in monetary aggregates for 1970.

      13 May   Dow Jones index of US stock market falls
                     to lowest since 1963; drop in London
                     market.

      29 May   Select Committee recommends publica-
                     tion of Bank of England accounts.

      31 May   'Temporary' floating of Canadian dollar.

      18 June   Conservative election victory; Heath
                     Prime Minister; Iain Macleod Chancellor.

      26 July   Barber Chancellor, following death of
                     Macleod.

      6–12 August   Carr and Barber emphasize duty of em-
                     ployers, including nationalized industries,
                     to resist wage inflation.

      20 September   Meeting of IMF in Copenhagen; fully
                     floating rates anathematized, but study of
                     greater flexibility to continue.

      27 October   Public expenditure cuts. 6d. off income
                     tax and lower corporation tax.

      29 October   Increase of 1 per cent in Special Deposits.

      5 November   Scamp Report concedes over 15 per cent
                     to municipal workers, admitting its pro-
                     posals 'are inflationary'.

5

ACHIEVEMENTS AND MISSED OPPORTUNITIES: FROM DALTON AND CRIPPS TO THE 1959 ELECTION

Three Labour Chancellors: controls without a plan: Labour's first wage freeze: Korean rearmament: the 1949 devaluation: 'Butskellism': expansion under Butler: the Robot plan: the 1955 error: the economics of Stockton-on-Tees: Thorneycrofts I and II: a change of priorities: the PM's position: shelving the issues: kissing the rod

THE aim of this and the following chapters is to look at some examples of the forces affecting Treasury policies rather than to provide a full and consecutive history. 'Treasury policy' in this context is the outcome of a complicated process of interaction between the Chancellor, Treasury officials and the Bank of England – with other economic ministers and ministries, and the Prime Minister himself, playing roles that have varied in importance from time to time.

THREE LABOUR CHANCELLORS

The immediate post-war years, which were very different in character from the subsequent period, are not our main concern. But a few fringe notes on the Labour government of 1945–51 may be helpful as background.

The era of Dr Dalton, the first post-war Labour Chancellor, who resigned after a minor Budget leak in the autumn of 1947, reads today almost like pre-history. He was the last Chancellor who was primarily a finance minister without responsibility for economic management; and a fascinating glimpse of the confusion and frustration which results from the divorce of finance and economics could have been obtained long before Labour's later experiences in the 1960s by anyone who had read the last volume of Dalton's autobiography, *High Tide and After*.

Dr Dalton was the most exuberant and least austere of all Chancellors. He was a noted egotist and his great booming voice saying 'Between you and me' to someone in the garden could be heard from a twelfth-floor hotel room. Astonishingly enough for a Chancellor of the Exchequer, he was the author of a well-known textbook on public finance (which he brought up to date after his retirement) and before the war had been an inspiring and surprisingly orthodox university teacher. Yet his Cheap Money drive, which for a time brought long-term interest rates down to as little as two and a half per cent, has become notorious as a misguided attempt to do the very opposite of what the postwar situation required.

It is often supposed that this was a personal policy which Dalton embarked upon in the teeth of official advice. But just before he died Lord Dalton revealed that all his Treasury and the Bank of England advisers had supported and even encouraged him at the crucial moment. Dalton's only adviser to warn him of the dangers was the late Evan Durbin, who was in the lowly position of Parliamentary Private Secretary.

Dalton's successor, Sir Stafford Cripps, knew far less about finance than people imagined from his resolute public manner. During his reign the idea of planning through the Budget first became established. The doctrines, however, were those of Sir Robert Hall and other advisers. It was Cripps who added the drive and the moral fervour.

Mr Hugh Gaitskell, who took over from Cripps in the autumn of 1950, probably understood his job better than any Chancellor before or since. He was, of course, a professional economist by training, but of a later vintage and more sophisticated in his approach than Dalton. His officials had a great respect for him; but they complained that he insisted on doing himself a great deal of detailed work, for example in relation to economic forecasts, which he would have been better advised to delegate.

CONTROLS WITHOUT A PLAN

It is a myth to suppose that the Labour government of 1945–51 engaged in detailed long-term planning of the country's production; and most of the blame and praise directed at it on these grounds were equally misdirected. The controls and regulations which caused so much controversy were basically a hangover, which probably lasted too long, from wartime restrictions.

The 1947 Economic Survey contained detailed manpower and output targets for particular industries, and a comprehensive import programme, but it did not say how the manpower targets would be achieved. They were meant neither as 'an ideal distribution nor a forecast of what will happen' but as an 'approximate distribution necessary to carry out the nation's objectives if the nation as a whole sets itself to achieve them'. It is hardly surprising that these targets were not achieved, and in the 1948 Survey they were simply referred to as a 'tentative Budget'.

Subsequent Surveys became less and less specific. The 1950 Survey was described by the *Economist* as 'a humble document, meek almost to the point of being meaningless'. According to a later study by A. A. Rogow, 'had there been no Korean War it is probable that Labour Government planning in 1951 would have been almost entirely confined to Budget policy and certain balance-of-payments controls'.[1] It was towards this goal – Butskellism as it later came to be called – that the Labour government was moving during most of its period of office.

Looking back on the documents and speeches of these years, one is struck by the extent to which economic policy was conducted on a year-to-year piecemeal basis. The

1. A. A. Rogow and Peter Shore, *The Labour Government and British Industry*, 1955, Blackwell, p. 42.

allocation of scarce materials and of factory permits was, in Mr Rogow's words 'more often the result of inter-departmental negotiation and amateur judgment than of consistent and scientific planning'. The whole system was probably modelled on the traditional annual haggles which the spending departments had with the Treasury. The Five-Year forward looks pioneered by the NEDC and the Treasury's long-term public expenditure surveys, both of which were started under a Conservative government, were much more ambitious examples of forward projection than anything Cripps ever did.

The Labour government did, it is true, produce in the autumn of 1948 one 'Long-Term Programme' to illustrate how the country could achieve 'economic independence' by the middle of 1952. Such a programme was more or less a condition of Marshall Aid, and was taken even less seriously than the subsequent NEDC and National Plans. It had little impact on day-to-day policy and was only mentioned once in all the Economic Surveys and Budget speeches of the period.

LABOUR'S FIRST WAGE FREEZE

Another fact that is often forgotten is that Sir Stafford Cripps had a wage freeze in 1948, some thirteen years before Mr Selwyn Lloyd and eighteen years before Mr Harold Wilson. In February 1948 the Treasury put out a *Statement on Incomes, Costs, and Prices*, which said, 'There is no justification for any *general* increase of individual money incomes', although there might be exceptions in the case of under-manned industries. Many of the doctrines of that White Paper have cropped up again and again in official pronouncements over the subsequent twenty years, irrespective of the Party in office – right down to the habit of saying 'incomes' when the writer really means wages.

One difference between Cripps and his later emulators was that Cripps did not interfere with arbitration in the public sector. Sir Stafford said in his 1950 Budget speech that wages had been left to free negotiations and the government had simply put its views before the country.

The TUC protested that it had not been consulted first; but, as in 1966 and in contrast to 1961, accepted, with a few qualifications, the principle of the pause. After the devaluation of sterling in September 1949, the TUC General Council went further still and even recommended the suspension of cost-of-living sliding-scale agreements, an idea which it never seems to have contemplated in 1966. By 1950 the policy had begun to crumble and in June of that year the General Council sent out a circular saying: 'There must be greater flexibility of wage movements in the future.'

By the end of 1950 the delayed effects of devaluation and the initial effects of the Korean war had combined to push the cost of living sharply upwards, and wages and prices were shooting merrily ahead. But for a two-year period the pause had been a great success, with wages rising by barely two per cent per annum.

KOREAN REARMAMENT

The most extraordinary episode in the Labour government's history was the cavalier way in which it embarked upon an enormous rearmament programme at the time of Korea. The first programme for spending £3,400m. in three years – or fifty per cent more than was originally planned – was sketched out in ten days in the middle of the summer holidays. A few weeks later General MacArthur took it upon himself to drive his forces to the Yalu river and the West to the verge of world war. The Chinese entered the Korean War and by the end of the year had captured most of the Peninsula, save for a small perimeter around the main Southern ports. In early December Attlee flew to Washington to intercede with President Truman not to use atomic weapons and, in this alarmist mood, the British govern-

ment announced a scarcely credible rearmament programme of £4,700m. for the same three-year period.

The Treasury, which is habitually pessimistic about the
capacity of the economy to bear civilian programmes which
are quite tiny by comparison, took the view that the nation
would just *have* to afford this extra arms bill. Mr Gaitskell
and his official advisers, who shared his devotion to the
cause of Western defence, made the mistake of assuming
that sufficiently strict budgetary planning, together with the
re-imposition of physical controls, would produce the raw
materials, machine tools, and components required for an
enormously enlarged defence programme. But, as Mr
Aneurin Bevan pointed out in his resignation speech, these
'were not forthcoming in sufficient quantities even for the
earlier programme'. In the words of Mr Harold Wilson,
who resigned from the government with Mr Bevan, 'the
financial programme of rearmament' ran 'beyond the
physical resources which can be made available'.[2] This experience in 1950–51 probably lay at the root of Mr Wilson's
later distrust of the Treasury as a super-ministry, and his
desire to put in charge of economic policy a minister who
would think in concrete physical terms instead of overall
monetary ones. The Bevanites proved right in the rearmament controversy – a fact which most politicians and Civil
Servants often wanted very much to forget.

The Labour government's rearmament programme was,
of course, severely cut by the Conservatives after their return
to office, but by then much damage had been done to the
British economy. As late as 1953 the Economic Survey
plaintively noted: 'Important sectors of the engineering
industries are heavily engaged in defence work when they
might otherwise be concentrating their main energies on
the export trade' (or, the Survey might have added, home
investment). An American economist, in an investigation

2. The best full-length account of the controversy is *Crisis in Britain*
by Jean Mitchell. Some useful lessons are drawn by Andrew Shonfield
in *British Economic Policy Since the War*, pp. 56–8 and 92–107.

of why the 1949 devaluation did so little to solve the British balance-of-payments problem, remarks that 'at least some of the substitutions which importers were forced to find for British goods during the Korean War continued' after British goods had once again become readily available.[3]

THE 1949 DEVALUATION

The 1949 devaluation does indeed look in retrospect a bad piece of tactics. The American study already quoted concludes that devaluation did not do much to improve British exports. 'Probably its strongest effect was the hidden one of softening the blow of Japanese and German recovery, since Japan remained with the dollar and Germany devalued by less than the UK.' It might have been better, the writer goes on to say, to have devalued 'a year or two later when the competition from these two countries began to make itself strongly felt'. Another argument for postponement was that 'exports could not have increased much more than they did because of the shortage of supply' induced by the Korean War.

The 1949 move also had the great political disadvantage of saddling the Labour Party with one devaluation and making it particularly anxious to avoid another, which helps to explain the delays and vacillations of 1964–7. The Conservatives, for their part, having had the good fortune to be out of office on both occasions, became determined to avoid being tarred with the same brush.

An important body of Whitehall opinion in fact wanted a different solution to the 1949 crisis. The idea, which had the support of the government's Economic Adviser, Sir Robert Hall, was that instead of fixing a new exchange rate for sterling, the pound should be left to float. This would have meant that the number of dollar bills or francs a businessman or tourist received in exchange for £1 would have

3. June Flanders, 'The Effects of Devaluation on Exports', *Bulletin of the Oxford Institute of Economics and Statistics*, August 1963, p. 196.

varied from time to time according to the state of the market – although the Bank of England would have intervened to iron out temporary fluctuations.

Such a solution would have dodged the whole problem of fixing a new exchange rate at a time when any figure was just a wild shot in the dark. (The actual devaluation from $4·03 to $2·80 for the £ was apparently far too large; but the competitive margin we gained was quickly eroded by overseas devaluation and inflation in Britain.) Some government economists wanted to find out if Britain could live with a floating rate in post-war conditions; and as Britain was in any case compelled to abandon the old $4 parity it seemed a good time to make the experiment.

They were defeated by the entrenched opposition of the Bank of England. The Bank has always bitterly distrusted exchange controls for reasons already discussed on page 86. It also dislikes floating rates intensely. Most traders, whether in goods or money, prefer fixed prices, whenever they can have them, to the risks and uncertainties of price competition, and central bankers are no exception. Their attachment to fixed exchange rates and their dire protestations of catastrophe if they are abandoned have some resemblance to the price ring and cartel mentality so common among ordinary businessmen, and which monopoly legislation has been designed to fight.

Although the Bank had to tolerate severe exchange controls in the post-war years and was prepared to put up with floating rates in the early 1950s, it was not prepared to accept both floating rates and exchange controls together; and its real aim was not to have either. In 1949 it argued that the extensive exchange controls, which at that time were supposed to prevent foreigners from converting their pounds into gold or dollars, could not be enforced if there was a floating rate. As no one in Whitehall was then prepared to sacrifice exchange controls for fear of a great capital flight from Britain, the Bank of England won the day.

'BUTSKELLISM'

These attitudes of the Bank of England affected economic policy both under the Labour government and under the Conservative government that succeeded it in October 1951.

Another link was the philosophy of 'Butskellism', a term compounded by the *Economist* out of the names of Butler and Gaitskell. Butskellism was already coming to the fore in the last few years of the Labour government, although its progress was interrupted for a little while by the Korean War. It was an interesting mixture of planning and freedom, based on the economic teachings of Lord Keynes. Planning during this period was concerned with one global total – the amount that was spent on goods and services – normally known as 'the level of demand'. (Subsequently the more precise expression 'pressure of demand' came into use, which is the ratio of demand to the country's productive capacity.) If production sagged, or unemployment looked like creeping up, extra purchasing power was pumped into the system through the Budget, the banks or the hire-purchase houses. If employment was overfull, or the pound came under strain, demand was withdrawn through these same channels.

Conservative economic policy in 1951–64 was characterized by some paradoxical features. On the one hand the Party always treated 'the man in Whitehall' with a certain detachment. The traditional Tory attitude to Civil Servants has been one of some disdain; one leading Conservative politician used to refer to them as 'clerks'. On the other hand, policy seemed to have originated largely from Civil Servants. I do not mean that official advice was always taken – far from it – but that ministers relied on Civil Servants to provide the intellectual framework on which their decisions were ultimately based.

In the thirteen years 1951–64 there were no less than six

Conservative Chancellors. Nearly all the Tory Chancellors who held office until 1962 were in every sense laymen. Not merely were they innocent of economic complexities, but they did not even have the practical financial flair that one might reasonably expect from a Party with business links. Conservative Prime Ministers, in fact, never risked putting a City personality or a leading business figure into No. 11. Most Conservative Chancellors were impressed, and even overawed, at their weekly meetings with Lord Cobbold, who was Governor of the Bank of England from 1949 to 1961. Cobbold, who had been a disciple of the mystery-mongering Montagu Norman, Governor for twenty-four years up to 1944, had acquired from Norman some very rigid convictions, especially about the proper role of the Bank of England in the scheme of national finance; but he made no claim to be a monetary thinker. 'If he had been faced by someone like John Anderson instead of the Chancellors we did have,' a Conservative minister once remarked to me, 'can you imagine who would have deferred to whom?'[4]

It is also noticeable that after Butler and Macmillan left the Exchequer none of the succeeding Tory Chancellors for many years after was a political heavyweight. Macmillan was long content to appoint to the Exchequer conscientious administrators, who cut no figure either at home or abroad. During most of the 1951–64 period financial affairs were treated by the government as an incomprehensible technical exercise, divorced from the mainstream of policy. Chancellors were more or less left to their own devices and

4. Sir John Anderson, later Viscount Waverley, was a most formidable administrative figure, who after rising rapidly in the Civil Service to become Permanent Secretary to the Home Office, later became Governor of Bengal, before entering Parliament. During Churchill's wartime coalition, he was Lord President of the Council, where he was the only successful economic coordinator without departmental responsibilities Whitehall has ever seen. After the death of Sir Kingsley Wood in 1943 he became Chancellor of the Exchequer. (*John Anderson, Viscount Waverley*, by Sir John Wheeler-Bennett.)

suddenly found themselves out of office for one reason or another when affairs went badly.[5]

When Winston Churchill formed his post-war government in 1951, he was generally expected to make Mr Oliver Lyttelton (now Lord Chandos) Chancellor. Lyttelton, a prominent City figure and industrialist, had been Chairman of the Conservative Finance Committee in opposition. He would, he says, have taken the Exchequer 'with zest' and believed he could 'make a contribution, perhaps even a decisive contribution' to the country's financial and economic problems.[6] After he had broken the news of Butler's appointment, Churchill told him: 'It was touch and go, but the Chief Whip thought the House of Commons stuff was a handicap to you.'

This was the second time in his life that Lyttelton nearly became Chancellor. After the death of Sir Kingsley Wood in 1943 Churchill actually suggested to Lyttelton that he should succeed him at the Exchequer. The following day he called Lyttelton to the telephone to tell him that Sir John Anderson would be much distressed if he did not become Chancellor. 'Having started life as a Civil Servant, it would crown his career to be head of the Treasury.'

Certainly Churchill would have taken a big gamble in 1951 if he had appointed Oliver Lyttelton, at a time when he had a Parliamentary majority of only sixteen. With his watch chain dangling aggressively from his waistcoat, and his difficulty in handling the House of Commons, Lyttelton seemed to many Labour MPs an incarnation of the spirit of big business. The effects of a Lyttelton Chancellorship are among the most interesting might-have-beens of history.

Churchill, having run away from the thought of Lyttelton as Chancellor, tried to keep check on Butler, of whom he was something less than a wholehearted admirer, by appointing a 'Treasury Advisory Committee' to 'assist'

5. At the time of going to press it looks as if the above paragraphs could apply unchanged to the Conservative government of 1970.
6. *The Memoirs of Lord Chandos*, Bodley Head, 1962, p. 342.

him. This consisted of a small group of ministers, including some of Churchill's trusted wartime colleagues such as Lords Woolton and Swinton. By all accounts they subjected the Civil Servants whom they summoned to quite an inquisition. Senior Treasury officials, including some who later became leading company chairmen, were asked what they knew about business. But for all their bark these committee-men had no power to bite. They had prolonged discussions on whether forecasting was in principle possible, discussions which were characterized by a degree of remoteness from reality of which only 'practical business-men' are capable. They tried very hard to abolish the Economic Survey, but even here they failed and the Survey survived until 1962. In the end, of course, Mr Butler and the Treasury knights were more than a match for what one politician irreverently described as 'those old battleaxes'. The Advisory Committee was diluted by increases in membership and eventually became absorbed into the Cabinet's ordinary Economic Policy Committee.[7]

EXPANSION UNDER BUTLER

Indeed the faults of the system of Civil Service thinking punctured by political intrusion were least apparent during the reign of Mr R. A. Butler, who held office for the unusually long period of four years. Butler had probably even less technical understanding than some of his successors of Treasury operations, and one official once suggested that he would have benefited from the purchase of one of the toy 'National Income machines' used for teaching students, in which the flow of money in the economy is represented by a stream of blue-coloured fluid. It was Butler's hunches as a political animal that on occasion enabled him to separate bad advice from good. Sometimes he would act for twenty-four hours as if he had taken a certain decision, so that he

7. See the Rt Hon. the Earl of Woolton, *Memoirs*, pp. 371–4, on which the above account is partly based.

could get the feel of living with it, and then if he did not like it he would change his mind.

Butskellism is a technique which can be used in an 'expansionist' or a 'restrictionist' direction, and Butler himself had a consistent bias towards expansion. His first, 1952, Budget proved in retrospect too severe; but nearly all the MPs listening were surprised that he did not make any net increase in taxation, as most outside commentators were urging him to do.

Although many consumer goods industries were already depressed, Mr Butler had to justify at considerable length in the prevailing alarmist climate of opinion his refusal to cut personal spending further. But the most interesting thing about the 1952 Budget was how Mr Butler managed to make a Budget that made no net change in the tax burden an interesting and exciting one. He cut food subsidies and put up a few minor duties, balanced this by improved social benefits and income-tax relief, and made many other offsetting changes. His Budget is still an object lesson, and one much misunderstood, for future Chancellors who have no net reliefs to offer. 'Restrictions and austerity are not enough,' he emphasized in his speech. 'We want a system which offers us both more realism and more hope.'

In 1953 Butler reduced taxation to take up the slack that had developed in the economy. 'The path of restriction has been so firmly fixed in people's minds,' he said, carrying on the theme he had begun the previous year, 'that it tends to be regarded as the inevitable line of conduct. But we can look to a more hopeful way. We can lighten our load and liberate our energies.' The following year was Butler's high noon. In his 1954 Budget he refused to apologize for the increase in personal consumption for which he had been criticized: 'The truth is that we must not be frightened at a little more ease and happiness, or feel that what is pleasant must necessarily be evil.' But he did supplement higher consumption by a new incentive to industrial investment. The Economic Section made a

proposal that twenty per cent of the cost of all new investment in plant and machinery should be deducted from a
firm's taxable income, over and above normal depreciation. Mr Butler accepted the proposed 'investment allowances' and forced them through against the opposition of
the Inland Revenue, who protested that they were a
'distortion' and a subsidy.

Interestingly enough, the intellectual quality of some of
the advice reaching ministers from permanent Treasury
officials and from the Bank of England (which was at that
time extremely influential) reached its nadir during Mr
Butler's period at the Exchequer. Monetary policy, for instance, was frequently spoken of as providing a sort of
painless discipline which would not slow down expansion
or be restrictive, but would nevertheless stabilize the
economy.

Although the quality of Whitehall analysis began to
improve after the mid 1950s, policy-making did not. An
idea of the increasing fatalism which overtook British
economic management in the later 1950s can be obtained
by comparing Mr Butler's Budget speech of 1954 with Mr
Heathcoat Amory's speech of 1958. Both men were speaking during US recessions, and both were speaking at a time
when it was not clear whether the American economy would
soon turn upwards (as in fact it did) or spiral downwards
into depression.

In 1954 Mr Butler stressed that the implications of the
American decline for the rest of the world must be closely
watched. If the need arose, action should be taken on a
national and international basis without delay. (He was
speaking at a time when *discriminatory* action by full-employment countries to prevent recession spreading was still
regarded as a possibility.) The Chancellor warned that we
must be prepared to act together with our friends. At home
he would not hesitate to take more radical measures should
'later in the year circumstances so demand'. In 1958 Mr
Heathcoat Amory, who was echoing contemporary official

doctrine, said: 'It is no use deceiving ourselves into thinking that we can carry the world on our shoulders or stem single-handed forces which are only to a limited extent within our control.' He went on to say that the strength of sterling remains 'the primary objective of our economic policy' and later emphasized 'that we must conduct our own finances with a special caution in difficult times'.

Nothing may have seemed to the many MPs more sound, cautious, and full of common sense than Mr Amory's remarks. Yet just this attitude, if adopted by every country, could send the world spiralling downwards into depression; and it is just what did happen before the war. Those who believe in surrendering to the world economic forces that they have often themselves had a share in creating, should not be allowed to take refuge in their favourite labels of 'outward-looking' and 'internationalist'.

The two far-reaching weaknesses of Butler's period at the Exchequer, which must heavily qualify the praise already given, concerned wages and sterling. On the wages front a quite deliberate policy of appeasement was adopted. Winston Churchill still had unpleasant memories of the general strike to live down. As Lord Woolton has put it in his *Memoirs*, 'he was determined that there should be no industrial strikes during his period as Prime Minister'. This was the era of Sir Walter Monckton at the Ministry of Labour, when all the ministry's energies were devoted to bringing the two sides together even at the cost of highly inflationary settlements. Appeasement did trade unionists little good, as higher wages were largely cancelled out in higher prices. Indeed, British workers were paying until 1967 for the Monckton policy, which by pricing British goods out of world markets slowed down the growth of the whole economy.

The government walked into these dangers open-eyed. The Treasury's Economic Survey for 1954 – a remarkably good one – was one of the first published documents to draw attention to Britain's falling share in world trade. The 1954 survey writer had a gift for gloomy exaggeration. 'If in present circumstances the prices of our exports generally were to be pushed up by a rise in internal costs, we should be taking a short cut to national bankruptcy,' he thundered. 'Our competitive power would be disastrously weakened and the consequent worsening of the balance of payments would destroy for the time being any chances of a further improvement in the standard of living.' And Mr Butler himself repeated the point, only a shade less dramatically, in his Budget speech.

A White Paper published in 1956 showed that Treasury economists had believed for many years in the theoretical case for an incomes policy, and Lord Woolton afterwards mentioned that the appeasement policy 'greatly disturbed some of us in the Cabinet'. (The judgement that appeasement was a mistake does not itself imply any great optimism about the positive effects of an incomes policy.) But as the government's Economic Adviser, Sir Robert Hall, frankly admitted to the Radcliffe Committee in 1957, 'the Cabinet', despite Lord Woolton's strictures, 'had ever since it came to office regarded the problem of the price level as one to be solved by a change in the climate of opinion.'[8] Or, as Butler put it in his 1954 Budget speech, 'we do better through relying on voluntary moderation'.

In his Budget speech of April 1955 Mr Butler listed the results of voluntary moderation. Between 1953 and 1954 output per man rose by two and a half per cent but wages and salaries rose by about seven and a half. In his speech on the emergency Budget of October 1955, he gave another progress report. Wage rates had risen by five points between December 1954 and March 1955. Between March and June they had risen by another three points and since then by a further point, making nine points in all. In December 1955 there was a Cabinet reshuffle and Mr Butler was replaced by Mr Macmillan. But it was not until

8. *Volume of Oral Evidence*, HMSO, 1960, 'Proceedings of 25 October 1957, Q. 1657'.

seven years after ministers had first identified the problems in their speeches that a Conservative Chancellor intervened to impose a wage freeze.

Another important criticism of domestic policy during Mr Butler's term of office is that the government tended to wash its hands of all concern for the performance of particular industries, or of problems such as industrial training, research and technology, salesmanship and quality of management of which we hear so much today. This neglect of such down-to-earth matters served, quite unfairly, to discredit the basic Butskellian ideas. Some *laisser faire* was an inevitable reaction to the negative post-war controls with which the Labour government had become associated, but the reaction which took place was too long and too indiscriminate. A concern for structural problems is perfectly compatible with a private-enterprise, free-market orientation. In the 1960s the pendulum swung to the other extreme and it became fashionable to exaggerate what the government could do in such matters and mistakenly see it as a substitute to Butskellite economic management.

THE ROBOT PLAN

The biggest confusion during Mr Butler's reign was on policy towards sterling. The story of Operation Robot, an abortive plan for making the pound convertible to non-sterling-area holders at a floating rate of exchange and freezing certain sterling balances, is now fairly well known. There were severe restrictions on the degree of convertibility. A large part of the sterling area's London balances was to have been blocked, and so were ninety per cent of the balances held by those who were neither in the dollar nor the sterling area. Convertibility was in fact to have been confined largely to dollar-area residents.

The plan was devised by the Treasury with the support of the Bank of England, soon after the Conservatives returned to office, without the participation of either Sir Robert Hall, the government's Economic Adviser, or Sir Edwin Plowden, the Chief Planning Officer. It gained Butler's support, but was vetoed by Churchill against his original inclination, on the advice of his wartime confidant Lord Cherwell (then back in office for a short period as Paymaster General) and also of Sir Arthur Salter, who was the second minister at the Treasury with the title of Minister of State for Economic Affairs. At first Cherwell and Salter argued against it independently, without knowledge of each other's positions, but they later worked together very effectively to defeat the plan. Cherwell himself turned for economic advice to G. D. A. MacDougall, who had been a member of his wartime staff. Salter worked closely with Plowden and Hall. He also gave strong encouragement to an independent but influential Chatham House Committee, which quickly published a report 'of considerable help'[9] to those opposing Robot.

At one point a suggestion was made that the sterling exchange rate should not be left to move indefinitely downwards, but should be supported in the market by the Bank – interestingly enough at $2·40. The original intention was to announce Robot in the Budget, which was advanced to 11 March 1952 partly for that purpose, and a decision to postpone it was taken only a few days beforehand. The project was not finally vetoed until June of that year. Churchill is said to have remarked at the end: 'I don't know much about these technical financial matters myself, but I can't help feeling that when Cherwell and Salter [who had been long-standing opponents in many contexts] agree there must be something in what they say.' This approach by the

9. *Slave of the Lamp*, by Arthur Salter, Weidenfeld & Nicolson, 1967, Chapter 15. This and *The Prof. in Two Worlds* by the Earl of Birkenhead, Collins, 1961, are the two main first-hand accounts of Robot. An account of Robot and the convertibility plans that succeeded it can be found in *The Management of the British Economy*, by J. C. R. Dow, Cambridge University Press, 1964, and *Britain and the Post-war European Payments Systems*, by Graham L. Rees, University of Wales Press, 1963.

veteran war-leader turned out no worse a basis for decision-taking than the *ad hoc* interventions of later premiers who professed greater economic expertise.

This brief account is enough to dispel any idea that devaluation has always been abhorrent to Conservatives as a cure for a payments crisis. (The supporters of a floating rate in 1952 had no illusions about the rate moving anywhere other than downwards.) It may not be entirely a coincidence that the two ministers who exerted themselves against Robot were 'outsiders' brought in by Churchill without any Conservative party political background. Salter had been a Civil Servant, and then an independent MP, while Cherwell was an academic who had become Churchill's scientific adviser.

Why however was the Bank of England, of all institutions, prepared to tolerate floating rates in the winter of 1951–2?

To explain this flirtation with unorthodoxy one must go back to the run on sterling which took place in the autumn and winter of 1951–2, just as the Conservatives were returning to office. The 1951–2 run on the pound was a particularly severe and somewhat mysterious one, due partly to the collapse of the Korean boom overseas and partly to overstrain caused by rearmament at home. Mr Churchill himself took a very alarmist view. 'I have seen', he told Oliver Lyttelton, 'a Treasury Minute and already I know that the financial position is almost irretrievable: the country has lost its way. *In the worst of the war I could always see how to do it. Today's problems are elusive and intangible*, and it would be a bold man who could look forward to certain success.'[10]

As usual the Bank projected the outflow into the future, and worked out how many months it would be before the reserves were exhausted. It seemed, therefore, to the Bank during that winter as if Britain would have to devalue or

10. *The Memoirs of Lord Chandos*, Bodley Head, 1962, p. 343. The italics are mine.

float in any case; it therefore wanted to make a virtue of necessity, and gain convertibility into the bargain. A fluctuating rate was seen as the price for moving to convertibility; and this in essence was the attraction of Robot. There were at that time people in the Bank who had experience of working a system of floating rates in the 1930s, and this weakened their resistance to the idea. But when the reserves did not run out in the way feared, and eventually began to return, the Bank could see no more point in floating. As the 1950s wore on personalities changed, memories faded, and opinion hardened in favour of fixed rates at any price.

The idea of floating rates did not, however, immediately die when Robot was rejected. Another secret plan or series of plans for a 'collective approach to convertibility' emerged by the end of the Commonwealth Conference in December 1952. These too provided for convertibility at a floating rate; but it was hoped to bolster up the sterling-area reserves with an American loan or at least obtain US support for an application for help from the International Monetary Fund. But when Butler presented the Treasury's ideas to the new Republican Administration early in 1953 he received a pretty unenthusiastic reception.

These plans hung fire for a while, and emphasis shifted towards import liberalization in concert with other West European countries. The anti-*laisser-faire* wing of the Treasury was never too keen on convertibility and wanted to make haste as slowly as possible, but the Bank of England, which was becoming more and more dominant in overseas financial policy, was gradually dismantling exchange restrictions. From February 1955, when the British authorities decided to support transferable sterling in the market, sterling was in practice convertible into dollars and other foreign currency for all non-residents at, or very near, the official rate of exchange.

The fashion had shifted towards a concerted move to convertibility on a European rather than a sterling-area basis; and by 1955 the Bank of England believed that it could achieve this goal. But some officials were still keen to have, if not a completely free pound, at least some exchange rate flexibility; and as late as July 1955 members of the British delegation to talks on the new European monetary agreement, which was to come into effect after convertibility, were arguing for a three per cent margin of freedom on either side; in other words, a rate which would move from around $2·72 to $2·88 to the pound.

Widespread gossip on the subject during the summer of 1955, at a time when sterling was already weak, caused a burst of speculation against the pound. The Bank of England finally put its foot down against the whole idea of floating rates, and persuaded Mr Butler and the Treasury that they must do the same if the run on the pound was to be stopped. On 14 September 1955 Mr Butler categorically denied all thought of a change in the sterling exchange rate at Istanbul, where the International Monetary Fund was holding its annual conference. The Bank of England, for its part, had to accept a postponement of formal convertibility, which did not come until December 1958 – and, of course, at a fixed rate of exchange.

Anyone looking at Robot with later controversies in mind might have expected the expansionist section of the Treasury around Hall and Plowden to have been its strongest backers. The reasons why it took the opposite view centred not so much on the floating rate as on the convertibility aspects of Robot. In 1952 the dollar shortage was still acute, and if sterling had become convertible foreign holders might well have rushed to switch their pounds into dollars at the expense of the British reserves, as happened during Dr Dalton's ill-fated experiment in the summer of 1947. On the trade side other countries might have been encouraged to cut down on UK imports in order to accumulate convertible sterling for use in making dollar purchases. A floating rate in the winter of 1951–2 might thus have meant a heavily depreciated rate and an unnecessarily severe fall in British living standards; moreover, owing to the industrial overstrain caused by rearmament, British exports might not have been able to respond to the stimulus that devaluation normally brings.

These were not the only arguments used. Lord Salter's account shows that the more familiar notion that devaluation meant default, together with horror at the idea of blocking the sterling balances, played a prominent part in the opposition to Robot. Nor should it be forgotten that progressive views were often identified – quite wrongly in my opinion – with opposition to economic liberalism.

It is questionable if the fierce hostility of the progressives to Robot was well judged even in 1952. The operation might well have led to a realignment of currencies which would have put an end to the dollar shortage. Although British living standards would temporarily have fallen, the authorities would have been left with an automatic balance-of-payments adjustment mechanism, and many of the 'stops' of the next decade and a half might have been avoided.

But even if the case against Robot is conceded for 1952 when the issue was fought out in Cabinet, in the following years the dollar shortage eased and defence spending was no longer pre-empting the resources that could have supported an export drive. If the economic planners in the Treasury had come out wholeheartedly in favour of convertibility at a floating rate in, say, 1954, the whole course of subsequent British economic history might have been changed immeasurably for the better. As it was, all they gained was a period of delay, during which Britain had most of the drawbacks of sterling convertibility and none of the prestige; and at the end of the day the Bank of England won a practically total victory.

THE 1955 ERROR

This account has strayed from Mr Butler and his mistakes of 1955, which were not confined to foreign exchange policy. During that year, his last at the Exchequer, Mr Butler passed through an unhappy phase after the death of his first wife. His political intuition failed him in his April Budget, when he made a serious blunder by handing out £135m. of tax reliefs in the middle of a raging boom.

The economy was expanding rapidly; unemployment (seasonally adjusted) had fallen over the previous year from 1·5 to 1·1 per cent, and there were nearly twice as many vacancies as men out of work. The gold reserves were under strain and the economy was suffering from a demand inflation of a severity that has never since been equalled. This is a situation in which even the most expansionist of economists might have argued for a touch of the brake. The government's Economic Adviser did not support an expansionist Budget.

The real blame for the 1955 miscalculation lay with what might be called the permanent side of the official Treasury, with the connivance of the Bank of England. Paradoxically it was just those sections of official opinion that are normally most cautious about expanding production when there is unemployment and slack in the economy who encouraged Mr Butler to introduce a tax-cutting Budget, and they did so at a time of overfull employment when extra consumer spending would be sure to have the most inflationary possible effect.

One normally very mild-mannered observer of these events has described them as 'entangled and discreditable'. Some senior Civil Servants (long since departed) seemed too preoccupied with Mr Butler's political difficulties on the eve of an election. This does not mean that the officials who advised Mr Butler were cynical or dishonest, for they certainly believed their own rationalizations. Having only recently rediscovered monetary policy, the Bank of England and Treasury officials overestimated its strength and speed. Early in 1955 Bank Rate had been raised in two steps from three to four and a half per cent; very moderate hire-purchase controls (with minimum deposits of only fifteen per cent and two years to pay for both cars and durables) had been introduced; and banks had been asked to limit finance for hire purchase and credit sales. There was, however, a tell-tale reference in the Budget to the 'resources of flexible monetary policy', suggesting a slight fear that all might not be well and that greater restraint might later be needed.

There were, in fact, many interesting sentiments in the speech with which Mr Butler introduced his unfortunate first Budget of the year. He said, 'productivity should benefit from the maintenance of prosperous conditions at home and from the added incentive to effort which the prospect of rising consumption affords; and an economy in which production and productivity are rising fast, and new lines of production are continually being developed, should be in a good position to hold its own in export markets'.

There would still be disagreement among economists about the degree of validity of these observations. They were in any case very different from what Mr Butler himself was saying the previous year when he talked about steering a middle course. They were also almost the opposite of the sentiments that Messrs Heathcoat Amory, Lloyd and Callaghan used to put in their speeches.

The type of Budget that is introduced must clearly vary according to the economic situation; but this is no justification for allowing the measuring rod by which situations are judged to shift its position in such a dazzling fashion. At one moment all the talk is of expansion; at another the public is told that easy times are gone, perhaps for ever, and that everything else will be subordinated to the overriding task of supporting sterling. It is hardly surprising that many businessmen, thrust into uncertainties they are not professionally equipped to handle, become resentful of the whole universe of politicians, officials and economists.

Mr Butler is reported to have come back after the 1955 election full of fury with the bankers who, he believed, had misled him; and well he might. By July he had introduced a package measure of further restrictions: hire-purchase deposits went up to thirty-three per cent, the nationalized industries were asked to cut their investment programmes, the banks were told to cut advances, and coal and steel prices were raised abruptly to mop up spending power. But this was not regarded as enough by the Treasury, as the pressure on sterling increased, and wages continued to soar; and in October Mr Butler introduced an autumn Budget which took back the greater part of his earlier reliefs. The damage done to Mr Butler's reputation by the advice he received in 1955 from permanent Treasury officials may have been at least a factor in his first failure to achieve the premiership early in 1957 and even (through its general effect on his standing at a crucial moment) in his second failure after Mr Macmillan retired in 1963.

THE ECONOMICS OF STOCKTON-ON-TEES

Mr Harold Macmillan, who succeeded Butler at No. 11 in December 1955, was regarded as an inflationist by Treasury and Bank officials and (after he became Prime Minister) by some of his own Cabinet colleagues. His views were indeed coloured by his acquaintance with mass unemployment at his old constituency of Stockton-on-Tees in the inter-war period; and this was a subject of some mockery in Whitehall. Officials were said to keep a mental tally of the number of times he mentioned Stockton-on-Tees in any one week.

He resented the restricting influence of sterling on British economic expansion, and would clearly have loved to have found a way of getting rid of the sterling-area 'bank' which the 'family firm' had inherited. He was passionately interested in the international liquidity problem, which (long before most central bankers) he rightly regarded as a matter of generating more internationally acceptable money to finance the growth of world trade; and he persisted in sending American Presidents notes on the subject. The simplest way of solving the problem, he always maintained, was to increase the price of gold; but the fetish that the American leaders made of the existing gold–dollar parity prevented a solution along these lines throughout his period in office.

Cynics always underestimated Macmillan's economic understanding. He was intellectually unhappy at the need to exhort people to export more. The occasional speech in which he recalled the vanished mechanisms of the nineteenth-century gold standard, and wondered why there was today no automatic system of bringing exports and imports into balance, again were not the platitudes that superficial listeners supposed. He always had a hankering after a floating exchange rate, and would have introduced one if given the slightest encouragement.

Macmillan was, however, rusty on the mechanics of economic control by the time he got to No. 11, and he had little intuitive feeling for economic timing. Yet he occasionally had a better understanding of the logic of the really major issues than either his Treasury or his Bank advisers; and it must never be forgotten that Macmillan was one of the very, very few Conservative politicians who had been right before the war both about unemployment and about the appeasement of Nazi Germany.

The interaction between Mr Macmillan (when he became premier), his ministers, and the Whitehall machine was responsible for much of what was wrong with British policy. It is therefore all the more necessary to emphasize that so long as Mr Macmillan was at the helm there were grounds for hoping that the bigger economic lunacies would never be allowed to happen. If the danger of large-scale unemployment ever became real and not just a fantasy it would have been very difficult for the Treasury and the Bank, by the usual lame cries of 'world situation beyond our control', to deter Mr Macmillan from vigorous action. The continuous changing of Chancellor showed the Prime Minister's determination on this point clearly.

Macmillan's friends might say that he came to the Treasury twenty years too late; he did not enjoy his stay and only went there because of an unsatisfactory relationship with Eden in his previous post of Foreign Secretary. He more or less acknowledged this in his one and only Budget speech in April 1956, when he began by mentioning that Churchill was said to have been quite surprised to find himself at the Treasury in the winter of 1924 – 'but not half so surprised as I was, thirty-one years later'. At the Exchequer he was no longer prepared to do the homework which would have enabled him to set forth a detailed policy of his own as an alternative to what his advisers were offering him.

Mr Macmillan's Budget speech was by far the most entertaining of the whole post-war series. The whole mood was buoyantly expansionist. There were long passages from Macaulay to show how the country prospered in the eighteenth century, despite increases in the National Debt to many times the level that earlier Cassandras had regarded as catastrophic. The National Debt stood at £645m. on 4 August 1914, £8,400m. on 3 September 1939, £27,000m. in 1956. Its servicing, Mr Macmillan pointed out, cost at the time he was speaking £638m. a year 'or nearly 3s. on the income tax'.

'No one who contemplates these [National Debt] figures can fail to draw the lesson,' said Mr Macmillan. 'Whatever the temporary difficulties from which we may suffer from trying to run too fast, if we stand still we are lost.' Runaway inflation was, of course, bad, but 'we must all be expansionists of real wealth. The problem of inflation cannot be dealt with by cutting down demand; the other side of the picture is the need for increasing production. The only question is at what rate, for what markets, and how best guided our expansion is to be.'

Cutting down demand is, however, just what Mr Macmillan did, and indeed there was a strong case for doing so at the time with unemployment scarcely 1·1 per cent. A few weeks before the Budget he had introduced a particularly stiff package dose of restrictions which, among other things, tightened hire-purchase restrictions still further, cut public investment, and suspended the investment allowance for private industry – the latter a move he eventually recognized as a particularly misguided decision. The Budget imposed no further net increase in the burden; but with the aid of cuts in government spending, aimed to increase the above-the-line surplus by well over £150m. The Economic Survey added threateningly, 'If the measures so far taken are slow in producing results they will be reinforced.'

Of all Conservative Chancellors Macmillan was the only one who really wanted a full-scale capital gains tax. But he was baulked by the Inland Revenue and hardly encouraged by his own Party. All that happened as a result of his measures was that instead of the increased production for which he had called, 1956 was a year of stagnation. It can be argued that this was part of the price that had to be paid for Mr Butler's boom, which made a subsequent period of pause inevitable. But the combination of an expansionist speech and a restrictionist Budget was symptomatic of Macmillan's whole conduct of economic policy, except when he was alarmed by the fear of recession (which was quite frequently, but not always at the right moments).

Mr Macmillan's two main achievements as Chancellor were (a) the introduction of Premium Bonds and (b) the improvement in official statistics, which he had castigated as 'last year's Bradshaw'. The fall-out from the second operation continued over many years and economic analysts are still feeling the effects today.

Macmillan's last few months as Chancellor were overlaid by the Suez crisis. A mystery still to be cleared up about this period is the identity (if any) of the ministry which gave Eden the misleading advice about the supposedly catastrophic effects on the British economy should the Canal be closed.

One critical writer recently remarked that the Treasury stopped a small war in Palmerston's day by refusing to agree to the required expenditure. He asked rhetorically whether one could imagine it happening today. One could. Treasury alarm at the rate at which the gold reserves were falling had a good deal to do with Britain's decision to bring the Suez operations to a sudden halt in early November 1956, only a few days after they had begun. As was usual on such occasions, Macmillan telephoned Washington in his capacity as Chancellor to ask for the American Administration's good offices in obtaining financial assistance for the pound. The Americans replied that there was no hope of any aid while fighting was going on in Egypt.

Macmillan had originally been the warmest cheer-leader of the Suez expedition, and had at first maintained, on the basis of a personal meeting with Eisenhower, that the Americans would not oppose it. But in a crucial Cabinet meeting in early November he suddenly changed his mind and threw all his weight behind those who wanted to bring the operation to an end, but he has since denied saying 'we can't afford it'. How much then had the run on the reserves really to do with his change of front?

People's motives are rarely entirely distinct, even to themselves, in the fever-heat of a crisis. There were a great many factors involved in the final decision: the threat of rockets from Russia, Britain's fantastic isolation from world opinion, and above all, the extreme separation from the US. America's refusal to help Britain financially in an hour of need was symptomatic of the rupture in Atlantic relations.

THORNEYCROFTS I AND II

Mr Peter Thorneycroft (now Lord Thorneycroft), who succeeded Macmillan at the Exchequer when the latter moved up to No. 10, was often compared to Mr Selwyn Lloyd; and there are certain obvious similarities. Both imposed tough financial policies in the teeth of fierce opposition and eventually earned Mr Macmillan's displeasure. Neither was a man of great guile or subtlety; and both pursued their policies with a dogged determination, irrespective of the effect on their own political fortunes, which won admiration even from their critics. Neither could fairly be written off as a Tory reactionary (Thorneycroft was, for example, a keen European and a free trader; Selwyn Lloyd supported the abolition of the death penalty), although both found their chief backing in the financially orthodox wing of the Conservative Party.

Yet there were also important differences. Peter Thorneycroft never claimed to be an intellectual high-flier; but he was rarely at a loss for words and was much more interested than the average politician in general economic ideas. After his resignation he contributed to a professional symposium on the Radcliffe Report on the monetary system.[11] Selwyn Lloyd, by contrast, was easily embarrassed both in public speeches and in conversation, and was ill at ease in general economic discussion.

Although Mr Thorneycroft was no intellectual heavyweight, he had a good many sound instincts. The argument over the Aswan Dam is a case in point; and during the Suez crisis he never took seriously the scare about a world tanker shortage that obsessed many other members of the Cabinet. In the very early days of the Common Market, around the time of the Messina meeting of June 1955, when the Six were still working out the treaty, Thorneycroft had written a paper saying that Britain should be associated with it in a free-trade area. If the Cabinet had accepted the idea then, instead of waiting a couple of years, the negotiations would probably have succeeded.

The Treasury did not suit him at all. The manoeuvring between rival knights, at which Butler had been so adroit, had no appeal for him. Thorneycroft was disturbed by the thought that he, as a lay minister, knew more about

11. *Not Unanimous*, Institute of Economic Affairs, 1960.

finance than Sir Roger Makins, his Permanent Secretary. This was very different from the Board of Trade, in which he had worked together very happily with Sir Frank Lee, with whom he had a very close sympathy.

Thorneycroft's reign is quite correctly associated with the first stop-go episode, in which the post-war objectives of full employment and economic expansion to which Butler and Macmillan had both been dedicated seemed for a time to have been abandoned.

The speeches Thorneycroft made in his first six months in the Treasury were so different from those he made in his second six months that it is difficult to credit them with the same authorship. The following utterances by Thorneycroft I and Thorneycroft II illustrate the point.

Thorneycroft I: Speaking about inflation, the Chancellor said

There are some who say that the answer lies in savage deflationary policies, resulting in high levels of unemployment. *They say that we should depress demand to a point at which employers cannot afford to pay and workers are in no position to ask for higher wages.* If this be the only way in which to contain the wage–price spiral it is indeed a sorry reflection upon our modern society. To slash production, to drive down investment, to push up unemployment to a level at which, despite high world demand, we have manufactured our own recession, is to say the least a high price to pay for stability. (Budget Speech, April 1957.)

Thorneycroft II: After outlining the measures to limit public investment in money terms and restrict bank advances, Mr Thorneycroft went on

Against this background, if an attempt were made to take out of the system in money income more than is put in by new effort and production the only result would be a reduction in activity and the employment of fewer men. The only other thing I would say about these measures is that I am confident they will be effective. They will be pushed to the lengths necessary for that purpose. If inflationary pressures grow inside the economy, other things may

alter, other aspects of policy may have to be adjusted, but the strain will not be placed on the value of the pound sterling.
(Speech at the Annual IMF Meeting in Washington, 24 September 1957.)

Thorneycroft I took the advice of Sir Robert Hall. It is not generally known that before switching over to his ultra-tough money approach, Thorneycroft did try to introduce an incomes policy. This was to have been a guiding light – similar to that proclaimed by Mr Selwyn Lloyd barely five years later and rechristened as a norm by the Labour government – giving the increase in wages compatible with stable prices, and stating some of the grounds for exceptions. The idea was rejected by the Cabinet for predictable reasons: there was a danger that the guiding light might become a minimum instead of a norm and it was wrong to interfere with collective bargaining.

The three-man Council on Prices, Productivity and Incomes appointed by Mr Thorneycroft in August 1957 to make reports to the public was the vestigial remnant of his attempt at an incomes policy. But as the one and only economist on the Council, the late Sir Dennis Robertson, was a distinguished representative of the school which believed in tough money alone, there was never any chance that the Council would take upon itself the odium of producing a guiding light. So it proved. The exercise in buck-passing failed, as it deserved, and the Council contented itself with arguing the case for monetary deflation.

Mr Thorneycroft's Budget of April 1957 was quite a cheerful one. The figures worked out in such a way that he could reduce taxation by £100m. (£140m. in a full year) and yet increase the above-the-line surplus substantially. Some relief in the burden of surtax, which until then came down suddenly on all earned incomes as soon as they reached the £2,000 point, was introduced via the backdoor of the earned-income relief; and this was accompanied by other reliefs for lower incomes. The one probable mistake was the special tax concession for companies operating abroad, which added a gratuitous strain to the balance of payments which did not come to an end until the 1965 Finance Act. The concession had been recommended by the Royal Commission on Taxation, and Mr Macmillan had given an undertaking on the subject the previous year.

It was, of course, a sudden traumatic run on the gold reserves during the summer that transformed Thorneycroft I into Thorneycroft II. In two months in the summer £186m. was lost and the sum would have been larger without some special payments. The main cause was a bout of currency speculation, triggered off by a partial devaluation of the French franc in August. Rumours were circulating that the German mark was to be revalued and sterling might be depreciated as part of a general realignment. Naturally, funds poured out of London, and traders delayed making payments in sterling and accelerated payments in other currencies. Sterling had already been weakened, first by the Suez episode, and then by the purchase of dollar securities through Kuwait by British citizens speculating against the pound. Mr Thorneycroft has publicly admitted that the Bank of England was opposed to direct action to close the Kuwait Gap,[12] and that this delayed action. Yet for all the Bank's technical objections, the gap was closed effectively enough in July. By then it had cost the reserves £70m.[13]

Mr Thorneycroft responded to the run on the pound with his famous deflationary package, raising Bank Rate from 5 to 7 per cent. Public sector investment was cut, a ceiling was imposed on advances, and the Capital Issues Committee was told to be more restrictive. The Chancellor, moreover, firmly announced his intention of stopping the rise in government spending. He did not want too much attention to be paid to Bank Rate alone and let it be

12. Radcliffe Committee: *Volume of Oral Evidence*, Q. 11255.
13. *The British Economy in the 1950s*, edited by G. D. N. Worswick and P. H. Ady, Oxford, 1962, p. 222.

known that he would like his package deal to be known as the 'September Measures'.

The language about stopping up the supply of money which Mr Thorneycroft inserted into his speeches had no effect on what he actually did, which was to impose another old-style set of deflationary measures to curb spending with a special emphasis on the public sector. He also threatened that any wage increases granted in the public sector would be at the expense of employment; but he was not long enough at the Treasury for anyone to discover whether such a policy could be implemented. It seemed to some Treasury officials that Thorneycroft had confused government expenditure with the quantity of money. The merits of what economists know as the Quantity Theory of money were never even put to the test. The money supply had been falling rapidly as a proportion of the GNP for several years before Thorneycroft acted; a table demonstrating this was rather maliciously inserted into the 1958 Economic Survey. During the twelve months after his measures the trend was, in fact, reversed. Even in absolute terms, the quantity of bank deposits plus notes in circulation rose more quickly in the year after the Thorneycroft measures of September 1957 than in the year before.

The Treasury itself presented a confused and divided picture during this period. Some Treasury officials saw no alternative to the September Measures even though they disliked the verbiage in which they were clothed. But the official Treasury advice which Mr Thorneycroft received from the Permanent Secretary Sir Roger Makins was opposed to what he did.

Mr Thorneycroft felt that his only consistent supporter near the top of the hierarchy was Sir Leslie Rowan, who was in charge of external finance. Thorneycroft formed the impression that Sir Roger Makins was against what he was doing, but had no alternative advice to offer except to ride out the storm. There may have been a case for doing nothing, but it would have had to be argued with great clarity, force and ruthless facing of possible consequences if it was to convince a Chancellor who had just seen nearly a quarter of his gold reserves disappear within a couple of months.

The Chancellor worked out the main lines of policy with the help of Mr Enoch Powell, the Financial Secretary, and Mr Nigel Birch, the Economic Secretary, who exercised a dominating influence extremely unusual for junior Treasury ministers. It was they who were largely responsible for turning the anti-inflationary policies into a crusade. Needless to say, the Bank of England sounded the alarm in the summer of 1957 and backed the Treasury ministers all along the line.

Thorneycroft's switch of policy became apparent in July when he gave instructions to the Treasury 'to consider possibilities of checking inflation by taking firmer control of the money supply'. On 7 August, before he went on holiday, he gave more precise directives that 'a study should be made in the Treasury of the possibility of bringing about a measure of deflation in the economy'.

The role of Professor (now Lord) Robbins in the affair has been exaggerated by those who believe in the conspiracy theory of history. In the period before the measures were announced, Mr Thorneycroft became very worried that neither his Department nor his Cabinet colleagues were supporting him. He telephoned Professor Robbins, who was on holiday in Switzerland, asking him to come back to London. The Chancellor, who knew and respected Robbins, wanted to make sure that the latter thought his proposed measures were sensible. He also wanted him to speak to Macmillan, who was far from keen on Thorneycroft's proposed measures; and, as the universities were later able to confirm, Robbins was an extremely impressive person to have on one's side.[14]

On Tuesday afternoon, 17 September, the Cabinet

14. Lord Robbins's actual views at the time were the subject of a great deal of newspaper gossip. Readers interested in what Robbins really did believe about the 1957 crisis are referred to his article in *Lloyds Bank Review* of April 1958, reprinted in *Politics and Economics*, Macmillan, 1963.

approved the Chancellor's measures apart from the Bank Rate increase. This was discussed at a 10 p.m. meeting at 10 Downing Street, attended by the Prime Minister, Chancellor, Governor of the Bank of England, Sir Roger Makins, and two other officials, but not Sir Robert Hall. After some discussion Mr Macmillan said he 'would not make up his mind whether the Government should agree to Bank Rate being raised, and if so, to what figure, until the following morning' – when, of course, he agreed to seven per cent.[15]

A CHANGE OF PRIORITIES

The September Measures of 1957 marked a turning aside from the road along which the country had travelled under successive Labour and Conservative governments. Mr Thorneycroft's supporters saw this better than some of his critics. At the time of Mr Butler's autumn Budget of 1955, or of the curbs imposed by Mr Macmillan in 1956, it could always be argued that the economy was genuinely overloaded. Unemployment (seasonally adjusted) was down to 1–1·2 per cent; and there were almost two recorded unfilled vacancies for every man out of work. A deflationary policy in these circumstances did not necessarily imply sacrificing the growth of the domestic economy for the sake of sterling.

But by 1957 the situation was radically different. Although still low, unemployment had been on a rising trend for two years and looked like moving higher. Despite several years of rising investment, production had only just regained its 1955 peak. Treasury economists who had supported the Butler and Macmillan squeezes of 1955 and 1956 saw that the pressure of demand on supply had already

15. A blow-by-blow account of the events leading up to the Bank Rate decision was extracted by Professor Ely Devons from the proceedings of the Tribunal of Inquiry into allegations of a leakage. It appears in a special issue of the *Manchester School* (Vol. 27, No. 1, September 1959) which contains three highly interesting articles on the political, economic, and sociological evidence which emerged from the episode.

eased and they expected more slack to develop in the coming months. They feared that the Thorneycroft measures would aggravate a recession that was already on the way. Even worse was the fact that the Thorneycroft measures were imposed in response to a flight of hot money when the balance of payments itself was in comfortable surplus.

In December 1956 government spokesmen said publicly that the best Britain could hope for was a bare current balance in the year ending mid 1957. A few months later Mr Thorneycroft told Parliament that he was looking forward to a current surplus of £125m. Speaking at the IMF meeting in September 1957 he announced that the surplus had worked out at over £200m. and he expected a bigger surplus in the following twelve months. By deflating the economy in the face of his own figures he was proclaiming to the world that production and employment in Britain would be held back whenever currency speculators decided to take a gamble against the pound, or traders delayed their payments – however unjustified their actions were. This was quite different from the runs on sterling of the 1960s which reflected well-justified alarm over the balance of payments. Public criticism of Thorneycroft's measures in Britain concentrated on peripherals and did not fully bring out the full extent of this change in economic priorities.

Supporters of the September Measures often maintained that they were justified by the speed with which wages were rising in Britain. This is hardly sustained by the figures published in 1958, by the Cohen Council[16] – who were the warmest supporters Thorneycroft ever had.

Not only is there no sign that Mr Thorneycroft was faced with a bigger problem of wage inflation than his predecessors; on the contrary, the pace of wage inflation was already beginning to decline when he decided to hit the British economy on the head. Indeed, most of the evidence suggests that even the reduced wage inflation of 1956–7

16. *Council on Prices, Productivity and Incomes*, Second Report, August 1958, HMSO.

was a delayed response to a boom that was fast fading away. As an ex-Treasury economist, Mr J. C. R. Dow, once pointed out, 'the pressure of demand twelve months ago may have an effect on the wage–price spiral that will take several years to work through'.

TABLE 10

PER CENT INCREASE

	Average Weekly Earnings	Index of Wage Rates
Oct. 1947–Oct. 1955 (annual average)	7·1	5·5
Oct. 1955–Oct. 1956	7·2	7·5
Oct. 1956–Oct. 1957	5·8	5·5

But the real tragedy of 1957 was the missed opportunity on the sterling side. In the later sterling crises, central bankers used the state of the dollar as an argument against allowing the pound to float or against tampering with the exchange rate in any way. If the pound 'went', it was claimed, there would then be a run on the dollar, and this would lead to a general flight from currencies into gold with untold consequences. This argument carried great force with a British Cabinet which regarded the special relationship with America as the mainstay of its foreign policy. It did not, however, apply at all in 1957, as the first signs of weakness in the dollar did not emerge until well on in 1958. Thus 1957 was the last sterling crisis when Britain could have abandoned the sterling rate fixed by Cripps in 1949 without any risk of rocking the international boat; and the opportunity was thrown away.

It was also the last sterling crisis for more than a decade in which a floating rate could have been honestly presented as something different in conception from devaluation. For in the 1950s the pound was not yet decisively over-valued at $2·80. Overseas payments were in balance, taking one year with another, even though the economy was on average being run at a high pressure of demand – considerably higher than in the 1960s.

The balance-of-payments surplus for 1958 was much larger than anything experienced for a decade on either side of it. Had a floating rate been introduced in 1957 it would probably have fallen temporarily, recovered strongly in 1958, and then moved gradually downwards from 1959 onwards, as the surplus ran off and became transformed into a deficit; and this would have provided both a warning and an incentive to move resources into exports and import-saving. The readjustment, which was attempted painfully in a short period after the 1967 devaluation, could thus have been accomplished earlier and more gradually, and without a crisis of national morale, in response to market forces.

The Treasury ministers were, however, engaged in the autumn of 1957 in a crusade to maintain the value of the pound at home and abroad. After the humiliation of Suez the sterling exchange rate – mere arithmetical ratio though it be – was one of the few status symbols we had left. In addition the Conservatives had had several by-election defeats, which they attributed to middle-class resentment over the rising cost of living.

THE PM'S POSITION

Yet this hardly explains why there was such a large gap on this and many subsequent occasions between Macmillan's own expansionist views and the policies of his Chancellors. Part of the answer is that by the then prevailing Conservative tradition the Foreign Secretary tended to be the Prime Minister's emissary, while the Chancellor occupied a more independent position.

Although, as we have seen, Macmillan had very pronounced economic views, his heart was, as the public realized, in foreign affairs. In the words of one of his ministers: 'Foreign affairs was his vocation, economics his hobby.' Officials were never quite sure how seriously to take some of the more unorthodox ideas Macmillan expressed in memoranda or over a drink in the evening. They usually found that he was satisfied with a well-reasoned brief defending the orthodox case and explaining why his heresies would not work. So long as the Chancellor of the Exchequer considered his arguments, the Prime Minister was not prepared to impose them on him – although after a while he would change the Chancellor. Moreover, for all his joy in teasing the Treasury, Macmillan did not think that Britain was doing all that badly in production and trade, considering the difficulties. His own brushes with the Treasury knights had given him a slight 'thing' about them which was not very easily turned into constructive criticism.

Another reason for Macmillan's lack of influence over his Chancellors was his lack of a technically qualified staff to write papers for him, develop his views in detail, suggest ideas, and refute the objections of the Treasury and the Bank. The Prime Minister is the one member of the Cabinet who does not have a Department to brief him; economic policy comes up for decision through the huge machine described in Chapter 2 and, as Mr Wilson's experiences were subsequently to show, it is too delicate and complicated a subject to benefit from *ad hoc* personal interventions.

There was also in 1957 an *ad hominem* point. Not having imposed a floating rate the previous year when he was Chancellor, Mr Macmillan could hardly force this course of action on Thorneycroft. As a result some of his memoranda in the 1957 crisis were, to say the least, uninspired, and were said to have raised questions such as whether there were any votes in road-building.

Nevertheless, the eventual victory, as so often in those days, was with Mr Macmillan. The three Treasury ministers played straight into the Prime Minister's hands by their theological stress on permitting no increase at all in government expenditure for the coming financial year in money terms (which meant cutting it in real terms). The actual increase in government spending over which they resigned in January 1958 seemed a triviality even to some of their supporters inside the Bank of England, who, as usual, became calmer once sterling was strong again. The ministers' resignations seemed inexplicable to many senior men inside the Treasury – although others subsequently sent private letters of support to Thorneycroft. The resignation speech of Mr Thorneycroft, when he warned that Britain was attempting too many commitments, external and internal, in relation to its ability to carry them out, was a good one, but was not closely linked to the particular financial policies over which he resigned.

SHELVING THE ISSUES

The choice of Mr Derek Heathcoat Amory (now Lord Amory) to succeed Mr Thorneycroft seemed an ideal way out of 'little local difficulties'. Amory had acquired a good administrative reputation as Minister of Agriculture. He belonged to the liberal-humanitarian wing of the Conservative Party, and was personally popular on both sides of the House, but was intellectually very cautious and would do nothing to upset the supposed susceptibilities of holders of sterling. For Macmillan, it was a way of shelving the underlying issues.

Mr Heathcoat Amory quickly dropped the fanaticism and the monetary metaphysics, but he did not reverse Mr Thorneycroft's economic priorities. He had himself supported the September Measures, though he would have preferred less drastic action earlier. It is, in fact, doubtful if Macmillan had much idea what Mr Amory's views were when he appointed him. The Prime Minister was about to go off on a Commonwealth tour and was anxious to find a competent person to leave in charge as quickly as possible.

Indeed, it was quite exceptional for Mr Macmillan to bother about a new minister's opinions on policy before appointing him ('That was the last thing he thought of,' a leading Conservative politician once ruefully remarked). A stress on character, reliability and loyalty as against declared intellectual position is, of course, a fairly characteristic High Tory attitude towards subordinates. But it made it even more difficult for Macmillan to have a satisfactory impact on economic policy.

Although Mr Amory held advanced views on social matters, Treasury officials found Amory the most conservative of recent Chancellors with the sole exception of Thorneycroft II. This fact was obscured from the public because most of Amory's period at the Exchequer was spent during the upswing of the policy cycle. He had a great sense of personal responsibility and was liable to attacks of conscience, which were especially apt to come on if he thought he had gone too far in an inflationary direction.

When Mr Heathcoat Amory arrived at the Treasury he was subjected to strong political pressure from his Cabinet colleagues and from Conservative circles in general to stabilize the cost of living above all else. He did not fail them, and he was careful not to re-expand the economy too soon for fear of starting off another wage–price spiral. In the two and a half years he was Chancellor retail prices rose by less than one per cent per annum, easily a post-war record. This was due mainly to the exceptionally steep fall in import prices, and to the fact that he left office before the full effects of the 1959–60 boom had shown in wages and prices. The purchase-tax reduction in the 1959 Budget also helped in this direction.

Many people assumed that Mr Amory had to change course gradually to avoid giving the impression of throwing overboard the Thorneycroft policies. Such a thought may have helped senior Treasury officials to close their ranks after Thorneycroft, but it never, in fact, entered Amory's head. He was one of the most unscheming of politicians, and approached the Treasury almost like a very high-grade Civil Servant.

Before the 1958 Budget Mr Amory's Treasury advisers told him, with varying degrees of emphasis, to avoid any expansionary measures that might upset foreign confidence.

This advice flew in the face of the current predictions in their own Economic Surveys of a substantial balance-of-payments surplus. Policy was dominated by fears of what speculators in the foreign exchange market might think of what we did. It was in the late 1950s that the mythical gnomes of Zurich, who were supposed to cherish a bitter hatred of the pound sterling, first appeared on the popular scene.

By the time Mr Heathcoat Amory came to introduce his first Budget in April 1958, production was already known to be declining slightly and unemployment rising. In his Budget speech he predicted that these trends would go rather further during the rest of the year, although he did not expect a sharp recession.

Yet in the face of his own diagnosis he maintained: 'We are not yet strong enough to give the economy more than a minor stimulus' – some small purchase-tax cuts in the context of a virtually neutral Budget. The Treasury in Heathcoat Amory's day did not yet aspire to the still unfulfilled objectives of *steady* expansion. The prospect of advancing by one per cent in one year and five per cent in the next did not fill it with any horror; although Mr Heathcoat Amory himself, as his tenure of office advanced, became more and more dissatisfied with the jerky methods of economic management he felt forced to employ.

An additional reason for this intense caution was the US recession already discussed. But, quite apart from the immediate diagnosis, the new Chancellor seemed to confirm the order of priorities introduced by Thorneycroft. He emphasized that 'provision of regular productive employment for all who are able and willing to work' was one of his main objectives. 'We want to see production and employment just as high as we can, consistent with maintaining the value of money.' Whatever else this is, it is not a full employment or a growth policy.[17]

17. There is a discussion of this point in the Introduction and Chapter 11.

KISSING THE ROD

The 1957 crisis had touched off a great debate on whether the sterling area was holding back Britain's growth. In the 1958 Budget speech the Treasury eagerly accepted these limits on our freedom of action. The sterling-area system was working well, the House was told. It would be preserved and developed, confidence would be fortified, and the intention was proclaimed of 'moving gradually towards still wider freedom'.

This passage bears all the hallmarks of the Overseas Finance Division of the Treasury. An official memorandum to the Radcliffe Committee in 1957, written before Mr Amory's Budget speech, speaks of the confidence in United Kingdom policy which 'needs to be continuously refreshed' – i.e. by not doing anything adventurous or unconventional. Pointing out quite correctly that 'widespread and persistent expectations of a change in the exchange rate, however ill based in the first place, can produce reserve movements on a scale which gives much more solid grounds for the initial expectation', the memorandum does not conclude that there is something wrong with the system, but reiterates the faint-hearted slogan: 'It is therefore all the more important that we should not take risks in the management of the domestic economy of the kind that affect the balance of payments.'

It is significant that the same outward-looking financial statesmen who attached most value to the building up of overseas confidence in sterling, even at the cost of domestic sacrifice, were most hostile to any British involvement in the movement for European unity – and this during a period before General de Gaulle came to office, when it was probably still possible to get in on acceptable terms. Sir Leslie Rowan, the Head of the Overseas Finance Division, was asked by Professor Cairncross at the Radcliffe Committee hearings in 1957 if there had been any suggestions about a pooling of reserves between the United Kingdom and European countries. In contrast to most other officials, Sir Leslie did not evade questions by sheltering behind ministerial apron-strings. He replied:

I think that the pooling of reserves is only another way of saying that you are going to have a common management of your currency, and if you have a common management of currency you are going to have a common management of economic policy; and if you have a common management of economic policy then you must have common legislatures, and so forth; therefore pooling our reserves is merely a way of saying federation or confederation. . . . The answer to your question is 'No'.

The Overseas Finance Division would have liked to see improvements in the international payments system which would have created more reserves, but which would not have involved any handing over of sterling balances to an international organization, or any 'funding' of them in other ways. The position of sterling as an international currency, with all the risks to which it exposed Britain, was regarded as desirable in itself, like a prisoner kissing the rod with which he is being beaten.

As 1958 wore on, the rigours of the sterling-first doctrines were abated, first by the growing strength of sterling and then by the fact that stagnation at home was turning into recession. The Treasury economists were warning Mr Heathcoat Amory of this by the end of May, and from June onwards Amory, whose actions were more generous than his words, began to introduce a trickle of concessions, which later broadened into a river.

There was first a minor increase in initial allowances for plant and buildings; then, in late summer, the banks were granted freedom to lend as much as they liked. Hire-purchase controls were first relaxed in September, and in October – when unemployment rose above the then magic figure of 500,000 – abolished. During the same period Thorneycroft's ceiling on public investment was thrown off and government expenditure was pushed up 'temporarily' to control unemployment. At about this time Mr Macmillan re-entered the economic arena with demands for vigorous anti-slump action; and was only appeased by the promise of a generous Budget in 1959. At that time the Treasury did not have all its present powers of reducing taxation in mid year, short of the full paraphernalia of an emergency Budget. Perhaps, too, Sir Robert Hall deferred excessively to the 'administrative convenience' of the career Civil Servants, who wanted to wait until the Budget.[18]

The bankers and hire-purchase houses had assured Mr Heathcoat Amory that the free-for-all in credit would have only a very slight effect, and for a time it looked as if they were right. In January 1959, just before the annual Budget decisions were taken, winter unemployment rose to 620,000. Production had, in fact, just begun to turn upwards, but this was obscured by the effects of winter and by the time-lag in statistics. Mr Amory was told by his colleagues that he was the one man who could lose the Conservatives the election. Britain had just earned the biggest balance-of-payments surplus since the Conservatives came back to office. The pound had been made officially convertible in a blaze of confidence, and economists inside and outside the Treasury assured the Chancellor that expansion was both safe and necessary and convinced him that £200m. of tax reliefs would not be nearly enough. Thus it came about that the most cautious of Chancellors was responsible for the most generous Budget ever introduced in normal peace-time conditions, which took ninepence off the income tax, cut purchase tax, returned post-war credits, and restored investment allowances. But it was the intervention of

18. See the Treasury evidence to the Radcliffe Committee on 30 April 1959 (Q. 13319 and 13320). Hall told the Committee: 'Last autumn we thought of what was at our disposal and what we could do. There is in a sense a bit of a conflict between my interests and the general administrative convenience; there has always to be a certain amount of give and take in it.' Sir Roger Makins afterwards added: 'The normal position is that major changes in purchase tax are made at the time of the Budget. They could be made at other times, but it would be straining the ordinary practice.'

Macmillan himself that was responsible for enlarging the income-tax cut, which was to have been 6d., to 9d. and thus enlarging the reliefs by an extra £60m. to £360m.

The Budget speech itself was as cautious as one would expect from Mr Amory. He spoke about 'encouraging a steady but not excessive expansion in production'. He referred to the fact that the problem of the wage–price spiral had not been solved, and this must influence his judgement. 'We must at all costs', he said, 'make it our business not to return to an overload on the economy.' There were many other passages in similar vein; and until a few minutes before he sat down many MPs had resigned themselves to a joyless safety-first Budget.

Even after he had announced his tax changes, Mr Heathcoat Amory went on to emphasize that he was not signalling 'Full steam ahead, but steady ahead with confidence. This is no spending-spree Budget.' He had not changed his priorities; it was simply that his advisers had underestimated the delayed-action effect of his earlier measures, and of the head of steam that was now building up in the economy. Inadvertently Mr Amory gave a sharp upward push to a boom which was already getting under way. As a result industrial production rose in a year by nearly eleven per cent – a rate far too rapid to be sustained for long.

Orthodox economists and officials have ever since regarded the 1959 Budget as an object lesson in the dangers of trying to go too fast. It was, however, impossible to be sure at the time that the wide margin of slack would be taken up without further government assistance, and after three years of stagnation it was understandable that the Treasury economists should want to take risks on the side of expansion.

The real error of the 1959 Budget is not so much that it gave away too much, but that it came too late. It is apparent from the chart on page 449 that if it had been introduced the previous year it would have alleviated or even stopped altogether the 1958 recession and led to a much smoother advance of production. The balance-of-payments arguments (as distinct from the 'men of Zurich' arguments) themselves told in favour of an earlier stimulus. As Mr Gaitskell remarked in the Budget-day debate: 'A year ago during the middle of the most favourable six months for the balance of payments there was far less danger of expansion involving us in a balance-of-payments crisis than there is now.' The Treasury made the very same error in delaying re-expansion all over again in 1962; by 1967 the pound had become so clearly overvalued that any domestic re-expansion, however well timed from the point of view of the domestic business cycle, would have brought on a crisis.

6

THE REAPPRAISAL OF THE 1960s:
THE SELWYN LLOYD ERA, 1960–62

The traumas of 1960: the effect of Selwyn Lloyd: the
Treasury and the Common Market: the Brighton revolution: the new look for state industries: the search for
regulators: the 1961 sterling crisis: the growth-rate controversy: an unfortunate Budget: reflation postponed: the
departure of Selwyn Lloyd

DURING the period after the 1959 election, events moved
on two different levels. Economic management continued
much as before, with the government trying to steer a middle
course between recession and overheating, but tending to
intervene too late both on the upturn and the downturn.

On a different level it was a period of great change. Many
of the new policies which Labour was later to proclaim as
distinctively its own had already emerged in the far-reaching reappraisal which went on inside the Treasury and other
government departments around 1960–61. It is doubtful
if even the officials taking part were aware of the full extent
to which they were changing the atmosphere of economic
policy for nearly a decade to come. The characteristic
themes of the Wilson government in its first three years of
office – whether the emphasis on incomes policy, the regional approach to unemployment, the National Plan, the
attempt to join the Common Market, long-term regulation
of government expenditure, the idea of continuous economic
regulation instead of merely annual Budgets, or even (in
embryonic form) the stress on physical 'supply' side problems had already been adopted by Conservative ministers
very early in the 1960s. Labour's contribution in the unfortunate 1964 election campaign and the period that
followed was to ignore or malign its predecessors' efforts in

these directions, and yet vastly exaggerate the potency of such ideas as a substitute for proper overall management of demand and the balance of payments, and present the whole package as purposive, technically advanced government.

The year which saw the greater part of the new thinking was 1960, although it is about the least remembered of all the years of that decade. On the surface it was an uneventful one. Businessmen were becoming more and more dissatisfied with government policy, but neither the public nor the Cabinet gave much attention to economics. Mr Amory would make some announcement after Question Time in the quietest possible way, and discussion of it would be chiefly confined to the financial columns.

The unpublicized policy reappraisal of that year is best approached by looking at the seemingly rather dull course of the economy at the time. In the first half of 1960 the post-election boom seemed to be going too far, and the economy looked as if it might suffer from genuine overstrain for the first time since 1955–6. Unemployment was falling rapidly towards $1\frac{1}{2}$ per cent; unfilled vacancies were rising. The Conservative victory had touched off a spectacular investment boom, imports were soaring, and it soon became apparent from the trade figures that Britain was heading towards a large overseas deficit. But the fact was hidden from many wishful thinkers among politicians and in the City by a flood of 'hot' money pouring into London from overseas – a flood which, judging by all past experience, was bound to go back home before very long.

Ever since the 1959 election Mr Heathcoat Amory had been worried that the economy was going to become overloaded; and in 1960 he wanted a severer Budget than either the Prime Minister or even his own official advisers. The Treasury apparently considered that, whatever the forecasts, it would hardly be feasible to deflate so soon after an election – another instance of the political sense Great George Street tries to develop on behalf of its masters.

1960 was the sort of year – 1964 was another – when economists want to apply a brake (for fear of stopping the vehicle altogether a year or two later), while normally cautious politicians and officials prefer to leave well alone. This was certainly the line-up in 1960 when even the National Institute (then at the height of its expansionist phase) saw the case for a restrictive Budget. During the 1960 pre-Budget discussions Mr Heathcoat Amory had to change his Budget plans at a fairly late stage as a result of the opposition he was meeting from the Prime Minister and other colleagues. The Budget itself was more or less neutral, although it raised Profits Tax, and contained a warning that the Chancellor 'stood ready to take any further corrective measures that may be called for in the near future in the monetary field'. The Bank of England raised many obstacles here, and put up a last-ditch emotional stand in favour of 'voluntary cooperation' with the joint stock banks, but eventually on 28 April had to restrict their credit forcibly by means of Special Deposits. The Chancellor himself imposed hire-purchase restrictions on cars and durables (20 per cent down payment and two years to repay). Sir Frank Lee, who had become Joint Permanent Secretary to the Treasury in succession to Sir Roger Makins on 1 January 1960, after seven years at the Board of Trade, had publicly declared his opposition to hire-purchase restrictions as an economic weapon in evidence to the Radcliffe Committee. But he was alone in the Treasury on the issue, and there was then no other weapon to hand.

The possibility of a guiding light or norm for incomes was under discussion in the Treasury throughout Mr Amory's tenure; this was an idea which Sir Robert Hall had always strongly supported. Hall's opponents inside the Treasury pinned their hopes on the two and a half years or so of largely fortuitous price stability which the country enjoyed during Mr Amory's tenure of the Exchequer, and which they hoped might restrain wage increases.

It is not generally known that when Mr Heathcoat

Amory resigned in late July 1960, a year before the Selwyn Lloyd Pay Pause, he gave the Prime Minister a very clear hint of trouble ahead when he came to say farewell. He warned that if he had been going to stay on – as Macmillan very much wanted him to – he would have insisted either on running the economy at a higher level of unemployment or, preferably, on the government accepting an incomes policy. But another year was to elapse before his warning was heeded.

THE TRAUMAS OF 1960

The period of economic rethinking began before Mr Amory left the Exchequer – unlike Mr Thorneycroft, voluntarily, and on genuinely personal grounds. Following the credit restrictions he imposed in April, production stopped rising but, to the great disappointment of the Treasury, there were few compensating benefits in other directions. This simple episode had a traumatic effect on Treasury thinking. As the months went by it stimulated three main lines of reflection, which were to be the source of all that followed:

1. After all the investment of the past few years 'either production should have increased or employment decreased', as Sir Robert Hall put it in an article in the *Economist* after he retired.[1] In the event the curbs on demand stopped production from rising, but did not cause any unemployment or even stop the increase in the labour force.

Later research, put in hand partly as result of such episodes, made this paradox easier to explain. It appears that in both recessions and booms the movement of employment normally lags behind production. At the top of the boom the labour force is usually not yet fully adjusted to the level of production; so employment may

1. 'Britain's Economic Policy', the *Economist*, 16 and 23 September 1961.

go on expanding for some months after output has stopped rising. Conversely employment can go on falling even after the bottom of a slump has been reached.[2] Yet the puzzle is not entirely removed. The British economy in the 1960s was prone to periods of high-level stagnation; another such episode occurred in 1965–6, and although these periods can always be explained in retrospect, their full extent seems a surprise at the time. Rightly or wrongly the 1960 experience prompted many reflections on the structural weaknesses of the British economy and proposals, such as the payroll tax, to discourage the wasteful use of labour.

2. The restriction of home demand failed to boost exports, even though world trade was for most of the time buoyant. This fact, together with the previous point, made many Treasury officials extremely critical of the efficiency and skill with which industry was run. It was about this time (around the end of 1960) that the first papers were written on the conditions of long-term growth, and that interest blossomed in French planning methods and in the Common Market.

3. Soon after the government reimposed hire-purchase controls in April the bottom fell out of the American car market and the consumer durable cycle turned downwards at home. Inadvertently the Chancellor had singled out for attack two industries that were already in trouble by the time his measures took effect. For these industries official stabilizing action turned out to be violently destabilizing.

This was probably the single event which did most to turn industrial opinion against stop-go and made it look with a less jaundiced eye on national planning. Within the Treasury it stimulated a search for general regulators that did not discriminate against one or two particular trades and which could be introduced between Budgets.

2. W. A. H. Godley and J. R. Shepherd, 'Long-Term Growth and Short-Term Policy', *National Institute Economic Review*, August 1964.

It also aroused interest in a whole family of theories – the best known of which was worked out by Professor Paish – for securing steadier growth with the aid of a moderate but fairly constant margin of unused capacity, and a less ambitious definition of full employment.[3]

The two key figures in the policy reappraisal were Sir Frank Lee, who became Permanent Secretary at the beginning of 1960, and Mr Selwyn Lloyd, who was Chancellor for almost two years after the retirement of Mr Amory. Sir Frank Lee was mentioned in earlier chapters as the first post-war Permanent Secretary to be familiar with economic issues. He had strong views on policy and, unlike more conventional officials, did not bother to hide them. Nevertheless, his own conduct was imbued with a fiery insistence on sticking to the practical and the politically possible, and anyone else who did not do so soon felt the force of his displeasure.

He understood both businessmen and bureaucrats too well to be starry-eyed about either and, both at the Board of Trade and at the Treasury, he saw more competition (he was the driving force behind the Restrictive Practices Act), rather than more planning, as the cure for British industry. The conversion of the government to 'Conservative planning' was certainly not his work. He told the Radcliffe Committee, 'If I believed that you could get an overall investment plan operated by people of undoubted vision and wisdom I would agree with that concept.' Because he was sceptical whether such a plan could be achieved he preferred a different approach.[4]

In the argument between the financial expansionists and the restrainers, Lee was most often to be found on the side of the restrainers. 'I have always felt', he told the Radcliffe Committee, 'that if the economy could be made only marginally disinflationary that would have quite an impres-

3. These doctrines are discussed in more detail in Chapters 10 and 11.
4. *Minutes of Evidence to Radcliffe Committee*, HMSO, 1960.

sive effect on business psychology . . . in such matters as concern for costs, attitudes towards wage claims, general willingness to fight wage claims, or negotiate longer periods for wage claims.' Lee wanted to tackle the wage-price spiral by dampening down demand and he was not enamoured of the arguments for an incomes policy when he arrived at the Treasury.

Lee had more achievements to his credit than most of his predecessors. As one senior ex-Civil Servant privately remarked, 'Anyone who could persuade the Conservatives to become a low-tariff party must be counted a great man.' His bias towards deflation remains controversial.

THE EFFECT OF SELWYN LLOYD

If Sir Frank Lee was an unusually controversial Permanent Secretary, his political master, Mr Selwyn Lloyd, was an even more controversial Chancellor. It is particularly important to judge Lloyd by what he did rather than by his public image. The view that his main fault was that he could not 'put his policies across' degrades the post of the Chancellor into that of a glorified Public Relations Officer.

Something has already been said about Mr Lloyd in the previous chapter (p. 207). His weaknesses were obvious enough. He did not have a large enough grasp to distinguish between big issues and minor points of detail, and, like most other Chancellors, he seemed to think about economic policy without the aid of any intellectual framework. Lloyd was sensitive to criticism, yet his sensitivity was combined with an endearing sense of humour about himself. But although Lloyd was intellectually dependent on his Treasury advisers, he was also somewhat suspicious of them. He sometimes gave them the impression that he did not quite realize the full implications of what they were asking him to say, but suspected that he would not like them if he did. Lloyd had many of both the virtues and defects of the better type of Tory backbencher. Yet, for all his defects, his period at the Exchequer was the most eventful since Cripps.

Was he a good Chancellor? On the one hand his management of the brake and the accelerator at home, and his handling of the sterling problem, seemed pretty inadequate at the time. But two points must be made in his defence. The first is that a severe deterioration had by then taken place in the underlying balance of payments, which made the task of economic management far more difficult than for his predecessors of the 1950s. (The National Institute was almost alone in early 1961 in urging devaluation as a remedy; it certainly received no support from the Labour opposition.) Secondly, Mr Lloyd's management of the cycle was genius itself compared with that of the Labour government in its first three years of office.

The real reason why Mr Lloyd's tenure of the Exchequer deserves to be remembered is for the changes he inaugurated which transformed the long-term environment in which day-to-day management took place. Some of these changes may have done some indirect harm in encouraging the notion, later to be seized on with such misguided zeal by Labour ministers, that new organizations and procedures could be a substitute for difficult policy choices. Many of the reforms were, however, in the right direction and his successors have reason to be grateful for them. It is worth listing a few of the main changes:

1. The setting up of the National Economic Development Council, which introduced indicative planning to Britain.
2. Long-term 'forward looks' for the government's own spending plans along Plowden lines.
3. Acceptance by the government – and later by the country – of the *idea* of an incomes policy.
4. The raising of the surtax starting point on earned income from £2,000 to £5,000.

5. The introduction of economic regulators giving the Chancellor power to vary tax between Budgets.

6. The reform of the archaic Budget Accounts.

7. A new policy towards the nationalized industries, which helped to transform their morale, performance and public standing.

As one official once privately remarked, a subtler person would have seen more difficulties and snags and not accomplished as much.

The regulators were due, in fact, largely to the persistence of Sir Frank Lee, and the White Paper on nationalized industries was thought out almost entirely by officials. But Lloyd does deserve the political credit for introducing both. The NEDC, moreover, was to a large extent Lloyd's own personal creation; and, to the surprise of some of his officials, Lloyd himself was also keenly interested in the reform of the Budget accounts.

He was not responsible for the Plowden Committee which was appointed by his predecessor, Mr Heathcoat Amory. But Lloyd himself wanted to go down in history as the Chancellor who reduced the burden of taxation. Lloyd did not succeed in his ambition; but in his attempts he gave an impetus to the long-term planning of government expenditure, which remained valuable.

The raising of the surtax starting point from its 1920 level of £2,000 to £5,000 was privately welcomed by almost everyone who understood taxation, irrespective of political party. Not only did the old starting point dampen incentives, but so far from promoting equality it helped to ossify the class system. For the high surtax rates did not affect people of established wealth, or those becoming rich by capital gains, but erected barriers against rising executives or professional men dependent on their own earnings. With the partial exception of Mr Thorneycroft, Mr Selwyn Lloyd was the only Conservative Chancellor in the whole 1951–64 period with the courage to tackle this particular problem.

THE TREASURY AND THE COMMON MARKET

Mr Selwyn Lloyd was, of course, at the Exchequer at the time of Britain's application to join the Common Market, which many people thought was a sudden response to the 1961 sterling crisis. This was a very common view on the Continent, but it was mistaken. In the first place, the principal motive of Mr Macmillan, who was personally responsible for the new European policy, was political rather than economic. Secondly, the basic rethinking of British foreign policy towards Europe was done when 'hot' money was still pouring into London and when most politicians felt no sense of economic emergency.

In the course of 1959–60 there had been a reappraisal by the Foreign Office of British policy towards Europe; and by the time Mr Macmillan came to make his decision quite a number of leading officials in various ministries were pleased with the way it went. But the decision was very much Macmillan's own. There was no official *éminence grise* behind the scenes.

Mr Macmillan seems to have made up his mind around Christmas 1960 after several months' contemplation. The Summit failure of May 1960 after the unfortunate U2 incident depressed the Prime Minister deeply and made him feel conscious of the need for a new role for Britain. Macmillan feared that a strong and growing Continental bloc would carry more weight in Washington under a post-Eisenhower Administration than an isolated Britain. The best way to preserve Britain's influence with the US, he and others believed, might be as leader of a united Europe – a trend of thought which explains why both his application and that of Mr Wilson in 1967 failed to make headway. Another factor was the changing character of the Commonwealth, which was symbolized by South Africa's withdrawal in 1961, but which was clear long before.

By the time he came to the Treasury, Sir Frank Lee was a convinced European. He was one of those who thought that the Common Market would give British industry a much-needed competitive impetus. But this was a personal view. The Treasury's overseas coordination unit, which was responsible for working out a common policy towards Europe among all government departments, had at the time practically a separate identity of its own, distinct from the rest of the Treasury. It was on behalf of this unit, rather than as a Treasury spokesman, that Lee took the lead, with all the zeal of a convert, in preparing Common Market briefs for the Prime Minister and Cabinet Committee. The Chancellor of the Exchequer was not during this period the minister responsible for Common Market questions.

The Treasury proper was sceptical of the Common Market venture, although there were, of course, individual exceptions. The Overseas Finance Division was opposed to it partly because it did not like the idea of a common monetary policy leading to a pooling of sovereignty.[5] In addition it was attached to the sterling area, which could hardly emerge unscathed from an economic fusion with Europe. Its idealism took the form of support for developing the poorer parts of the Commonwealth rather than any enthusiasm for the Six.

Many academic economists, especially in Cambridge and Oxford, thought that the arguments both for and against entry were overblown, and this was also Mr Gaitskell's view. The predominant advice that ministers received from the Treasury's Economic Section during 1960 was on these lines.

Basically, however, the European negotiations were begun for political reasons by Macmillan and terminated for political reasons by General de Gaulle. The real reason for the failure was that Macmillan (like Wilson after him)

5. A quotation from an earlier Head of the Overseas Finance Division, Sir Leslie Rowan, is given on p. 223.

tried to graft the Common Market on to existing foreign and defence policies – policies which gave priority to a profoundly desired special relationship with America which often embarrassed the Kennedy administration. If Britain had joined, the relationship with the US would certainly have changed in due course, but in the meantime the General had a better justification for keeping this country out than is usually admitted (although not for deliberately misleading the whole of Europe).

THE BRIGHTON REVOLUTION

A few days before Mr Macmillan announced Britain's application to join the Common Market Mr Selwyn Lloyd announced that he was going to set up new machinery for national planning. It so happened, moreover, that the spiritual father of the European Common Market, M. Jean Monnet, had also been the first head of the French Planning Commission immediately after the war. Later M. Monnet became chairman of the unofficial but influential Action Committee for a United States of Europe, and by 1960 he had become an active protagonist of British membership of the Common Market.

During 1960 and 1961 he was telling his many British contacts in politics, administration and industry that if planning was to survive in the Common Market it would have to be on a supra-national basis. He hoped Britain would throw in its weight as a pro-planning country in an enlarged Common Market, and that Britain and France together would tilt the balance against the *laisser faire* Germans. This was certainly one of the reasons, apart from propagandist zeal, why the French Commissariat Général du Plan was so helpful during this period in arranging visits and conferences for British economists and officials to study French planning methods.

But despite these connections the move towards planning and the move towards Europe were on the British side completely separated strands of policy and, indeed, largely the work of different people. It was mainly among some journalists that equal enthusiasm could be found for both.

Planning of the kind Mr Selwyn Lloyd introduced to Britain involved three basic ingredients, the order of importance of which varied according to taste:

1. A national growth target stretching over a period of several years, the possible implications of which are worked out in some detail for a number of industries.

2. A Council where ministers, business leaders and trade unionists could consult each other regularly on current problems, including incomes policy, and try to hammer out solutions. This was to be supplemented by lower-tier groups for particular industries, known as Little Neddies.

3. An office, separate from the Treasury, to work out forecasts and targets, and suggest ideas for removing obstacles to growth. (This was first attached to NEDC, but under Labour the major part of the work was switched to Whitehall.)

When Mr Selwyn Lloyd entered the Treasury he already thought that long-term planning of government expenditure was, like his other beliefs, common sense. He was converted to the view that planning had something to offer for the private sector as well by a conference of the Federation of British Industries, held in Brighton at the end of November 1960, to consider 'The Next Five Years'. At this time he had not even seen any of the Treasury's own ruminations on the subject.

The conversion of the Federation of British Industries to the idea of planning is a strange story. It was almost entirely the work of a tiny minority among British businessmen. The Brighton Conference was attended by 121 leading businessmen and 31 guests, including the heads of government departments and of the nationalized industries, and a few economists. The conference divided into five groups, and it was not altogether a coincidence that a like-minded set of people found themselves together in Group III which discussed 'Economic Growth in Britain'. The group was reinforced by Mr Reay Geddes, the managing director of Dunlop, who had made a speech the previous February which foreshadowed NEDC in a remarkable way. In the chair was the veteran managing director of Guinness, Sir Hugh Beaver, himself something of an industrial radical.

The group's report, presented by Sir Hugh at the end of the conference, argued that there was 'room for a more conscious attempt to assess plans and demands in particular industries for five or even ten years ahead', as had already happened in the case of steel. Government and industry might also, the report suggested, see 'whether it would be possible to agree on an assessment of expectations and intentions which should be before the country for the next five years'. The report vigorously attacked rapid switches of government policy for their effects on confidence and particularly on investment plans.

Most remarkable of all, Sir Hugh went out of his way to express his disagreement with the priorities reiterated at the opening of the conference by the ex-Chancellor, Viscount Amory, who had expounded official doctrine with his usual charm and lack of evasion. In deliberate contrast to the ex-Chancellor, Sir Hugh stressed that the achievement of a faster rate of growth might be the best way of achieving stable prices and a sound balance of payments, and not the other way round.

This report, by one group out of the five into which the conference was split, was by no means FBI policy at the time. But somehow, without any specific resolution at any time, the doctrine of Group III emerged as FBI policy. In the course of 1961 there were a number of meetings between Mr Selwyn Lloyd and other ministers and the FBI; and at these meetings Sir Hugh Beaver took the lead, gradually steering the discussion in favour of indicative planning.

Discussions of indicative planning were by no means confined to these informal meetings. There was, for example, a dining club started early in 1960 by a mixed group of industrialists and economists to discuss various topics, including growth. The leading spirit was Mr (now Sir) Hugh Weeks, the chairman of the FBI's Economic Policy Committee. But the dining group was a purely private one separate from the committee. In the end it published no papers and there were considerable differences among its members. Nevertheless, its discussions were symptomatic of the concern which had been aroused by the league tables then coming into vogue contrasting Britain's economic performance with that of other countries.

Reports of the French Four-Year Plan, which were only just beginning to become known in opinion-forming circles, were another big influence. A PEP book, *Growth in the British Economy*, published in 1960, drew attention to French experiences; and a joint PEP–National Institute conference in the spring of 1961 was devoted exclusively to the subject.

It would be too cynical to regard all this activity as a reaction to the effects of Mr Amory's reimposition of hire-purchase controls during a bad phase in the durable cycle. Indeed the pioneering spirits among the FBI had begun their activities while the economy was still in a period of 'go', which they rightly suspected would not last. What the hire-purchase controls, which hit cars and durables so severely, did do was to win them supporters among a wide circle of businessmen who would not normally have bothered about anything as esoteric as 'indicative planning'.

Soon after the FBI conference Mr Selwyn Lloyd mentioned the planning idea to Mr Macmillan. The Prime Minister, who had been well known since the 1930s for his belief in planning, welcomed the idea with alacrity. He may have suggested something like it himself to Lloyd informally at an earlier date. But there is no sign that Macmillan ever tried to initiate anything himself on these lines before his Chancellor took up the idea, and it is Lloyd who must be regarded as the key figure.

During the course of 1960 some of the Treasury officials had, quite independently of the FBI, become interested in new ideas for adding some drive to British industry. A very popular conclusion from the disappointments of 1960 was 'how little the government can do' and that everything depended on a change of habit and outlook on the part of both management and trade unions. The tendency for Civil Servants to blame industry for British economic shortcomings, and for industry to blame Civil Servants, unfortunately continued for many years.

Officials who thought in this way were looking, above all, for an effective channel of communication with both sides of industry, and were often just as sceptical about planning itself as was Sir Frank Lee. Many of them welcomed the idea of a so-called planning body simply as a possible way of involving the unions in an incomes policy. During the course of the negotiations with the TUC the Treasury at first played this point down. It was confident that any impartial investigation of the obstacles to growth would bring the question on to the agenda without any forcing. Its confidence was justified, partly as a result of NEDC's own inquiries, and partly because Mr Lloyd's successor, Mr Maudling, and Mr Brown after him, insisted again and again that incomes policy was central to the whole exercise.

There were, it is true, a very small number of officials, more genuinely interested in indicative planning, who thought that it was worth putting together the forecasts and plans on which individual industries were already working to see if they fitted together. At the very least they thought this might throw up problems and suggest methods of tackling them, and, in the course of 1960, some Treasury officials made unpublicized visits to Paris to study at first hand what the French were doing.

There had been in existence since the days of Sir Stafford Cripps a small Planning Board (whose title was extremely misleading) on which a few Treasury officials and business and trade-union leaders discussed economic subjects once a month, with very little follow-through. After the FBI conference, the Planning Board discussed 'conditions favourable to growth' at four of its meetings in the first few months of 1961.

At these Planning Board meetings one well-known official, speaking for a large section of Treasury opinion, strongly opposed the creation of an independent office. He thought that the best way to embark on long-term studies was to expand the Economic Planning Board and enlarge its staff – a recipe which, in the prevailing climate of opinion, would have failed to attract the publicity the exercise required.

Mr Lloyd ran into a great deal of opposition to the NEDC concept from other ministers. Most of the Cabinet was, in fact, opposed to him on this issue. Among Lloyd's few supporters were Lord Hailsham and Mr Hare, the Minister of Labour (now Lord Blakenham). Some ministers said that contacts already took place with industry through existing channels, and Mr Lloyd should work through these. Another argument was that NEDC might duplicate the work done by government departments and even cut across the responsibilities of the Cabinet. The feature which gave rise to as much opposition in the Cabinet as in the Treasury was the independent office.

On this point Mr Lloyd dug in his heels. He thought, as he wrote later,[6] that an independent body was much more likely to be successful in bringing together the views of people inside and outside government. An independent office, he maintained, would give its studies a value and authority which they would not have were they just another government department. Last, but not least, Mr Lloyd is believed to have wanted another source of advice to which he could turn as an alternative to the Treasury. The constitution of NEDC (and that of the Department of Econo-

6. 'NEDDY and Parliament', *Crossbow*, October–December 1963.

mic Affairs afterwards) cannot be understood in isolation from the mood of profound distrust which had gathered round the Treasury by the time of the 1961 sterling crisis. From the day it was set up the NEDC office consciously tried to establish a different order of priorities. Members of the office in their off-guard moments jocularly referred to the Treasury as 'the other side'.

One of the main opponents of the NEDC concept at the time was Mr Reginald Maudling, then President of the Board of Trade. He could see little point in an independent office distinct from the Whitehall machine, and was suspicious that too many get-togethers by industrialists would lead to market-sharing agreements and other restrictive practices.

If matters had been left to the slow machinery of Cabinet and Civil Service Committees, NEDC might have been buried beneath delicately balanced memoranda. There was still no Cabinet agreement on the subject until the sterling crisis forced the issue. When Mr Lloyd introduced his 'Little Budget' on 25 July 1961 something had to be inserted urgently to show that the government had some long-term ideas apart from stop-go. A fortnight later Mr Macmillan allowed Mr Lloyd to invite both sides of industry to join a national planning council, on the grounds that his statement of 25 July had in practice committed the government. Cabinet rumblings continued for a long time afterwards, but to little effect.

It took several more months of delicate negotiations before the Council and office were finally established. From the outset Lloyd had intended to make Sir Robert Shone, the former head of the Steel Board, whom he had known for years, Director General, and he was appointed on 18 December. It was not until 24 January 1962 that the TUC agreed to serve. During these months of delay it would have been very tempting for Mr Lloyd to have gone ahead without the unions, as many commentators advised him to do. In the end the real weakness of the Council was on the employers' side. The six industrialists chosen were above average in quality, but because of the division then prevailing between the three employers' organizations they were simply chosen as individuals and had no power to commit anyone else.

Without Sir Frank Lee NEDC would have remained a paper dream. He was ill in Paris during the July crisis; when he came back to London and found that the planning decision had been taken he spared no effort to make it work, whatever he might personally have thought about planning. Lee was fully behind Lloyd's insistence, against the advice of many senior Treasury officials, that the NEDC office must be distinct from the Treasury if the unions were to have confidence in its independence.

THE NEW LOOK FOR STATE INDUSTRIES

Another rather different product of the economic rethinking of 1960 was the approach to the nationalized industries. A great many of the changes since 1960 have, of course, been due to developments in the nationalized industries themselves; all the same the Treasury has never received the praise due to it for its undoubted share in the transformation.[7] The new policies were heralded in July 1961 by a White Paper, *The Financial and Economic Obligations of the Nationalized Industries*, the very title of which ensured a minimum of publicity.

The basic principle of the White Paper was that state industries were not a form of social service, but must earn a return on their assets to justify their existence. This approach led, for example, to the closing down of high-cost pits and uneconomic rail services. The White Paper was a pioneering document, some of whose inadequacies were corrected by a later White Paper, published in 1967. But compared with what went on before it was an immense

7. Although no one would suppose that the Treasury suggested Dr Beeching's £25,000 salary.

change for the better. In 1960 most state concerns were demoralized and uncertain of where they were supposed to be going, like animals in a maze. The most important need was to give them a visible goal; the rest could come later.

The new policy was achieved in spite of, rather than because of, the committee of ministers which asked for the study to be made. The ministers were chiefly interested in organizational forms. Politicians chronically pay too much attention to the question of who should take decisions, and to whom they should report, rather than the criteria on which decisions should be based. For a long time many Conservative MPs had an obsession with regional decentralization as a shortcut to commercial principles. Ministers and MPs found it easier to talk of geography and lines of command than of the pricing policies and rates of return which were implied by the free-enterprise principles in which they professed to believe. Most of the nationalized industries had been reorganized over and over again; and it was the Treasury that managed to give the 1960–61 discussion a constructive and less organizational twist.

THE SEARCH FOR REGULATORS

Although the new thinking on economic planning and the nationalized industries emphasized the case for longer horizons, there was a pressing need for better short-term weapons. The last six months of 1960 were accordingly taken up with the search for fairer ways of regulating consumer spending between Budgets than the industrially unpopular hire-purchase restrictions.

The characteristics of a tax which is to be moved up and down as an economic regulator were simply stated at the FBI Brighton Conference by one of the groups (not Group III) of which Sir Frank Lee happened to be a member. Such a tax should be, according to the group, speedy in its effects; it should cut right across the board; it should cause the minimum disruption to business plans and, if possible, should attack or at least 'be inimical to' the rigidities which hamper change in British economic life.

One of the most interesting suggestions was for a PAYE regulator. The idea was that income-tax rates might be varied part of the way through the year if economic conditions changed. One simple method, which would not require fresh tax tables, would be a straight percentage change in everyone's tax bill from the date on which the regulator is applied. But the suggestion never got as far as a definite proposal. The Inland Revenue predictably objected on the grounds of administration and equity, and politicians disliked the idea, ostensibly because income-tax changes by Order in Council would detract too much from the authority of Parliament. The tax surcharge concept, in one form or another, will not be killed so easily. President Johnson's 1968 tax increases took this form and it could be revived in Britain at any time.

Another idea, and one on which Sir Frank Lee had always been keen, was a uniform sales tax in place of purchase tax, over a wide range of consumer spending, which could be varied up or down by a point or two as the economic situation changed. This idea was defeated partly by the Customs and Excise, who made great play with the difficulties of taxing services, and partly because of the political embarrassments involved in taxing food. A value-added tax was also considered as a possible substitute for a sales tax. This would have been a tax on business turnover minus purchases from other firms. This was fiercely resisted by the Customs and Excise on the grounds that it would have meant several hundred thousand points of collection.

Finding such ideas repulsed, the Treasury understandably asked the Customs and Excise for its own suggestions for regulating consumer spending, and, surprising though it may seem, the Customs produced a device within a very few weeks. This was accepted the first time round with very little argument and was included in the 1961 Budget. It has since become known as the 'regulator' or (inaccurately) as the 'purchase tax regulator'. It is simply a power that the Treasury renews every year to vary all consumer taxes – drink and tobacco duties as well as purchase tax – by up to ten per cent in between budgets. The ten per cent does not, as is often supposed, refer to the taxes themselves, but is a percentage of the previous rates – for example, a fifty per cent purchase tax is raised by five per cent to fifty-five per cent when the regulator is brought into full operation.

Another concept which first came into vogue in the 1960 reappraisal was the payroll tax. Two different ideas, with different histories, were involved here, although this was not sufficiently appreciated at the time. One was a surcharge on payrolls as a temporary economic regulator to stimulate or restrain private spending. The other was for a payroll tax as a permanent part of the tax system, which would not add to the tax burden, but replace other imposts.

The latter idea arose from a study of the supposed structural weaknesses of the British economy. Sir Robert Hall's disappointment, expressed in his *Economist* article, that the 1960–61 investment boom had had so little effect on productivity, has already been mentioned. In the short run he attributed it to labour hoarding. But he also diagnosed deeper defects. A great deal of new investment, he suggested, had been of the wrong kind. Too much had taken the form of simple additions to productive capacity and too little took the form of modernization or new processes. As a result there was not enough labour to man the new plant and equipment; and in a time of boom, overfull employment of labour was reached when there was still a great deal of unutilized industrial capacity. Sir Robert concluded that the labour hoarding should be discouraged and investment given a more labour-saving twist.

The supporters of a permanent payroll tax hoped it would do just this. They pointed out that in other European countries, especially France, a far higher proportion of the cost of the social services fell as a charge on employers' payloads.

The idea that any tax on labour will encourage manpower-saving – or any subsidy labour-hoarding – is superficial. If employers can pass the tax on in higher prices there is no inducement to labour-saving left; and the measure has the same effect as an extra increase in money wages – or, to be accurate, an increase in money wages combined with a general reduction in demand achieved by some combination of monetary and fiscal policy.

For there to be even the possibility of a labour-saving effect, a tax on payrolls would have to be not a new imposition but an exchange for some existing form of taxation (or just conceivably a selective tax confined to some sectors, such as the Selective Employment Tax discussed on p. 324). The more thorough-going supporters of the payroll tax in 1960–61, such as Sir Robert Shone, saw it as a reform of company taxation; and envisaged it as a substitute for some of the tax on corporate profits. The arguments of the Richardson Committee, which rejected the idea of a value-added tax in 1964 on the grounds that it would be entirely passed on in higher prices, even if it was imposed in place of profits tax, apply – if valid – to a payroll tax as well. For a value-added tax is simply a tax on payrolls plus profits. The difference – which counts against the payroll version – is that the value-added tax alone can be remitted on exports.

The possibility of a permanent payroll tax was, in fact, raised by Treasury economists. Their idea was much less radical than Shone's. It was simply to impose a payroll tax in exchange for a reduction in purchase tax and other indirect taxes, and the incentive to labour-saving would have been at most a psychological one. But it was rejected by ministers on the grounds that it was a tax on employment which – in a full-employment economy – was what it was intended to be.

The second idea, of using payroll tax variations as a short-term weapon for regulating the business cycle, has a long history. As far back as 1944 the wartime coalition government's White Paper on employment policy contained a scheme for varying both employers' and employees' National Insurance contributions, to increase purchasing power in a slump and reduce it in a boom. The variation of the *employees'* contributions in such a scheme would be the most effective in both directions. If anti-inflationary action were desired, workers' spending power would be immediately reduced and in a way that did not raise prices. The increase in *employers'* contributions on the other hand would take a long time to affect consumer spending, and this would only happen to the extent that industrialists passed on the higher contributions in the form of higher prices.

During the search for regulators in 1960, the Treasury was asked by Lee to take another look at the 1944 idea, which the National Insurance authorities had insisted was impracticable. The result of its researches was the 'second regulator' which gave the Treasury power to impose a surcharge of up to 4s. per week on employers' National Insurance contributions. As a regulator it had all the wrong qualities. It was very slow-acting. There would be delays of nearly three months before the surcharge could be introduced, and the choice of the *employers'* contribution showed that the whole scheme had either been misunderstood or denuded of much of its economic value to make it politically acceptable – probably a bit of both. For an economy with deep-seated balance-of-payments problems it was positively harmful, as the only way it could work would be through pushing up industrial costs, including export costs.

The payroll regulator had only one strong supporter among senior officials; the rest were either strongly opposed or at best lukewarm. Yet, to everyone's surprise, Mr Selwyn Lloyd accepted the idea, and asked for the necessary powers in his 1961 Budget speech. The main argument in its favour that appealed to the ministers was that two regulators were better than one. The hope of its official supporters was that if it had a trial run as a regulator it might later become more acceptable as a permanent tax.

Just how misguided their hopes were became clear within a matter of hours. The very, very slight discrimination it introduced against firms which were heavy employers of labour in relation to their output was enough to set off a storm of protest from industry. An embarrassed FBI was deluged by telephone calls and telegrams and had to back-pedal very quickly on its earlier sympathy for the idea. Once again the lesson was learnt that those who lose from any change in the structure of taxation always create far more sound and fury than those who gain; equity is always judged in terms of the *status quo*. Mr Selwyn Lloyd himself lost faith in the second regulator within a few days of his announcing it; and the concept of a permanent payroll tax was retarded rather than enhanced by the attempt to combine two different ideas.

THE 1961 STERLING CRISIS

All the new thinking about Britain's industrial structure and on economic regulators was taking place against a gathering sterling crisis, which was itself handled by traditional stop-go methods. This originated, like everything else in this chapter, in 1960, when Britain had the worst balance-of-payments deficit for a whole decade, although this fact was not then apparent because of the influx of short-term funds to London. There was something to be said for softening the blow by attracting some foreign footloose funds to London by high interest rates. But in 1960 so much 'hot money' was attracted to London that the gap was filled to overflowing and the reserves rose substantially.

The current account deficit in 1960 was £258m. (It looked even worse in the April 1961 balance-of-payments White Paper.) Taking capital payments into account the overall payments deficit came to £450m. Faced with a gap of this kind, one might expect to have seen a big fall in reserves; instead they rose by £177m. The inflow was swollen by the distrust of the US dollar in front of the presidential elections, and by the barriers that Germany and Switzerland had put up against the entry of short-term funds into their own money markets. Thus, even making allowances for unrecorded earnings hidden in the balancing item, over £500m. of 'hot money' was attracted into London during 1960 – almost exactly the amount that went out again in the sterling crisis of the following year. Can there be any doubts that Britain would have been better off on this and similar occasions if the bulk of this money had never arrived and never left? It is a sad, but well-established, paradox of international finance that an inflow of funds does much less good than an outflow of the same amount does harm – if only because bankers and speculators will always project the outflow to the point where a country's reserves are completely exhausted.

The Treasury and Bank of England were both involved in this dangerous policy. Neither deliberately wanted to attract so much hot money. Bank Rate was raised from 4 per cent to 5 per cent in January and to 6 per cent in June, to reduce demand at home. But the British authorities were seriously at fault in not realizing soon enough that they were playing with fire; and the issue of a new government stock, tax-free to foreigners, aggravated the situation. Bank Rate did go down by half a per cent in October and again in December, but by then it was far too late to repair the damage. The cavalier attitude towards the risks involved was epitomized by Mr Cameron (now Lord) Cobbold, the Governor of the Bank of England, at the Lord Mayor's Banquet in 1960 when he said: 'I see no cause to cheer when these short-term money movements cause our reserves to rise; nor shall I see any cause to complain if our reserves fall because they go the other way. This is what reserves are for. And a good deal of what now looks like short-term money may in fact turn out to be more permanent investment.' Just how permanent it was soon to become apparent in the months that followed.

The signal that reversed the hot-money flow was the 5

per cent upward revaluation of the German mark, announced on 5 March 1961. It was widely thought that this was only a first stage and that sterling would be devalued as part of a general realignment of currencies. Rumours of this kind were responsible for a big run on the British reserves which began as soon as the German revaluation was announced. The outflow was hidden for a while by the Basle arrangements under which the Continental central banks stockpiled over £300m. of sterling. Towards the end of June the central banks indicated that they had reached their limits and in July came Mr Selwyn Lloyd's crisis measures.

In some ways the 1961 crisis was a repeat performance of Mr Thorneycroft's 1957 experience, but in other ways it was a trial run for the July 1966 crisis, when Mr Wilson imposed a pay freeze and deflated the economy. As in 1957 the exodus of short-term funds was touched off by speculation in favour of the German mark. As in both 1957 and 1966 the deflation was imposed when the pressure was already beginning to come off the economy; and on all three occasions the government measures made sure that an easing of business activity turned into a near recession. In contrast to 1966 the statistical balance of payments was in 1961 already more or less satisfactory (although not as good as in 1957) when the measures were imposed; and the spectacular outflow in part reflected the delayed reaction to a deficit that was already passing. The relevant comparisons are brought out by Table 11.

In fact the published figures understate the deterioration both between 1957–61 and 1961–6. In 1961 the inflow of private capital into the UK was perhaps £150–175m. greater than normal as a result of some special American takeover transactions. In 1966 the extent of the deficit was understated both by the deferment of imports in advance of the removal of the surcharge, and also by a fortuitous bulge in exports at the end of the year.

The main point about 1961, as the right-hand side of the

TABLE II

	Current Balance £m.	Current and Long-term Capital Account, £m.	Current Balance, £m. (seasonally adjusted)	
1957	+233	+127	1960: 3rd quarter	−98
1961	− 4	+ 73	4th quarter	−60
1966	+ 64	− 48	1961: 1st quarter	−24
			2nd quarter	−33
			3rd quarter	+42
			4th quarter	+11
			1962: 1st quarter	+28
			2nd quarter	+45

Source: *Economic Trends*, September 1966

table shows, is that the balance of payments was on an improving trend throughout the year and by the time Mr Selwyn Lloyd acted in July there already was – whether his advisers knew it or not – a current surplus.

There was one difference between 1957 and 1961 of which the public was unaware. Whereas in 1957 it was the Treasury ministers who became alarmed, in 1961 it was the officials who became agitated and exerted pressure on Mr Selwyn Lloyd. Part of the explanation may be that the Treasury was in the process of changing economic advisers. Mr Cairncross arrived only in June 1961 and could not possibly have acquired enough power in the following weeks to stop the deflationary package even if he had wished to. Then again, the chance of securing a margin of excess capacity, in accordance with a recurrent intellectual fashion, was too tempting for some Treasury officials to resist, whatever the circumstances in which this came about.

It is, however, easy to overrationalize crisis measures with the aid of Economic Section doctrines. The Treasury mood was prompted on this, as on other occasions, by the sight of reserves rapidly running out, which it interpreted as 'the money running out of the kitty'. It was calculated that, at the current rate of loss, the reserves would have disappeared completely by Christmas (a rather moderate outflow judged by the standard of later crises). Sometimes in such situations papers are drawn up in deliberately strong terms to alarm ministers, and the official authors become infected by the atmosphere they have themselves created.

Mr Selwyn Lloyd's unofficial Budget of 25 July raised by its full 10 per cent the consumer tax regulator, imposed a curb on government spending and bank advances, and raised Bank Rate to 7 per cent. These measures caused an outcry when they came and helped to ensure almost two years of near-stagnation in production. Yet it was not generally known that the Treasury, and even more the Bank of England, considered them not nearly severe enough. The Treasury originally wanted to raise income tax in addition to all the other measures (for the whole of the fiscal year and not through any mid-year regulator of the kind earlier rejected). When it failed to persuade the government on this front, it then advised the use of the second regulator – the 4s. levy on payrolls – as well as the first, to take another £200m. of spending power away. A levy on payrolls, even though extracted from employers, on top of a pay pause would have been a particularly explosive combination.

Mr Lloyd resisted this extremism doggedly; and the last stage of the battle was fought at Chequers the week-end before 25 July. An *Express* photographer managed to obtain a picture of Macmillan and Lloyd. An observant person looking at the photograph would also have noticed the back of a third person's head. No one realized at the time that this was the Earl of Cromer, the new Governor of the Bank of England, who had arrived to put the case for sterner measures. Mr Lloyd had also at the time to fight off even more extreme advice from Dr Per Jacobsson, the Managing Director of the IMF, who would have liked a cut in government spending of £500m. (What exactly this meant was far from clear.) Although he did not receive satisfaction on this particular point, there is no doubt that – as on other occasions – a supporting deflationary programme was a condition of the IMF credit Britain was then given.[8]

There was in fact nothing in the July 1961 measures which could not have been enacted with better timing and, therefore, less subsequent damage to the economy in the ordinary Budget in April, which, apart from surtax relief, confined itself to an increase in profits tax and the imposition of a fuel-oil tax. The net disinflationary effect of the measures was trivial. The official Treasury view would have preferred a straight tax increase of £100m. levied on consumer spending rather than the fuel-oil tax. But it is difficult to see these small differences of opinion as a timely warning to Lloyd of the dangers ahead. Looking back on the events of 1961 (or for that matter early 1962) the Treasury's advice on the management of the cycle does not seem to have been more impressive than the instincts of a lay politician with no economic pretensions. In some ways, indeed, it was more misguided.

In retrospect a number of those involved recognized that they had been wrong to cut demand in July 1961. Contrary to what was claimed at the time, demand was not rising at all quickly in the middle of 1961 and unemployment would probably have risen even without the July measures. Yet no one in the Treasury or the Bank apparently voiced dissent from the severity of the advice given, which if accepted would have increased the severity of the July measures.

Just as their Labour successors in the 1966 crisis were to be, many ministers were most unhappy with the deflationary bent of policy, but – like the majority of their successors – they could think of no alternative. The crisis came to them as a bolt from the blue. Throughout a large part of the 1960s ministers of both political parties, although

8. A published Treasury document of September 1967 acknowledges that strings are normally attached to IMF drawings.

continually talking of planning, were reacting to events, and hardly ever anticipating them. Labour ministers might have been more inclined than members of the Macmillan Cabinet to assert that men can be masters of their fate, but on neither side were the necessary Promethean qualities on display.

With Selwyn Lloyd, as with Wilson after him, popular reaction concentrated on the pay pause. Popular reaction was, as is so often the case, deeply misguided, as on both occasions the freeze was the most defensible part of the whole package. Having said this one must add that the timing and tactics of policy on the wages front, in the months before the July 1961 measures, were remarkably uninspired.

During the early part of the year it was the Bank of England that was quickest off the mark in urging a pay freeze (as it was in the 1966 crisis, the 1967 devaluation, and on almost every other relevant occasion). Wage negotiation is the section of economic policy furthest removed from the Bank's operational responsibilities, and thus the area where radical action is easiest to advocate. No doubt the Ministry of Labour was equally radical on international liquidity.

Very early in 1961, long before the April Budget, the Bank gave the government a warning that the wage settlements already in sight would give Britain an overvalued currency, and that the only cure for an overvalued currency was devaluation. This, it was said, would set off a train of unpredictable events outside Britain's control. Whenever it gave such a warning the Bank was shrewd enough to point out that devaluation would weaken our foreign policy. Of all the possible consequences, the one that could be relied upon to inhibit the Prime Minister most (whether Macmillan or Wilson before 1967) was the effect on Britain's relations with the United States of any move that affected the dollar, as a devaluation of sterling was bound to do.

The fact that wages were rising with alarming rapidity

was obvious well before the April Budget. The Economic Survey pointed out that earnings per head in the second half of 1960 were $6\frac{1}{2}$ per cent higher than in the previous year – a rate far higher than productivity can ever be expected to rise. The Budget Speech itself mentioned the Treasury's fear 'that the cost inflationary process will speed up further. That I feel is the principal menace at present, and one which it is impossible to exaggerate.'

Yet in the face of this menace the Chancellor did nothing but warn and more precious months were lost. Not merely did he take no action, either of a deflationary or of a more direct kind, but his whole Budget showed no recognition that he might have to deal with wages later. I do not share the facile view that the surtax concessions were badly timed. If Mr Selwyn Lloyd had not made them then, they would then have been very difficult to enact during the rest of the 1959–64 Parliament. But they should have been balanced by some other measure to redress the social balance, such as a full capital gains tax, which was being widely advocated at the time on its own merits, and not only among Socialists.

The two attempts which were made in the 1961 Budget to give the appearance of a *quid pro quo* to the union side could hardly have attracted less popular attention if they had been deliberately drafted with that end in mind. One was the further increase of $2\frac{1}{2}$ per cent in profits tax to 15 per cent in the Budget of the previous April, following a similar increase in 1960. But the very impersonal and obscure nature of such a change defeated its own object. The public hardly knew that it had happened and did not weigh it in the balance at all when judging the surtax reliefs which had a spectacular effect on individual people. This experience did not prevent the Labour government from making the same mistake and raising corporation tax twice after the November 1967 devaluation without the slightest return in terms of union goodwill.

The second 'social justice' measure in the April 1961 Budget was the promise of a tax on short-term gains realized within six months. Whether a well-conceived tax or not, it was a minor matter which the unions were right to ignore. A promise to introduce it was inserted at the last moment in the April 1961 Budget speech as a result of a revolt at the pre-Budget Cabinet involving Maudling, Macleod, and Heath.

The Wilson freeze six years later was in fact much harsher than the Lloyd one, as it postponed the implementation of agreements already made and was backed by statutory sanctions. It is difficult to believe that the much greater public acceptance was due to the pointless temporary surcharge on surtax in 1966, the existence of which was hardly known except to those affected. Much more relevant is that it takes the public – and even more the organs of opinion – a long period to get used to new ideas, after which they become second nature. By the time of the devaluation winter of 1967–8 the press was positively clamouring for a pay freeze which the government was reluctant to impose.

Among the events leading up to the Selwyn Lloyd pay pause was a report entitled *The Problem of Rising Prices*, written, in the early part of 1961, by six economists to the Organization of European Economic Co-ordination, supporting the wage-push theory of inflation. Published between the Budget and the July crisis, this helped to convince many sceptics in the Treasury and elsewhere of the case for tackling wage inflation by intervening directly in industrial settlements, and not relying exclusively on financial policy.

The Treasury's Joint Permanent Secretary, Sir Frank Lee, was in hospital in Paris when the crisis measures were prepared. It was a Civil Servant, then at Under-Secretary level, Matthew Stevenson (later Permanent Secretary of the Ministry of Housing), who was instrumental in persuading the government to grasp the wages nettle. Another key to the conversion of the government to an incomes policy in July 1961 was a change of front at the Ministry of Labour, which had previously been the main source of resistance to the idea. After a long line of Permanent Secretaries who mostly saw the job in terms of conciliation, the ministry was now headed by Sir Laurence Helsby, a former economics don with a Treasury background who later became Head of the Home Civil Service. Although he was no revolutionary, under his reign the ministry decided as a conscious act of policy that it could no longer automatically step in to conciliate irrespective of the economic damage it produced in the process. With much equivocation and many backslidings, this view has continued to colour Ministry of Labour policy afterwards.

Equally important was the accident that the Minister of Labour, Mr John Hare, was a personal friend of Mr Selwyn Lloyd's and willing to listen to the Treasury point of view. When Lloyd was dismissed by Macmillan in July 1962, Hare offered his own resignation, pointing out to the Prime Minister that he too was involved in all Lloyd's actions on the wages front.

Why, as the TUC so bitterly complained, did not Mr Lloyd consult the unions before acting? His reason was that he could not put them in the picture without mentioning his other measures, including the 7 per cent Bank Rate. If he could have had his time over again, Mr Lloyd would have introduced the financial measures first and then held emergency talks with the unions over wages. One may wonder why no one in the Treasury suggested that Mr Lloyd should try this course; but it is difficult to believe it would have made any fundamental difference.

The first major defeat for the new wages policy was an electricity pay settlement in November to which Mr Lloyd was violently opposed. The Prime Minister was in Scotland and Mr Lloyd in Paris. The chief negotiator for the Electricity Council telephoned Mr Richard Wood, the Minister of Power, who told him: 'You must take the responsibility', which he did. Later Mr Macmillan gave the Electricity Council a headmasterly rebuke in the House of Commons. But the breakthrough showed quite clearly that relations between the Chancellor and ministers responsible for particular industries were not then organized in the way that would be necessary to make an incomes policy work.

The fact remains that, for all its inept handling and occasional breaches, the pause had some notable results. It first shocked people into an awareness of the wage–price problem, in a way that a whole decade of ministerial sermons had failed to do, and for good or evil paved the way for all the developments of incomes policy under Labour. It is probable too that the pause, which ended on 1 April 1962, had some effects in slowing down the wage–price spiral for a few months although, because of the implementation of previously agreed settlements, this is difficult to demonstrate.

The Cabinet had endless difficulty in agreeing on a long-term incomes policy to follow the pause. The statement which was issued in February 1962, and which set forth a 'guiding light' stating that money incomes should not rise by an average of more than $2\frac{1}{2}$ per cent per person each year, had been in existence for well over five years and draft after draft had been sent back by ministers for re-writing. The document which appeared was a triumph of obscurity and an object of derision even in the Treasury corridors.

To Macmillan the White Paper was not a policy. He wanted, above all, an institution which would help decide priorities among different kinds of workers, and different kinds of income. Many suggestions were aired. Some officials hoped to find a way of introducing national economic considerations into the actual processes of wage negotiation or conciliation. This idea was not regarded as workable. Others wanted ministers to pronounce in public on wage settlements which were against the national interest as soon as they were made or even before. But this was too forthright a solution for British governments, which preferred to pass such questions to outside bodies. In the end Macmillan lost his patience with the argument and delay and himself summoned a group of officials, including Sir Laurence Helsby, to Admiralty House in the spring of 1962 to hammer out the main lines of the National Incomes Commission – an extremely unconventional kind of initiative for a British Prime Minister to take.

There is a curious tailpiece to the story. Mr Selwyn Lloyd was holding talks in the summer of 1962, just before he was dismissed, with Mr Victor Feather, then Assistant General Secretary of the TUC, on the establishment of the NIC. Some misunderstandings seem to have arisen at this stage. For although Feather was non-committal, it seemed to the Treasury that the talks were going reasonably well, and there seemed no hint of the furious TUC objections which were later to develop. Later on, in July, Mr George Woodcock came back from a meeting of the International Confederation of Free Trade Unions and treated the project as a personal affront. By then the Prime Minister was determined to introduce it in the Vote of Censure debate of 26 July, and the Whitehall preparations had acquired a momentum difficult to stop. Although the NIC was boycotted by the TUC it was the precursor of the Aubrey Jones Prices and Incomes Board, which indeed inherited the NIC staff and many of the NIC objectives.

THE GROWTH-RATE CONTROVERSY

The other and more popular of the planning bodies, the National Development Council, held its first two meetings in March and May 1962. An expanded version of the Treasury's earlier papers on obstacles to growth was placed before the Council at one of these early meetings. This was abruptly turned down without consideration on the grounds that the Council wanted to hear from its own office and not the Treasury; and it was incidentally one of the employers present who took the lead in this. The words 'Treasury trash' were heard to cross the table.

Some Whitehall officials felt rather bitterly about this incident, and claimed that their own documents made nearly all the points in NEDCs own report on *Conditions Favourable To Growth* which appeared a year later. There were undoubtedly many points in common; both sets of documents put considerable emphasis, for example, on the need for incomes restraint. The Treasury papers put the emphasis on the obstacles and the difficulties; the NEDC papers started with the assumption of a growth programme and looked at the problem in that perspective. The main apparent triumph for the NEDC office came, however, in the acceptance of the 4 per cent growth target. Where, the question was often asked, did the 4 per cent target come from?

A hint was provided by the target of 50 per cent growth in ten years (equivalent to 4 per cent per annum) set for the West as a whole by the Kennedy Administration soon after taking office at meetings of the OECD (the Organization for Economic Cooperation and Development, the successor to the Marshall Plan organization which included the US and Canada as well as Western Europe). This target was based partly on the assumption that the US would move nearer to full employment under Kennedy than under the Eisenhower Administration and partly on the Common Market's growth record, allowing here for some slowing down.

The main point, however, was that the NEDC office believed that 4 per cent also suited Britain's particular requirements for the period 1961–6. On an analysis of past statistics the Treasury thought that Britain's productive capacity was growing annually by 3 per cent. NEDC hoped, however, that Britain would be able to do better in the future than in the past. It was also thought that NEDC should aim higher than the Treasury, which, because of its concern for the balance of payments and government spending, was bound to take a cautious view.

Some Treasury officials were in favour of using 4 per cent as a basis for NEDC's studies because they thought that a figure higher than was likely to be achieved would bring out all the objections and snags they wanted to see discussed. Too late they realized that once the magic figure of 4 per cent was announced it would inevitably become a target from which it would be highly embarrassing to draw back.

At NEDC's second meeting, in May 1962, 4 per cent was accepted as 'a reasonably ambitious figure likely to bring out problems that have to be solved if faster growth is to be achieved and as a help in focusing thinking on the problems of faster growth'. Long before the industrial inquiry was completed near the end of the year, the 4 per cent was prematurely treated in the press as a target, an error which the office did not over-exert itself to correct. This insistence on a 4 per cent growth target wrongly seemed at the time a major victory for economic radicalism.

AN UNFORTUNATE BUDGET

When Mr Lloyd introduced the 1962 Budget the government was not yet formally committed to the 4 per cent target. But it is doubtful if this was the main reason for the disappointing nature of the Chancellor's measures and unemployment in the following months. A few commentators hoped the 1962 Budget would produce some ingenious device for stimulating exports; some thought it would provide incentives for private investment, by then obviously on the downturn; others thought that it would give some stimulus to purchasing power. Hardly anyone believed that the Budget would contain none of these three things and that the only innovation would be a tax on confectionery and ice-cream.

The 1962 Budget judgement is one that has ever since been regarded inside the Treasury with embarrassment.

So far from foreseeing the unemployment that was to come, the Chancellor in his Budget speech actually worried that total spending would make 'too great a call on our resources'. The buoyant forecast was mainly due to an extremely optimistic view of exports, which emanated from the Board of Trade. The Treasury in its own analysis of what went wrong put most stress on the surprise it received when, contrary to expectations, exports levelled out and then fell slightly after the middle of the year. As a secondary factor it blamed the fall in private investment, which was much steeper than the Treasury had thought it would be. These two setbacks helped to generate a typical deflationary cycle, which led to lower employment, shorter hours, and a fall in industrial stock building.

An important contributory factor at the political level was that Mr Selwyn Lloyd was led to think that success in the Common Market negotiations would be apparent by July 1962, and that an agreement would be on the table by September. This news, he envisaged, would stimulate an investment boom. On a more intellectual level the trouble was that the Treasury economists over-estimated the growth of demand just at one of those periods when they were most captivated by the theory of maintaining a margin of spare capacity, and when forecasting errors were therefore most dangerous.

Mr Lloyd became personally worried about the Treasury's 1962 forecast a week or so after his Budget speech. So in time did the Board of Trade and the Ministry of Labour. In June Mr Lloyd allowed hire-purchase deposits on durables to be reduced from 20 per cent to 10 per cent, a relaxation which the Treasury considered unnecessary.

The April Budget was badly received by some of Lloyd's colleagues, and the promise to abolish Schedule 'A' at some future date was inserted after the pre-Budget Cabinet as a concession to critics. During the months after the Budget a number of ministers wrote personal papers for the Cabinet voicing concern about a possible recession and attacked the

Treasury's complacency. The critics are said to have included Lord Mills, the Prime Minister's confidant, Sir David Eccles, Mr Marples, and, to some extent, Mr Macleod and Lord Hailsham. Yet, despite these dissatisfied voices, Lloyd's dismissal on 13 July came as a bolt from the blue, both to Lloyd himself and to the Treasury.

REFLATION POSTPONED

On 11 July, the day before Lloyd heard the news of his dismissal, a junior Treasury minister, Anthony Barber, gave the Press a Lobby briefing which showed no change of heart whatever. *The Times* headlines ran: NO ECONOMIC STIMULUS LIKELY YET; TREASURY CONFIDENT OF STEADY GROWTH; OUTPUT, EXPORTS, AND HOME DEMAND ALL RISING. No one has found a method of avoiding even quite major forecasting errors. But there was in the summer of 1962 an extremely ivory-tower element in the Treasury's misinterpretation of the existing situation. Stock Exchange prices had just slumped after a Wall Street crash; industrialists were nervous, uncertain, and deferring investment plans; retail sales had been stagnant for eighteen months running, and unemployment (adjusted for seasonal changes) had already been rising for a whole year. It was difficult to remember a time when business and Whitehall were so far apart in their economic assessments. Even the Bank of England was far more conscious of the dangers of recession than the Treasury and (sterling being fairly strong) was gently urging more expansionist policies.

The most questionable part of this briefing was the view reported in the *Financial Times*: 'Fears of repeating the 1958 error of stimulating the economy too soon out of fear of recession still sway the Government more than the doubtful outlook for the American economy, or the failure so far to get any steam behind a revival of business confidence in Britain.' As one City editor wrote at the time, 'Too soon! How it can seriously be suggested that after three years of stagnation the economy was re-expanded *too soon* in 1958 I find utterly bewildering. After all, the Treasury has never done anything too soon (nor probably has any other Government department for that matter). Its actions fall neatly into two categories, too little too late and too much too late.'[9] So it proved both in 1958 and 1962.

As the minor post-Budget relaxations showed, Mr Selwyn Lloyd had himself been raising queries about the Treasury advice. At a meeting during his very last week as Chancellor, Mr Lloyd heard for the first time of a new forecast that winter unemployment would reach 525,000 instead of 450,000 as originally expected. The news came as a shock to Lloyd, and he told Macmillan that if the economy really proved to be running at a standstill during the summer, he would want in the first few days of October, the earliest Parliamentary rules allowed, to move the regulator downwards. This would have reduced all purchase tax and other consumer taxes by a tenth and injected an extra £250m. or so of extra spending power.

On the eve of his dismissal Lloyd had made tentative plans for a Bank Rate reduction to 4 per cent for early August (this did not in fact happen until 3 January 1963) and a release of another 1 per cent of Special Deposits (which did not happen until October). Mr Lloyd also authorized an extra £70m. of public investment, over and above what he had originally planned, which would mostly take effect in 1963–4. This he regarded as making a virtue of necessity.

As soon as Mr Lloyd had gone, the Minister of Labour, Mr Hare, became worried that the change of Chancellor would delay measures to fight unemployment. At his request Lloyd sent a letter to a member of the Cabinet outlining all the plans just listed, as examples of the sorts of action which he would *not* regard as a repudiation of his own policies.

9. Nigel Lawson, *Sunday Telegraph*, 15 July 1962.

THE DEPARTURE OF SELWYN LLOYD

The reasons for Lloyd's dismissal have never been adequately explained. It would be misleading to report that it was just because he was too late and too timid in switching over to re-expansion. Most of the evidence suggests that any such feeling was only one element in a much more general belief that Macmillan had gradually acquired that Lloyd was no longer the right man for the Treasury and had become a political liability. The dismissal came not very long after Orpington and a whole series of really shattering Conservative defeats.

The unfairest of reasons given for Lloyd's dismissal, but one that is all too likely to be important, is the two words 'pay pause'. Lloyd paid the price for an unpopular policy which quite a few eminent men of a Labour and trade-union background privately believed to have been essential – 'saved the nation' was one, albeit exaggerated, remark actually made.

Another factor was that Lloyd could not take part to Macmillan's satisfaction in ruminative general economic conversation. On complex Treasury matters Lloyd seemed to the Premier and to some of his colleagues to be too dependent on his brief, and to look at a loss when unexpected questions turned up. Whether these criticisms did justice to Lloyd as a minister or not, they were perfectly predictable when he was moved to the Exchequer after five years as Foreign Secretary. This deficiency was, however, aggravated in Mr Macmillan's eyes by the Wall Street crash of May 1962, and renewed talk of the difficulties of the dollar. These events had revived the Prime Minister's concern with the liquidity problem, i.e. the inadequate amount of gold or alternative types of international money to finance world trade. He wanted a Chancellor who could force the Treasury and the Bank into taking some initiative on the question.

But probably the most important reason of all was Macmillan's extreme irritation that Lloyd carried on talking about an incomes policy, after the end of the pay pause, without, as the Prime Minister thought, taking any visible steps towards it. If there was one specific incident which turned the balance against Lloyd it was the inaction which led Macmillan to set up NIC himself. Subsequent events were to show that neither the dismissal of a Chancellor, nor even a change of government, could produce a long-term incomes policy with any demonstrable effect on the movement of money incomes.

7

AN UNFINISHED EXPERIMENT:
THE MAUDLING PERIOD, 1962–4

*Making haste slowly: does Nature move in leaps?: Mr
Maudling's reflation: the £800m. deficit: an abortive
Statement of Intent: Tory modernization*

WITH the arrival of Reginald Maudling at the Exchequer
on 13 July 1962 we are no longer in the region of history,
but of controversies which are likely to remain current
for some time to come.

Two opposed views are often put forward about his two-
year reign. One is that by embarking on a profligate
growth policy he created the severe balance-of-payments
problem which was responsible for most of Britain's trouble.
This was the 'legacy' view assiduously canvassed by Labour
spokesmen after the 1964 election; but those who believed
it most strongly and sincerely were the financial conservatives in the City of London and elsewhere. The opposite
view, which became more fashionable after the failure of
Labour's own early economic policies, was that Maudling
had embarked on a courageous expansionist experiment
designed to break out of the stop-go cycle, which might
well have succeeded – and without devaluation – if only
the incoming Labour ministers had not shattered confidence
in sterling.

Both views seem to me a great deal too *simpliste*. But before embarking on this controversy it would be best to
begin with some of the main events of Maudling's tenure of
the Exchequer. Unlike Mr Selwyn Lloyd he had never been
personally close to Mr Macmillan. The Prime Minister
brought him in at a low point in Conservative fortunes
when he wanted, above all, someone who had some notion
of economic policy and was able to express himself on the

subject in public. Mr Maudling had these qualities. He did not find the intellectual framework within which policy is discussed by Treasury economists and outside commentators as incomprehensible as some of his predecessors. At his best Maudling would give birth to a flow of ideas in the hope that if his own turned out to be impracticable they would at least provoke his advisers to think of preferable alternatives. His speed of work and his casual conversational manner sometimes gave a false impression of laziness.

Maudling was relatively independent of his officials, because he could rapidly absorb and even anticipate their advice. But he had too equable a temperament to be a ruthless administrator steamrollering his way through colleagues and advisers. Although he was appointed Chancellor at the comparatively early age of forty-five, in one sense he was appointed several years too late. He had been associated with the Treasury in one capacity or another for the best part of a decade. He had been Economic Secretary under Butler, and had supported successive Chancellors of the Exchequer in economic debates, first as Paymaster General, then as President of the Board of Trade, and had seen many policies tried and fail. Then, too, he came to office after his Party had been in power for eleven years and was hardly in a position to repudiate the heritage of his predecessors. He was appointed in the second half of a Parliament – never a good time to introduce heretical ideas, which in the first instance usually lose more votes than they gain.

The month of July 1962 saw not only the announcement of a new Chancellor, but a new Permanent Secretary as well. The appointment of Mr William Armstrong, who was promoted from the ranks of Third Secretaries over the heads of his superiors after the retirement of Sir Frank Lee, was in many ways more surprising than Lloyd's replacement by Maudling. Armstrong was not even a knight when his appointment was announced.

Armstrong, who has already been referred to on page 71, was a strong contrast to Lee. The latter was an expansive extrovert, while Armstrong was more of an introvert, although of an exceptionally approachable variety. While Lee would take charge of an investigation from the beginning, Armstrong would, in his early years at least, let his subordinate officials pursue their own course before coming in with his comments. Armstrong was careful not to become associated with strongly defined ideological attitudes. He disliked shibboleths and insisted on basing policies on facts and logic. His favourite motto was Leonardo da Vinci's 'He who controls the weather controls the world.' He was probably the first Permanent Head of the Treasury to have a sophisticated and contemporary approach to economic management. But he was very conscious of the widespread criticisms that the Treasury had tried to foist certain doctrines on governments; and he was careful not to arrogate for himself the choice of policy goals, perhaps being even a shade too scrupulous in this respect.

There is rarely any direct connection between Cabinet and Civil Service changes in the lifetime of a government. Armstrong's appointment had certainly been approved by Mr Selwyn Lloyd before being confirmed by Mr Maudling. But at a deeper level the two sets of changes had a common origin in a strong feeling of dissatisfaction that Mr Macmillan and one or two of his close personal advisers had long had with the workings of the Treasury. As so often, dissatisfaction with *policies* made itself felt in a demand for organizational changes. Politicians find it hard to free themselves of the hope that better information, or improved administrative machinery, can prevent the policy dilemmas which they so much dislike from emerging. Maudling himself was too realistic to have such illusions, but understandably he did not want to face these dilemmas any earlier than was avoidable.

MAKING HASTE SLOWLY

Nothing could be further from the truth than the popular picture of Maudling arriving at the Exchequer, putting his foot on the economic accelerator and immediately embarking on the 'Maudling experiment'. In fact the transition from Lloyd to Maudling actually delayed re-expansion by several months. Although Mr Maudling was sometimes a bold conversationalist he was cautious in his actions. As President of the Board of Trade, he was on the side of moderation during the 1961 crisis. As Chancellor a year later, he was equally moderate about re-expansion, and was again very moderate in the Budgetary restraints he imposed on the 1964 boom.

The Treasury, to do it justice, had by the summer of 1962 an expansionary package in reserve, which could be introduced very quickly should its view of the situation change. At the very same time as the Lobby correspondents were being given the highly over-optimistic briefing mentioned at the end of the last chapter, officials at a middle level were already revising their forecasts downwards – an illustration of the drawbacks of the lengthy processing and discussion through which papers go before they are placed in front of ministers.

By the late summer of 1962 the Treasury was already advising Mr Maudling to use the Regulator – as Mr Lloyd had contemplated. It wanted the Chancellor to announce this at his Mansion House speech on 3 October. To give Parliament time to discuss the move within twenty-one calendar days, as the Finance Act then demanded, the House of Commons would have had to be recalled one day early. This project ran into trouble when Mr Maudling came back from the annual IMF meeting feeling that too early a reversal of Mr Lloyd's policy would be bad for sterling. His international liquidity initiative had been rebuffed; sterling had suffered a short, but unpleasant, shock after a Telstar broadcast by President Kennedy in defence of the dollar, and Maudling was in a very cautious mood.

All that was announced at the Mansion House was a small release of post-war credits, the increase in public investment that Mr Lloyd had already approved, and the end of the credit squeeze. But as Lord Plowden remarked in the House of Lords in a speech the following February, 'Cheap credit is no help when there is a short and declining order book. It is like a fuel that will catch fire only when the fire is burning well.'[1] The same remark could also be applied to the improved investment allowances announced a month later.

As the business situation worsened during the course of the autumn, Maudling was still unwilling to use the regulator. One reason was that more than half of its effect would have come through lower drink and tobacco prices. This was not a strong argument, as a surcharge imposed by the regulator would not have changed the existing distribution of taxes between different items, but simply lifted the whole scale up or down. In any case a reduction in the price of tobacco and drink would simply have compensated for the earlier increase when the regulator was used in an upward direction in July 1961. The use of the regulator was also disliked by Macmillan, who found it difficult to believe that 'making a glass of sherry a bit cheaper' could do much to restore prosperity.

Mr Maudling eventually decided to act on purchase tax. A separate attack on all the different rates provided a highly complicated affair. In the end the Chancellor and his advisers came to the conclusion that it would be better to reduce all tax rates in the highest 45 per cent category to 25 per cent. (The special stimulus to the motor industry was mainly a *post hoc* justification.) The total value of the purchase-tax cuts was about £90m., less than half of what the regulator would have been. Yet even these modest relaxations were staggered in two stages. The cuts for

1. *House of Lords Hansard*, 19 February 1963, column 1284.

cars were announced on 5 November (together with increased investment allowances) and the reductions for cosmetics, records, radio and TV were held over for two months until New Year's day.

Mr Maudling did have one economically very attractive idea which proved abortive. This was to pay out the higher pensions and other National Insurance benefits which the government had promised for 1963 several months before the increase in contributions. If Maudling's idea had been accepted, a large temporary stimulus worth several hundred million pounds a year would have been applied when it was most needed. Later, when contributions were raised, the stimulus would have been much reduced in a way that everyone would have regarded as fair, and could not possibly have denounced as stop–go. The Chancellor took the unusual step of asking the Ministry of Pensions officials personally to his room to discuss the problem, but he was defeated by the seemingly irreducible time-lags affecting any change in benefits or rates.

The same unfortunate time-lag applied to the rise in public expenditure which Mr Maudling had authorized for the financial year 1963–4. As Sir Robert Hall subsequently pointed out, a substantial increase in public expenditure, however justified from a social point of view, was a method of expansion notoriously slow to take effect, and one which tended to get out of phase and exert a destabilizing influence.[2] A gradual step-by-step approach may often be good politics, but economic policy is in this respect different. For the golden rule in trade-cycle control, if it is attempted at all, is to act with maximum speed as soon as signs of slump or excessive boom appear. The longer the Chancellor waits, and the greater the time-lags in the actions he takes, the more likely he will be to aggravate the fluctuations he is trying to cure.

During the winter of 1962–3 many people refused to listen to any explanation of the high unemployment in these

2. 'Incomes Policy – State of Play', *Three Banks Review*, March 1964.

terms at all. The popular view was that there was something wrong with specific geographical areas. In a sense this was right. These were the areas that felt the brunt of any recession and did not quite fully share in any recovery. Their problems certainly needed tackling. But the cause of the sudden deterioration in their condition was the general economic down-turn. Table 12 shows that the regional problem was only slightly worse than in the 1958 recession. The trouble both in 1958 and in 1962 was the movement of demand in the country as a whole, difficult though this was to demonstrate over the TV screen. By the 1967 recession the regional aspect had become slightly less severe than on either of the two previous occasions.

TABLE 12

Thousands of Workers

Unemployment	December 1958	December 1962	December 1967
Northern Region	40·7	64·9	58·7
Scotland	95·5	100·6	86·2
Wales	39·5	36·6	41·9
N. Ireland	39·7	36·9	38·6
Total Depressed Regions	215·4	239·0	225·4
Total UK	571·4	603·0	621·3
Depressed Regions as Percentage of the Total	37·8%	39·6%	36·2%

Mr Maudling did in fact do a great deal to help longer-term development in the high-unemployment areas. The most important example was the introduction of free depreciation in high-unemployment areas. This allowed an industrialist to write off against tax all he spent on new plant in the first year of its life – the equivalent, according to one large firm, of a 10 per cent subsidy on new capital expenditure in the development districts. It was Maudling personally who pressed the idea. Originally he thought of it for the country as a whole, but was defeated by its cost – perhaps £400m. per annum. (This showed how incomplete was the conversion of even the most sophisticated of politicians and officials to the Keynesian approach. In terms of real resources the extra load on the economy would have been very much less.[3]) The Inland Revenue accepted the scheme with some misgivings as a lesser evil to profits tax discrimination in favour of development districts – which it had also been asked to consider.

Quite apart from his special help for unemployment areas, Maudling increased tax incentives for capital development for the country as a whole, first in November 1962, and then in the 1963 Budget. Britain's fiscal incentives to investment were by then about the best in Europe. The Chancellor also had a number of special schemes. A minor success was the £75m. of Exchequer loans for shipowners willing to place orders in British yards. The loans were just enough to tide the shipbuilding industry over a trough and bring into operation labour and capacity that would otherwise have lain unused, but not enough to put the industry on a permanent subsidized basis. The scheme, which was announced by the Minister of Transport, was a personal notion of Mr Maudling's which ran into great scepticism from both officials and other ministers, but it was revived in various forms by the Labour government. The proposal which interested him most, however, was for special aid for developing countries that were willing to place contracts in depressed areas in Britain. Loans were given, to a modest total, for example to India for the purchase of steel plates, to Pakistan for sugar processing machinery and to Ghana for cargo ships. The scheme was never formally cancelled although it was not much publicized after Maudling's departure.

3. Provided that the extra government borrowing could have been accommodated without an increase in the money supply.

DOES NATURE MOVE IN LEAPS?

Although the Treasury wanted Mr Maudling to be more expansionist than he was in the summer of 1962 and the winter of 1962–3, its views on the country's long-term possibilities were conservative. As we have seen in earlier chapters, it had all along been extremely sceptical of NEDC's 4 per cent growth target for 1961–6. Among the ministers and career Civil Servants involved the real doubt was whether export volume could rise by the 5 per cent a year then believed necessary on average to achieve this target. NEDC's Industrial Inquiry showed little hope among the firms questioned about expanding overseas sales in line with this requirement – a point glossed over in its first report. But the Treasury economists who argued with NEDC at ground level did not, it is most important to appreciate, base themselves on the export argument at all, but on the historical figures of productivity mentioned in the previous chapter. These threw serious doubts on the 4 per cent target.

The long-term trend of productivity reflected in the Treasury view the fundamental working habits and pace of innovation of the whole nation and could not be changed overnight, least of all by stoking up the flames of demand. The motto which governed its reactions appears on the title page of Alfred Marshall's *Principles of Economics*, first published in 1890: *Natura non facit saltum*: Nature does not move in leaps. Here, in this symptomatic quotation, there was a welcome point of contact between the economists and the Treasury officials with a classical background.

The NEDC economists on the other hand believed that the underlying trend of productivity had speeded up in recent years, and that this had been hidden from view by the depressed conditions of 1961–2. They also argued that the high investment of 1960 and 1961 had not yet found expression in the output figures because demand had been held down. It was moreover suggested that many firms had

had a big competitive shakeout, and had launched drives against the wasteful uses of labour. Experience of NEDC's premature optimism did not prevent Mr Harold Wilson from claiming a big rise in productivity on identical statistical grounds in 1967.

The novelty of NEDC's approach was that it tried to find out from industrialists what they could actually do in the present and the future, if the demand were there for their products and the different sections of the economy moved in phase. Its first inquiry, completed near the end of 1962, was admittedly a crude and pioneering affair. It appeared to suggest, however, that a 4 per cent growth rate was regarded by industry as physically possible. This kind of questionnaire arithmetic is prone to errors of over-optimism and bristles with technical statistical difficulties. But if one remembers that the working population was still increasing, NEDC's conclusion was not nearly as misguided as it later became fashionable to believe.

Mr Maudling did not lose much sleep over any of this statistical theology. As has been explained earlier, he had not been a great supporter of the NEDC organization in Cabinet, and at its earlier meetings some Council members had the very strong feeling that (like the regulator) it was 'not his baby'. On the other hand he was personally quite well disposed towards the 4 per cent growth target. Although Maudling was a cautious man, he was also temperamentally an optimist; and looking at other European countries 4 per cent did not seem too absurd as a benchmark at which to aim. Long before the NEDC formally approved the 4 per cent objective, on 4 February 1963, the Chancellor was supporting the target in his public speeches. He subsequently made it clear inside the Treasury that the 4 per cent target could not just be dropped without inducing a national mood of frustration and disappointment. He determined to go on as long as he could playing it by ear and not attempting to define too closely over what period the 4 per cent target was meant to be achieved.

MR MAUDLING'S REFLATION

Maudling's relations with NEDC as an organization went through several phases. After his early scepticism he began to hope that the Council, with its representatives of both sides of industry, would give him an opportunity to mobilize support for the government's objectives, above all, for an incomes policy; and he took a very active part in the Council discussions around the beginning of 1963. His Budget speech of that year followed very closely, almost in the order of contents, the NEDC *Report on Conditions Favourable to Faster Growth*.

The Budget itself aimed to give away an extra £250m. in reliefs. It did so through higher income-tax allowances for married couples and families with children. It abolished Schedule 'A', introduced further improvements in industrial investment incentives, and reduced stamp duties. The main aim of the Budget, apart from general reflation, was to obtain union support for an incomes policy. The tax reliefs Maudling gave were equivalent for many workers to a wage increase of 2 per cent. For the same cost he could have reduced income tax by well over 6d. in the £; if he had done this the Chancellor would have obtained better headlines and pleased many Conservative supporters a great deal more than he did. Instead he achieved the satisfaction of having his Budget praised by the TUC Economic Committee – probably the first time ever for a Tory Chancellor. But for all the subsequent cooperation he received, he might as well have saved himself the bother.

Although Mr Maudling stressed the element of a personal judgement in the £250m. figure, it was in fact little different from the recommendation he had been given by the Treasury's Budget committee. There was apparently no support on that committee for the £400m. in reliefs urged by the National Institute, but the Chancellor and his advisers were delighted with the Institute's recommendation, as it made anything they did seem moderate by comparison.

The decision to give away only £250m. turned out right in the end, as the National Institute itself subsequently admitted. Yet the actual assumptions behind the Budget judgement were, at Maudling's insistence, surrounded in mystery at the time. They eventually emerged in a little-noticed *OECD Report on the UK Economy*, published during the summer holidays, which revealed the very gradual pace at which the Treasury envisaged the return to full employment. In fact the economy was recovering more rapidly before the Budget's stimulus took effect than either the Treasury or its critics realized; and production rose and unemployment fell in the closing months of 1963 with unexpected speed.

One unfortunate aspect of the Budget was its timing. We have seen that Mr Amory's expansionist Budget of 1959 came too late, and added fuel to the flames of the next boom. But in some ways Mr Maudling's Budget was even more unfortunate. For while Amory's reliefs had their full impact straight away, Maudling's reliefs were not expected to have anything like their full effect until the financial year 1964–5, when, as became all too apparent, the economy was much more likely to need restraint than stimulation. (The main tax reliefs were not even paid until July.) The following figures (although set out in Budgetary rather than economic terms) do make a valid comparison.

The fuel for the overheating of the economy in the elec-

TABLE 13

Tax Reliefs (in £m.)

	Estimated Value in Budget Year	Estimated Value in Following Year
Mr Amory in 1959	366*	361
Mr Maudling in 1963	269	446

* Including £71m. post-war credits.

tion year of 1964 was provided not by anything that Mr Maudling did in that year, but by the delayed-action re-flation of 1963 – when many of the Chancellor's critics, including Mr Callaghan, were worried he had not reflated enough. Even with hindsight it would be difficult to argue that Mr Maudling was wrong to reflate by as much as he did in the Budget of 1963, whatever one may think of the time-pattern of his measures. On the basis of the knowledge then available, with total unemployment reaching 873,000 in February (the proportion due to the abnormal winter was a matter of guesswork) and a depressed business psychology, it would have been far too risky to have given a smaller stimulus.

A more serious question was whether Mr Maudling was right to have reflated via the home market at all, or whether he should have devalued and relied on an export-led boom to provide the stimulus. Professor Kaldor was one of the very few who criticized Mr Maudling's strategy on this basis right from the beginning. My own view at the time was that we were possibly – even probably – in a fundamental disequilibrium, and that the forthcoming re-expansion might easily run into the familiar payments difficulties. But this was far from certain. There had been only one recent year of severe payments deficit (1960); there was some evidence that Britain's costs had recently been rising more slowly than those of her main European competitors. No one could be sure how successful the much-discussed incomes policy would be, nor whether a sustained home market expansion would spill over into exports or not, as some reputable economists believed. Given the political inhibition on tampering with the exchange rate, a case could be made for taking a calculated risk and attempting a home-based expansion, *provided that there was an ultimate willingness to devalue should this prove necessary to sustain expansion.*

THE £800M. DEFICIT

By the time of the 1964 Budget it was obvious that some slowing down in tempo was necessary to avoid overheating, although no one then predicted an £800m. overall deficit. The official estimate was indeed more in the nature of £400m. As far as internal policy was concerned the main question was how far the boom would slow down of its own accord and how far official restraining action needed to be taken. Mr Maudling decided that only mild restraint was required and raised taxation by only £100m. by putting up the duties on drink and tobacco.

It would be wrong to overplay the role of electoral considerations in that decision. Temperamentally Mr Maudling was inclined to do less than many economists advised, in both a reflationary and a deflationary direction. Nor should it be forgotten that even some very senior Treasury administrators were influenced by the atmosphere of the 'growth experiment', were anxious to avoid giving a shock to business confidence by too large a tax increase and wanted to persuade sceptical industrialists that stop-go had at last been abandoned in favour of steady growth.

For a time in the middle of the year it seemed that the Chancellor's judgement had been right about the internal, although not the external, economy, as production seemed to have levelled off on to a plateau. The moral of this misreading, as of others since, is that the industrial production index is a dangerously misleading guide to short-term trends. Moreover, by mid summer something was clearly going very wrong on the balance-of-payments front. Mr Maudling was extremely sensitive to any suggestion that he was refraining from corrective action for electoral reasons; and before the summer recess he asked his most senior advisers if they advocated any new measures. None was suggested. The whole episode shows the disadvantage of the system whereby Chancellor after Chancellor received his advice only from the most senior Civil Servants and – in contrast to the Foreign Secretary – had very little contact with officials at working level actually doing the calculations.

Basically, however, whether corrective action should have been taken in July, or in October, or whether the April Budget should have been slightly harsher, are secondary questions. The real issue is whether the whole Maudling growth experiment was a misguided venture, a solemn lesson in the consequences of putting growth before the balance of payments. An answer can only be given in hypothetical terms, for it depends on what Mr Maudling and his colleagues would have done in the hypothetical (and always unlikely) circumstances of a Conservative victory in 1964.

It is in fact clear that Mr Maudling would have been prepared to use import restrictions rather than resort to stop-go. Indications of a major change of policy were given in his 1964 Budget speech when he said:

I do not object to import controls on doctrinal grounds, but on grounds of practical policy. Certainly there could be occasions when their use would be justified and permissible under international agreements, that is, if we should be facing severe balance-of-payments difficulties which could not be dealt with in better ways.

He had subsequently explained that he had put work in hand on two alternative schemes, import quotas and a surcharge, and would have utilized these rather than reverted to stop-go.[4] Such schemes had been examined in previous crises but pigeon-holed in the end.

This solution did not work for two reasons. First, the payments deficit turned out to be so large that the savings from the surcharge (which was prematurely reduced in April 1965) seemed almost like a drop in the ocean. There is a second point which was not made as explicitly as it

4. See Reginald Maudling: 'The Economy: What are the Facts?', *Sunday Times*, 25 October 1964.

should have been in the original Pelican edition of this book. *Temporary* import restraints, imposed for a year or two, are only of use in dealing with a *temporary* deficit, due say to the re-stocking phase of a boom. In this sort of situation they act like an IMF credit and can be regarded as a substitute for international liquidity. Such temporary restraints cannot remove an underlying deficit which outlasts any restocking period and emerges whenever the economy is allowed to grow at a normal rate.

The crucial question then is whether if the Conservatives had been returned they would have devalued, rather than imposed a severe 'stop', once temporary import restraints had been shown to be insufficient. If the answer is 'No' then it would have been better never to have embarked on the Maudling experiment, but to have stuck to a Paish-type policy of running the economy at a higher margin of unemployment. This is a question to which the answer will never be known. There was a scarcely credible interchange of correspondence at the end of 1967, when Mr Wilson suggested in a debate that the contingency plans found waiting by the Labour government included devaluation, and Mr Maudling wrote a letter indignantly denying that he had asked officials to consider such a possibility. As a subsequent letter in *The Times* pointed out, Mr Wilson seemed to be trying to score a point out of Mr Maudling's doing what should have been common prudence under any Chancellor, while Mr Maudling was insisting that he had never done it.

During the crises of 1967 suggestions were made in the Press, and even belatedly by some Conservatives, that the Maudling growth experiment might not have deserved the vilification poured upon it and might even have been successful if it had been allowed to continue. It was unfortunate that Mr Maudling himself undermined the intellectual credibility of his own case by insisting that it could have worked with the aid of just a voluntary incomes policy, maintained international confidence and the use of central bank credit facilities, but strenuously denying that it would have meant devaluation – and not even mentioning in his 1967 version the possibility of direct controls over imports.[5]

This view seems to overlook the amount of red ink in the balance of payments in the mid 60s. It is difficult to see how even the most perfect handling of overseas confidence could have averted the series of deficits Britain was running in 1964, 1965, 1966 and 1967, which came to a total of nearly £1,500m. (Whether a more severely deflationary policy begun much earlier would have stopped the deficit is a debatable question, but such a course would have been quite inconsistent with the 'Maudling experiment'.)

By the time of the change of government in October 1964 it was clear that while part of the year's deficit was due to temporary factors such as stockpiling or abnormally high overseas private investment, there was a substantial part which was liable to persist. Indeed the end-1964 forecasts turned out to be too optimistic about the size of the persistent element.

One of the few near-certainties of recent history is that if Mr Maudling had remained Chancellor, he would have had to face the same choice, between devaluation and relying solely on a much more deflationary internal policy, which confronted the Labour government.

AN ABORTIVE STATEMENT OF INTENT

Mr Maudling's main interest in 1964, apart from overall financial policy, was in securing a Statement of Intent from employers and trade unions in favour of wage and price restraint. He made considerable efforts to secure this at NEDC meetings early in the year, but the TUC refused, either to cooperate or to suggest an alternative approach. In the course of the talks, Sir Norman Kipping, then Director General of the FBI, tentatively suggested, as a *quid pro quo*, a price-review body to comment on contro-

5. See his letter to the *Observer*, August 1967.

versial increases. (This, together with the much-abused NIC, was the germ of Mr Aubrey Jones's Prices and Incomes Board.) But the idea was then rejected by the employers' own representatives.

There is nevertheless little doubt that the Conservative government would have gladly gone as far as Mr George Brown's Statement of Intent, in making an incomes policy acceptable to the unions. The promise to deal with excess *aggregate* profits by fiscal means was made in more than one Conservative Budget speech; and there is little doubt that Mr Maudling would have accepted some form of price-vetting, and would have persuaded the employers to agree, if the unions had moved on wages. The fact is that neither side wanted to give away its bargaining position in advance of the election. Nor would it be realistic to suppose that any Conservative minister could have made the same personal appeal to the union leaders that Mr George Brown was able to do on behalf of a Labour government in his early days of office.

Even when it was clear that no Statement would be forthcoming, the enthusiasts for an incomes policy still hoped that the government would try to keep wage increases as near as possible to the $3\frac{1}{2}$ per cent 'norm' (then called a 'guiding light'). It hoped to do this by its influence on public-sector wages and by not stepping in too quickly to conciliate in the private sector. Indignation was expressed by many, including the present author, at the weakness ministers showed in holding the line. The engineers were granted a 5 per cent increase in rates; and this was followed by a statement from employers that this would mean higher prices. Postmen, electricity workers, busmen and other workers in state industry all received increases which were a good deal above the guiding light. It could be argued that the public sector was once again taking the lead in an inflationary breakthrough. An endemic weakness in the period up to October 1964 was that the Ministry of Labour was rarely regarded as a senior political office, worth holding for its own sake rather than as a stepping-stone to higher things. Sir Alec Douglas-Home if anything reinforced this unfortunate tradition by appointing Mr Joseph Godber, an amiable man who had made a favourable impression as Britain's disarmament negotiator, but was hardly a heavyweight, at the Labour Ministry.

TORY MODERNIZATION

Many of the themes that were later to figure so prominently in Labour's modernization programme were already being enacted by the Conservative government in 1963–4. As explained in Chapter 8 they had their roots in the re-appraisal of 1960–61 when a more 'structural' approach to economic policy came into fashion in official circles. The electoral needs of the Conservative Party accelerated, but did not cause, the appearance of many new policies such as the acceptance of the Robbins Report on Higher Education and the plans for the North-East, Scotland and the South-East.

A much-discussed innovation was the appointment of Mr Edward Heath in October 1963 as President of the Board of Trade with the additional many-worded title of Secretary of State for Industry, Trade and Regional Development. The Board of Trade was for most of the post-war period officially responsible for promoting industrial efficiency as well as for the government's relations with particular industries; and it was also in charge of Britain's overseas trade policy. Yet it had hitherto occupied a surprisingly lowly place in policy-making. The title of Secretary of State, of which only a limited number can be created without a special Act of Parliament, together with the appointment to the post of an energetic politician, who was clearly a front-runner for the Tory leadership, was meant to redress the balance. Yet with the exception of regional policy there was no change in the actual function of the Board of Trade or its role in broader economic policy-making.

When Mr Heath was first appointed every political columnist speculated about a coming clash between him and Maudling. The two, of course, were rivals for the Conservative succession and – although broadly in the same segment of the Party – were temperamentally poles apart. The stock witticism was that the Conservatives would now provide a preview of the fight confidently expected between Mr George Brown and Mr James Callaghan, who were being groomed for the Economics Ministry and the Exchequer respectively in a Labour government. Yet the promised Maudling–Heath clash failed to materialize, partly because of the painstaking diplomatic efforts of the two men's Permanent Secretaries to keep them from wandering into each other's gardens.

Another reason was that temperamentally Mr Heath's interest was in detailed micro-economic problems, and he made no real attempt to direct economic strategy from the Board of Trade. With a growing payments deficit, and an election looming which the Tories were not expected to win, there was in any case little incentive to become involved in strategic issues of economic management. The resale price maintenance issue apart, Mr Heath's heart was in the regional-development aspects of his job, where he had a greater impact than was generally realized.

An unfortunate effect of Mr Heath's experience is that it encouraged him later to overestimate the potential influence, especially in the short- and medium-term, of structural reforms, and to underestimate the importance of broader economic management. This was a similar error to that made by Mr Wilson. It was a national misfortune (although not entirely a coincidence) that both Party leaders since the middle 1960s have been ex-Presidents of the Board of Trade neither of whom had had the experience of being Chancellor.

An impediment to change in 1963–4, as at other periods, was the national hypocrisy about modernization and change. The fashionable belief among both parties for a long time was that if a country was to get moving it needed not a new financial policy but more fundamental changes in its industrial and business structure. Yet whenever any such structural change was proposed opposition immediately burst out from all sides, as Mr Heath found out when he brought in his famous Bill to abolish resale price maintenance. The Labour Party, to its discredit, simply abstained while large numbers of Conservative MPs – Cabinet colleagues as well as backbenchers – made no attempt to conceal their opposition.

A number of other worthwhile reforms were introduced in the last year of the 1959–64 Parliament. Industrial Training Boards were set up, more generous grants were provided for training in the high-unemployment areas, 'Little Neddies' were set up for individual industries and new agencies were formed to promote industrial building, all achievements for which the Conservatives were oddly reluctant to claim credit later. Much of the small print of the 1965 National Plan, and Mr Wilson's own 'purposive physical intervention' had already been enacted before Labour came to office.

8

THREE TRAUMATIC YEARS: THE LABOUR GOVERNMENT, 1964 TO THE 1967 DEVALUATION

Labour's economic philosophy: the initial phase: the collapse of confidence: the attack on the capital account: uncreative tensions: a Statement of Intent: the DEA's work: the first false dawn: the selective employment tax: blown off course: the July measures: the second false dawn: home-based expansion: a regional payroll subsidy: the beginning of the end: physical intervention – a last attempt: 'The centre cannot hold': the devaluation timetable: 'The pound in your pocket'

THE verdict reached in an earlier chapter on Mr Selwyn Lloyd's record at the Treasury was that his management of the economy was undistinguished, but that he deserved to be remembered for the changes he inaugurated in the long-term environment in which that management took place. The same can be repeated *fortissimo* of the 1964 Labour government in its first three years in office.

The Bank of International Settlements, in an analytical summary of the events that led up to the 1967 devaluation, remarks: 'It is likely that sterling was an overvalued currency by the beginning of the 1960s and that the situation had remained tenable only because of the improvement in the terms of trade.'[1] Nor were such opinions reached only with hindsight. Mr Callaghan confessed to the House of Commons that a month after taking office on 16 October 1964 he was advised by a 'very senior monetary authority in Europe'[2] that sterling was in fundamental disequilibrium and ought to be devalued by 10–15 per cent. It subsequently turned out that the authority in question was no less than

1. *38th Annual Report, 1967–8*, Basle, June 1968, p. 18.
2. *Hansard* for 20 November 1967, columns 945–6.

Emile van Lennep, then chairman of the EEC Monetary Committee and of OECD's key Working Party Three. He was accompanied by Thorkil Kristensen, the OECD's Secretary-General.

Most published accounts suggest that the initial 'irrevocable' decision not to devalue was taken within a day or two of the formation of the new government and taken largely on political grounds.[3] It was apparently thought that another devaluation would be disastrous for Labour, as well as alienate the Americans. Harold Wilson himself also held the view that it was an inappropriate remedy, as the basic problems of the British economy were physical and structural. From then all reference to the subject was forbidden and it became known as 'the great unmentionable'.

If the Prime Minister's mind was closed to argument on the exchange rate,[4] irrespective of any new facts and figures which might be produced, his best course would have been to have deflated in October 1964, and then proceeded to run the economy at a higher margin of unemployment. Quite how severe a loss of production and employment would have been required to remove the fundamental disequilibrium by deflationary measures in 1964 is debatable. It certainly cannot be assumed that an increase in unemployment to the 'Paish' margin of $2-2\frac{1}{2}$ per cent would itself have been sufficient. For it is wishful thinking to suppose that internal and external equilibrium necessarily are the same thing. But at least relative money wages, costs and prices would have been considerably lower than they were when Mr Wilson deflated in July 1966, and international indebtedness would not have reached the same proportions.

The really serious mistake of the Labour government,

3. See, for instance, Henry Brandon: *In the Red, The Struggle for Sterling*, André Deutsch, 1966.

4. Or on long-term trade controls, if these really were an alternative, which I doubt.

after both the 1964 and 1966 elections, was to refuse to admit that a choice between devaluation and relying on unaccompanied deflation had become necessary. The result was an eventual devaluation, which in all but the technical sense was forced, at the worst possible time internationally, when resources not only of foreign exchange, but of confidence, patience and credibility had all been nearly exhausted. Trying to get the best of both worlds, the government succeeded in achieving the worst.

Although no one involved can contract out of some share, the primary responsibility for this policy – or rather non-policy – rested during the crucial period of 1964–6 with the political leaders, rather than with Civil Servants, whether regular or irregular. Despite the ban on discussion of the subject, the ministers concerned were given ample warning of the implications of a refusal to devalue, and all options had their spokesmen among officials and advisers. But the Prime Minister, with support from enough of his colleagues to allow him to continue, persisted in believing in the face of accumulating evidence that there was some mysterious kind of 'direct physical intervention' which could provide a 'third way' to enable him to avoid both devaluation and deflation. From this mistake all else followed.

It is unnecessary to look around for Hungarian scapegoats for the disappointing performance of the Labour government after 1964, when a Prime Minister could say, as Mr Wilson did to the New York Economic Club in April 1965: 'If an incoming Government were at any time likely to consider devaluing the nation's currency, political considerations would have dictated doing it on that first day, when the fault would clearly and unequivocally lie with those who had charge of the nation's affairs for 13 years. So that decision, once taken, was a decision for good.'

This is a remarkable approach to a major decision of policy – as if it were possible to give a once-for-all answer to the question of whether the currency is overvalued in a few hours on the first day of a government. There were in act numerous occasions in 1965 when the government could (truthfully) have said that the fundamental disequilibrium it inherited was larger than it at first realized and that devaluation would after all be necessary. After the second election of March 1966, when the government had a majority of 97, there was no further justification for inaction, even of a political kind. The result of this refusal to choose between alternatives was that the government had to deflate much more severely in July 1966 – and at a much more unsuitable time in the cycle – than if it had acted earlier. Then in 1967 it became alarmed at the severity of its own deflation and embarked on a home-market consumer-based Macmillanesque revival of just the kind which Harold Wilson had vowed never to emulate. Finally, in November 1967, the government was forced to embark on the devaluation which it had been the main object of its policy for the previous three years to prevent.

LABOUR'S ECONOMIC PHILOSOPHY

To ascribe everything that went wrong entirely to lack of courage, or to misguided political manoeuvring, would be a gross oversimplification. Mr Wilson and some of his leading colleagues sincerely and profoundly believed that a direct 'physical' attack on the economy's weaknesses could succeed where 'financial tinkering' had failed. This belief was compounded of several elements. There was (and still is) a strong current of opinion, represented in Conservative as well as Labour circles, which was impatient of Keynesian (or any other type of) management of demand and the balance of payments, and saw 'more fundamental' structural reform as an alternative. To this was added a strong bias against the global approach in favour of an industry-by-industry and firm-by-firm attack. Thirdly there was a preference for direct 'physical' methods over financial forms of regulation. Interestingly enough, apart from a few highly emotive areas such as housing and rents, the Labour leaders of the mid 1960s had no great liking for controls as such; they believed that once 'theology' was cast aside, industrial and trade union leaders would be prepared to cooperate on a common-sense basis.

There were certain contradictions in this approach from the beginning. Much of Labour's appeal to some of the younger members of the managerial classes in 1964 was based on the belief that it was on their side against 'board-room deadwood'. Yet Labour leaders were still deeply ambivalent about the profit motive (whether corporate or personal) which strongly motivated this new generation. Ministers were aware at the back of their minds that many of the new techniques which their departments preached, such as 'Discounted Cash Flow', were primarily devices for maximizing profits and meaningless on any other assumptions; but, despite several speeches in favour of profits, a residual suspicion of the market economy remained, and appeared to the business community greater than it really was.

At a more personal level there was a contradiction between Harold Wilson's economic thinking, which put most emphasis on long-term structural change, and his political penchant for playing things by ear. This presupposed a dichotomy between political decisions and economic planning which did not exist in reality. The conflict was symbolized by the contrast between the Prime Minister's warm endorsement of Fulton's criticism of the amateur Civil Service administrators, who were said to move through a series of disconnected jobs without time to learn any of them, on the one hand, and the record turnover among his own ministers, on the other.

Despite these contradictions a number of Labour's structural reforms were well worth while and some were indeed an extension in a major key of the new-look policies adopted by the Conservatives in the early 1960s. The failure of the Labour government's overall economic strategy in 1964–7, with which this chapter is largely concerned, is not the whole of the story.

THE INITIAL PHASE

The first economic actions of the Labour government followed directly from the plans laid by its Conservative predecessors. Of the two import-saving schemes prepared during Mr Maudling's tenure – an import surcharge and import quotas – the incoming ministers chose the surcharge, levied at a rate of 15 per cent. This was the main new measure in the statement *The Economic Situation*, issued on 26 October 1964, ten days after the new government had taken office with a majority of three.

A subsidiary measure was the direct rebate on exports equivalent to the average amount of indirect tax paid. International agreements allow countries to refund indirect taxes such as purchase tax or oil duties which fall on export costs, but not direct taxes falling on incomes, profits or payrolls. The average value of the rebate was nearly 2 per cent. The idea had been in existence since at least the early 1960s, but had previously been rejected because of fears that the rebate method of compensating for indirect taxes might be challenged by Britain's trading partners. The export rebate was, however, extremely small by comparison with the import surcharge, which formed the greater part of the package. Mr Maudling's comment that the new government inherited 'our problems and our remedies' was basically correct, however much it irritated partisan myth-makers on both sides.

The text of the White Paper contained some strange features. Paragraph 7 stated: 'Apart from special problems of individual areas and a limited number of industries there is no undue pressure on resources calling for action.' By the standards of judgement normally used by Treasury economists and explained in Chapter 3 of this book, there certainly was excess pressure on resources. Unemployment was $1\frac{1}{2}$ per cent and shortages of capacity or manpower were reported as bottlenecks in several industries. The statement was a gratuitous present to Conservative spokes-men, who subsequently quoted it, times without number, as proof that the inflationary pressures were entirely a product of the change of administration. The same paragraph also proclaimed: 'The Government reject any policy based on a return to stop-go economics' – an extraordinarily self-con-fident assertion for ministers who had just summarily re-jected devaluation on political grounds and whose own 'physical' remedies were completely untried.

Another feature of the White Paper was the extreme haste with which it was launched (labelled by some as 'the hundred-days itch'). A new set of ministers might have been expected to take a little time for reflection, especially as there was surprisingly little pressure on sterling in this initial period. One unfortunate result of this excessive speed was the remark about re-examining urgently the Anglo-French supersonic Concorde, from which it did not in the end prove possible, for legal reasons, to withdraw.

The most controversial feature of the White Paper was the decision to prolaim to the whole world the new official estimate of an £800m. balance-of-payments deficit for 1964. When all allowances have been made for the continu-ing election atmosphere, the trumpeting of the 'inherit-ance' made the government's own task far more difficult. Not only did it have an immediately damaging effect, but it contributed to a more *conservative* climate of opinion in which economic policy was judged entirely by the balance of payments, and international borrowing was regarded as a sin. There is no doubt that ministers were genuinely shocked by the size of the deficit. Yet in one sense they appeared to underestimate its true magnitude. Ministers put all the emphasis in their pronouncements on the 1964 figure, which was swollen by an exceptionally heavy net outflow of long-term capital and abnormally rapid stock-building, instead of on the element of the deficit that was likely to continue. In this way they gave the impression (not least to many 'sound finance' Tories) that the balance-of-payments problem was simply the result of a pre-election aberration by Mr Maudling, which could easily be corrected by stricter policies.

THE COLLAPSE OF CONFIDENCE

Within a month of the publication of the confident White Paper of 26 October one of the most savage of all sterling crises had erupted. There were so many items in the confused train of events that preceded the collapse of confidence that an indefinite number of rival explanations can be offered, and the most illuminating course may be to set out first the bare chronology of the crisis.

Monday	26 October	White Paper: *The Economic Situation*
Wednesday	11 November	Autumn Budget
Monday	16 November	Prime Minister at the Mansion House talks about not hesitating to take further steps to secure strength of sterling
Thursday	19 November	(*a*) Bank Rate not raised (*b*) EFTA Ministers Council Meeting
Sunday	22 November	Crisis week-end meeting at Chequers
Monday	23 November	Bank Rate raised from 5 to 7 per cent
Wednesday	25 November	$3,000m. package of standby credits
Thursday	2 December	UK draws $1,000m. IMF standby credit
Wednesday	8 December	Squeeze on bank credit.

The story goes back in fact to the way in which the surcharge was handled before publication day. According to Henry Brandon,[5] American leaders had a personal briefing

5. op. cit.

the previous weekend from Sir Eric Roll, the retiring British Economic Minister, who had just been appointed Permanent Secretary of the Department of Economic Affairs. By contrast European capitals were informed by 'diplomatic cables arriving on a Saturday, when Foreign Offices in any case are reduced to duty officers'. Brandon even suggests that two members of the US Administration themselves suggested that the Germans and Dutch should be informed, but too late to have any effect. The doctrine of the special relationship with the US, which had contributed so much to Macmillan's downfall, was working its unfortunate spell on a Labour Administration which had not appreciated how much the balance of financial power had shifted towards Europe since it had last been in office in 1951.

International hostility towards the surcharge was further aggravated by the fact that it was illegal according to both the GATT and EFTA Treaties. In fact an import surcharge – which gives every overseas supplier the same hurdle to jump over – is much less arbitrary and protectionist than quota restrictions. But because of a legal anachronism quotas are permissible as a temporary measure for countries with a payments deficit, while a surcharge is not.

The popular belief inside Britain that the surcharge was ineffective was wide of the mark. It was based largely on the simple observation that there was no *reduction* between 1964 and 1965 in the volume of imports affected by it. The correct comparison is with what would have happened in the absence of the surcharge. With domestic demand rising, both absolutely and in relation to capacity, imports would almost certainly have risen a good deal more without it. The effect was, however, lower than had been hoped, because importers, believing it to be temporary, absorbed some of it themselves. Domestic producers had, for the same reason, little incentive to develop substitutes. With hindsight it would probably have paid Britain to have stuck to the letter rather than to the spirit of the law and also obtained a more predictable result by using quotas.

The desirability of overhauling the list of internationally permitted balance-of-payments actions remains. If flexible exchange rates are regarded as too risky, import surcharges and export rebates – now rechristened 'border tax measures' – are probably the least disruptive alternatives.

Despite the rumbling about the surcharge in GATT and EFTA, relative calm prevailed until the autumn Budget of 11 November. The aim of the Budget was to off-set the potential inflationary effects of the increases in pensions and other benefits, and the abolition of Health Service charges, also announced by Mr Callaghan in his Budget Speech. In crude revenue terms the Budget was more than enough for the purpose. The increase of 6d. in the standard rate of income tax, combined with the higher petrol duty, was expected to yield £215m. in a full year – more than the Exchequer would have to find for the new benefits.[6]

The economic arithmetic was, however, very different. The increase in benefits, as the National Institute pointed out at the time, was almost entirely reflected in consumer spending. The increase in income tax (which was not extended to the reduced rates) was to a considerable extent at the expense of personal and company savings. The higher employers' National Insurance contributions could only be expected to reduce demand indirectly and belatedly, as they worked through into price increases. It would, however, be equally wrong to go to the other extreme. The November 1964 Budget, together with the surcharge and the social service changes, was intended to be neutral in economic terms. If it in fact turned out inflationary, it was so by only a small margin and could have played only a minor role in the overheating of the economy in 1965 and early 1966.

It was not any such fine economic arithmetic that

6. The import surcharge itself was deflationary to the extent that it removed spending money from people's pockets, but inflationary to the extent that it directed demand to home producers.

upset the financial markets. The feature of the Budget that caused the greatest outcry was Mr Callaghan's foreshadowing of his proposals for Corporation and Capital Gains Tax, due to be revealed in full the following April. The uncertainty created was transmitted to the foreign exchange market, both directly and via the gilt-edged market.

This episode has sometimes been used as an argument against any advance discussion of Budget proposals. But the main reason for the outcry was not that the proposals were disclosed before Budget Day and comments invited, but that the initial announcement did not make clear the precise nature of the government's own proposals.

A more important query is whether ministers were right to give such priority to two such highly complicated measures, which had no direct bearing on the deficit which they had themselves highlighted. The Capital Gains Tax might have been justified as a social measure to buy union support for an incomes policy – even though such gestures do not seem ever to have had any practical effect on wage settlements. The Corporation Tax lacked even that degree of justification; but it was much the more complicated of the two measures, and for years afterwards the Inland Revenue (and private accountants) were too busy digesting it to contemplate more worthwhile reforms. The most that could be said for it was that it might have had some modest long-run effect on the balance of inward and outward investment. This was an incidental bonus which could have been obtained more simply.

Overseas opinion, especially on the Continent, was probably as much influenced by the social service benefits as by the proposed new taxes. Some holders of sterling did not realize that higher National Insurance contributions would finance the greater part of the new benefits; but it is doubtful if the growing hostility to the new government in European political and financial circles can be explained by such technical misunderstandings. The hostility reflected a more generalized resentment that, after having shouted from the rooftops about the mess they inherited, the new ministers were showing that they still put welfare benefits above economic recovery. In this syndrome free prescriptions played a role out of all proportion to their very trivial Budgetary importance. They became a symbol to financial opinion at home and abroad of Labour's alleged tendency to put party doctrine before urgent economic needs.

The two days after the Budget were followed, in the words of the Bank of England Bulletin, by 'heavy sales of sterling from Europe and North America'. The Prime Minister tried to stem the tide by proclaiming at Guildhall the following Monday his 'determination to keep sterling strong'. He expressed a degree of enthusiasm for the sterling area and the Commonwealth, which his Conservative predecessors would have been embarrassed to voice. He added that he 'would not hesitate to take any further steps that at any time are, or become, necessary' to protect sterling. These words were taken as the conventional formula preceding an increase in Bank Rate. Yet Mr Wilson's words – which some commentators thought Churchillian – were not followed by any action, and on Thursday 19 November, Bank Rate was still at 5 per cent. From then on, in the Bank of England's words, the 'pressure on sterling intensified'. On the Friday sales were 'exceptionally large'. The panic was further intensified by the belief in the City and foreign centres that the advice of the Governor of the Bank of England, Lord Cromer, had been overridden. Henry Brandon believes that Mr Wilson's reluctance to raise Bank Rate was due to a doubt about how President Johnson would react. This was partly a fear that the President would find an increase embarrassing, because of the probable impact on American rates, and partly a hope that Johnson would help him out with a loan.

On that very same Thursday there took place one of the worst in the series of international meetings on the surcharge, that of the EFTA Ministerial Council. The subsequent communiqué included an undertaking that a beginning would be made in reducing the surcharge 'in a matter of months'. The *Financial Times* diplomatic correspondent reported that the Foreign Secretary, Patrick Gordon Walker, and the President of the Board of Trade, Douglas Jay, had to telephone London at 4.15 a.m. on 20 November to obtain approval for this undertaking.

By the following weekend the run on sterling had reached a point at which action could be delayed no further; the newspapers reported that a Chequers ministerial meeting over the weekend of 21–2 November, originally called to discuss the defence review, had been attended by Lord Cromer as well as the service chiefs; and on the following Monday Bank Rate was raised from 5 to 7 per cent. Yet, instead of slowing down, the flight from the pound accelerated, and on the Tuesday and Wednesday sales of sterling were, in the Bank of England's words, 'massive and growing'.

Some City critics attributed the perverse reaction to the fact that Bank Rate had been raised on a Monday instead of the normal Thursday – which the market, not unreasonably, regarded as a sign of panic. Others, going a little deeper, already spotted the government's growing habit of talking with two different voices to two different audiences. While the Bank Rate increase was presented to overseas and financial opinion as a sign of the government's readiness to take harsh measures, it was presented at home as a technical adjustment, which was not intended to deflate demand. Indeed, special arrangements were made to insulate local authorities from the higher borrowing costs. The run on the pound was due to the very natural desire of holders of sterling to protect themselves against the threat of devaluation; and signs of government panic only increased their fears.

On 25 November there was a dramatic announcement from the Bank of England that eleven central banks, together with the Bank for International Settlements and the

US Export-Import Bank, had arranged a further $3,000m. of short-term credits which Britain could draw upon to protect the pound. The exercise seems to have been a combined operation, arranged almost overnight by the US and British monetary authorities.

Even this unprecedented credit did no more than slow down the outflow of funds from London. The Bank of England stated that 'throughout December' there was 'a very heavy demand for foreign exchange for forward delivery'. Outright sales of sterling were much less than in November, 'although still substantial by normal standards'. On 2 December Britain drew its £357m. ($1,000m.) from the IMF and used the proceeds to pay off the bulk of the central bank credits. But by the end of the year the amount of central bank aid outstanding had risen to £188m. ($526m.). In addition the reserves had fallen by £122m. over the year.

The last pretence that the government was not deflating was dropped by 8 December 1964, although the first move was extremely mild. The clearing banks were told that they could expect no relief from their liquidity troubles in the period of seasonal pressure in March, as it was official policy to slow down the rate of growth of bank advances.

THE ATTACK ON THE CAPITAL ACCOUNT

The pressure on sterling abated a little in the New Year of 1965 after the publication of better December trade figures. But a further outflow began in February under the combined impact of US measures to repatriate liquid funds from abroad and a deterioration in the January trade figures. The Bank of England's announcement in February of a renewal of the $3,000m. central bank credits, pending a fresh approach to the IMF, did not remove the underlying unease.

Meanwhile, another EFTA meeting on 29 January demanded an immediate cut in the surcharge and denounced the export rebate into the bargain. Admittedly the import surcharge was intended to be temporary. But the government's haste in acceding to this request was remarkable, and on 22 February it announced a reduction to 10 per cent to take effect from the end of April. The decision was extremely difficult to reconcile with published forecasts, such as those of the National Institute, which predicted an overall deficit of well over £200m. for 1965, even with a 10 per cent surcharge, and one of over £350m. for 1966 without the charge.

As the Budget approached, sales of sterling became very heavy again, and rumours grew that the Chancellor would announce devaluation. But the rumours overestimated the willingness of ministers to draw the right lesson from the inheritance about which they spoke so much. By this time the government was working to announced targets. There was the growth target, on which the National Plan was based, of a 25 per cent increase in output between 1964 and 1970, involving an average annual increase of about 3·8 per cent; there was also a short-term balance-of-payments target. This was to move out of deficit (without the aid of the surcharge) by the end of 1966. The Budget turned out to be sufficiently deflationary to undermine the credibility of the National Plan targets, but not nearly deflationary enough to eliminate the payments deficit at the $2·80 exchange rate.

The 1965 Budget was supposed to 'take £250m.' out of the economy at an annual rate. But only half this amount (expressed in revenue terms) came from the higher drink and tobacco duties and other consumer taxes. The remainder came from a miscellaneous variety of measures such as the abolition of entertainment allowances as a business expense, and the Capital Gains Tax; even the cancellation of the TSR2 was brought into the calculation. The Budget did not, however, rely entirely on reducing the growth of domestic demand to tackle the balance of payments. Direct measures to improve the capital account were also announced. The most important of these was a requirement that 25 per cent of the proceeds of the sale by UK residents of overseas securities had to be handed over to the authorites in exchange for sterling at the official rate, whereas previously the entire proceeds could be reinvested overseas (or sold to other investors in the 'investment dollar' market). This innovation probably saved £70–100m. of foreign exchange per annum. It was also hoped that the Corporation Tax would discourage outward investment and encourage the inward variety. Further measures to reduce net overseas investment followed in later economic packages. After July 1965, for example, direct investment outside the sterling area had to be financed from overseas borrowing on the investment currency market, as official exchange was no longer made available. In April 1966 a 'voluntary programme' was announced to slow down the outflow of direct investment to developed sterling-area countries. This was initially intended for two years, but later renewed. By 1967 the net outflow was down to about £60m. Without the controls it would certainly have been running at a much higher level.

Such actions admittedly carried with them a threat to the growth of investment income from abroad. The continuing annual gain to the balance of payments, including both profits and induced exports, for every £100 of direct overseas investment worked out according to the Reddaway Report on average at only about £9, assuming that it was financed entirely from the reserves.[7] (The greater the resort to local borrowing the greater is the balance-of-payments return for Britain.) Saving the £100 on the reserves here and now was regarded as more important, so long as the balance of payments remained in fundamental disequilibrium.

Altogether the Labour government showed itself more ready to take direct action on the balance of payments than its predecessors. Apart from the capital account and the

7. *Effects of UK Direct Investment Overseas*, Cambridge University Press, 1967.

export rebate already mentioned, the growth of government overseas spending was brought to a halt in 1966, after which it fell slightly. There were also a number of minor measures, which together must have had a marginal effect, such as the increased sums for export promotion, including subsidies for trade missions and industry-wide market research, and improvements in export credit. The Selective Employment Tax originally contained a very small inbuilt export subsidy; and the investment grants which replaced the old allowances were deliberately concentrated on manufacturing industries, because, on average, a high proportion of manufactured goods was sold abroad.

The impact of direct action of the peripheral kind attempted by the Labour government was thus inadequate to the scale of the problem. Economists, and commentators writing on government economic policy, pointed this out frequently enough. But the full implication took time to dawn on the foreign exchange market. The Budget on 6 April was followed on 14 April by the Prime Minister's address to the Economic Club of New York, already cited, when he spoke of the government's 'unalterable determination to maintain the value of the pound' and that those who doubted this determination were 'today licking their wounds'. He was, of course, speaking 'with absolute frankness as befits a representative of Britain talking to an audience of friends, not least because as a Yorkshireman who believes in speaking his mind I sometimes get a little tired of the cant and mumbo-jumbo with which issues of this kind are cloaked'. The temptation to carry on quoting must be resisted. The speech made a deep impression on a supposedly hard-boiled audience of bankers and industrialists.

Afterwards the authorities actually took in some foreign exchange and a modest inflow continued until nearly the end of May. Meanwhile the Budget was followed by a call to the banks for Special Deposits on 29 April, and on 5 May a 5 per cent ceiling was imposed on the growth of advances in the year up to March 1966. On 25 May a further drawing of \$1,400m. (£500m.) was made from the IMF, together with a parallel Swiss credit of £14m. The greater part of this sum had to be used to repay the fresh central bank borrowings which had been made since the December Fund drawing. Nevertheless, the Bank of England took advantage of the lull in the foreign exchange market to reduce Bank Rate to 6 per cent on 3 June, which was offset by a slight stiffening in hire-purchase regulations.

The lull was short-lived. Exports stopped rising between the first and second quarters of 1965, while imports continued to grow and the trade deficit was nearly as large as in 1964, despite the surcharge. Wages were continuing to rise much faster than the recommended norm of 3–3½ per cent under the voluntary incomes policy. Foreign opinion was disturbed by very heavy local-authority borrowings from the Public Loans Works Board (not quite appreciating that this represented mainly a change in the source of finance). The government's earlier deflationary measures seemed to be slow in working through to the labour market, and unemployment remained, even on a seasonally corrected basis, at the extremely low level of 1·2 per cent. Many of the same industrialists who had been behind the earlier growth agitation became alarmed by labour shortages and began to press for further deflation. They soon had their way.

The exceptionally bad trade figures published in the middle of June set off another heavy burst of sterling sales, and this was followed by another bad period in the second half of July. Press reports at the time also suggested that there had been a change of front in Washington. Previously the US had wanted Britain's growth experiment to continue and had supported the surcharge as an alternative to a domestic clamp-down. But now, according to these reports, President Johnson's Administration was urging heavy curbs on home demand as the only way of saving the pound. Mr Callaghan, who flew to Washington on 29 June, had the opportunity to confirm this.

In any case, on 27 July the Chancellor announced what was intended to be the severest package of restrictions so far introduced by the Labour government. Hire-purchase restrictions were tightened further; the starting dates on some public-sector capital projects were postponed for six months; loan sanctions for local authorities were limted. These, together with other restrictions made in local-authority and government investment, were supposed to amount to £200m. in a full year. In addition building licences were introduced for commercial projects.

It was as a result of the July 1965 package – a full year before the more famous 1966 measures – that many close students became finally convinced that the government had abandoned its growth and employment objectives, and would be prepared to deflate to the extent necessary to maintain the exchange rate. Thus the National Plan was written off by many people two months before it was published. The National Institute, in its August 1965 issue, forecast that unemployment would rise to $2-2\frac{1}{2}$ per cent by the end of 1966 and that there would also be, by that time, a small balance-of-payments surplus 'at the cost of slowing down the rise in national output nearly to a stop'. Things did not in practice work out that way; but economic opinion clearly believed that a decision in favour of uninhibited deflation, as the alternative to devaluation, had been taken in principle.

It took time for the package of July 1965 to affect the foreign exchange market. Indeed, pressure on sterling continued for most of August, aggravated by the excessive frankness of the published July reserve figures. Instead of offsetting nearly all the true loss by central bank borrowing, as had become normal custom, the authorities decided to show an actual loss of £50m. in addition to undisclosed borrowing.

Towards the end of August the selling pressure on sterling appeared, according to the Bank of England, 'to have exhausted itself'. It also became known at about that time that the government was talking to unions and employers about a compulsory 'early warning' system for notifying the government of prospective wage and price increases. After a marathon day-long session with the TUC General Council at the Metropole Hotel in Brighton, Mr George Brown was able to announce the plan on 2 September with official union blessing. This was endorsed by the full TUC annual conference on 8 September. Press reports suggested that the Americans were pressing for some direct action on wages as a *quid pro quo* for the latest package of central bank standby credits. This was announced by the Bank of England on 10 September. Ten central banks were participating in the latest package to replace the earlier support that had lapsed.

The sterling rate, which had already begun to recover, rose further after the announcement. Even if the initial rise was due to central bank buying, as was widely suggested at the time, the recovery soon took on a momentum of its own. Some of those who had gone short of sterling, for speculative or precautionary reasons, hurried to buy back pounds, and some of the adverse 'leads and lags' began to be reversed. In the remainder of the year the reserves rose a little and considerable amounts of central bank assistance were repaid. The autumn of 1965 and subsequent winter saw the first false dawn to be experienced by the Labour government. It was left to a few academics and journalists to point out that the problem of combining reasonable growth and employment with balance-of-payments stability was as far from solution as ever.

UNCREATIVE TENSIONS

This lull at the end of 1965 provides a convenient opportunity to look at some of the changes in the machinery of government, as well as at some of the longer-term policies of the new ministers. Five new departments were established immediately after the 1964 election – the Department of

Economic Affairs, the Ministry of Technology, the Overseas Development Ministry and the Ministry of Land and National Resources (the latter was disbanded in 1967) and the Welsh Office.

The most important of these was, of course, the DEA, under Mr George Brown, who was First Secretary of State, and *de facto* deputy Prime Minister. The respective roles of the DEA and Treasury were dogged by confusion and misunderstanding from the very beginning. Mr George Brown's concept of the DEA, as he subsequently explained, was that of a single major overlord department, in charge of all aspects of economic policy; the other economic departments, such as the Treasury, the Board of Trade and the Ministry of Labour, would have been specialized executive arms, carrying out the policy laid down at the centre.[8] (An analogy would be that of the relationship of the revenue departments to the Treasury under traditional arrangements, or the Service ministers to the Minister of Defence.)

It was not my impression, even before the 1964 election, that Mr Wilson thought of the matter in these terms. The impression he gave was that rival views on economic strategy, instead of being argued out in the depths of the official machine, would be represented by different ministers, which would bring the Prime Minister into the picture in a way that had not happened under the Conservatives. In any case Mr Brown's original conception, as he subsequently wrote, 'never really went into effect'. It could hardly have done so when the Treasury was given to the Number Three man in the Labour hierarchy who had himself been a candidate for the leadership in 1963, and who could not reasonably have been expected to act as an executant to the policies of another minister.

The result was a dual system of economic control with the Department of Economic Affairs and the Treasury enjoying overlapping responsibility over a wide field. Thanks

8. 'Why the DEA lost to the Treasury Knights', *Sunday Times*, 31 March 1968.

to the energy of Mr George Brown, and to the spirit that reigned among the staff in the early days, the DEA did a much better job than might have been expected from the confused logic of the situation. Established Civil Servants were forced to re-examine many of their long-held assumptions and many of them were – in retrospect at least – glad of the experience. The DEA under Mr Brown was the least politically doctrinaire of departments; it was the first to appoint 'industrial advisers' seconded from senior management posts, and it was normally the spokesman for industry, when industrial needs conflicted with other objectives of policy. Yet it would be wrong to disguise my view that these aims would have been better achieved without the catastrophic experiment of two rival economic ministers locked together in uncreative tension, with the Prime Minister swinging sometimes one way and sometimes the other on no known principle.

The division of responsibility between the two departments, eventually laid down in a 'Concordat' between them, was supposed to be that (a) the DEA would concentrate on the long term and the Treasury on the short term; and (b) the DEA would concentrate on 'physical resources' and the Treasury on finance.

The distinction rested on a combination of conservative illusions about the supposed autonomy of finance, and equally old-fashioned socialist ideas about the physical control of industry. This was apparent well before the 1964 election, when the Wilsonian form of the idea was first floated. There seems no reason to change the original conclusion on the subject in the 1964 edition of this book:

Much in the preceding pages would point in the same direction as the Production or Economics Ministry favoured by the Labour and Liberal Parties. But the snag in most of these plans is that they assume that there is something called 'finance' quite apart from economics and production. In fact, of course, the instruments by which production is influenced in this country are the Budget, monetary policy, exchange rate policy, and one or two very general controls. Despite all the talk of 'physical intervention', this is likely to remain the case. If the Treasury remains responsible for the balance of payments, for taxation, for the Bank Rate, and for the use of devices like the Regulator, it is likely to remain the effective economic ministry, whatever nominal changes are made.

Even before 1964 the interaction between Chancellor, Treasury officials, and the Bank of England, with the Prime Minister in the background, produced a worse result than if any one supreme authority had been given its head. If this was the situation before 1964, it was *a fortiori* worse during the years of the Wilson–Brown–Callaghan triumvirate. If any one minister had been placed in charge of the economy, the result would certainly have been at least a little better than what actually transpired.

Interestingly enough, both George Brown and Douglas Jay – who are often believed to represent opposing points of view on the subject – have been at one in emphasizing the need for unified control over economic management. Mr Jay envisaged that minister as the Chancellor.[9] Mr Brown envisaged a DEA in ultimate control of short- and long-term economic strategy with a subordinate Ministry of Finance carrying out the details in a 'mechanistic' way. Neither, however, advocated the institutionalized conflict of views which Mr Wilson actually established.

There is no art in giving the balance of payments priority and leaving it to the man down the corridor to make a fuss about growth and employment. Equally there is no art in giving expansion the maximum priority, if you do not have the responsibility for the balance of payments and sterling. The art is to find a way of managing demand and the balance of payments which will combine satisfactory expansion with price stability and external solvency. It is difficult to think of a worse way of achieving this than the artificially fostered ministerial rivalries of Labour's early years.

9. 'Government Control of the Economy', *Political Quarterly*, April–June 1968.

A STATEMENT OF INTENT

Within this system of unsatisfactory departmental relationships there were certain tasks where the DEA took the undisputed lead. The first of these, which took up a great deal of the personal time of the First Secretary, was prices and incomes. The zest and energy with which Mr George Brown threw himself into the task of obtaining a voluntary policy won the admiration of many on both sides of industry. Moreover, he won the consent of the unions to the principle of wage restraint with far fewer concessions to the anti-profit tradition of the Labour movement than were made later when the policy came under different control. In the Statement of Intent, as well as in all the First Secretary's speeches, the principle was accepted that profits were a different kind of animal from wages and were best regulated at an aggregate level through the tax system. For this was the only way of enabling the more efficient firms to increase their profits and dividends at the expense of the less successful, while still providing a backstop to make sure that wage restraint did not lead to an increase in the share of *total* profits in the national income.

The government faced two choices in October 1964. It could either have gone for a temporary wage freeze or attempted to lay the basis for a long-term incomes policy. Those who argued that the government should have gone for a wage freeze in 1964 were, in my view, correct. A freeze in 1964 would not have been enough to restore Britain's international competitive position, but it might have prevented it from deteriorating further during a crucial period. It would have done more good than the freeze imposed in 1966 after two further turns of the inflationary spiral. In rejecting this point of view George Brown was quite deliberately giving up the chance of a spectacular short-term success in the hope of establishing a new system of wage determination which he believed would be of permanent value for the future.

Granted Mr Brown's original choice of objective, the signature by management and trade union representatives of the Joint Statement of Intent on 16 December – two months after the government had taken office – was a notable achievement. It does not detract from the achievement to say that this approach was very much a continuation of the previous government's attempt at a voluntary incomes policy; Mr Maudling, it will be recalled, had tried very hard to obtain a similar statement earlier in the year.

The text of the Statement of Intent is reprinted on page 316. Someone reading the document without prior knowledge would not have been able to guess under which party it had been issued; but he would have a much better chance of guessing the period in British history when it was issued. The elaborate prices and incomes machinery probably had to be given a trial, and the highly desirable measures mentioned in Paragraph 7 for helping market forces to work may have been given some impetus because of their presumed role in incomes policy. The Declaration's main fault was the assumption that individual behaviour could or should be determined by a national purpose in normal peacetime conditions. Too much was expected from entities such as management and unions which had no real power to deliver what they promised.

Another main activity specific to the Department of Economic Affairs was the preparation of the National Plan. The fact that the government had no real strategy for fulfilling the balance-of-payments requirements of the plan, and that there was a contradiction between its requirements and those of the non-devaluation pledge, was pointed out by practically all outside economists, some of whom queried the internal objectives as well. It would indeed have been remarkable if economists inside government service had been blind to these obvious points.

Although there was undoubtedly strong political pressure to secure quick publication, it is difficult to believe that the plan had any influence, one way or the other, on the outcome of the 1966 election. Perhaps the biggest draw-

JOINT STATEMENT OF INTENT
ON PRODUCTIVITY, PRICES AND INCOMES

THE OBJECTIVES

The Government's economic objective is to achieve and maintain a rapid increase in output and real incomes combined with full employment. Their social objective is to ensure that the benefits of faster growth are distributed in a way that satisfies the claims of social need and justice. In this way general confidence will be created in the purpose of the national plan and individuals will be willing to make their utmost contribution towards its implementation.

2. Essential conditions for the achievement of these objectives are a strong currency and a healthy balance of payments.

THE ECONOMIC SITUATION

3. The economic situation, while potentially strong, is at present extremely unsatisfactory. Drastic temporary measures have been taken to meet a situation in which the balance of payments was in serious deficit, with exports falling behind imports. But these measures can provide only a breathing space.

4. To achieve a more permanent solution we must improve the balance of payments, encourage exports and sharpen our competitive ability. Our longer-term interests lie in reducing the barriers to international trade. We must take urgent and vigorous action to raise productivity throughout industry and commerce, to keep increases in total money incomes in line with increases in real national output and to maintain a stable general price level. Unless we do this we shall have a slower rate of growth and a lower level of employment.

*　　　*　　　*　　　*

5. We – Government, management and unions – are resolved to take the following action in our respective spheres of responsibility.

THE GOVERNMENT

6. The Government will prepare and implement a general plan for economic development, in consultation with both sides of industry through the National Economic Development Council. This will provide for higher investment; for improving our industrial skills; for modernisation of industry; for balanced regional development; for higher exports; and for the largest possible sustained expansion of production and real incomes.

7. Much greater emphasis will be given to increasing productivity. The Government will encourage and develop policies designed to promote technological advance in industry, and to get rid of restrictive practices and prevent the abuse of monopoly power, and so improve efficiency, cut out waste, and reduce excessive prices. More vigorous policies will be pursued designed to facilitate mobility of labour and generally to make more effective use of scarce manpower resources, and to give workers a greater sense of security in the face of economic change. The Government also intend to introduce essential social improvements such as a system of earnings-related benefits, in addition to the improvements in national insurance benefits already announced.

8. The Government will set up machinery to keep a continuous watch on the general movement of prices and of money incomes of all kinds and to carry out the other functions described in paragraph 10 below. They will also use their fiscal powers or other appropriate means to correct any excessive growth in aggregate profits as compared with the growth of total wages and salaries, after allowing for short-term fluctuations.

MANAGEMENT AND UNIONS

9. We, the representatives of the Trade Union Congress, the Federation of British Industries, the British Employers' Confederation, the National Association of British Manufacturers, and the Association of British Chambers of Commerce, accept that major objectives of national policy must be:

to ensure that British industry is dynamic and that its prices are competitive;

to raise productivity and efficiency so that real national output can increase, and to keep increases in wages, salaries and other forms of incomes in line with this increase;

to keep the general level of prices stable.

10. We therefore undertake, on behalf of our members:

to encourage and lead a sustained attack on the obstacles to efficiency, whether on the part of management or of workers, and to strive for the adoption of more rigorous standards of performance at all levels;

to co-operate with the Government in endeavouring, in the face of practical problems, to give effective shape to the machinery that the Government intend to establish for the following purposes:

(i) to keep under review the general movement of prices and of money incomes of all kinds;

(ii) to examine particular cases in order to advise whether or not the behaviour of prices or of wages, salaries or other money incomes is in the national interest as defined by the Government after consultation with management and unions.

11. We stress that close attention must be paid to easing the difficulties of those affected by changed circumstances in their employment. We therefore support, in principle, the Government's proposals for earnings-related benefits and will examine sympathetically proposals for severance payments.

* * * *

12. We – Government, management and unions – are confident that by co-operating in a spirit of mutual confidence to give effect to the principles and policies described above, we and those whom we represent will be able to achieve a faster growth of real incomes and generally to promote the economic and social well-being of the country.

On behalf of the Trades Union Congress	On behalf of H.M. Government	On behalf of the Association of British Chambers of Commerce
		(Signed)
		RICHARD WILLS
		CHARLES HEY
		On behalf of the British Employers' Confederation
(Signed)	(Signed)	(Signed)
COLLISON	GEORGE BROWN	MAURICE LAING
GEORGE WOODCOCK	JAMES CALLAGHAN	GEORGE POLLOCK
	DOUGLAS JAY	
	RAY GUNTER	On behalf of the Federation of British Industries
		(Signed)
		PETER RUNGE
		NORMAN KIPPING
		On behalf of the National Association of British Manufacturers
		(Signed)
16th December, 1964.		LESLIE JENKINS
		HAROLD GRAY

back of the whole exercise was that DEA officials, who should have been working on *policies* for faster growth, had to devote too much of their time to the arithmetic and presentation of a document which assumed that the policies had already been found and accepted.

THE DEA'S WORK

The third DEA activity was industrial policy. In the early period this was based on a sector-by-sector search for ways of improving efficiency and international competitiveness. The approach soon became known to initiates as 'Catherwoodery' after Mr Fred Catherwood, a former managing director of British Aluminium, who became the first Industrial Director of the DEA, and later Director General of NEDC. The limitation of this approach in its early stages was that it worked mainly through 'Little Neddies' – part-time voluntary committees, which had neither direct powers over the industries concerned nor incentives to offer them. The market economy does not work so perfectly that the ear-stroking activities of the 'Little Neddies' can be ruled out of court *a priori*, and on a long view some of these committees have played a useful part. The government's mistake was to exaggerate both the magnitude of their influence and the speed with which it could take effect.

The fourth main field of DEA activity was in regional policy. Here a large part of the work in the first year or so was organizational, in particular the setting up of Regional Boards of government officials and Regional Councils of nominated representatives. The new bodies were inevitably a stop-gap, which could not be a substitute for the reform of local government and the creation of elected regional authorities.

Indeed, the DEA's most important contribution to regional policy lay not so much in the work for which it was directly responsible, but in its role as a central coordinating department in the general evolution of government decisions which were announced by a wide variety of ministers. Among the key decisions taken by the government as a whole were the exemption of the development districts from the various cuts in public expenditure, the extension of these districts from the unemployment black spots to whole regions suitable for development, the loading of the investment grant in favour of these regions and the regional employment premiums announced before the 1967 Budget.

This general observation applies over a much wider field. The most valuable reforms carried out by the new government were due not to the DEA's specific actions, but to certain collective government decisions in which the DEA must in its heyday have had a say, in view of its coordinating role. Examples include the cancellation of the TSR|2 and the reduction in the bloated commitment to the aerospace industries, which was so heavily criticized in the Brookings Report on the UK. An absolute ceiling on defence spending at the 1964 level of £2,000m. (measured at constant prices) was announced in August 1965, and there were several reviews of overseas commitments, which put a stop to the rise in government overseas spending and eventually led to the decision to withdraw from East of Suez.

If such changes might seem easier for a Labour than for a Conservative government, the same could not be said of the willingness to face a heavy rundown of manpower in older industries such as the mines, the railways and textiles. Even more remarkable was the way in which Labour ministers actively encouraged the 'take-over kings', whom they had denounced in opposition, even when the expressed object of bids was to cut out unnecessary labour. The smallness of the compromise made with the Luddite form of anti-capitalism was probably the single most courageous feature of Labour rule – except, alas, in its later stages.

In a good many areas, of course, structural reform was a continuing process going from one government to the next. The outgoing Conservative government introduced Industrial Training Boards; the incoming Labour one brought in wage-related unemployment benefits and redundancy compensation. The DEA deserves, however, special mention for its part in the creation of two bodies: the Prices and Incomes Board and the Industrial Reorganization Corporation. The IRC was one of Labour's most notable innovations. Despite some controversial aspects of its work it accelerated mergers and regroupings which an imperfect and protected market might have taken much longer to accomplish. How far the PIB was really able to slow down the increase of wages and prices is debatable. Much more important was the boost that it gave, under the leadership of Aubrey Jones, to productivity bargaining. Inevitably, however, the effectiveness of the PIB reports became subject to rapidly diminishing returns as their number increased and belief in incomes policy waned.

A good many of the reforms just mentioned were ones in which the Treasury and the DEA would have had a joint interest in speaking up for the country's long-term economic interests when these conflicted with prestige activities. Looking back over these years it is difficult to escape the conclusion that economic (and especially industrial) policy was much closer to the hearts of the leading Labour ministers than it had ever been to most of their predecessors; and this may explain the initial goodwill which Labour possessed in some industrial and business circles. Of course, preoccupation with a subject is not identical with success. For a long time the potential benefits of Labour's structural reforms were more than offset (*a*) by the feeling among the mass of business managers and executives that the government was biased against both profits and personal financial success and (*b*) by the mismanagement of policy towards demand and the balance of payments. As all these adverse influences are likely to pass with time, the effects of the structural changes will become more apparent. Many items on the Conservative reform agenda, such as trade union law reform or personal tax incentives, are complementary rather than competitive to what has gone before; and a good deal of the work of the abolished Labour institutions still continues under other bodies.

THE FIRST FALSE DAWN

These reflections have moved ahead of the historical narrative, which was left in the autumn of 1965. The government faced the winter with what was generally imagined to be a set of deflationary measures behind them, backing from the central bankers, and the setting up of an early-warning system as a task for the immediate future. For a time the tide seemed to have turned. There was a sufficient return of reserves to London in September to give a net inflow over the third quarter as a whole, despite the balance-of-payments deficit. In the final quarter of the year even this narrowed dramatically as a result of one of those erratic movements away from trend to which the trade figures are subject. The political and journalistic habit of looking at individual monthly figures could not have been more misleading. Figure 4 shows how irregular the trade movements were even on a quarterly, let alone a monthly, basis, and even taking a seasonally adjusted average including invisibles. Subsequent revision of the figures underline this moral still further.

It was, however, obvious even at the time that the improvement in the trade balance in the course of 1965 owed a good deal to an exceptionally rapid growth of world trade, which could not be expected to last. Moreover, of the 7 per cent rise in the value of exports between the years 1964 and 1965, nearly 5 per cent represented higher prices. Although this helped the trade balance temporarily, it had ominous implications for the future. But the foreign exchange market seemed to repent of its earlier hysteria by going to the other extreme and ignoring the underlying weaknesses altogether. Mr Callaghan was able to tell the House proudly on 1 March 1966 that the entire outstanding short-term debt to the Federal Reserve Bank of New York had been repaid; without this repayment there would have been a gain in reserves of £380m. between the end of August 1965 and the beginning of February 1966.

But the most remarkable feature of all was that the increase in unemployment which most economists had expected as a result of the earlier deflationary measures did not occur. So far from rising, unemployment once more dropped on a seasonally adjusted basis to a low point of

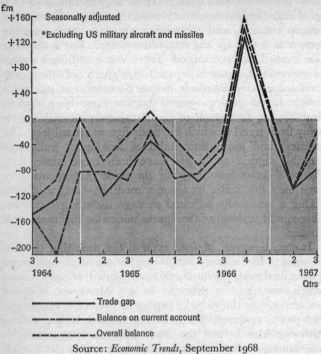

Source: *Economic Trends*, September 1968

Figure 4. Trade and payments fluctuations

below 1·2 per cent in March. Instead of the anticipated problem of too many people out of work, the problem had become one of a labour market that was overheated, even from the point of view of the most extreme expansionists.

It was, moreover, apparent that the voluntary incomes policy was not making any contribution to immediate problems. If anything it was encouraging the unions to move in more quickly before detailed scrutiny of industrial claims could begin. The surveys of both October 1965 and

April 1966 showed an increase of $9\frac{1}{2}$ per cent over the previous year in average hourly earnings. Retail prices, on the other hand, rose by an annual rate of only about 4 per cent. The increase in real personal disposable income was rather less owing to higher taxes and social security payments; between the winter of 1964–5 and that of 1965–6 it was around 3 per cent. Real consumers' expenditure went up by only 2 per cent owing to an increase in the savings ratio, partly brought about by credit restrictions. The failure of their 1965 deflationary measures to work on anything except production was probably as much a surprise to ministers as to outside economists; but they were not slow to seize the electoral opportunity this failure presented.

A further tightening of hire-purchase controls was announced on 8 February 1966, which was meant to reduce consumer spending by £160m., and banks were asked to stick for the time being to the previously fixed ceiling on advances. After this the Chancellor felt able to preface the election campaign with a full-scale Budget-type oration in which he solemnly announced that he did not 'foresee the need for severe increases in taxation'. There was a case for this dovelike attitude from an internal point of view on the basis of forecasts such as those of the National Institute, which suggested that the economy would soon come off the boil and unemployment rise without further measures. But it was quite astonishing in view of the balance of payments. The National Institute's central estimate was for a continuing moderate deficit at the end of 1966 (an assessment which, it confessed, erred if anything on the side of optimism); and its projection for 1967 showed no sign of the move into surplus required for medium-term debt repayment.

Apart from his general economic review, the Chancellor also promised an 'option mortgage' scheme to cheapen home purchase for the lower ranges of taxpayers to be financed by a Betting Tax. Both the expenditure and revenue sides of the account could be expected to meet with electoral approval. The net result was good enough to justify fighting an election called for 31 March 1966 on the slogan 'You know that Labour Government works'; and not all the Conservative chanting of '9:5:1' (their estimate of the ratio increase in earnings, prices and production) could prevent Labour from being returned with a majority of 97.

THE SELECTIVE EMPLOYMENT TAX

The election was held not a moment too soon. Sterling was already under intermittent pressure towards the end of February and from time to time in March. There was a further weakening in April despite the strengthening of the government's majority. This was partly a reflection of dearer and tighter money in New York, which was attracting funds from London, and partly of renewed concern about Britain's own balance of payments. The trade figures for the early months of the year suggested that the apparent disappearance of the current deficit in the final quarter of 1965 was indeed a statistical fluke. The pressure on sterling was, it is true, fairly moderate compared with what had gone on before and was subsequently to ensue, but there was still no sign of the much predicted easing of the pressure of home demand. Unemployment was still at 1·2 per cent. It was clear that the Budget, which had been postponed to 3 May, would have to be deflationary. The terminology of doves and hawks was introduced for the first time into economic debate by William Rees-Mogg to describe the differences of opinion about the right degree of Budget severity.

The actual Budget judgement was somewhere in the middle of the range, with perhaps a slight bias towards the doves. The surprising feature was the announcement of the Selective Employment Tax as the Chancellor's main instrument for reducing demand; this was expected to have a net yield of £240m. in a full year. If people received the impression that the new tax had been hastily drafted, they were not far off the mark. An orthodox deflationary Budget, prepared by the Treasury, had at the very last moment apparently been rejected by the Prime Minister and the leading economic ministers, because they thought that it looked too much like a repetition of familiar Treasury medicine, and because they believed that a tax with a structural aspect would seem less like a breach of the pre-election declaration. As a result, officials had to work into the small hours of several mornings to put Professor Kaldor's basic idea into operational form; and when Mr Callaghan got up to announce his Budget many of the details had still to be decided.[10]

The subsequent discussion of SET was marred by a failure to distinguish between administrative anomalies – which arose from the machinery employed – and the intrinsic merits and defects of the measure. The basis of the tax was a surcharge on all employers' National Insurance contribution amounting to 25s per male employee (increased in two successive steps to reach 48s in the 1969 Budget). These sums were to be refunded completely to employers in transport, agriculture and the bulk of the public sector, and repaid, with the addition of a premium, to manufacturing industry. The burden of the tax thus fell exclusively on services and construction. But because the National Insurance authorities were incapable of making any industrial, occupational or regional distinctions they had to collect £1,060m. from the public sector, and the Ministry of Labour to pay back £820m., so that the Chancellor could receive the difference of £240m.

There were three important aspects of the tax: the efforts to spread the tax net wider, the backdoor export subsidy and the poll-tax method of assessment. Professor Kaldor's arguments for encouraging labour to move from services to manufacturing were undoubtedly a motive behind SET.[11] But the measure was not dependent on these arguments

10. The above paragraph is based on general impressions gained at the time, which are strongly supported by a detailed scrutiny of the relevant speeches and documents. My own period as a temporary Civil Servant came to an end in January 1966.

11. *The Causes of the Slow Rate of Growth of the United Kingdom*, by N. Kaldor, Cambridge University Press, 1966.

and was supported by some regular Treasury economists simply as a method of removing the disparity between the treatment of goods and of services under the existing system. While many manufactured goods were subject to severe purchase tax or excise duties, there was no tax at all on services before 1966, except local rates and the motoring taxes. The Chancellor indicated that SET was equivalent to a 3–4 per cent tax on services (or a 7 per cent tax after the 1969 increase). For the unlucky concern where labour was a high proportion of turnover it amounted to about 7 per cent (or 13 per cent after 1969). Purchase tax rates on the other hand were 10, 15 and 25 per cent of wholesale value (and had risen by 1969 to $13\frac{3}{4}$, 22, $36\frac{2}{3}$ and 55 per cent).

Clearly SET was a rough-and-ready tax method of spreading the burden – it actually increased the spread between services and those goods not subject to tax at all. If fresh peas were served in a restaurant, the work of shelling and washing was subject to tax. If the restaurant bought tinned peas this work had already been done by the manufacturer, who paid no such tax. On balance – and very much on balance – this aspect of the tax was one which could be supported by economic liberals as a way of reducing tax discrimination between the different sectors of the economy.[12] Whether SET increased or decreased discrimination in the tax system depended on whether *retail distribution* was regarded as already taxed by imposts such as purchase tax. If they were, then SET simply removed the bias in favour of personal services such as hairdressing, laundry, banking and insurance, or professional services, and the discrimination in favour of food, transport and miscellaneous untaxed manufactured products then stood out all the more.

Supporters of SET would argue, however, that retail

12. SET is discussed in more detail in my article 'The Selective Employment Tax', *Banker*, June 1966. A more sceptical view is taken by Lady Margaret Hall in 'Are Goods and Services Different?', *Westminster Bank Review*, August 1967.

distribution, which accounts for about a tenth of the working population, was not hitherto subject to tax in an economically significant way. For, before SET, the amount of tax paid did not vary whether a product was purchased at Harrods, with a great deal of personal service attached to it, or whether it was picked up in a self-service discount store. The result was that retail services received an artificial boost and took up more manpower than if they had paid a *pro rata* share of the indirect tax burden. Ultimately, one is up against the problem of how to assess a tax change which increased the differential between some of the thousands of relevant categories and decreased the differential between others.

The basis of the premium to manufacturing industry was that *on average* the export content of manufacturing output was much higher than that of those services covered by SET. The premium was thus a minor backdoor substitute for devaluation; but after taking into account all offsets the stimulus was very low and amounted to well under 1 per cent of manufacturing turnover. When the government devalued by the front door the premium was abandoned (except for the development districts).

The most controversial aspect of the tax was its poll-tax method of assessment. This was dictated in the first place by the need to work out in a couple of weeks a tax which could be implemented in the course of 1966. The fixed charge per head, which bore especially heavily on the more unskilled, older or handicapped workers, was both ethically monstrous and bad economics. It could, however, be remedied eventually by levying the tax on a genuinely payroll basis, proportionate to the wage bill, instead as a fixed sum per head.

Why, however, use the payroll basis at all? Why not go over to a general value-added tax, taking in services? The economics of payroll taxes have already been discussed in relation to Mr Selwyn Lloyd's abortive attempt in this direction (see Chapter 6, pp. 248–51). The argument of SET supporters was that while a general payroll tax would simply be passed on in higher prices,[13] in services like retailing such a tax is initially met out of profits and eventually leads to a reduction in the labour force employed. Some of the opposition to SET reflected the national dislike of paying any tax, rather than a preference for an alternative; and it is worth pondering the very considerable overlap between the more hysterical opponents of SET and the lobbies that opposed Mr Heath on resale price maintenance.

But whatever its longer-term merits or defects SET was a singularly ill-chosen measure for the particular needs of the 1966 Budget. One point on which doves and hawks agreed was that the economy was working under very high pressure that spring, but that it might cool off later in the year. Therefore, what was required was a measure with the quickest possible impact and the minimum delayed-action effect. SET was just the opposite. As collection did not start until September (and the first repayments were made in February 1967), it could not even have *begun* to affect demand until the autumn, and its main effects were still further delayed. The episode once again reflected Labour's lack of feel for demand management in its first few years of office. When the Chancellor sat down, it required no genius to predict that still further measures might be required before many months had passed. The prediction could be made all the more confidently because of the announcement in the 1966 Budget speech that the surcharge would go completely the following November with nothing to take its place. This seemed scarcely credible at the time in view of the balance-of-payments outlook, and the fact that it was made was a sad commentary on the influence of the overseas lobby (described on p. 470).

13. Including export prices; for unlike a value-added tax it cannot be remitted under GATT.

BLOWN OFF COURSE

Indeed, trouble began within a few days of the Budget. The first sign was the visit of an IMF team to London in early May for one of its regular consultations. It soon became known that it took an extremely sceptical view of the likelihood of reaching the Chancellor's target of a payments balance by the end of 1966, and its scepticism was widely shared in British economic circles. The really heavy blow to sterling came with the seamen's strike, which began on 16 May and lasted six and a half weeks. The strike reflected the government's determination to encourage employers to resist wage claims made in defiance of its incomes policy. But in selecting for a showdown the industry that most immediately and directly affected the whole of Britain's trade, the government had not chosen its ground well and the overseas holders of sterling were the opposite of impressed. When a government is reduced to guessing which kind of toughness will make the most psychological appeal to half-informed observers abroad, it is a sign that the currency is fundamentally weak and more fundamental treatment is required.

The publication of the May reserve figure, which did not conceal the whole of the true loss, further upset the foreign exchange market. The devaluation of the Indian rupee at this time stimulated the imagination of many nearer home. Even the announcement from Basle on 13 June of new swap facilities designed to offset fluctuations in the sterling balances failed to help for more than a few days. The pressure on sterling was aggravated by the extreme tightness of money in New York. This prompted London-based banks, who had previously converted dollar deposits into sterling for loans to British local authorities, to switch them back into dollars for use in the US. Foreign exchange, which had been attracted to London by high interest rates and had helped to finance earlier payments deficits, now went back across the Atlantic. A sign of the international money squeeze was the increase in Bank Rates throughout Western Europe. But the large size of the movement out of Britain reflected a loss of confidence in sterling as well as the attractions of the US money market.

Mr Wilson later made much of these overseas pressures in defending his July measures, and tried to make the TUC's blood curdle with talk of 'another 1931'. But if the flight from sterling simply reflected international financial movements, rather than the British balance of payments, what was the relevance of deflation in Britain? The analogy with 1931 has been made so frequently on so many occasions that it is about as useful as summoning the spirit of Dunkirk (which the Prime Minister also did). But if it is pressed, what turned a financial crisis into a world depression in 1931 was the attempt of so many countries to preserve an outmoded system of gold and exchange parities by clamping down on their home economies. It is noteworthy that Mr Callaghan put much less emphasis on Eurodollar mysteries, and much more on Britain's payments position, in his own speeches after 20 July.

This, however, is to anticipate. By the middle of June it was clear that further measures would have to be taken. The publication of the much larger first quarter deficit at the end of June, and the subsequent publication of a reserve figure that revealed £51m. of the June gold loss, led to heavy sales of sterling. Most important of all, the regular Treasury forecasts, which were beginning to emerge from the machine at the beginning of July, made it clear there was little hope of getting out of deficit at the end of 1966, or even in 1967, on existing policies; Mr Callaghan was alerted at an early stage and work began in the Treasury on a new deflationary package.

Mr Brown had begun to change his attitude well before the 1966 crisis. He had discussed with his senior officials early that spring a possible 'outline package' which included devaluation and the application to join the EEC, as well as the conventional deflationary measures. Apart from Mr Brown a small pro-devaluation group had begun to form in the Cabinet, including Roy Jenkins, Anthony Crosland and Richard Crossman. None of them had economic posts at the time; and their discussions had to be held with little more information than was available to the general public. Mr Callaghan himself, who was on good personal terms with Crosland, wavered for a short time in the summer of 1966 in his support of the parity, but was soon back in the loyalist fold.

The Prime Ministerial veto on the mere mention of the word 'devaluation' meant that the DEA's 'outline package' could not have been worked out as carefully as would have been desirable. Indeed it was largely unknown, not only in the Treasury, but even in the DEA itself. Mr Wilson was easily able to outmanoeuvre his economic ministers as well as the other members of the Cabinet who possessed some expertise on the subject. As the *Sunday Times* remarked, 'his determination to avoid devaluation had become an obsession'.

Not that Mr Wilson was at that stage the lion-hearted apostle of deflation that he afterwards became. Indeed, until the very last moment he continued to oppose further restrictive measures with examples from his well-stocked fund of analogies from the past. His statement, at the beginning of July, that he would be going to Moscow in ten days' time to talk about Vietnam, was regarded by many critics as an illustration of his complacency in the face of the imminent crisis at home. Nor did his decision in the same month to stay away from a dinner for the French Prime Minister, M. Pompidou, to attend a Vietnam debate, help matters. M. Pompidou formed his own impressions which he was not slow to convey to others.

From then on the course of events is worth listing day by day.

SUNDAY 10 JULY 1966 The *Observer* published a brave leading article on the case for devaluation. Most of the papers carried stories foreshadowing a deflationary mini-Budget. Then came the most amazing step of all. Indignant denials were put out, from 10 Downing Street, of any such measures. The pressure on sterling was declared to be purely temporary.

MONDAY 11 JULY The foreign exchange market naturally concluded that the pound's prospects of survival at $2·80 were now very much less and there were heavy sales of sterling. But the attitude of No. 10 remained unaltered.

TUESDAY 12 JULY The Chancellor announced that the existing ceiling on bank advances would remain at least until March 1967 and that no relaxation would be made to finance the interval between the payments and refunds of SET. That evening the Prime Minister attempted to blame the crisis on the Press. At a dinner for the Australian Prime Minister, Mr Harold Holt, he remarked:

You, Mr Prime Minister, well recognize how remote from the realities of Britain's economic situation are the defeatist cries, the moaning minnies, the wet editorials – yes, the Sundays as well – of those who will seek any opportunity to sell Britain short at home or abroad.

WEDNESDAY 13 JULY Another set of bad trade figures was published (distorted, of course, by the seamen's strike). The Chancellor was already discussing the details of a possible deflationary package with other ministers and officials.

THURSDAY 14 JULY Bank Rate was raised from 6 to 7 per cent and increased calls were made for Special Deposits. In the words of the Bank of England *Bulletin* this was regarded in the foreign exchange market 'solely as reinforcing the tight restrictions already imposed on bank credit; and when other measures which the market had expected were not immediately forthcoming, heavy selling of sterling was resumed'. The Prime Minister made the further mistake of telling the House that he would be announcing deflationary measures in about a fortnight's time.

FRIDAY 15 JULY So far from reassuring the market this

statement gave rise to even more speculation about devaluation, and sterling had its worst day of the entire crisis.

Mr Wilson now tried to limit the damage by making it clear over the weekend that the package would be brought forward to Wednesday 20 July – after his return from Moscow. The Prime Minister's personal influence was suddenly switched to the side of maximum severity. Mr Callaghan had been sceptical whether it would be politically feasible to save the parity by deflating production and employment to the required extent, and it was Mr Wilson rather than the Chancellor who forced the July measures through the Cabinet and announced them to the House. The result of the Prime Minister's repeated denials and delays was a much more severe package than would have been imposed if he had acted earlier. Yet Mr Wilson himself was reported in 1967 to have come to the private conclusion that the July measures had been overdone.

From any point of view, the domestic economy was still overheated in July 1966. The main argument against relying on deflation, unaccompanied by devaluation, was that the old difficulties were likely to arise as soon as expansion was resumed. It also seemed to the critics that the government had once again waited to impose its heaviest dose of deflation until the economy was in any case on the verge of turning downwards.

The question remains why all the many deflationary measures before July 1966 had so little effect – especially on the labour market, where the June unemployment figure was still only just over 1·2 per cent, seasonally adjusted. A four-part answer is required. The first point is that the earlier deflation was less than it appeared. The rise in public expenditure was working in the other direction to the tax increases and credit restraints. Secondly, the prices-and-incomes policy was more successful on the prices than the incomes side, and consumer demand for that reason too was not depressed as much as had been intended. These were the two offsets most stressed by the Conservative opposition. But despite them the deflationary measures were effective enough to reduce the growth of output to a rate of only 2 per cent per annum between the end of 1964 and the middle of 1966, and this should have led to an increase, rather than a decline, in unemployment.

The reason why this did not happen brings us to the third part of the answer – the reductions in the normal working week that occurred between the end of 1964 and the beginning of 1966. During this period, average normal hours for manual workers fell from $42\frac{1}{2}$ to $40\frac{1}{2}$, but, in contrast to previous similar reductions, it was nearly all reflected in a cut in hours normally worked, instead of leading to more overtime. This most important element was completely left out of the public debate at the time. But even this did not entirely explain the level of employment, which was still very high in relation to output in the first half of 1966. The disparity can only be fully understood with the aid of a fourth assumption – that there had been labour hoarding by employers in excess of their actual needs. This was confirmed by the rapid reduction of work forces after the July measures, which was sharper and more rapid than would have been expected on the basis of past relationships. The bad habit of telling two different stories about government intentions to the home and overseas audiences must bear some of the blame for this labour-hoarding. Business opinion did not believe that ministers were in earnest about deflating the economy until July 1966. The soft-pedalling presentation in the end made it necessary to administer a deliberate shock to domestic business confidence before any impact could be made on the labour market. Unfortunately, the opportunity provided by this shake-out was wasted in the months that followed.

THE JULY MEASURES

The contents of the July 1966 measures could have been easily guessed. After having first neglected overseas and financial opinion, by Friday 15 July Mr Wilson had gone to the other extreme and decided, before departing on his Moscow weekend, to put every known variety of restrictive measure into the package in order to placate it. In this way he hoped he could at last bring to an end the almost non-stop series of sterling crises that had dogged his administration – an exciting idea which overlooked the fact that economic management is a continuous matter, and not one of suddenly taking over the bridge when the ship is on the rocks.

The measures to reduce demand were prepared by the Treasury in the normal way, making use of the standby packages which that department often has ready for occasions of this kind. At the time the Press made great play with the fact that three knights – Sir Burke Trend, the Cabinet Secretary, Sir William Armstrong and Sir Eric Roll – were told to wield the hatchet over the weekend while Wilson was away in Moscow. This three-man operation appeared to be concerned mainly with the public expenditure side of the package, which in the end proved the opposite of effective, as real expenditure rose by 9 per cent in 1967–8.

Mr Brown's alternative outline package was initialled a couple of days after Mr Wilson had instructed his top Civil Servants to prepare an orthodox batch of stringent measures; and it was the latter that formed the agenda of an afternoon Cabinet meeting held on Tuesday 19 July. The Prime Minister did not have an entirely smooth passage at this meeting; and it was Mr Crossman who first insisted on raising the question of devaluation, which the Cabinet did discuss, but without the aid of papers of any kind. The pro-devaluation group was heavily outvoted. Mr Brown, who had decided to resign, pushed back his chair from the table, but was not allowed to leave the room until the end of the meeting.

The main ingredients of the 20 July package were the 10 per cent 'regulator' surcharge on consumer taxes, a quite severe tightening of hire-purchase credits, £150m. of cuts in public expenditure for 1967–8, and intensified building controls. These were estimated 'to reduce demand on the domestic economy by more than £500m.'. As usual, there was no indication of how this figure was defined or the period to which it applied. In addition there was to be a six-month statutory freeze covering wages, salaries and dividends, to be followed by a further six months of 'severe restraint'. Prices were also to be frozen, except to the extent that they reflected increases in taxes or import costs, which could not be absorbed. The machinery of the freeze was simply to add reserve powers of actual control for twelve months to the 'early-warning Bill', then going through Parliament, which had originated in the crisis of the summer before.

The package also contained a few politically motivated additions with negligible economic impact, designed to show that the better-off were being hit. One of these was the 10 per cent surcharge on surtax for one year. Characteristically, it was a tax which hit earned income more than capital. At the upper end of the range some taxpayers actually paid more than 20s. in the pound for the year in question. The other measure of this kind was the £50 Travel Allowance, which was imposed more for psychological reasons than for its effect on the balance of payments. For the sake of a pseudo-egalitarian gesture, one of the most important ingredients in personal liberty was removed, leaving Britain the only country in the Western world at the time with comparable restrictions on travel. Yet so determined was the Conservative leadership to support the $2·80 exchange rate at all costs, and still at the time so fearful of Wilson's tongue-lashing if it did anything that could be misrepresented as being 'pro-rich', that it did not divide the House on the measure. Nor indeed did it challenge the logic of the whole package. In this masochism it was in tune with public opinion to a degree that amazed and impressed the Prime Minister himself.

The advisability of attempting to save the exchange rate in July 1966 by running the economy at a 2–2½ per cent unemployment rate was something on which reasonable men could hold more than one opinion. What was a little difficult to bear was the absence of any indication by Wilson that he had undergone any process of intellectual conversion. This was not merely a matter of his scathing condemnation of stop-go when in opposition. The contrast between his attack on the Conservatives in the 1966 election for wanting to solve the country's problems through higher unemployment and his own policies of 20 July required a little explanation, even from a political realist.

Nevertheless, this was Mr Wilson's finest hour in the upper reaches of the City and among the 'sound money' school of commentators, who actually believed that he had adopted the Paish theory with a courage denied to his Tory predecessors. At a somewhat lower level of sophistication, conventional middle-class opinion up and down the country was delighted to see the Prime Minister 'have a bash at the unions' by means of a wage freeze with legal sanctions, and the implied threat of imprisonment for those who disobeyed. In many respectable circles Wilson was hailed as the best Conservative Prime Minister the Party did not have.

But it was only Sir Leslie O'Brien – and to some extent Mr Callaghan – who were prepared to risk trouble with Labour MPs by explaining frankly that the new policies called for a larger margin of unused manpower, as Professor Paish had all along recommended. The Prime Minister coined the word 'redeployment' for what was being done; the vast majority of articulate public opinion discussed the measures in this newly invented language.

Even if it agreed with the policy, the Conservative opposition had nothing to lose from exposing 'redeployment' as a euphemism for unemployment. Yet so far from stripping off the verbal disguise, official opposition spokesmen themselves discussed the government's policy as if it could have worked without unemployment, given only a little more placing and training by the Ministry of Labour. In a deeper way, too, this line of approach played into the hands of the government, in the implicit assumption that there was a superior pattern of employment to that determined by the market, which the government ought to know and enforce. The person who deserved most sympathy was Mr Selwyn Lloyd, who had suffered so much abuse in 1961 because he had not been able to think of a comparable verbal disguise for his own very similar measures.

Another similarity to the Selwyn Lloyd period was that public controversy centred mainly on the temporary wage freeze which was the most justifiable part of the whole package, and indeed should have been imposed a long time before. Despite the many arguments inside the Labour movement, the freeze was accepted by a large majority of the population. Mr Lloyd's earlier pause had done a great deal to accustom the public to the idea; and the Labour government was able to use its in-built advantage in dealing with the unions to impose an absolute freeze with no exceptions.

Precisely because of this public willingness to accept sacrifices, July 1966 would have been the ideal time to devalue. This is not a mood which can be recreated to order; the squeeze on home demand and a modified form of wage freeze would have been the ideal complement to devaluation, as George Brown was arguing at the time. Instead the opportunity was wasted; and when devaluation did come a year later, people were much more reluctant either to reduce spending or to have incomes curbed for the second time round. Mr Brown was persuaded by a large number of MPs and Ministerial colleagues not to resign on the issue, and he stayed in the government, influenced by the difficulty of carrying out a public campaign on an issue of this type. Later that summer he changed places with Mr Michael Stewart, the Foreign Secretary, who took over the DEA.

One of the *sotto voce* arguments against devaluing in July 1966 was that it was better to wait until there was some surplus capacity to support an export boom. It is difficult to see why the reduction of domestic demand and the expansion of export production could not have gone hand in hand. Admittedly the reduction in home demand would then have had to be bigger to reduce domestic overheating, and this would probably have meant a still larger deflationary package. But public opinion was in a mood for harsh medicine in July 1966 and might well have been prepared to take a single large dose of medicine then, rather than have had to swallow one supposedly final dose from Mr Wilson, and several others from Mr Jenkins in succeeding years.

Nevertheless, the argument for 'first digging the hole' and then filling it was used vigorously to persuade waverers in the Cabinet and elsewhere to fall into line. The real snag about this counsel of patience was that it overlooked the strong possibility of a sharp temporary improvement in the balance of payments after the July measures, which would make it seem for a while as if the measures had worked on their own. In due course such a breathing space did indeed arrive, marking the second false dawn since Labour returned to office. There were in fact so many crises, July measures and false dawns in the period 1964–7 that the following list may be a useful *aide-mémoire*:

1964	16 October– 8 November	*Taking over 'the inheritance'.* White Paper publicizes £800m. deficit; surcharge.
	9 November– 5 December	*The first sterling crisis.* Autumn Budget; surcharge controversies; $3,000m. of credits for £.
	December 1964–May 1965	*Indeterminate phase.* No one clear characteristic. Intermittent trouble with sterling. Met by mixture of mild deflation and direct measures on, e.g., overseas investment.
1965	June– September	*Second sterling crisis.* First July measures. Early warning Bill on wages promised. National Plan.
	September 1965–May 1966	*First false dawn.* Confidence returns; central banks repaid; economy not deflated; Labour increases majority at second election (31 March).

339

1966	June–September	*Third sterling crisis.* Second July measures. National Plan abandoned; wage freeze.
	September 1966–May 1967	*Second false dawn.* Confidence returns; central banks repaid; economy *is* deflated ('shakeout'), 'Regional Employment Premiums' announced; official acceptance of Paish theory; hopes for 3 per cent growth and payments surpluses.
1967	May–November	*Fourth sterling crisis.* Practically uninterrupted; moderate at first but becomes severest ever. Suez Canal closed (5 June); unemployment worries. HP relaxations and social security increases. June–September: domestic interlude of selective physical intervention. Wilson 'takes over' DEA (end August). Common Market talks go badly. Adverse European comments on sterling. Pound devalued from $2·80 to $2·40 (18 November). Second de Gaulle Veto (27 November).

THE SECOND FALSE DAWN

Confidence did not, however, return immediately after the government acted. The 'hot' money outflow slackened, but did not stop until September 1966. The signal for the change in sentiment was – as in September 1965 – another support operation for sterling. This consisted of an increase from $750m. to $1,350m. in the 'swap' facilities with the US Federal Reserve and further undisclosed new central bank facilities. Together with sterling-area credits negotiated the previous June, the pound seemed moderately well protected against purely short-term movements; and in the final quarter of the year there was a dramatic return of funds. By the end of March 1967 practically all previous central bank assistance had been repaid. The sum involved, £463m., gives some idea of the run the previous summer.

Nor was this gain all obvious 'hot money'. A sudden

surplus of £141m. appeared in the overall balance of payments in the final quarter of 1966, and there was a large visible trade surplus for about the first time anyone could remember. It was no use pointing out that the knowledge of the surcharge removal on 30 November had caused a postponement of imports; or that there was an abnormally rapid rise in imports by sterling-area countries in that same quarter, which was an exceptionally good one for world trade generally. Ministers were unwilling to take heed of their own official warnings against going by a single month's or a single quarter's figures.

Looking at the recovery in sterling, the better trade figures, and the standstill in the wages index, they were convinced that the corner had been turned. It was true that they worried about the increase in unemployment. But the 2 per cent level it reached in the first quarter of 1967 was a good deal less than some of the more scarifying talk the previous July had suggested. The alarmists had forgotten that the danger of unemployment getting out of hand is usually greatest not one, but two, winters after a government has taken severe deflationary action.

In more sophisticated form the optimism even affected the official forecasters. In his Budget speech Mr Callaghan predicted a surplus in 1967 as a whole with an even bigger one in 1968. In fact he expected to be just on the right side in 1967 and to achieve a £200m. surplus in 1968. These forecasts did not seem unreasonable to independent experts, such as those at the National Institute. Previous experience had always suggested that sufficiently determined deflationary action could secure a temporary breathing space. The real payments trouble had in the past come after re-expansion had been under way for some while. Few of the government's economic critics thought that the balance of payments would be in deficit the year after the severest deflationary measures ever inflicted in the postwar period. The warning they did give was a more general one: as a result of the deficit and debts of the previous three or four years the government was walking a tightrope, and could not afford a deviation on the wrong side of the central forecast, even well within the range of error of the exercise. The part of the official machine that seems to have carried balance-of-payments optimism to the furthest extreme was the Bank of England. This was hardly surprising in view of its enthusiasm for the July measures. The Bank had a natural desire to show that sterling was not in fundamental disequilibrium; and like all human institutions tended to pay more attention to those straws in the wind which supported its belief than to those which did not. The March 1967 *Bulletin* waxed prematurely lyrical about the benefits of an 'easier supply position at home' and persuaded itself that – because of Rhodesia and the seamen's strike – the 3 per cent rise in export volume in 1966 was 'no mean achievement'.

The really extraordinary feature of the assessment made in early 1967 was not the forecast for that year, but the view taken of the medium term; and this was the really important part of the Chancellor's Budget Speech. Mr Callaghan spelt out to the House the belief that it would be possible to earn a series of payments surpluses in the years up to 1970, at the existing rate of exchange, with a growth rate of 3 per cent (in place of Mr Brown's target of nearly 4 per cent) and an average unemployment rate no higher than 2 per cent. A very similar view was taken by the National Institute in its own medium-term projections to 1970.

The National Institute model assumed that the gap of over 1 per cent between the average annual increase of British export prices and those of competitor countries would be almost closed as a result of operating the economy with a higher margin of unemployment, incomes policy, or both. It also assumed a moderate improvement in the competitiveness of home-produced manufactures against imports for the same reason. The official forecasts, in which the Board of Trade played a large role, were apparently more optimistic still about the effects of the new policies on the British competitive position. One widely circulated set of estimates showed a gradually increasing surplus, eventually reaching £500–600m. on the basis of the old rate of exchange, thus providing enough to cover the estimated balance-of-payments costs of joining the Common Market, given by Mr Wilson to the House of Commons. Such extravagant views emanated from the very nature of medium-term projections mechanically applied. For once a basically optimistic view is taken of export and import trends, geometrical progression will eventually yield larger and larger improvements in each successive year.

The authors of these projections would have been the first to concede that they were subject to a large margin of error and that, as already pointed out in connection with the short-term forecast, Britain could not afford deviations on the wrong side. The strategy proclaimed in the 1967 Budget speech was really a gamble. Not merely did it depend on the absence of overseas disturbances, but it also presupposed an absence of error in domestic demand management, as well as an optimistic view of the effects on costs of maintaining slightly higher unemployment percentages than in the past. These qualifications, together with the doubts of some of the principal economic advisers about the central projections themselves, were certainly expressed in Whitehall. But somehow their full force was never appreciated by ministers who, for all the scorn they sometimes poured on forecasts, basically preferred a single-figure guess to a more complex discussion of ranges of possibility and the resulting balance of risks.[14]

HOME-BASED EXPANSION

If the purely domestic side could have been viewed in isolation, reflation in 1967 was rather better timed than in previous cycles. Ministers and officials were now aware that corrective measures had been too long delayed in the past,

14. This subject is discussed further on pages 134–6.

both in the upswing and the downswing. The ceiling on bank advances had ceased to bite in the autumn of 1966, because of the fall in demand for loans. On 1 November the Bank of England took the unusual step of drawing attention to the availability of credit, especially to priority borrowers. At the beginning of December the government announced a temporary increase in investment grants, for 1967 and 1968 only, from 20 per cent to 25 per cent; and from 40 per cent to 45 per cent in development areas. This was a sensible innovation in trade cycle control. For the first time industrialists were given an incentive with a fixed time-limit attached. The President of the Board of Trade also helped by announcing several accelerations in the payment of these grants. Bank Rate was reduced to 6 per cent in two successive stages early in 1967; and Mr Callaghan was able to give the apparent world-wide trend in favour of lower interest rates a nudge at a finance ministers' meeting at Chequers in January.

The 1967 Budget was presented by the Chancellor as a neutral one because it involved no net tax change. His slogan at the time was 'steady as she goes'. This was, however, hardly an apt description in view of the rapid rise in total public expenditure. This in fact increased by 9 per cent in real terms between 1966–7 and 1967–8 – more than both the government's long-term public expenditure target of $4\frac{1}{4}$ per cent per annum and the estimated underlying rate of economic growth of 3 per cent. The Treasury was, of course, aware that the net effects of its policy were expansionary. Indeed public investment had been deliberately allowed to increase faster to offset the expected fall in private investment. But the department had no wish to broadcast this fact to the foreign exchange market. As it was, the figures for government spending contrasted oddly with the much-publicized axe-swinging of the three knights the previous July, and helped to increase the scepticism towards public expenditure cuts in general.

The Budget was followed by a statement from the Minister of Economic Affairs, Mr Michael Stewart, that the compulsory powers under Part IV of the Prices and Incomes Act would lapse with the end of 'severe restraint' in the summer. Reliance would be placed on 'early warning' and the power to delay settlement by up to seven months in the light of the PIB findings. In practice these powers were hardly used at all.

A REGIONAL PAYROLL SUBSIDY

One reason why the Budget appeared so uneventful was that the Chancellor's main proposal was published a few days before on 5 April as a Green Paper. This was a welcome new device for publishing proposals in tentative form so that public discussion could take place while there was still time to influence policy. The Green Paper suggested a Regional Employment Premium (eventually fixed at 30s per week for males, for a minimum of seven years) for manufacturing workers in the development areas. The background to it was that the policy of running the economy at a higher national unemployment percentage would raise the number of jobless in the less fortunate areas to intolerably high levels, where unemployment had for long averaged twice the national total.

The REP was an ingenious idea, which originated in combined pressure from a number of economic advisers including Sir Donald MacDougall, the DEA Director General and Professor Kaldor in the Treasury. But it also fascinated some of the Treasury career economists, and Sir William Armstrong was instrumental in getting it through Whitehall. The basic thought was that the degree of inflationary pressure depended largely on the demand for labour in areas of low unemployment such as the Midlands or London. This would not be affected by an increase in the demand for labour in the high-unemployment areas, provided it did not spill over into the rest of the country.

The wage subsidy in the high-unemployment areas

would give their products a competitive advantage over those of the rest of the country, where – it was concluded – unemployment would actually rise slightly as a result. An estimated sum of £100m. per annum was to be spent on REP without any compensating increases in taxation. The higher volume of national economic activity would, it was true, generate a small increase in the import bill; but this would be offset by giving the 20 per cent of British industry situated in the development areas a competitive advantage in foreign export markets, as well as in other parts of Britain, arising from lower labour costs.

The REP was received with considerable scepticism, even by many industrialists whom it was designed to benefit. Some of the opposition dwelt on details such as the use of the SET machinery or the case for extending the premium to non-manufacturing activities in the tourist areas. This last concession was made in the 1968 Budget, and the use of the SET machinery was an administrative convenience which could later have been dropped. The new premium was also opposed from a somewhat *simpliste* dislike of subsidizing labour, which ignored the fact that capital was already far more heavily subsidized in those areas by investment and other grants. Many of the arguments used against REP were really arguments against any form of discriminatory regional policy – which would, of course, have been perfectly legitimate if their proponents had followed them through to their logical conclusions. The view that more help should be given through public expenditure on transport, education and other 'infra-structure' activities cannot be entirely dismissed. But the effect of such expenditure on cost levels – and therefore on the competitive advantage of the regions – would have been longer in coming, and probably less in amount. Some increase in demand would probably have spilled over to other parts of the country and the effect on exports would have been less. For both these reasons £100m. of extra public expenditure would have had to be partially offset by higher taxes. It was remarkable that this kind of objection came from many businessmen and politicians, who in other contexts tended to regard public expenditure and high taxes as the root of all economic evil. The REP was roughly equivalent to a regional devaluation combined with a cash transfer. It thus involved the maximum use of the price mechanism, and also the minimum direct government intervention, consistent with having any regional policy at all.

The discussion of the Green Paper was in the end a one-way affair. The government wanted a quick decision which could be put into operation before the winter came; few regional representatives were, when it came to the point, prepared to say 'no' to a government subsidy; and the first REP payments were accordingly made in September 1967. Official economists hoped that over three to five years it would lead to a reduction of 50,000 in the number of un-employed in the affected regions compared with what that figure would otherwise have been. Without making any real study of its effects the Conservatives subsequently announced the abolition of the REP in 1974.

THE BEGINNING OF THE END

Meanwhile, despite the large increase in public expenditure, it became clear that the economy was not expanding by the 3 per cent forecast by the Chancellor. Partly for this reason and partly because productivity was, for the time being at least, expanding faster than in the past, seasonally adjusted unemployment was creeping upwards from the 2 per cent level it had already reached before the Budget. A sinister feature was that the most important single reason for the slow growth of output was that exports levelled off in the first quarter and then started falling. Imports, more-over, quickly recovered from their artificial dip before the end of the surcharge. Visible trade was again in deficit in the first quarter of 1967 and, in the second quarter, the trade gap had widened to an average of nearly £50m. a month, even before the Middle East war had had any real impact on the figures.

Nevertheless, confidence in sterling held up until the middle of May. Short-term funds continued to return to London; there was a reduction in Bank Rate from 6 to $5\frac{1}{2}$ per cent as late as 4 May, and during the month as a whole there would have been a small rise in the reserves had it not been for a repayment to the IMF. The sharp turnround in the sterling market occurred, in fact, in the middle of May – about three weeks *before* the Arab–Israeli war. Although the increase in tension in the Middle East and in other parts of the world contributed, these were probably not the main reasons. The announcement of increased electricity charges – meant as a highly orthodox move to limit Exchequer lending – was badly received by the foreign exchange market; but this too was mainly a catalyst for other anxieties.

More significant was the publication in mid May of a particularly bad set of trade figures, which increased suspicion that the economy was off course again. (Indeed from the middle of May 1967 until well into 1969 the course of sterling and the reserves was almost one continuous slide.) But probably the most important reason for the disquiet was Britain's second application to join the EEC, finally presented on 11 May 1967, and under discussion since the previous autumn. Even in the preliminary soundings the French – and to some extent the EEC Commission in Brussels – had stressed the sterling area and the British balance of payments as obstacles.

The view that Britain could not possibly accept EEC obligations at the current rate of exchange was held not merely by Europeans, but also in the very highest reaches of the British Treasury, where the highly optimistic projections for 1970 were not believed. The thought was expressed that if too many weights were put into a boat the vessel was bound to sink. For a long time there was no official estimate of the balance of payments cost of EEC entry; and Mr Douglas Jay, who was still President of the Board of Trade, wrote a personal paper which put the annual cost in the range of £500–750m. A pretext was found to stop the circulation of this paper to the Cabinet. As an alternative, the group of top economic advisers who occasionally met in a body to consider various subjects were asked to look into the question. Their own estimate was of a payments cost of £450–900m.

Sir William Armstrong himself was now sure that at some point the Prime Minister would have to choose between rival objectives, and informed him of this in unusually categorical terms at the end of April Chequers weekend before the decision to apply for EEC membership. But once devaluation became thinkable in one context, it became thinkable in another. The application to join the EEC was thus the real origin of the Treasury's change of attitude towards the $2·80 parity.

The balance-of-payments history of the rest of 1967 is all too well known. The trade deficit remained extremely high in the second half of the year, and shot up to freak levels in the closing months as a result of a dock strike. For the year as a whole the overall payments deficit came to £417m. In its Economic Report on 1967 the Treasury attributed about half the 1967 deficit to the 'hump' of imports following the surcharge, the dock strikes at the end of the year and the temporary effects of the closure of the Suez Canal in June.

British exports were also adversely affected by the pause in US economic activity in the first half of 1967, which coincided with a German recession. As a result, the growth of world manufacturing exports levelled off in the first nine months of the year. But all these special factors taken together could not explain away the whole deficit. Despite the combined effects of the wage freeze and the squeeze on the home market, the British share of world exports continued to slip back before they were hit by the dock strikes.

Moreover, one or two abnormal events must be expected in every year; the fact that Britain was in no position to meet them showed that something was badly wrong.

Despite the renewed outflow of gold and foreign exchange, fresh reflationary measures came thick and fast in the course of June and July as ministers grew alarmed by the highest summer unemployment figures for 27 years and forecasts of a total winter unemployment peak of 750,000 began to appear. On 7 June, some car hire-purchase reliefs were introduced, which added about £100m. annually to demand. Mr Callaghan had already had the possibility of these at the back of his mind when he rounded upwards the Treasury's forecast in his Budget speech. Nevertheless, quite a few people were surprised that the relaxation should have been announced two days after the start of the war, and on the same day that the Suez Canal was closed. On 21 June the government went on to announce higher pensions and other benefits to take effect at the end of October. At the end of July increased family allowances were announced, some of which were to come in October and the remainder in the following April.

The defence for these moves was that up to the middle of July the pressure on the reserves had been less than in previous crises, and it was hoped that the vastly extended network of central swap facilities would provide sufficient protection. The real objection to this argument was not just the state of the foreign exchange market, but also the persistent balance-of-payments gap to which temporary borrowing was no solution. The Chancellor's announcement at the end of June that the Travel Allowance would stay at £50 in 1968 showed that he had been informed of the deteriorating payments outlook, even though this may not yet have been fully reflected in the official forecasts. By this time too it had become a little more difficult to stifle public discussion of devaluation, and editorial references to the subject became a little less indirect. The Treasury itself now regarded it as a very real possibility, despite the political capital that had been invested in $2·80, and Mr Callaghan was warned of this before he replied to the economic debate on 24 July. But despite his doubts of the previous year, he now felt personally involved in the defence of the old parity, and in his speech passionately denounced devaluation, remarking 'Fortunately the Government's position is too well known for this to become a serious matter.' (It is only fair to add that he was also at the time heavily engaged as Chairman of the Group of Ten in trying to secure agreement for a new international monetary unit to supplement gold and the reserve currencies; and the compromise agreement in August on the Special Drawing Rights owed a great deal to his patient diplomacy and that of Dr Emminger, the German chairman of the official Deputies.)

PHYSICAL INTERVENTION:
A LAST ATTEMPT

Before they went away for their 1967 summer holidays, ministers asked for contingency plans to be prepared for improving the trade balance by direct intervention; and in the course of August a number of plans for acting directly on exports and imports, or the reserves, were examined. These included import quotas, prior deposits on imports, a Labour Party scheme for an official importing agency and plans for voluntary acquisition of some of the privately held dollar portfolio. Virtually all the government's regular advisers were against nearly all of them. The Whitehall view was that if the government did not wish to devalue, it would have to try to sit through the crisis and face the domestic consequences. Officials did not believe there was any third way.

For the time being, at least, this assessment was accepted. But the Prime Minister was still determined to intensify direct physical intervention in other ways. On 28 August the newspapers reported that he was to take personal direction of the Department of Economic Affairs, with Mr Peter Shore in charge as Secretary of State. This was Mr Wilson's final attempt to use detailed industrial intervention as an alternative to devaluation. Whether or not this could ever have been feasible, it was three years too late. As the one senior member of the Cabinet with a real enthusiasm for this approach, he should, if he had wished to give it a fair trial, have taken over responsibility for economic and industrial policy three years before in 1964, and left the role of world statesman until Britain's external finances were stronger.

By 1967 it was much too late and the experiment was unworkable. The *Economist* explained the inherent contradictions of the situation rather well the previous year, when it remarked about Mr Wilson:

He has an aversion to market forces, and a preference for trying to get round them by administrative devices. This is a perfectly defensible philosophy for a reasoning man to have. But it is nonsense to try to run a country by having a great machine of officialdom whose object is to devise economic policies that would make the best use of market forces, and then to have a Prime Minister sitting on top, taking wholly isolated decisions, motivated by a personal inclination to move things in a quite opposite direction.[15]

The day after the Cabinet changes the government announced another set of substantial HP relaxations, extending this time to durables as well as cars. These had been decided upon about a month earlier, before the summer holidays. This was just the kind of consumer credit reflation which Mr Wilson had earlier – and with undoubted sincerity – vowed would not occur again. But it so happens, as Whitehall economists had made clear, that consumer and government expenditure are the only elements of home demand that are subject to direct and reasonably rapid government influence. Industrial investment lags rather than leads in a cyclical recovery.

While the Treasury and, more particularly, the Bank of

15. The *Economist*, 13 August 1966.

England were somewhat unháppy about the June and July relaxations, the opposition of these two institutions to the August measures was strong and unmistakable. They saw that the state of the balance of payments and sterling could not support the existing level of home demand, let alone a further stimulus. From then on, Treasury policy-makers began to see devaluation as a probability rather than a strong possibility. But the view sometimes voiced in City quarters, that devaluation could have been avoided if it had not been for these relaxations, is self-deception. The relaxations merely set the seal on a sentence of execution which had already been written much earlier. The trade gap had already widened alarmingly in the first three quarters of the year before even the earlier consumer relaxations could possibly have had much effect. Even if all the stimuli administered from June onwards had been blue-pencilled there would still have been a large payments deficit in 1967 and another one predicted for 1968 at the old exchange rate. The real argument against the relaxations is not that they caused devaluation, but that they had stimulated by the end of the year a strong consumer boom which had to be reversed in mid-stream to give devaluation a chance of working. Mr Jenkins's task would have been easier, and fewer tax increases required, if the boom had never been started.

'THE CENTRE CANNOT HOLD'

Until the summer of 1967 it would have been incorrect to have spoken of a 'Treasury view' on devaluation. The department accepted that ministers had ruled it out altogether, and that it was up to officials to advise on the implications of this decision. Naturally the degree of enthusiasm or reservation towards this basic decision varied from person to person. (There was probably a modest correlation between age and attitudes to this question, as there was among outside opinion.) It was, however, possible to identify a more definite view among a central core of 'regular' economists and officials concerned with economic policy, which was already in existence under the Conservatives in the early 1960s and persisted right up to 1967. This was, very briefly, that it was not worth the risks and dislocation of a devaluation, if the parity could be preserved by running the economy with a margin of up to about 2 per cent unemployed; but it was not desirable to go much above this level for long just for the sake of the exchange rate. This body of opinion was important, because it stood in the middle between those who had long been advocating devaluation and those who saw it as a dishonour or disaster which it would be worth paying a very high price to avoid. By August or September most members of this central school of policy-planners had switched sides and had come to the conclusion that the $2·80 parity could not be saved at this moderate price in unemployment.

The Commonwealth finance ministers were informed at the regular annual meeting in the third week of September that there would be an overall surplus of £100m. in the year from mid 1967 to mid 1968. Rarely could a forecast have been more misleading – the actual *deficit* over the period worked out at around £700m. But the figures, which had been calculated the previous June, were no longer believed by British officials and economists. In August and early September Mr Callaghan was given strong hints that he might be advised to devalue, and when he returned from the Rio meeting of the IMF at the end of September he knew that this was probable.

In the six months up to the end of that September the increase in liabilities to central monetary institutions outside the sterling area – a fair measure of central bank assistance – was nearly £500m. By then the question about devaluation was 'When?' rather than 'Whether?', although a final recommendation had to wait for the full autumn forecasts.

By the time of his strikingly successful performance at the Labour Party Conference in the first week of October Mr Callaghan had come to the personal conclusion that only a major long-term credit to reinforce the sterling balances – such as the $2,000m. afterwards negotiated in 1968 in Basle – would prevent him from devaluing. Having become so personally committed to the defence of the parity, the Chancellor was still hoping against hope that such a long-term loan might be offered in time. As such a loan would have done nothing to remove the payments deficit, it is as well that it did not appear at that stage to confuse the issue. Meanwhile Mr Callaghan's conference speech was mostly devoted to prices and incomes and contained very little about the balance of payments. The delegates did not seem to notice or worry about the omission.

The cat was finally set among the pigeons by the Common Market Commission's explicit strictures on the sterling area, and the implied strictures on the sterling exchange rate, in its report on the UK application. The crucial section became available in London at the beginning of October, and this message was heavily underlined by the then French Foreign Minister, M. Couve de Murville, in a speech on 25 October. On top of all this one must add the monotonous refrain that the foreign exchange market was also disturbed by the latest trade figures published in mid month.

A dubious move, announced on 10 October, was the acceptance of a 12-month loan of £37½m. from a consortium of Swiss commercial banks at 5½ per cent. This was seen not only as a humiliation, but as manifestly inadequate to the gap that would have to be bridged. The next stage in the escalation of the crisis came on 19 October, when the Bank Rate was raised from 5½ to 6 per cent, ostensibly to keep British rates competitive with American. The sinister feature, reminiscent of November 1964, was that the exchange market, which had been expecting a 1 per cent rise, reacted perversely and sterling weakened further.

During October the Treasury was hard at work both on a devaluation plan and preparing the ground for its reception by Labour ministers who had made the preservation of the parity the one unalterable pillar of their policy. An extremely small group of regular and trusted officials and economists from the Treasury and Bank had in fact been meeting for over two years to work out contingency plans for devaluation. The tempo and degree of detail of their work gradually intensified in the course of 1967.

The existence of this group was compatible with the Prime Ministerial ban on the mention of devaluation, even in top-level discussion of economic strategy. If he knew of this group, the Prime Minister thought of it in the context of the emergency plans that must always exist somewhere for wars and other catastrophes. Thus, although advance thinking on devaluation had been done, no account was allowed to be taken of this work in discussion of economic strategy, at least until the final few weeks.

Overseas finance ministers and central banks had also been engaged in similar contingency planning; and discussions had been held in organizations such as the EEC's Monetary Committee and (informally and privately) among the topmost OECD economic staff. Anyone who had travelled at all in Continental financial centres would have known that a devaluation of 15 per cent had long been regarded as tolerable and not one to be followed *en bloc* by the rest of Europe. Whether or not this figure would have been the British Treasury's first choice, it seemed from its initial pre-devaluation calculations to give a sufficient margin of safety, if given time to work.

The die was finally cast when the final version of the autumn economic forecasts became available at the end of October or beginning of November. Not only was a £500m. 'basic' deficit correctly forecast for 1967,[16] but a figure of not

16. This was afterwards reduced to £417m. as a result of the discovery of missing exports. (See p. 397.)

much less was forecast for 1968, despite the prospective improvement in world trade and the gradual return to normal in the oil and freight markets after the Middle Eastern war; and there was no real reason to be confident of a surplus even in 1969. With unemployment already 2·3 per cent, the domestic cost of using deflation alone would have been prohibitive; and it was no part of the philosophy of the dominant middle-of-the-road wing of the Treasury to make the attempt. At the end of the day, the Bank Governor, Sir Leslie O'Brien, loyally accepted the decision and the nation was spared a dramatic resignation or calls for a national government to save sterling, from this particular source.

The two elements in the change of front of the Prime Minister and Chancellor were the forecasts and the sheer size of the drain on reserves after several years of continuous borrowing. By the end of 1967 the total amount of central bank assistance had – judging by the net increase in liabilities to official monetary institutions outside the sterling area – risen to well over £1,000m. Both the forecast and the reserve drain were necessary elements in the change of front, and the two together were sufficient. The forecasts probably weighed more with Mr Callaghan, while the reserve drain may have counted more with Mr Wilson. The Cabinet itself was not in the picture until the Thursday before devaluation, and even the other principal economic ministers received no hint until a day or two before.

THE DEVALUATION TIMETABLE

A tentative decision to devalue was taken very early in the week beginning 6 November. How long the Prime Minister stood out is unknown. The strong conviction of both Mr Callaghan and the official Treasury machine in November 1967 that it would be wrong to carry on defending the parity any longer was a very different matter from the Chancellor's temporary hesitancy about the parity in the summer of the previous year. Given the state of sterling it was scarcely conceivable that the Prime Minister could have overruled the advice he was given.

That week messages were sent on a personal basis to about half a dozen key figures in the international financial system on whose discretion the Treasury could rely. These men – labelled the 'Praetorian Guard of the international monetary system' by one very highly placed British official – included Pierre-Paul Schweitzer, the Managing Director of the IMF, F. Deming, the US Under-Secretary of the Treasury, E. van Lennep of the Netherlands Finance Ministry, Dr Otmar Emminger of the Bundesbank, and Sr Ossola of the Bank of Italy. They were asked in a non-committal way how they would react either to a change in the rate, or to a request for a short- or long-term loan to support the parity.

Three types of reaction came back. One school of thought believed devaluation appropriate; a second favoured supporting the old parity, and a third wanted to temporize with short-term standby credits for a few more months. All three courses would have had to be backed by a further deflationary package. Meanwhile the market position of sterling continued to deteriorate. Talk of devaluation increased not as a theoretical argument, but as an imminent possibility. A further Bank Rate increase to $6\frac{1}{2}$ per cent on 9 November, designed to forestall a disastrous set of trade figures, affected by the dock strike, produced another perverse reaction.

It so happened that from Saturday 11 November the leading central bankers and finance ministry officials of the West were due to be in almost continuous sessions at a series of routine meetings, which had been arranged a very long time beforehand. Although these meetings gave the men concerned an excuse for gathering openly, such was the state of sterling that dramatic announcements were expected from them; and their failure to materialize weakened sterling further.

The first of these occasions was the regular monthly meeting of central bankers at the BIS in Basle on 11–12 November. Sir Leslie O'Brien was authorized to continue the discussions there on the same hypothetical basis. At this meeting an unprecedented telephone call was put through to the IMF's Managing Director, M. Pierre-Paul Schweitzer, on the possibility of fresh credit to support the sterling parity. M. Schweitzer played for a time with the idea of providing Britain with $3,000m. of loans or standby credits from the Fund by means of a special operation going outside its normal lending limits. But reflection on the onerous conditions which would have to accompany such a loan at the old exchange rate very quickly persuaded the Fund Director to drop this idea.

On Monday 13 November reports from Basle correctly predicted that a $250m. credit (then worth £90m.) would be extended to Britain for up to 18 months to finance the repayment of the remainder of the IMF credit drawn in 1964. This had been under negotiations for some months, but its announcement at this time only weakened confidence, as the sum seemed so derisory in relation to the pressure on sterling.

Later the same day, Sir Leslie O'Brien appeared particularly gloomy when he spoke to reporters at London Airport on his return from Basle. He remarked that he always received the 'moral support' of his colleagues and that he was not looking forward to the following day's trade figures. That evening the Prime Minister omitted his customary lion-hearted defence of sterling at the Guildhall dinner; but the Press was too slow, or too anxious not to rock the boat, to pick up this clue.

The venue of the international discussion now shifted to Paris where OECD's key Working Party Three was meeting on Tuesday 14 November. This was followed on the Wednesday and Thursday by a meeting of OECD's Economic Policy Committee, a group with a much less restricted membership. Although devaluation could not even be hinted at the larger gathering, the key personalities could continue to meet behind the scenes.

The general reaction to the British feelers was that a devaluation of around 15 per cent would not be met by retaliation. There were, however, two difficulties. One was the unhelpful attitude of the French representatives. The British approach was discussed by the Monetary Committee of the EEC at a lunch in Paris on the Tuesday at which the French Treasury representative, R. Larre, seemed to be opposed to a devaluation of sterling. There was a further acrimonious evening meeting of representatives of the Six, at which the French refused to give a definite idea of how they would react if Britain moved. A second difficulty was that the USA was alarmed by the idea of a change in the sterling parity. Because other countries fixed their parities in relation to the dollar, there was no question of the USA retaliating, but the Americans did try to persuade other countries to join in a support operation for the $2·80 parity. The will to support the parity, however, no longer existed in London; and for the first time for many years a British government was prepared to part company with the Americans on a major international issue.

On the night of Wednesday 15 November the BBC broadcast a Continental rumour of possible fresh $1,000m. credit for Britain. The report was probably an echo either of the American overtures or of the proposal that M. Schweitzer had briefly considered and rejected. Such reports could have been helpful to the British authorities, because the implication that there was an alternative to devaluation might have helped to reduce the rush out of sterling, had it not been for the mishandling of a Parliamentary situation.

On Thursday morning, 16 November, the British Cabinet approved the devaluation of the pound. An immediate problem facing the Cabinet was that Mr Robert Sheldon, the Chairman of the Labour backbench Economic Committee, had tabled a Private Notice Question to the Chancellor about the reports of fresh credits, which the

Speaker had accepted. The Question could have been stopped by giving either the Speaker or Mr Sheldon (who was a staunch devaluationist) a hint. The failure to do so was yet another example of the price paid for the obsession with secrecy in the governmental process. In the end Mr Callaghan refused either to confirm or deny the reports from Paris and advised Members not to believe everything they read in the Press.

Late Thursday afternoon the floodgates were opened and funds poured out of London. Some observers wondered why neither the Chancellor nor any of his advisers thought of saying that talks were going on (as they were in connection with standby credits to back devaluation), and that the House would obviously not expect a statement while they were still proceeding. Yet one wonders whether any of the critics would have done better, if they had been themselves involved, in an atmosphere of secrecy and tension, with hundreds of matters to arrange, and knowing of the great risks to the world, as well as the British economy, if the international arrangements had gone wrong. These are situations when each day should have had far more than twenty-four hours for all the tasks to be performed.

There was subsequently a controversy whether, following Mr Callaghan's answer, it would have been possible to have brought the announcement forward from Saturday night, 18 November. Another question was whether the IMF Executive Board could have been summoned any earlier than Saturday morning. With hindsight one wonders, too, whether it would not have been possible to close on Friday some of the world's leading foreign exchange markets, as was done in the gold crisis of the following March. These are not questions on which it is easy to dogmatize. All I would emphasize is that they were *not* the most important questions about the conduct and planning of the devaluation operation. It was essential to obtain some understanding about supporting credits, as well as to widen the discussions designed to prevent British devaluation being copied by the other leading countries. If a once-for-all loss of 16⅔ per cent of the value of the foreign exchange which left London on that Friday was the price of securing an internationally supported devaluation, it was well worth paying.

After the British Cabinet had already decided to devalue, the Bundesbank Council considered a US request for a loan to Britain; it was, of course, too late. The devaluation decision became irrevocable on Friday 17 November at 6 p.m. London time, 1 p.m. Washington time, when President Johnson was informed. The same evening, M. Schweitzer was given formal notification and told the amount of the change. The IMF Board met on Saturday at 10 a.m. Washington time, having been summoned only two hours before. The Board sat for three hours, by which time it was, of course, 6 p.m. in London. It was not until that Saturday afternoon that the French government, after a Cabinet meeting, decided not to follow Britain's devaluation. The UK Treasury statement, which was issued at 9.30 p.m., announced that the official parity against the dollar had been lowered from $2·80 to $2·40. This represented a 14·3 per cent reduction in the price of sterling, but a 16·7 increase in the price of dollars and of all other currencies which did not follow sterling. The British statement was able to say that devaluation would be backed by approximately $3,000m. of standby credits – $1,400m. from the IMF and the remainder from central banks, and this was what really mattered.

The really unhappy side of the devaluation decision was the domestic one. The Treasury had prepared a comprehensive programme of domestic restraints to accompany the decision. These were designed to build up in impact, so that the home market was progressively restrained, as the rise in exports gathered strength. But having made one major unpopular decision ministers were not prepared, despite the advocacy of the Treasury, backed by the Bank of England with the most strenuous support it knew how to give, to inflict another full-scale squeeze. The demand restrictions contained in the devaluation statement on Saturday 18 November were mainly confined to a moderate increase in HP restrictions, a ceiling on bank advances and an increase in Bank Rate from $6\frac{1}{2}$ to 8 per cent. Promises were made of £200m. of cuts in public expenditure, including defence and the nationalized industries, but these were not found immediately convincing. The withdrawal of the export rebate and the SET premium for manufacturing (except in the development areas), which was to save £200m., were not really measures to restrict demand, but the abandonment of minor backdoor devaluation devices, widely disliked abroad, which Whitehall thought it discreet to jettison now that front-door devaluation had been adopted. The increase in Corporation Tax from 40 to $42\frac{1}{2}$ per cent was not expected to restrict demand, but was mainly a political move to trim the increase in profits expected to follow from devaluation. The whole package was a good deal less than had originally been put up to ministers.

'THE POUND IN YOUR POCKET'

Was this a forced devaluation? In the technical sense, no. Apart from the foreign exchange market fiasco on the Friday, the operation was well planned and well carried out. For the first time the devaluation of a reserve currency had been internationally agreed and accepted beforehand. Only a handful of countries followed; and many of the major sterling-area countries, including Australia and South Africa, did not follow the British pound downwards. For this reason the devaluation – although it was not realized at the time – was probably larger than the 1949 move from $4 to $2·80, when most of the rest of the world devalued as well.

But in any except a technical sense the move was forced on the government in flat contradiction of its intended strategy and at a particularly bad time both nationally and internationally. (While July 1966 was the best time to have devalued psychologically, early 1967 would have been the best time economically.) Mr Callaghan insisted that devaluation had been a defeat, and his letter of resignation was in the Prime Minister's hands by the time of the announcement. Having had to give so many assurances about the parity to his overseas colleagues, he did not wish to stay on as Chancellor, and on 29 November moved to the Home Office. He was a victim of the Bretton Woods system, under which exchange rates do occasionally change, but do so in single jumps, and which requires finance ministers to give false assurances of the immutability of their currencies in the intervening period.

Mr Harold Wilson's attitude was strikingly different. In the first few days following the announcement, he spoke of devaluation with all the exaggerated enthusiasm characteristic of the convert,[17] and when pressed on television about his biggest past mistake, said it was to underestimate the power of speculators. His remark about the 'pound in your pocket' not being devalued, did not, however, deserve quite all the obloquy it received. It was an attempt – albeit exaggerated and unsuccessful – to refute the surprisingly common notion that the internal purchasing power of everyone's money would automatically fall overnight by the full extent of the devaluation. Much more open to attack was his mention to the Parliamentary Labour Party of the possibility of 6 per cent growth in 1968. If this had been attempted, it would have meant frittering away most of the benefits of devaluation in a domestic boom and this idea was soon abandoned. But when it was suggested it alarmed the international economic bodies, especially OECD in Paris. It seemed as if the Prime Minister himself regarded devaluation as the soft option which he had previously accused its advocates of seeking.

17. So adamant had been his refusal even to hear of devaluation that he had been dubbed as 'Parity Harold' by one of the government's economic advisers.

For three years the public had been taught to believe that devaluation was a disaster, a disgrace and a dishonour. The government line on the subject was reiterated by the opposition, the organized leaders of industry, almost every City banker (at least in public) and the TUC. The Press had been excessively discreet in analysis, prediction and prescription alike. Even many economists had felt inhibited by excessive respect for the supposed political constraints. Professor Harry Johnson put it rather well when he wrote:

Though from the autumn of 1964 on more and more economists came to regard devaluation as a prerequisite to a solution of the country's problems, this was revealed to the public only after devaluation actually was forced on the Government. Meanwhile the economists who were free to speak devoted most of their policy efforts to preaching the virtues of an incomes policy which it was hoped – on the basis of no evidence whatever – would avoid the necessity of a devaluation.[18]

A week after devaluation General de Gaulle announced his veto on Britain's second attempt to join the Common Market. Here again the Labour government had failed to learn from the experience of its Conservative predecessor, and once more tried to graft membership of the EEC on to existing foreign and economic policies, assuming that Britain could join against French opposition with the aid of the Five. The blow to national morale, when a mistaken European strategy and a mistaken three-year attempt to support an overvalued parity both collapsed at the same time, was severe.

The opposition's reaction to devaluation did little to help. There was surely enough material in the events leading up to an unplanned devaluation, at a time not of the government's choosing, for an all-out and deserved attack in which floaters, devaluationists and deflationists could all have joined. Having given the government only tame and peri-

18. *Encounter*, January 1968.

pheral opposition for so long, the Conservative front bench then used all its suppressed venom to attack the first big decision the government took that pointed in the right direction.

The real question was whether the change of policy was radical enough. Having subordinated every other objective and distorted the whole of economic policy in a misguided attempt to maintain one particular exchange rate, there was a risk of the whole process being repeated at a different rate. The events of the preceding years had painfully and expensively established that $2·80 was too high; but they had not established what the correct rate was. By fixing a new rate at $2·40 on the basis of the most hazardous and uncertain international trade elasticities the government was taking a very great gamble for the years ahead.

9

THE APPROACH TO THE 1970s

The argument about exchange rates: policy in a new era: the Washington gold agreement: the Basle sterling-area arrangements: further traumas: The 1969 Budget: the nadir: the news of 12 June 1969: the mark saga: the Fund studies reform: the pre-election Budget: dawn, true or false?

A BENEVOLENT cynic could easily argue that Britain should be grateful to President Nasser and to General Dayan for the Middle Eastern War, which magnified the 1967 deficit to a frighteningly high figure and triggered off the succession of sterling crises which led to devaluation. Without it the government might have struggled on hopelessly and desperately for some time longer at the old $2·80 parity, kept going by injections of overseas credit and drifting gradually into a siege economy with no visible prospect of emerging into solvency.

This gratitude would have been greater if the war and the attendant sterling crises had come a little earlier. For the lateness of the 1967 devaluation was not merely a matter of lost opportunities; as will be shown below it made the whole exercise more difficult, more risky and more unpleasant than it need otherwise have been. But more serious even than the technical disadvantages of acting so late was the effect that it had on public attitudes.

THE ARGUMENT ABOUT EXCHANGE RATES

Some of the most popular arguments against any parity change – for example that it was impossible because other countries would follow to the same degree – were later exploded by events. So was the belief that a parity change was politically impossible. But controversies of this kind are never quite settled by evidence, and a whole fresh crop of misconceptions has been fostered by the circumstances surrounding the 1967 move.

Devaluation was undoubtedly a defeat for the Labour government and for the more conservative sections of financial opinion; but it was widely hailed as a defeat for the nation as well. A possible result of this feeling, together with the unpopularity of the government in the period that followed, could have been to reinforce the prejudice against exchange rate changes until they are forced by events. Such a reinforcement would be harmful for even if foreign exchange is rolling into the reserves by the time this book is published, it would take a very bold man to claim that sterling could never become overvalued again, as a result either of events in this country or parity changes abroad.

The more reasonable advocates of exchange rate changes do not regard them as a panacea. They would simply argue that they are the best method of bringing about balance-of-payments adjustment in a world of diverse national currencies, diverse movements of wages and prices and where money costs are strongly rigid to downward pressures (but where surplus countries are not indifferent to the rate of domestic inflation). In these conditions a change in the international price of the currency involves a smaller check to living standards – when the problem is one of deficit – than the alternative of relying on deflation alone. Exchange rate changes can in the longer run enable a country's output to rise as fast as the underlying increase in efficiency; but they cannot magically produce a faster increase than that; and they need to be supplemented by appropriate internal policies if they are to produce the desired results.

Most of the anti-devaluation arguments based on the check to real wages resulting from it were really arguments against eliminating the deficit at all. A country wishing to cure a current payments deficit has by one means or another to export goods and services it would otherwise have used at home and/or import less.[1] Unless there is a large margin of unused capacity this is bound to mean a temporary check to public or private expenditure at home. It would be unfeasible as well as undesirable to allow the main burden of the adjustment to be borne by investment; but whether consumption actually has to fall, or there is just a lower rate of increase for a time, depends mainly on (a) the size of the move from surplus to deficit required, (b) the time allowed for making the move, and (c) the deterioration in the terms of trade required to persuade other countries to take more of the exports of the devaluing country and to persuade its citizens to buy less from abroad.

The reason for the attempted severity of the squeeze on real incomes in 1968 was the very large size of the turn-round required in the balance of payments. A legitimate cause for complaint is that an adjustment, which should have been made gradually, had to be squeezed into a year or two. As a result of the delay in acting a jump had to be made from a large underlying deficit not merely to a balance, but to a continuing surplus of substantial size to repay years of borrowing. Of the £1,000m. per annum once-for-all shift in resources away from the home market officially believed necessary after the 1967 devaluation, only £300m. was due to the loss on the terms of trade consequent on devaluation. The other £700m. was due to the arithmetical effect of moving from deficit to the target surplus.

But to regard the £300m. as 'the cost of devaluation', which could have been avoided if we had not devalued, would be superficial. Ultimately, there is no way, short of a retreat into protectionism (which itself has its costs), of avoiding the sacrifice in the terms of trade *as well as* the shift of resources. Indeed devaluation, incomes policies and unaided deflation are all in the last analysis devices for reducing British prices *relative to foreign prices* on both home

1. I leave out the textbook cases where supply elasticities are so low that devaluation improves the terms of trade, or where demand elasticities are so low that appreciation can cure the deficit.

and overseas markets. (Just as important in practice, they allow British exporters to maintain their overseas prices, but increase their profit margins. Importers who maintain their prices will, on the other hand, reduce their profitability).

It is, incidentally, no use rejecting all these price mechanism remedies in a deficit situation because 'British costs and prices don't seem to me any higher than those abroad', or 'It isn't prices that matter, but service, design and delivery dates.' No matter how low British prices are, if, owing to bad management, unimaginative salesmanship or original sin, we are not selling enough to pay our way, they have to be reduced still further – or export profit margins increased.

Mr Wilson's physical intervention, or the Conservative penchant for trade-union reform and tax incentives, could have been alternatives only if (a) they could have had not merely a *generally beneficial* effect, but a sufficiently large specific impact on *sales of British goods in export markets and in competition with imports at home,* and (b) they could have had this impact quickly enough to bring the balance of payments into surplus before our reserves and borrowing power ran out. Both of these hypothetical propositions take a great deal of believing in the light of experience in the 1960s.

Devaluation reduces British prices and/or increases British profit margins, relative to competitors, directly and automatically. The hope behind both incomes policies and conventional deflation was that over a period of years British costs and prices could be made to rise *less rapidly* than those of our competitors, and thus bring about the equivalent of a slow-motion devaluation. The trouble was that incomes policies would have worked too slowly, if at all, while unaccompanied deflation would have worked only at the cost of a long period of wasteful stagnation and unemployment.

It is worth asking how much extra loss of output and employment would have been necessary to have avoided devaluation in November 1967. When a currency is correctly valued it is sufficient to make a hole in the economy by curbing home demand. The hole will then be automatically filled, before too long, by exports and import-saving production. (Indeed this is the generally accepted criterion, in IMF circles, for determining whether an exchange rate is correct or not.) Experience in Britain suggested, however, that at the old $2·80 exchange rate the hole tended to stay a long time unfilled, and the main effect of deflation, unaccompanied by other measures, was to reduce output and employment. In so doing it also reduced imports, but the effect on exports was controversial and in any case smaller. As not much more than a fifth of all expenditure went to imports, the depression of business activity would have had to go a very long way to turn the deficit into a surplus.

The Treasury's target improvement in the balance of payments of £700m. per annum, *compared to what it otherwise would have been*, was equivalent to nearly £600m. at the old rate of exchange. According to the relationships estimated by the Brookings Institution, for every £100m. per annum reduction in total demand, imports would fall by £24m. and domestic output by £76m. To secure the required £600m. improvement at the $2·80 exchange rate would have involved cutting total demand in 1968–9 by about £2,500m. per annum, of which about £1,900m. would have been reflected in a shortfall in output. This would have reduced the gross domestic product by a good 5 per cent below what might otherwise have been expected. The resulting downturn would have been more like a prewar slump than a post-war recession.

Because many people would drop out of the registered labour force in these circumstances, and the overhead labour force is relatively stable, the increase in unemployment would not be as great. But on the basis of the Brookings relationships it would still have been $1\frac{1}{2}$–2 per cent. This additional unemployment would probably have been superimposed on an annual average of a good $2\frac{1}{2}$ per cent, thus bringing the total to more than 4 per cent, or an annual average of well over 900,000 (and over a million at the winter peak).[2] Apart from its human consequences, a setback of this kind would have had a catastrophic effect on profits and investment, and seriously impaired future growth projects for a long time to come. The illustration brings out the misleading nature of the slogan 'Devaluation is not an alternative to deflation.' It is not. But with a properly managed devaluation only home demand need be deflated; without it output and employment are deflated as well.

Let us, however, take the discussion one stage further and assume that it would have been politically feasible to persevere with a deflationary policy long enough to secure the same effect on international competitiveness as the November 1967 devaluation. A heroic assumption would be that the effects of a lower pressure of demand, together with inflation in other countries, would have brought about such an improvement in relative costs and prices over a period of five years that, at the end, this country would have been back in underlying balance and able to pay its way without any more undue slack in the domestic economy.[3] The annual loss of output initially would have been £1,900m., as calculated above, but would have fallen gradually to zero at the end of the period. It would have averaged just

2. *Britain's Economic Prospects*, 1968. The relationship I have used is derived from Equation (4) on page 160. (Strictly speaking the Brookings calculations assume also some new exports gained as a result of the reduction in the pressure of demand, balanced by a loss of exports to countries whose own purchasing power has been cut down by Britain's reduction in imports.) The Brookings calculations may slightly exaggerate the proportion of marginal expenditure absorbed by imports, and also the effect on unemployment of any given reduction on output. But from the point of view of the calculations given above, these would tend to offset each other.

3. This assumes that additional unaccompanied deflation could have led to an improvement in relative costs of nearly 3 per cent per annum over the five years – a very big assumption starting from a time when there was little overheating and unemployment was actually over 2 per cent. (The offsets that reduced the effective value of the devaluation below the nominal 14 per cent would equally have applied to the deflationary alternative.)

under £1,000m. per annum during the five years, and the total loss would have amounted to a little less than £5,000m. This sacrifice would have been over and above the once-for-all £1,000m. per annum switch of output to exports and import-saving, which would have had to take place irrespective of whether the government devalued or not.

Clearly deflation is not likely to be taken in practice that far. The calculation assumed that the government was in earnest about moving into surplus and did not intend to go in for a protectionist policy. In fact the tendency in such circumstances is to restrict overseas investment severely, even to the extent of net disinvestment, to adopt anti-libertarian measures such as the Travel Allowance and to resort to every variety of back-door protection. In addition, deficits are allowed to run and the international begging-bowl is passed round for as long as possible. Thus a country that will neither devalue nor deflate sufficiently limps along, an object of international pity.

POLICY IN A NEW ERA

There were three queries that those who accepted the need for devaluation could have raised about the November 1967 change. These were whether the devaluation was large enough, whether the move should have been to a floating rather than a fixed rate, and whether it should have been accompanied by temporary import controls.[4]

4. One reason why press discussion of all three questions was somewhat muted in the period immediately following devaluation was that Mr James Callaghan in one of his last acts as Chancellor personally appealed to financial journalists to suppress any doubts – just for once – on patriotic grounds. As a general rule such considerations should not have a place in the writings of independent commentators. The assumption behind a free society is that there is a long-run value in the *principle* of open discussions which transcends the immediately visible drawbacks. If the case for frank discussion had to be argued on its merits on each occasion, free speech would be at an end. But November 1967 seemed to me then (but does no longer) one of the extremely few occasions when

The potential price or profit margin advantage from the 1967 devaluation move was less than the 14 per cent figure would suggest. A deduction had to be made for the increased cost of the import component in output, and the withdrawal of the export rebate and SET premiums. There had just been an increase in employers' National Insurance contributions and a further smaller increase was in the pipeline – but strictly speaking these should not have been counted as part of the devaluation package, as they would have happened in any case. There was also the vexed question of whether the Corporation Tax increase was to be counted as a slight addition to costs or not. The net result was that the devaluation advantage was worth about 9–10 per cent, calculating it the official way, and about 7 per cent the way many industrialists preferred to reckon it.

This advantage certainly seemed sufficient at the time not only to Whitehall, but to independent forecasters such as the National Institute, and also to qualified overseas observers such as the Brookings Institution. Such distinguished bodies can often be wrong, especially when they speak with one voice. But whether or not it should have been larger, a potential 7–10 per cent price advantage – or its equivalent in profit margins – was a worthwhile gain and not the chickenfeed the critics supposed.

The Treasury actually supposed at the time that it had a margin in hand. But given the enormous margins of error in such calculations, it was unwise to throw away the 2 per cent export rebate before being absolutely certain it would not be needed. The fact that the Americans were making threatening noises even before devaluation, and were apparently talking about a countervailing duty on

---

it was right to make an exception. Having secured what they had so long been vainly advocating, the advocates of devaluation thought it fair that they should allow the government some discretion on the particular measures taken and to help avoid the extremely unpleasant situation which would have arisen had the devaluation proved an immediate failure.

British whisky, does not automatically mean that Britain should have given way.

A form of floating exchange rate is at the heart of the long-term strategy suggested in the concluding chapter of this book. November 1967 was not, however, the ideal time to launch such an experiment. Suspicion and distrust of sterling were then so strong that the free market rate might well have fallen below what could have been justified on any reasonable view of the elasticities of international trade.

This is not all. A big downward plunge in the sterling rate might then have taken the dollar with it and led to a massive upheaval in gold and currency parities generally. It can be argued that sterling was not the only problem that had been postponed for too long, and that a general re-alignment was overdue and could only have been brought about through an international crisis. But there would undoubtedly have been risks to the UK in a *Götterdämmerung* of this kind, and it was prudent, if unheroic, of the government's advisers to want to avoid unnecessary international disturbances until Britain's own balance of payments was in better shape.

Another puzzle is why devaluation was not backed by temporary import controls. Devaluation is not an instant remedy. Changes in price and profitability take time to offset both export and import volumes; and until volumes have changed by a certain minimum amount, the arithmetical effect of devaluation is to make the balance of payments worse. A simplified illustration can be given by supposing that the *foreign exchange* price of all imports is unchanged after devaluation, and that there is no import substitution in the first year. The import bill in foreign exchange therefore stays the same. One might assume, for the sake of illustration, that the foreign exchange price of all British exports falls immediately by 7 per cent. Then, until the volume of exports reaches a level 7 per cent higher than it would otherwise have reached, the current balance is actually worse.

Unfortunately, the one commodity that Britain lacked even more than gold in November 1967 was time. In the five years up to the end of 1967 a total deficit of nearly £1,500m. had been accumulated on current and long-term capital account. Moreover, the UK started 1968 with reserves which were about half Britain's debt to the central banks and the IMF. The government would therefore have had a perfectly good case for imposing temporary import controls, as part of the total package, to bridge the interval before devaluation could produce results. It decided, however, not to do this and to rely on IMF and central bank credits to see it through the difficult initial period. The argument for this strategy was that it was less disturbing internationally, and helped to secure a better reception for devaluation abroad. But it was always vulnerable to the risk either of the 1968 deficit being larger than expected (on a pre-devaluation basis) or of devaluation itself being slower to work than originally hoped.

The reflux of short-term funds, which might normally be expected to follow a devaluation and help to bridge the transitional period, lasted in fact only a few days, and by December 1967 there was a renewed outflow of foreign exchange. The British devaluation came at the worst possible period for the dollar. The US economy was, for the first time for many years, suffering from severe domestic overheating; and the Vietnam war was imposing a particularly heavy burden of overseas military expenditure. The US had been losing gold for many years and her stocks were falling towards the $10,000m. level (valued at $35 per ounce) which many Washington authorities regarded as the minimum to which they could be allowed to go. Here was the real cause of the widespread belief that the Americans would be forced to 'devalue' the dollar against gold – and possibly against other currencies. The devaluation of sterling thus triggered off a gold-buying rush for which the ground had already been well prepared by other events.

Sterling itself suffered from the backwash of this gold speculation. The most usual explanation was that, as sterling was a reserve and trading currency, large amounts of it were available for sale. But a much more likely cause is that market operators expected that sterling would go down at least as far as the dollar in any international adjustment, despite the fact that it had already been devalued.

This brings one to the real fear behind the renewed outflow of sterling in the winter of 1967–8 – the belief that there would be a second devaluation. The perfectly reasonable criticism was made, both at home and abroad, that the government had not curbed home demand enough to make room for the export boom which devaluation was intended to bring. The government soon realized that curbs must come; Mr Wilson's earlier optimism about 6 per cent growth vanished as if it had never been, and the pressures to act were strongly reinforced by the IMF team which came to London to finalize the $1,400m. standby credit. The pledges were spelt out in detail in the first of the published Letters of Intent signed by Mr Callaghan, and disclosed by his successor on 30 November. The IMF understandably had no wish to see yet another credit frittered away and in the ensuing months Mr Richard Goode, the leader of the Fund mission, assumed bogyman proportions in British political mythology. Many years too late the House of Commons had woken up to the fact that IMF credits were conditional.

The Confederation of British Industries misunderstood the economics of the operation; and a circular letter to members actually claimed that industry would be 'out of pocket on the whole deal' – although the one certain fact about devaluation is that it is good for company profits, and so it proved. The constant rumours throughout the winter of 1967–8 of a second devaluation were not based on a sober disagreement with the Treasury on international trade elasticities, or on the appropriate measures of demand restraint, but had a large emotional and even hysterical element about them. One could hardly go to social gatherings, even in circles where international currency was not normally discussed, without being asked when the second devaluation would take place; and it was often just those who had most vigorously contested the need for any devaluation at all who were most firmly convinced that a fresh one was imminent.

For a time in late November and December the pressure on sterling was aggravated by a French war of nerves, primarily designed against the dollar, but which did not hesitate to use sterling as an instrument; and rumours about difficulties in negotiating the IMF credit flowed out thick and fast from Paris. On top of all this members of the sterling area, particularly in the Middle and Far East, appeared to have been genuinely shocked by devaluation. In contrast to the Continental countries, they had accepted earlier British denials. The urge of some sterling-area countries to diversify their reserves reflected less, however, moral indignation than a belief that sterling was more likely to depreciate again than appreciate – and perhaps to do so quite soon.

In this atmosphere the new Chancellor, Mr Roy Jenkins, was anxious to show that he meant business; and the early days of the New Year were devoted to arguing out in full Cabinet a programme of public expenditure cuts. A bargaining session with over twenty people at table is hardly the most rational way of deciding public expenditure priorities; the procedure was partly a political operation to help rebuild the government's shattered internal morale.

The expenditure changes, which were announced by the Prime Minister in a speech, were undoubtedly genuine. Yet as the original programmes for the year in question were announced for the first time, public opinion could be forgiven for being a little sceptical. This scepticism was increased when it was found that because changes in the public sector have a long gestation period, public spending in real terms was expected to rise by $4\frac{3}{4}$ per cent in 1968–9 but by only 1 per cent in 1969–70.[5] The effects of some of the more important military cutbacks were not expected to be felt until 1970–71, for which no overall figures were given. Confusion was further increased by the publication of what seemed very different and much more alarming figures in the Vote on Account presented to Parliament a month later. A useful semantic reform for future occasions would be to refrain from using the word 'cuts' to describe reductions in a planned rate of increase.

By January 1968 these faults of presentation and detail no longer deserved to be at the centre of public attention. For the first time since it came to office the government had a rational strategy which at least had a chance of working. The $2·80 parity had been abandoned, however belatedly; the main feature of the public expenditure review was a planned withdrawal from the Far East and Persian Gulf by the end of 1971, by which time there would be no major military bases outside Europe and the Mediterranean.[6] The public speeches of the Chancellor, and even of the Governor of the Bank of England, emphasized the need for a carefully negotiated reduction in sterling's role as an international reserve currency. Thus the illusions about Britain's financial and military role in the world – of which Mr Wilson had originally been the foremost exponent, and which had held the country back for so long – were at long last jettisoned. The public expenditure announcement even moved a few steps away from the old Labour principle of universal welfare payments. The key decision here was not the re-imposition 'with the utmost reluctance' of prescription charges; this was the ritual slaughter of a sacred cow. It was rather the decision to take back via the tax system the increase in family allowances for those who did

5. In the event, progress was ahead of target and public expenditure rose by only 1·6 per cent in 1968–9. (*Public Expenditure 1968–9 to 1973–4*, Cmnd 4234, Table 1, HMSO, 1970.)

6. *Public Expenditure in 1968–9 and 1969–70*, Cmnd 3515, HMSO, 1968.

not need them. Clumsy and round-about though the method was, it was at least a first move towards selective benefits.

The economic forecasts which preceded the 1968 Budget proved surprisingly controversial. The first version, as it emerged from the official machine, suggested that there would be little rise in consumption even on the assumption of a neutral Budget – as the rise in prices following devaluation, and the previous deflationary curbs, would be sufficient to hold it back. These forecasts were received extremely critically, both by the specially recruited outsiders who formed the 'Group of Economic Advisers' (see p. 98) and by one or two very senior regular officials. For once the forecasts really were hammered out across a table by the higher-level committee in whose name they were issued. Part of the argument centred on whether the personal savings ratio would fall as consumers tried to maintain the accustomed annual rise in living standards in the face of devaluation. The final figure was a compromise between the various opinions.

Mr Jenkins's first Budget aimed to increase revenue by £923m. in a full year. The government's net borrowing for 1968–9 was estimated at £358m. compared with £1,449m. in 1967–8 and £1,164m. if the Budget changes had not been made. These figures were spotlighted to impress overseas and financial opinion. The Budget was actually expected to take just over £500m. of spending out of the economy.[7] This was just consistent with the range of recommendations presented by the Treasury. The difference between the Budget and the economic arithmetic was partly accounted for by changes such as the previously foreshadowed increase in Corporation Tax, and the 'special charge' on investment income, which were expected to have little effect on actual spending.

An important innovation was the publication for the first time of part of the official economic forecasts in the Budget

7. What this might have meant is discussed on page 137.

Speech. These showed that after the tax changes the Treasury was now expecting a 3 per cent rate of growth (measured at an annual rate) between the second half of 1967 and the first half of 1969. An alternative, deliberately optimistic, version showed that a rate of growth of nearer 4 per cent was possible if exports performed better than expected.

The way in which Mr Jenkins raised the sums he required was as interesting as their total amount. He went out of his way not to introduce anything that would traditionally have been regarded as 'a Socialist Budget'. There was no increase in Capital Gains Tax and (except for the recovery of family allowances) no increase at all in direct taxation on income. The Chancellor's main instruments for reducing spending were increases in taxes on goods, in SET and in the vehicle licence duties. Mr Jenkins tried to give purchase-tax increases a 'progressive' twist by increasing the width of the bands from 11, $16\frac{1}{2}$ and $27\frac{1}{2}$ per cent to $12\frac{1}{2}$, 20, $33\frac{1}{3}$ and 50 per cent, with the highest rate on so-called luxuries. But the main effort to tax the wealthy was a special charge on investment income. A once-for-all affair, it was really an expedient for taxing capital at a time when a wealth tax was out of the question for administrative reasons, and it was carefully designed to do the least possible damage to the 'effective functioning of a mixed economy'.

There were hints in the Budget speech of a new tax philosophy. Mr Jenkins hoped that he would eventually be able to reform personal taxation and added that his inclination was 'towards fewer loopholes and somewhat lower rates'. He added words which not many Labour Chancellors would use: 'The high rates breed the relentless search for loopholes which occupies a good deal of the time of our more skilled accountants and ever more ingenious rich.' Unfortunately the political and economic situation did not allow Mr Jenkins's objectives to be realized during his term of office. Taking the 1968 Budget on its own, it scored highly for ingenuity and inventiveness in a difficult situation, but the resulting goodwill soon evaporated under the influence of events.

A new Prices and Incomes Bill was also foreshadowed in the Budget speech. The new policy suggested a $3\frac{1}{2}$ per cent ceiling for wage, dividend and salary increases, and the government took powers to delay pay and price increases for up to twelve months to enforce PIB recommendations. Both enthusiastic supporters and opponents of a prices and incomes policy wrongly supposed these new measures important and controversial. The real clue to their nature was the forecast that prices would increase during 1968 by 7 per cent, owing to the combined effects of devaluation and the Budget; even though unemployment was historically high, the econometric evidence suggested that the price increases could feed back into wages and thus take a couple of points off the devaluation advantage. The new-style prices and incomes policy was thus really a holding operation to restrain the rise in wages for the time being. Ministers did not, of course, seriously expect to keep the rise in hourly earnings down to the nominal target; a 6 per cent increase in the course of 1968 would have been regarded as a reasonable success. The actual rise turned out to be about 7 per cent.

The Chancellor was much criticized for not announcing a curb on private consumption at the same time as the public expenditure measures, and for waiting instead until the Budget, which was brought forward to 19 March. The consumer spending spree in the first quarter of the year indeed outran all expectations. There were two reasons why Mr Jenkins waited so long as he did. He was anxious not to dig too great a hole in the economy by domestic restrictions until exports could expand to fill it. Secondly, and at least as important, if Mr Jenkins had acted in January, he would have had to use bulldozer methods, involving across-the-board increases in consumer taxes and an announcement of higher income-tax rates for the following financial year. He

was anxious to avoid these (especially the latter) and to prepare a more carefully assembled Budget.

The new Chancellor was in fact wrong to wait so long,
as he came to realize later.[8] It turned out that there was in
fact much more steam in the domestic economy at the
beginning of 1968 than the Treasury or most other forecasters realized at the time; and earlier action would
undoubtedly have helped to hold down imports without
involving a prohibitive cost in domestic unemployment.

THE WASHINGTON GOLD AGREEMENT

These domestic arguments were taking place against a
highly excitable international background. In the early part
of 1968 the rush into gold continued. The link between gold
and the American balance of payments was that the USA
was the one major country which undertook to buy gold
from, and sell gold to, overseas monetary authorities at
the official $35 price. Thus a large and continuing US
deficit led either to a drain on the country's gold stock or to
a potential drain from the accumulation of convertible
dollars by other countries.

The appetite of speculators had already been whetted by
General de Gaulle's call for a return to the gold standard
a couple of years before. It was aggravated by the increasing
American payments difficulties in 1967, of which the most
immediate cause was the Vietnam war. The much-publicized departure of France at the end of 1967 from the 'Gold
Pool' (set up at the beginning of the decade to stabilize the
private market) further influenced the situation. A rumour

8. Although a very quick-witted and economically literate politician,
Mr Jenkins had been carefully kept off the Cabinet's economic committee for two years, prior to November 1967, until he was suddenly
pushed in at the deep end. Mr James Callaghan in his turn was excluded
from this same committee for a long time after he went to the Home
Office, despite an earlier assurance that he would continue to be in the
government's innermost economic councils.

that Mr William McChesney Martin, the chairman of the US Federal Reserve, was going to attend the monthly BIS meeting in Basle in March helped to light the tinder-box. The statement afterwards issued from Basle on 10 March – a brief reaffirmation that the Gold Pool would continue to support the $35 price – merely increased suspicions; and by the end of the following week the Gold Pool countries had to stop supporting the market. Friday 15 March was declared a Bank Holiday, and the remaining Gold Pool countries – Belgium, Italy, the Netherlands, Switzerland, USA, UK and West Germany – met at the weekend in Washington.

Much popular comment made the mistake of identifying world prosperity with the preservation of the then existing monetary system and, above all, of existing gold and dollar parities; and the spectre of mass unemployment was conjured up in front of millions of people on the basis of no evidence – behaviour which the need to popularize could perhaps explain but not excuse. It later transpired that the months of the gold crisis had coincided with a vigorous re-expansion of world trade after the slowdown earlier in 1967.

The Washington Conference predictably led to a decision to wind up the Gold Pool. Some $3,000m. of central bank reserves had been handed over to private gold buyers in the previous months, and the drain clearly had to stop. A two-tier system was established. The US continued in theory to buy and sell gold from central banks at $35, provided that the gold was not unloaded at a profit on the private market. The central banks represented undertook not to buy or sell gold from non-monetary sources (the application of this provision to South African gold was later a source of controversy), and other central banks were invited to co-operate in this policy of isolating the private from the official market.

The far-reaching implications of the Washington agreement took time to dawn on many people, including some of those who had been present at the conference. After Washington a drain of gold from official into private stocks was no longer possible. Official reserves were insulated from the private market. Thus neither a fresh change in the sterling parity, nor any other psychological shock, could lead to a run on the US gold stocks or those of any other country, unless *official* holders of dollars asked Washington to convert them into gold. This gave countries, as they gradually came to realize, a new degree of freedom in managing their exchange rates.

The US continued to buy and sell modest amounts of gold from governments and central banks after the Washington agreement. But it was understood that major demands for conversion would be extremely unwelcome. National authorities which accumulated dollars had the option of holding on to the dollars, lending them on the Eurodollar market, or selling them. This last option was equivalent to allowing their own currencies to appreciate against the dollar. It was because there was no alternative and superior medium into which currency holdings could be converted that the world was said to be on a dollar standard.

After the reopening of the London gold market in April 1968 the free market price hovered around the $40 level for well over a year and reached a peak of $42·8 in March 1969. At no time in 1968–9 was it ever at a sufficient premium over the official price to tempt major countries into breaking the Washington agreement. The free market price kept above $41 until about the end of August 1969. Then with the mark and franc changes, the impending issue of Special Drawing Rights and South Africa's need to sell gold to balance her overseas payments, the price came tumbling down and reached $35 by November. At the very end of 1969 a compromise agreement was reached under which South Africa was enabled to sell gold to the IMF to meet her foreign exchange needs whenever the free market price fell to $35 or below or to finance a payments deficit.

THE BASLE STERLING AREA ARRANGEMENTS

Just as important for the UK as the Washington gold agreement of March 1968 were the Basle arrangements for the sterling balances, which were made a few months later. Agreement was announced in principle in July 1968 on a $2,000m. package of sterling standby credits, available up to 1971 and repayable over 1974–8, to be provided through the Bank of International Settlements, with the backing of a dozen central banks. These were not designed to meet a British payments deficit, but to offset the effects on the reserves of demands for conversion by sterling-area members. The credits were equivalent to about two-sevenths of gross liabilities to the sterling area. About $600m. of the available sum was used to finance diversification that had already taken place by the summer of 1968. In addition the British government gave a dollar-value guarantee on the bulk of officially held sterling-area balances in return for an undertaking by the countries concerned to keep approximately constant the proportion of their reserves held in sterling.

The sterling-area countries received in fact a generous bargain. For they received both a gold guarantee and a normal interest payment on their balances which made no allowance for that guarantee. In other words the UK was paying twice over to insure them against further sterling depreciation. It is therefore hardly surprising that the arrangements were very successful and that by March 1969 UK gross liabilities to official monetary institutions in the sterling area exceeded the pre-devaluation total, and the special Basle credits had been repaid. Even if better terms could have been obtained in a calmer atmosphere, the fact remains that the threat of a withdrawal of official sterling balances, which had hung like a sword of Damocles over successive Chancellors and inhibited countless policy initiatives, had been removed.

The Basle arrangements did not, of course, remove Britain's own payments deficit, nor the adverse leads and lags due to fear of a second devaluation or a forced downward floating of the pound. This had to be met by drawing, in June 1968, the IMF standby credit granted after devaluation, and by further use of 'swap' credits with central banks.

Although the 1968 balance of payments was not as bad as the original figures made it appear, it did take much longer to respond to devaluation than the Treasury had forecast. Exports of goods and services rose in fact rather faster than the authorities expected. But so – and to a much greater degree – did imports of goods and services. The increase in import volume between the second halves of 1967 and 1968 was 8·6 per cent against a forecast of 0·6 per cent. About 2 per cent of this jump could be explained by 'abnormal' shipments of silver bullion and diamonds. It was also possible that devaluation was superimposed on an economy with a larger import propensity than was realized at the time. But the biggest single factor in the discrepancy was undoubtedly home consumption which rose by 1 per cent over this period compared with the Chancellor's estimate of a 2 per cent drop.

Various explanations could be given for this disappointment. The official forecasters took insufficient account of 'permanent income effects' – i.e. the tendency for consumers to try to maintain a long-run upward trend in their real spending, and to compensate for sudden changes in their post-tax income by adjusting their savings ratios.[9] There was also the failure of home prices to rise by as much as forecast in relation to wages, which in turn may have been partly due to businessmen subsidizing home prices from their higher export margins.

An actual reduction in consumption, as distinct from a check to its rate of increase, is probably very difficult to

9. See Brian Reading and David Lomax, 'Too Little Saving', *National Westminster Bank Review*, August 1969.

engineer in normal peacetime conditions; and to that extent Mr Jenkins was over-ambitious. But it is difficult to escape the conclusion, to which he and Sir Douglas Allen eventually came, that Britain's difficulties were aggravated by the perverse way in which monetary expansion was offsetting fiscal restraint. In 1967, Domestic Credit Expansion (explained on p. 165) was £1,758m. and the money supply increased by 9·8 per cent. This was all part of the disastrous home-based expansion preceding devaluation, which was discussed in the previous chapter. Despite the hire-purchase restrictions and the bank advances ceiling of November 1967 (the latter redefined and intensified in May and November 1968) Domestic Credit Expansion rose even further – to £1,898m. in 1968; and despite the drain on reserves the money supply rose by 6·6 per cent, with exceptionally rapid increases in the second and fourth quarters. Although the central-government borrowing requirement was reduced in 1968, this was more than offset by official purchases of gilt-edged securities from the public, which helped to inflate the money supply. It was the large purchases of gilt-edged by the Bank of England in November of that year which alerted the Chancellor to the fact that something was going wrong on the monetary side; and from then onwards he began to receive daily instead of fortnightly reports on the Treasury's gilt-edged dealings.

There is no lack of possible routes by which the increase in the money supply could have affected actual spending: credit not subject to the overdraft ceiling, increases in portfolio values (there was a Stock Exchange boom in 1968) or 'real' interest rates themselves. A calculation by the OECD (not normally regarded as a monetarist stronghold) shows how misleading nominal interest rates can be in inflationary circumstances. The average nominal yield on company debenture and loan stock was 7·93 per cent at the end of December 1967 and was climbing slowly throughout 1968 to reach 9 per cent by the end of the year. If this is corrected for inflationary expectations by deducting the average increase in prices over the preceding four quarters, the resulting real rate of interest shows an opposite movement – from a high of 6·8 per cent in the first quarter of 1968 to a low of 4·5 per cent in the third quarter of the year.[10]

FURTHER TRAUMAS

By the end of 1968 £3,100m. was owed to the IMF and national monetary authorities. How had the country got into such a position? As briefly and as impartially as possible the summarized answer is as follows:

1. There was first the failure, out of pride, to fund the sterling balances when we could have done so in the immediate post-war period.

2. Instead of earning a sufficient payment surplus to meet the rundown of the wartime balances, the gap was filled by keeping interest rates sufficiently high to attract new balances to London, thus maintaining an approximately constant total of short-term liabilities.

3. There was an underlying payments deficit in the whole of the 1960s. In the five years 1964–8 a total deficit of about £1,800m. had accumulated.

4. As a result of the delay in tackling the deficit there were a series of confidence outflows from London over the same period.

5. By the time of devaluation confidence had been so far eroded that sterling balance-holders believed that the pound was more likely to go down further than to appreciate; and some balances which previously carried no repayments obligations had to be exchanged for repayable credits.

Factors 3, 4 and 5 were the result not of devaluation, but of devaluing too late.

10. Report on the UK, OECD, November 1969.

The components of the reserve drain can be seen from the following table, derived from the figures in the 1969 Balance of Payments 'Pink Book', and Financial Statements.

The increase in short-term claims represents mostly export credit and should in part at least be added to the basic deficit, as a measure of what would have happened

TABLE 14

THE 1964–8 OUTFLOW
£m. (rounded)

Borrowing from IMF	1,100	
,, ,, central banks, etc.	2,000	
Use of reserves and sale of Treasury dollar portfolio	500	
Total official financing		3,600
Current Account deficit	900	
Private investment, net outflow	600	
Official long-term capital outflow	300	
'Basic' payments deficit		1,800
Increase in gross sterling claims	700	
Reduction in gross sterling liabilities	500	
Other short-term outflows	600	
Total outflow of short term funds		1,800
Total to be financed		3,600

had other short-term movements been neutral. The figure for the basic deficit is deceptively low. For it would have been much higher without the import surcharge, severe controls on overseas investment and the below-capacity growth, which could hardly have continued indefinitely.

Sterling's difficulties were aggravated towards the end of 1968 by fresh international currency uncertainties. The chronic German surplus made it more difficult for other countries to get their own balance of payments right and gave rise to speculation about revaluation. The franc on the other hand was a devaluation suspect ever since the large wage increases which M. Pompidou, as General de Gaulle's Prime Minister, had been forced to grant after the student and union unrest the previous May. It seemed likely that one or other currency would eventually give way. The suspicion came to a head in the outburst of speculation in favour of the mark and against the franc in November. The backwash of this crisis was extremely painful for sterling, which was hardly expected to increase in value in any international realignment. The Bonn conference, which was hastily summoned at the suggestion of Henry Fowler, the outgoing US Secretary of the Treasury, simply attempted to paper over the cracks. A system of border taxes on exports and import rebates was introduced in Germany equivalent to a 3 per cent back-door revaluation and measures were taken to discourage the entry of hot money into the country. But these were regarded as a holding operation until the German elections of 1969.

Meanwhile Mr Roy Jenkins hurried back early from the Bonn conference to announce a fresh set of restrictions. Hire-purchase controls had already been tightened a few weeks before. Consumer taxes were increased by the full use of the regulator power, which was expected to reduce demand by £200m. per annum. Bank credit was tightened further; and import deposits of 50 per cent for six months were imposed on a wide range of manufactures. This latter measure was as important for its effects on the government accounts and the credit situation as for its direct impact on imports.

The end of 1968 was as gloomy as possible. The basic payments deficit for the year as a whole seemed on the first estimate to be no better than in 1967. Despite a big improvement between the two halves of the year it still appeared to be running, after all allowances, at an annual rate of well over £300m. The November measures, so far from restoring confidence, were followed by a further weakness in gilt-edged, and a fortnight later markets were shaken by unfounded rumours that Mr Wilson and/or Mr Jenkins were resigning. Press calls for a national government reached their peak, and a mood of near-hysteria developed in many 'establishment' circles.

THE 1969 BUDGET

During the first quarter of 1969 sterling recovered slightly and there were some net repayments of overseas debts. This was not because of any underlying confidence in the pound. The published trade figures remained poor; but the confidence outflow had for the time being spent itself. Overseas members of the sterling area were earning particularly good surpluses at what was in any case a seasonally favourable period, and, encouraged by the Basle arrangements, were adding to their London reserves. Funds also came in from other countries to finance UK import deposits. The inflow was also helped by an effective clampdown on credit expansion and a sharp rise in interest rates both nominal and real. Bank Rate, which had been reduced in two successive stages to 7 per cent the previous year, was raised again to 8 per cent on 28 February 1969. The rise in interest rates was world-wide; but the movement in Britain was particularly sharp in the opening months of 1969.

These short-term monetary inflows did not deceive the Treasury. Arrangements for the recycling of speculative short-term flows by means of central bank swaps were strengthened at the beginning of 1969. But Mr Jenkins was not prepared to use such credits indefinitely to finance a basic deficit. The Chancellor gave himself a deadline for the autumn of 1969. A large proportion of the Greek alphabet was used up in Whitehall with contingency plans for what should be done if the UK were not in surplus by then, or if an unmanageable run on sterling developed before. These included a downward floating of the pound, and, in some versions, provided different rates for different types of transaction.

The 1969 Budget was basically a holding operation designed to give devaluation and the internal measures of 1968 a further chance to work. There was a considerable conflict between the trade figures and industrial evidence, for example the engineering order book, which suggested very large increases in export orders, which seemed to be limited mainly by supply difficulties. The attraction of waiting for the autumn was, however, not entirely domestic. For there was the widespread expectation in international financial circles that the long-delayed German-mark revaluation would come after the elections of September 1969. A further British change, if it should prove necessary, whether to a new fixed rate or to a floating rate, might be made to seem less like a second devaluation if wrapped up in an international realignment.

Mr Roy Jenkins's second Budget was a deliberately low-key affair. The increase in revenue in a full year amounted to rather over £300m. But over £100m. of this came from an increase in Corporation Tax from 42½ to 45 per cent. The main measures with a direct effect on demand included an increase in petrol tax, higher duties on wine, and an extension of the purchase tax net (which was now to cover potato crisps!). The biggest single increase was in SET. The latter was chosen as an alternative to extending purchase tax further into the food range, which many Treasury officials would have preferred. The effect on demand calculated on either of the orthodox methods described on page 165 was £200–250m. p.a., appreciably less than the official Treasury and Bank of England would have liked.

The formal economic arithmetic played a smaller part in the Budget judgement than on previous occasions. The Budget judgement was determined in large part by the feeling of Mr Jenkins that an attempt to raise taxes by very much more would largely have been offset by lower savings. He was also influenced by the desire to avoid raising prices

– the whole Budget was expected to add only $\frac{1}{2}$ per cent to retail price index, and this over a period of several months. Both the Chancellor and the Treasury were quite favourably surprised by the reception of the Budget. They expected a much greater outcry at the additional round of tax increases, not realizing that the public had got into a mood where it was relieved simply to get off as lightly as it had.

There were two particularly unpredictable measures. One was the withdrawal of tax relief for interest payments on personal loans other than for housing. This was designed to reinforce the credit squeeze by making it much more expensive for the surtax payer, who could previously borrow at very low real rates, to obtain credit. It was also meant to be a sweetener to the Labour backbenchers. Very little allowance was made for it in the economic forecasts, although it could be argued that it would have a substantial effect on the demand for credit.

The other unusual feature was the 'save a you earn' contractual savings scheme, with a rate of interest of 13 per cent for those who stayed in for 7 years. This was to start in the autumn of 1969; but the Treasury wisely decided not to count on anything from this in advance. If one looked at the savings scheme, the withdrawal of tax relief on loan interest, the rise in gilt-edged yields, and the high Eurodollar rates, they all fell into place as aspects of a general increase in interest rates, reflecting the sudden and belated recognition on an international scale of the falling value of money. But frank recognition of this – which would have involved rationing bank credit by pricing and allowing banks to compete with each other for deposits – was still regarded as too revolutionary and a series of back-door moves was preferred.

The biggest uncertainty related however to the turnround in the government accounts. The conventional economic arithmetic ignored this completely – strictly speaking it was regarded as implicitly embodied in the economic forecasts. The Financial Statement showed a dramatic change in the net borrowing of the central government of over £1,500m. from the calendar year 1968 to fiscal 1969–70. In the latter an £807m. *repayment* was forecast. There were officials at the top of the Treasury who believed that – either directly or through its monetary effects – this made the Budget much more deflationary than the economic forecasters allowed. Thus all the uncertainties about assessing the economic impact of the Budget, discussed on pages 137–56, suddenly came to the surface.

THE NADIR

In the spring of 1969 the trade figures seemed to get worse rather than better. A dramatic narrowing of the visible deficit in January proved yet another false dawn. February, March and April were three months of unmitigated gloom with published trade gaps of £64m., £52m. and £59m. respectively. Although the public panic was less than at the end of 1968, Whitehall's anxieties were much greater. The nadir was reached in May when the publication of the April deficit came just after yet another burst of speculation in favour of the mark.

Professor Karl Schiller, the Social Democrat Economic Minister, had now become converted to revaluation – which the Bundesbank had favoured the previous autumn. But his suggestion was voted down early in the spring by the Christian Democratic majority in the coalition government. The new run into the mark was provoked by some incautious comments of Herr Franz-Josef Strauss, the Finance Minister. Although publicly identified as the arch-opponent of revaluation, Herr Strauss seemed to suggest that it might nevertheless take place as part of a general currency realignment. The combination of the new mark crisis and the latest British trade figures put sterling under very heavy pressure again.

It was at this time too that very tricky negotiations with the IMF over another Letter of Intent came to a head. An

IMF drawing of $1400m. made in December 1965 was due for repayment in 1968–70. In the spring of 1969 some $1,000m. was still outstanding and a further extension was clearly required. The agreed formula was that a fresh standby credit of $1,000m. would be drawn in instalments as the 1968 drawings were repaid. The net effect was to refinance the credits until 1974–5.

The most famous of the IMF conditions was the £400m. ceiling on Domestic Credit Expansion for the financial year 1969–70 (this is explained on p. 165). Sir Douglas Allen and a few officials on the Treasury finance side had for some time been convinced that an uncontrolled growth of the money supply could undermine their attempts to control demand. A change of emphasis had already begun in gilt-edged market policy, to reduce the amount of official support purchases even at the cost of sharper falls in gilt-edged prices. But for many in the Bank of England it was a shotgun conversion. Nor did the leading Treasury economists see the DCE ceiling as more than a necessary diplomatic gesture to secure the IMF standby. Apart from the DCE target, the Letter of Intent contained a new balance-of-payments target for a basic surplus of £300m. in the same financial year.

The politically sensitive part of the Letter was, however, the 'trigger clause'. Under this clause any failure to observe the agreed terms would require consultation with the Fund before any more of the standby could be drawn. Mr Harold Lever, the Financial Secretary regarded such 'banana republic' conditions as politically unacceptable to the UK. In an unannounced visit to Washington over the weekend of 9–11 May he succeeded in swapping the trigger clause for regular quarterly consultations to which no stigma would apply. The Lever mission was authorized by a somewhat reluctant Chancellor against near-unanimous Treasury advice to sign on the dotted line. Human nature being what it is, the success of the visit was not received with unqualified joy by everyone in Great George Street.

The most alarming problem arising that May was not, however, medium-term refinancing, but the persistent weakness of sterling a year and a half after devaluation. For all the attempts to gloss over the subject, there was obviously a real debate in IMF and American circles about whether it would be better to let the pound float downwards rather than shore it up with further credits. Mr William McChesney Martin, the then chairman of the Federal Reserve, thought that the UK was 'skating on very thin ice'. He believed that the $2·40 parity had 'a chance' of survival – no more than that – and in Washington gloomier voices could be found. The consensus was, however, in favour of giving the policies set out in the Letter of Intent a few more months to work.

THE NEWS OF 12 JUNE 1969

The firmness of the new German revaluation denial – 'final, unequivocal and forever' – which followed the May crisis, was helpful to sterling. But the real turnround in British fortunes was sudden and unexpected. It can be dated, as far as published evidence is concerned, to 12 June 1969. Three important items of news appeared that day. The provisional May trade figures showed that the visible deficit, measured in the traditional way, had narrowed to £20m. (later revised to £14m.). By itself this could have been as misleading as the transient improvement the previous January which the Prime Minister had been so ready to proclaim during a visit to Bonn. Much more important, therefore, was a second piece of information – the discovery of under-recording of exports subsequently estimated at £12m. per month.

As a result of the simplification of export documentation, a gradually increasing proportion of British exports had passed unrecorded since 1964. Contrary to what a purely accounting approach would suggest, this under-recording did affect the reserves by undermining confidence and provoking adverse movements of capital. Inquiries had been going on since 1968. The Board of Trade statisticians, however, anxious to avoid premature conclusions, played their cards very close to their chests; and not even the Permanent Secretaries of the Treasury and the Board of Trade – let alone ministers – knew of these 'missing exports' until near the end of May. This piece of comfort was therefore available neither to the Chancellor in his mid-month anxiety, nor to Mr Harold Lever, nor to the British Economic Minister in Washington, during the crucial negotiations on the Letter of Intent.

The third piece of good news published on that fateful 12 June was that net invisible earnings were running at a monthly rate of £50m., which meant that the UK was already in current surplus in the first quarter, despite the visible deficit. The significance of these items was not appreciated at the time by the general public, nor even by the financial markets. The story of the missing exports was treated with considerable scepticism – understandably in view of the number of misleading announcements of recovery that had been made by the government over the past few years.

The June trade figures were still very encouraging, although not quite as good as May's. A few perspicacious observers, including Geoffrey Bell and Peter Jay, had the courage to proclaim that the corner had been turned.[11] But this was very much a minority view. The Chancellor himself was inclined to suspend judgement for a little while longer. Sterling had still to go through a difficult summer of renewed talk of currency realignment.

In a still highly charged atmosphere some common-sense remarks by Mr Harold Lever at a Federal Trust Conference in July created a storm. Mr Lever noted the folly of pretending that the UK had in its coffers in July 1969 the money to repay debts theoretically regarded as short-term. He pointed out that the bulk of Britain's debts had been

11. 'The End of a "Vicious Circle"', *The Times*, 23 June 1969.

incurred on short- and long-term capital account (see p. 390) and called for a funding operation on an international scale, remarking that 'damaging impressions' had been 'created at home and abroad by Britain's failure to meet unrealistic debt repayment schedules'. The speech had been approved by responsible Treasury officials; but Sir Leslie O'Brien evidently felt that his pledged word to other central banks was put at stake by such frankness; and the Governor's explosive reaction was shared by the Chancellor. It was sad that temperamental differences prevented two men, such as Jenkins and Lever, with essentially complementary qualities, from achieving a smooth relation-

TABLE 15

THE POST DEVALUATION RECOVERY

Quarterly Rates Seasonally adjusted (£m.)
Current Account

	Original Figures	*As Later Revised**
1967 (net quarterly rate)	−129	− 76
1st Qtr 1968	−134	−112
2nd Qtr 1968	−169	−107
3rd Qtr 1968	− 80	− 10
4th Qtr 1968	− 77	− 68
1st Qtr 1969	− 20	+ 23
2nd Qtr 1969	+ 75	+ 74
3rd Qtr 1969	+141	+147
4th Qtr 1969	+140	+171
1st Qtr 1970	+144	+144

* Up to June 1970.

ship. The departure of Harold Lever (he went in the October reshuffle to the No. 2 position at Technology with a seat in the Cabinet) was by then inevitable; but the British political system is not so rich in ministers with a feeling for international finance that it can afford to make them feel unwelcome at the Treasury.

At the beginning of the 1969 summer holiday season
confidence in sterling was still far from strong. The US
monetary squeeze was at its height; Eurodollar rates were
climbing towards their peak; and interest rate differentials
were particularly unfavourable to sterling both on a covered
and uncovered basis. On 8 August the franc was suddenly
devalued by 11 per cent. The timing of the move took everyone by surprise. The general reaction of those members of
the London financial community who were still in town was
one of admiration. The French government had not waited
until the last possible moment and had little, if any, prior
consultation with other countries 'unlike we British who
always obey the rules'. The French move touched off
substantial selling of sterling. The shock was aggravated
by the publication of a July visible deficit of £37m. Allowing
for invisibles and under-recording, the current account was
still comfortably in surplus, but the market was not in a
mood for fine calculations. The reception of the news was
not made any easier by a misguided Bank of England
tactic – lowering the operative support price for the pound –
which gave the market the impression that the July figures
would be especially good and that the Bank was preparing
a 'bear squeeze'.

The public change in sentiment came practically overnight when the published *visible* trade balance for August
swung into a surplus of £40m. with a particularly large rise
in exports. This was partly the result of catching up with
under-recording of earlier months, and partly of an erratic
fluctuation in a favourable direction. Nevertheless it was
the August result which persuaded the world of 'practical
men' and the Chancellor personally that the corner had
been turned. Mr Jenkins himself received the preliminary
count when he was feeling particularly depressed after
reading the last of the series of doom-laden articles by Cecil
King, solemnly published on *The Times* leader page, in
which the author had inquired of his 'friends in the city'
how the economy was doing and could find 'no responsible

person' who thought a £300m. surplus possible and mentioned the possibility of 2·5 million unemployed which was foreseen 'by some experts'.[12]

The published monthly trade figures were not so freakishly good in the remaining months of 1969, but still indicated a large payments surplus. The current surplus was running at an annual rate of £600m. in the second half of the year; and the IMF target of an overall £300m. surplus for 1969–70 was almost achieved by 30 September, halfway through the financial year and four weeks after the King article. The Chancellor was helped by a big improvement in the capital account, due partly to the new policy of encouraging the nationalized industries to finance part of their capital needs overseas.

Any number of explanations can be found when affairs go well, as well as when they go badly. Nevertheless it was a remarkable coincidence, to say the least, that devaluation began to work in the same year that the money supply was brought under control. Domestic Credit Expansion in 1969–70 was *minus* £600m., and the growth of the money supply slowed down to a gentle crawl. (Some may wonder what would have happened if there had been the turnround in the public sector accounts and the monetary squeeze without devaluation. There would then probably have been some balance-of-payments improvement, although not as large, but more slack and unemployment at home.) With overall credit under control, the squabbles between the Chancellor and the clearing banks about the failure of the latter to bring overdrafts back to the level existing in November 1968 were of trifling importance.

There were several abnormal features in 1969. World trade was rising at above average rates for the second year in succession. British output on the other hand was rising rather more slowly than normal, probably by $1\frac{1}{2}$–2 per cent, stock accumulation was abnormally low and imports

12. 'Wishful Thinking Obscures Grim Financial Outlook', 2 September 1969.

were also held down by prior deposits – an effect which was magnified near the end of the year by the false belief that they were about to be lifted.

THE MARK SAGA

From the middle of September 1969 international interest shifted to the German mark, where revaluation was becoming an active election issue. As election day, Sunday 28 September, approached, the run into marks gathered momentum, although sterling was less affected than in previous mark crises. Paradoxically those economic commentators who believed in adjustments through the price mechanism and the profit motive prayed for a Social Democrat gain. They went to bed on Sunday night feeling very depressed, as the early results had been interpreted by the computer as a Christian Democrat victory. Not merely would this have been a setback for a rational exchange rate policy in Germany, but British politicians of a fixed rate mentality would have been delighted to rub in the lessons of a Social Democrat defeat. On the following morning, the radio announced the good news that a 1 per cent shift in the swing changed the comparative position of the parties, and it looked as if the Social Democrats would after all be able to form their promised coalition with the small Free Democratic Party.

To stem the inflow into marks the Bundesbank persuaded the outgoing German Cabinet to agree to contingency plans, and on 29 September, Germany was officially on a floating rate of exchange for a temporary period until a Cabinet could be formed and a new rate fixed. In fact the floating mark experiment had really begun on the previous Thursday, 25 September, before the election, when the Bundesbank closed the German foreign exchange markets to prevent speculation. As the German authorities were under no obligation under the IMF Charter to stabilize the rate outside their own country, the mark was thus on a *de facto* floating basis. The German foreign exchange market reopened at the old parity for a little while on Monday the 29th, but the inflow of funds was so large that the Bundesbank was soon allowed to withdraw from the market.

The chaos that many predicted did not materialize. Indeed, conditions were far more chaotic during the speculative runs before the rate was let free. The rate rose fairly quickly, with some prodding by the Bundesbank, to a premium of nearly 7 per cent at the end of September. There was another smaller climb in the last few days of the free market, when fresh hints were given, and a fixed rate revaluation of just over 9 per cent was announced in October.

THE FUND STUDIES REFORM

Exchange-rate reform was one of the main items on the agenda at the annual IMF meetings in both September 1969 and September 1970. The main impetus for the study of compromise forms of flexibility was provided by the Nixon administration which assumed office at the beginning of 1969. It was, of course, largely impelled by the hope that upward flexibility by surplus countries would help correct any overvaluation of the dollar. But there was also a sincere conviction – shared by many in the Treasury and Federal Reserve as well as the Council of Economic Advisers – that the failure to adjust exchange rates by moderate amounts in good time was a grave defect which threatened to undermine that freedom of trade and payments which the Bretton Woods system was designed to establish.

The chief opponents of more flexibility were to be found among the Common Market Six, especially the French, the Belgians and the Brussels Commission, who feared that it would threaten their premature dream of EEC monetary union. On the other hand, German and Italian central bankers were among the intellectual leaders of the flexibility movement – in the German case largely from a desire to avoid imported inflation from the rest of the world. The Japanese were opposed on principle, but unlikely to block an American-supported and optional change of the rules. Many of the developing countries were anti-flexibility mainly through misunderstanding of the implications for commodity prices. But they were hardly in a position to prevent the main industrial countries from moving; and their own exchange practices hardly put them in a good position to lay down the law. The UK played a muted role in the discussions. British officials did make one abortive attempt in the spring of 1970 to obtain agreement on an immediate amendment of the IMF articles, hoping to have the issue settled while calm still prevailed in the exchange markets. But fear of taking any line that would alienate any section of the Six on the eve of yet another round of membership talks was a powerful inhibiting influence.

Most of the speeches and meetings in this period emphasized the virtues of 'fixed parities', but also spoke of the need for parity adjustment. Thus both camps could claim they were winning, and the minor shifts of nuance from one 'Group of Ten' meeting to another added to the confusion. By the 1970 IMF meeting the Executive Directors were able to list specific proposals even though they were still divided on their merits. They announced accordingly that they would continue their studies. It was all very reminiscent of the earlier long-drawn-out saga leading to the establishment of Special Drawing Rights.

More important than the detailed proposals at this stage was the emphasis on prompt adjustment of exchange rates when this was appropriate without necessarily waiting, in M. Schweitzer's words, until evidence of a disequilibrium had proved 'overwhelming'. For all the protestation about preserving fixed rates, this willingness to accept exchange-rate changes as a normal method of adjustment was a far cry from the way that the Bretton Woods system had previously been operated. The main specific proposals were

(a) smaller and more frequent parity changes, including as one variant a modified 'discretionary crawling peg' which would allow countries to move their parities by say 3 per cent in twelve months and 10 per cent in five years, (b) provision for temporary floating in special cases so that countries who did this remained, in Dr Emminger's phrase, 'within the law', and (c) a slight widening of margins – hardly worth doing except as an adjunct to the first proposal.

It will be seen that all these suggestions were purely permissive. It was up to individual countries to take their own decisions – as Canada had done by 'temporarily' floating at the end of May 1970. The IMF would not be in a position to block a determined and well-prepared move on Britain's part. Unfortunately, the Treasury and, even more, the Bank of England, remained sceptical and negative up to the time this book went to press. There was a fundamental failure on their part to ask the right logical questions. Instead of comparing the likely costs and benefits of alternative systems, officials tended to put up lists of snags in the various reform plans and not face the question of a choice among alternative courses of action, none of which could be perfect. Yet it was my impression that a prime minister or chancellor who really wanted to float, knew his own mind, and did not see this as a pretext for letting things rip at home, would have found a sympathizer surprisingly high up in the Whitehall hierarchy. As it was, the best chance to float from strength in the winter or spring of 1969–70 – when the current payments surplus was running at over £600m. p.a. and confidence was high – was lost.

THE PRE-ELECTION BUDGET

In the opening months of 1970 the coming election over-shadowed these more far-reaching questions. The situation was in some ways uncannily similar to 1959 and 1963. As in previous Parliaments the government had deflated too late and then somewhat overdid it. Having allowed monetary expansion to get out of control in previous years, the authorities went to the other extreme in 1969 and brought monetary expansion to a near halt. Thanks to devaluation and the rapid rise in world trade, export demand took up some of the slack, but not all. The British authorities, like the US Federal Reserve, brought trouble on themselves by ignoring the lesson of history and continuing the clampdown too long. The result was that a powerful body of respectable and non-partisan economic opinion, including the National Institute, was urging a reflationary Budget as it had done in 1959 and 1963 with well-known results.

The main psychological factor pointing the other way was the rapid rise in wages around the turn of 1969–70. It was more rapid than would have been predicted from the state of the labour market, even allowing for expectations of inflation. It was possible that trade unions were pushing especially hard in reaction to the recent abnormally low rise in their living standards – in the two years up to the end of 1969 consumption had grown by less than 1 per cent per annum.

Yet when all qualifications were made, inept government tactics contributed to the 1969–70 wage push. While incomes policy may have little positive contribution to make, its mishandling made the problem worse. The trouble began in a minor way as early as the 1969 Budget Speech, when Mr Jenkins announced that the power to defer settlements for twelve months would be dropped at the end of 1969. The decision may have been right. The power had hardly been used; and too many distortions – such as dividend controls – were being imposed on the economy for the sake of incomes policy. But the news that the powers were being dropped acted as an advertisement for wage claims.

More serious was the fate of the Industrial Relations Bill, with its provisions for a conciliation pause and its financial penalties. This was a brave attempt by Mrs Barbara Castle to introduce some elements of law into the industrial relations jungle. It was also meant as a psychological substitute for the incomes legislation. The Bill was dropped, as a result of opposition among the Parliamentary Labour Party, on 18 June 1969. There were arguments for and against the Bill. But the worst possible course was first to announce it and then to abandon it. The disastrous impression was created that, until the election, the trade unions had only to emit the gentlest puff of breath and the government would give way.

Having been defeated in her attempt both to control incomes and to reform industrial relations, Mrs Castle turned her efforts to pushing up the wages of low-paid workers. The human objectives she had in mind would best have been achieved through the social-security system. With other workers reluctant to accept a narrowing of differentials, the net effect was that of anti-incomes policy, which actually pushed up money wages.

Partly because of these new doctrines, and partly out of a Wilsonian desire to avoid labour trouble before the election, an all-round policy of appeasement had been adopted in the public sector, where settlements averaged 12 per cent by the late winter of 1969–70.

One should add, however, that the most fundamental difficulty of all was that having for so long seen every issue in balance-of-payments terms, politicians, officials and informed public opinion had given very little thought to how much importance they attached to price stability, now that the fear of overseas deficits had receded. In fact neither the UK nor the world could tolerate an indefinite acceleration of the rate of inflation; and the higher the rate was allowed to go, the more 'temporary' unemployment would afterwards be required to pull price increases back to a tolerable amount – as the Americans were already discovering.

Roy Jenkins's last Budget was brave rather than imaginative. He was under considerable pressure to give a large handout, both because output was sluggish and unemployment historically high, and because the more naïve lobbyists imagined that the payments surplus was a budgetary sum available for distribution. He stoutly resisted these pressures, but tax reform along the lines foreshadowed in his 1968 Budget was conspicuously absent. This was partly because a short Finance Bill was required in case of an early election, but one also had the impression that some of the zeal had gone and that Mr Jenkins was already thinking of the post-election period when he hoped to go to the Foreign Office.

The main Budget change was an increase in the personal tax allowance. The full-year revenue cost of all the measures was put at nearly £200m. But these concessions did basically little more than offset the effects of rapidly rising money incomes in bringing more people into the income-tax range. Allowing for distortions, such as the phasing out of import deposits, the overall public sector balance was more or less unchanged and the Budget was no more than neutral.

There were two reasons for the Chancellor's caution. One was his extreme concern to err on the side of safety on the balance of payments, which had become an absorbing preoccupation with him after his traumatic experiences of 1967–9. The other was that according to the Treasury forecasts the economy was expected to grow by $3\frac{1}{2}$ per cent in the year to the first half of 1971. This was a good $\frac{1}{2}$ per cent faster than the expected growth of productive capacity and – if correct – this would have made some inroads into unemployment.

The Budget was right for the wrong reasons. For even though the forecasts turned out optimistic, it would have been folly to have given a stimulus at a time when earnings were rising by 10–15 per cent per annum, prices by 7–8 per cent per annum, and the rate of inflation accelerating. Many otherwise first-rate economists and commentators fell into the trap of supposing that because demand for labour was not the *only* factor influencing wage settlements, it could safely be pushed up without making the situation still worse.

From April onwards policy was in neutral gear. The

fiscal balance was unchanged; and the new DCE limit of £900m. for the fiscal year 1970–71 was associated with an estimated growth of 5 per cent in the money supply. It was unfortunate that the policy still worked to some extent through directives on bank lending rather than by operating on liquidity ratios. But, if everything had gone according to plan, monetary growth would have been on a long-run path consistent with sustainable growth at moderate rates of inflation. The logic of the policy – even though it was not how the Treasury economists thought of it – was that if runaway wage inflation came into collision with the limited growth of the money supply, and the fiscal balance were unchanged, then the eventual result would be higher unemployment and depressed business conditions. When this ultimately worked its way through to wages and prices, more normal growth might be resumed.

All this, however, was for the future. An election was called for 18 June in a fit of euphoria based on highly optimistic opinion-poll findings – before even the Budget concessions, planned for July, came into effect. There will be many post-mortems on the totally unexpected Conservative victory. But the economic facts explain a good deal about the result, if not the opinion polls. The Treasury had expected that real personal incomes, which had been squeezed in the post-devaluation period, would now start growing at a normal rate. Unfortunately for Labour, the rise in prices was greater than expected both absolutely and in relation to incomes. The government suffered not only from lower than anticipated real growth in spending power, but also from the discontent resulting from a rise in the rate of inflation, which altered the distribution of incomes (within as well as between families) and of which the losers were more conscious than the gainers. Interestingly enough the Finance (Home) side of the Treasury warned that prices would rise faster than the economists expected, as a result of the squeeze on corporate cash and profitability.

The main backroom work carried out by the Conservatives in opposition had not been on price stability, but on the structure of taxation and public expenditure. The tendency of their programme, which was conceived several years earlier, was to shift some of the burden from the taxpayers to the consumer. Whatever its other merits, this was likely to raise prices somewhat further. Yet by an irony of history the Conservatives won the election on the inflation issue.

Economic policy, in the sense of monetary and fiscal policy, inflation or the balance of payments, or international financial issues, had, in fact, little appeal to those Conservatives most closely associated with Mr Heath. Their heart was in issues such as tax reform and the machinery of government. This was a legitimate set of preoccupations, but left the new government without a strategy for the immediate inflationary crisis; and the Civil Service had less difficulty than it expected (or than it had in 1964) in laying down the broad economic course; and this was for the best, as the top permanent officials were less wrong than most politicians in their view of what needed to be done, if not in the reasons for their views.

The death of Iain Macleod was a tragic blow to the government. This was not so much for narrow Treasury reasons, but because Iain Macleod would have been one of the main voices to speak for liberal principles in a Tory Cabinet. He combined this with a political flair and imagination which was not easy to replace. On economic management as such his main contribution would have been, above all, realism and a temperamental inability to worship fetishes. He had little intellectual interest in exchange-rate reform, as such, and thought the subject politically unrewarding. But it is inconceivable that he would have been guilty of the ultimate immorality of making a 'moral' issue of a mere ratio such as the price of the pound.[13]

13. This is a good opportunity to record my gratitude for the courtesy and friendliness with which he allowed me to put the case for devalua-

The new ingredient which the Conservative government brought to the financial guidelines inherited from Roy Jenkins was a proclaimed desire to stand up to extremely inflationary wage claims in the public sector and not to lean on employers in the private sector to make them concede. Ministers seemed almost to relish the thought of one or two strikes in the autumn in key sectors which they hoped would bring symbolic victories. The aim was not to secure non-inflationary settlements overnight, but to make a gradual move from 'double-figure' awards to something more reasonable.

One could only wish them luck with this policy which had the warm support of officials and advisers who were far from Tory in their inclinations. Historical experience suggested that, unlike concordats, norms or guiding lights, it was at least worth trying. But both on the industrial front and in the even more important fiscal and monetary areas, it was necessary to suspend judgement on brave resolutions. There were innumerable dangers on the horizon: the siren songs of the 'expansionist' economists unwilling to adapt their thinking to changed conditions, the vulnerability to change of a Treasury line which still owed more to forecasts than to long-term philosophy, the possibility of excessive gilt-edged support by the government broker interfering with the monetary guidelines, the rogue-elephant tendencies of some nationalized-industry chiefs and the possibility of a headline-catching defeat for the government line on incomes in some unexpected sector.

It was also difficult to judge the effect of the appointment of a Chancellor, Mr Anthony Barber, who was an effective administrator and loyal to the Prime Minister, but not well known for his economic thinking. One obvious danger was that the public expenditure-cutting exercise might run into difficulties – partly through the lure of prestige pro-

tion and floating rates to Conservative gatherings in 1967 without making me feel the *odium theologicum* to which one was subject from other quarters in his party.

jects in the aerospace field – and, that there would then be a temptation to cut taxes by more than the spending cuts strictly justified.

Indeed there were those who argued that this is just what happened in the Barber 'Mini-Budget' of October 1970, when £329m. of cuts in public spending were announced to pay for a 6d. reduction in the standard rate of income tax. The demand-reducing effects of the cuts were queried on a number of grounds; and on balance the package was probably inflationary. This came at a time when the public-sector balance was in any case swinging back into deficit and the outturn for 1970–71 looked much less favourably than originally predicted. The fears about the effects of official gilt-edged operations also proved amply justified and in the six months from April 1970, the money supply was growing much faster than allowed for in the Jenkins guidelines. On the wages front too the new government ran into predictable bad luck and the policy of 'standing firm' came to be interpreted as an unofficial norm of over 15 per cent.

Just as Labour in 1964 was slow to realize the true nature of the inherited balance-of-payments problem which it exploited so much for electoral purposes, the Conservatives in 1970 were slow to realize the true nature of the inherited inflationary problem which they had exploited in the same way. The increase in Special Deposits, which the Bank of England wanted at the end of July, did not come until 29 October, and even then the government was still opposing the Bank's proposal to raise Bank Rate.

For most of 1970 both the Labour and Conservative governments had been protected from international pressures by the strength of the balance of payments. But by the end of the year the OECD Secretariat in Paris was convinced that prices in Britain were rising considerably more quickly than those of our main competitors.

DAWN, TRUE OR FALSE?

Mistakes of timing, and political influences, are inevitable in most countries. Much the most important question at the beginning of the 1970s was whether it was now possible to run a substantial payments surplus not in particular years, but over the economic cycle as a whole.

The real arguments were threefold. Quite apart from debt repayment, a surplus of perhaps £250–300m. was required on a conservative basis to make up for the net extension of medium-term overseas credit by British firms in a typical year.[14] Secondly, and perhaps more debatably, was the need to increase Britain's 'owned' international reserves. The decade started well with the first allocation of $3,500m. of the new Special Drawing Rights at the beginning of 1970, which was to be followed by another distribution of $3,000m. in both 1971 and 1972. The UK's own share in the first distribution amounted to $410m., or £171m. A continuing allocation at the 1970–72 rate would, if unspent, take Britain's annual reserves from £1,053m. at the end of 1969 to over £2,500m. by 1980. But a large part of the increases would be required to cope with the growth in the value of Britain's overseas transactions; and there were arguments for a more rapid rate of improvement earlier in the decade. These were connected with the third powerful argument, the need to build up a strong balance of payments in view of possible EEC membership, which on the most favourable assumptions would have a large balance-of-payments cost.

It cannot be sufficiently emphasized that the test of balance-of-payments success will not be the statistical outcome in a particular year. It will be the ability to pay our way in a normal year, when output is growing in line with productive capacity, and stockbuilding is of average

14. This is after offsetting the understatement of the surplus due to the financing of long-term overseas investment in the Eurodollar market.

size, and when world trade is growing at its long-run average, and without measures such as import deposits, which we are pledged to abolish. Unless we pay our way under the conditions just mentioned, the familiar troubles will surely recur. Even then we will only be in full equilibrium and escape the balance-of-payments constraint if we can also dismantle all those other aspects of policy, such as some of the overseas investment controls, or back-door export subsidies, which distort the allocation of resources, or restrict the freedom of individuals.

What then are the prospects? At the head of the list of favourable factors are the sterling and mark parity changes of 1967-9, which enabled the UK to start off from a much better competitive position than for many years past. The long-overdue levelling out of government overseas spending, which rose sharply in the decade up to 1967, will also be of great importance – provided there are not too many expensive reversals of the East of Suez policy. The increased willingness to tolerate less than brimful employment and to keep the money supply in check will also help the balance of payments – if these policies survive.

There are, however, plenty of forces which we can see acting in the opposite direction. Historically British export prices have tended to rise appreciably faster than our main competitors'; and if this trend reasserts itself the de-valuation advantage will be eroded. There is, moreover, some suggestion that even under comparable price and profitability conditions, British exporters have tended to do less well than their competitors for all the usual reasons of inadequate salesmanship, delivery dates and servicing.

Internally the move to equal pay and the spread of earnings-related pensions schemes, which are very much to be expected, will add to British labour costs in the next few years. A shift to indirect taxation, whether or not involving VAT, will in the first place affect the internal price level. But wages – and therefore export costs – are responsive to cost-of-living changes in any given state of the labour market. The same point applies to increases in food prices, whether brought about by the EEC or by an independent British switch from deficiency payments to levies.

It is impossible to forecast the underlying balance of payments in the years ahead. Some kinds of forward projection are, despite the sceptics, perfectly feasible. But the ability to predict tiny differences between flows of £12,000m. in either direction, over a four-, five- or six-year cycle, is not given to the late-twentieth-century economist. Yet this, and more, would be involved in any attempt to give a definite assessment of the $2·40 exchange rate.

Much more sensible than any such attempt would be long-term policies which do not depend on being able to foresee the unforseeable. The whole balance of payments problem is an artificially created one due to the co-existence of different national currencies, the prices of which are frozen by governments. If this artificial rigidity were removed, governments would be free to concentrate on their real economic problem instead of on the pseudo-problems which have loomed so large in this book. But British political inertia being what it is, I fear that instead of floating the rate as a freely chosen policy at a time of our choice, we shall be forced from weakness to devalue again or adopt some form of flexibility. Although this is infinitely better than hanging on to a wrongly valued rate, it will result in a much more painful and disruptive transition that would otherwise have been unnecessary.

Part 3

ANALYSIS AND CONCLUSIONS

On human actions reason tho' you can,
It may be reason, but it is not man;
His Principle of action once explore,
That instant 'tis his Principle no more.

Pope, *Epistle to Cobham*

10

THE LESSONS OF EXPERIENCE

Welfare, reserves and living standards: 'underlying' performance: misplaced fundamentalism: the balance of payments: overseas spending: Britain's competitive position: sterling's international role: was policy destabilizing?: the pattern of stop–go: a constraint on growth?: demand and wages

HEGEL once remarked that history teaches that people have never learned anything from history, or acted on principles deduced from it. Nevertheless the temptation to examine the forces affecting British economic policy is irresistible. Similar episodes appeared to recur far too frequently to be the product of chance, and certain influences appeared to be at work for long periods at a time. An analysis of the 1950s and 1960s in terms of a few fairly simple economic and political forces not only helps to make sense of what otherwise would be a confused succession of crises and controversies; it also sheds some light on why Britain's experience differed from other countries' and may even give a few clues to the prospects in the years ahead.

Most of the discussion that follows is based on the period up to the November 1967 devaluation. More recent material is used, where appropriate, especially towards the end of the chapter. Devaluation is a fairly recent historical occurrence, and the balance-of-payments turnround that succeeded it is more recent still. Not nearly enough time has passed to see the post-devaluation years in perspective. The period from the end of the Korean war to devaluation is to some extent a natural unit for examination, almost a laboratory experiment, all the more instructive because it did not go as planned. There is no reason to think that the forces affecting the British economy have changed their nature;

the reader will have to decide for himself if the policy response has changed for the better.

Table 16 is a conventional 'league table' comparing the growth of national income per person employed in several countries. A little later on in this chapter I am going to suggest that the sterling crises of the 1960s concealed at least some underlying improvement. None of this can conceal the fact that Britain was near the bottom of the growth stakes over the whole of the period 1950–67. The USA, which came below Britain in the table, had of course a much higher absolute level of income per head from the beginning. Comparisons of absolute levels of output are subject to even greater statistical uncertainties than rates of growth. The available estimates do suggest, however, that both output and consumption per head of population, in several Continental countries, overtook Britain some time in the early 1960s.

TABLE 16

AVERAGE ANNUAL GROWTH OF REAL NATIONAL
PRODUCT PER PERSON EMPLOYED

	1950–5	1955–62	1962–7
Japan	n.a.	8·6	7·9
Italy	5·3	5·4	5·4
France	4·7	4·9	4·0
West Germany	7·1	3·8	3·8
Netherlands	4·9	2·8	3·7
UK	1·4	1·8	2·6
USA	2·7	1·7	2·3

Source: National Institute compilation from international sources

At this point some will query the underlying assumption that economic growth rates are a valid measure of relative success, even among countries at a comparable stage of development.[1] The assertion that growth should be an

1. The case is well presented in E. J. Mishan, *The Costs of Economic Growth*, Pelican, 1969.

important objective of policy is in fact a deliberate plati-
tude, provided that it refers to the growth of welfare
rather than crude physical output. If people choose to take
increased wealth in the form of more leisure rather than
more goods, it is not a check to growth in the sense in which
I should prefer to use the term. Gross National Product per
hour worked (if such series were available on an international basis) would be a better index of welfare than total
GNP. But even then it could be a misleading approximation. Healthy city environments, comfortable travel conditions and other public amenities are part of welfare; and
an addition to physical output incurred at the expense of a
greater cost in noise, smell, dirt or destruction of beauty is
not a growth of welfare, but a diminution of it. One very
attractive way of taking out the fruits of faster growth
would be to make the working environment itself less
abrasive, even at the cost of some sacrifice in production;
indeed one of the best arguments for more rapid growth in
the more fundamental sense of the term is that we could
then more easily afford to be a little less 'efficient' in the
businessman's sense of efficiency.

For these reasons the figures shown in Table 16 are a very
crude measure of the kind of growth at which it is rational
to aim. There would, nevertheless, have had to be an
extremely large systematic bias against Continental
countries and in favour of Britain in changes in leisure, or in
other unmeasured amenities, or in the statistical comparability of the figures, to bridge the gap shown in growth
rates for the period as a whole.

Britain's relatively poor performance in the growth of
measurable output was hardly due to any deliberate sub-
ordination of material to social and cultural objectives. A
preference for a more relaxed tempo of work may have had
some relevance, but is unlikely to explain the whole difference. Britain's relative economic failure over the period
in question was not the result in my view of any conscious
preference for other values. Britain was at least as material-

istic as any other Western country (one only had to look at the issues which counted in elections) but inefficient in its materialism. It is even possible that if wealth had been increasing more rapidly the country might have been slightly less materialistic.

Under full-employment conditions there is a trade-off between future and present welfare. Faster growth may require more investment at the expense of current consumption. It would be irrational either to maximize present welfare and neglect the future, or to go for the maximum feasible rate of growth irrespective of present sacrifices. The optimum rate of growth lies somewhere between the two extremes. (The correct way of measuring public preferences between present and future satisfactions, not to speak of the interest of people yet unborn, and translating them into economic decisions is a subject of lively, and still unresolved, academic debate.)

Clearly expressions such as 'maximum expansion of real wealth' used by advocates of faster growth (and which turned up in the first Pelican edition of this book) are carelessly phrased. But I do not think that this affects the range of questions with which economic management has been chiefly concerned. Fear of neglecting the present through over-investment was hardly the cause of the opposition that 'growth first' doctrines encountered in some orthodox circles. Still less was expansion held back to preserve the cathedral cities, or to protect the countryside from sprawl. The purpose of policy up to 1967 was to safeguard sterling and it failed even in its professed object, leaving sterling actually weaker than if the towel had been thrown in, and the pound devalued earlier.

WELFARE, RESERVES AND LIVING STANDARDS

The official post-war aim of building up the reserves was never achieved and gold and foreign exchange holdings hovered, throughout the period up to the 1967 devaluation, on either side of the $3,000m. mark. During the same period the reserves of European countries increased several-fold.

While American, German, French and Italian reserves were sufficient to pay for about half a year's imports, Britain's were not quite enough to pay for two months'. Even Japan managed to achieve a better ratio. As an international currency, it would have been normal for sterling to have had a better reserve ratio than other currencies. In the last three years of the period, moreover, from 1964 to 1967, the official figures of gold and foreign exchange holdings gave an altogether misleading impression, as they were only maintained at that level by extensive borrowings from central banks and medium-term drawings from the IMF. By the time devaluation came, these credits substantially exceeded the published reserve figures, and real reserves were negative. By contrast the leading Continental countries had a substantial 'reserve position' in the Fund, on which they could draw unconditionally and automatically – a cushion which France found very useful after the 1968 political crisis.

The fierce arguments of the early 1960s over the relative priority to be given to growth and other objects of policy could, with hindsight, have been expressed less tendentiously in terms of the rational pursuit of welfare. Most so-called objectives, whether the preservation of the exchange rate, the growth of reserves, stable prices, or the expansion of the GDP, are in fact valuable only for the contribution they make to the welfare of the inhabitants of this country (or whatever other body of people constitutes one's reference group). Whenever conflict arises between goals rational choice involves evaluating, however crudely, the cost in terms of welfare of alternative marginal sacrifices.

If they had been expressed in terms of the trade-off in *all* costs and benefits between alternative policies at the margin, the arguments against immutable exchange rates would have been stronger still. For they could then have taken into account non-economic factors, such as the effects on national morale and self-confidence of the continual recourse to the international begging-bowl that marked the years after 1964, and the semi-public scrutiny of our affairs by our creditors. The effects on our foreign policy of the years of dependence on the USA to protect sterling would also have been relevant. (The fact that many people outside and inside this country believed that, from 1964 to 1967, the British government had no option but to support the American Vietnam war was humiliating enough irrespective of one's views on south-east Asia.) A more comprehensive analysis would also have enabled one to take into account the psychological effects of a succession of crises and economic stops in inducing a sense of failure and frustration, over and above any impact that they may have had on the long-run growth of output.

These psychological aspects go some way to explain an interesting paradox. This is that during the first half of the period, in the 1950s, when the growth rate was very low, the national mood was symbolized by the phrase 'You've never had it so good.' By the mid 1960s, when taking one year with another the growth rate had considerably improved, the mood was one of gloom and despondency.

There are, however, equally important materialist explanations of this paradox. In the 1950s personal income and expenditure were able to grow considerably faster than output for a number of reasons. Between 1952 and 1959 (when the Conservatives won the third successive election victory with an increased majority) net national output measured in constant prices rose by 20 per cent, yet personal consumption rose by 25 per cent and personal disposable incomes by 28 per cent in real terms.

The two main reasons for the disproportion were the fall in defence spending and the improvement in the terms of trade. When the Conservatives came to office in the early 1950s they inherited the rearmament programme which the post-war Labour government had embarked upon at the time of Korea. This programme, which the Conservatives reduced, reached its peak in 1953; in the following seven years defence spending *actually dropped by a quarter* (allowing for changes in prices) and fell even more as a proportion of the National Product. The declining burden of defence spending was probably the main reason why taxation could fall as a proportion of the national income for so many years running.

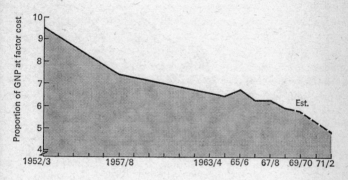

——————— own estimate based on 1968 policies

Source: Ministry of Defence

Figure 5. Defence expenditure

In addition the country enjoyed a windfall from the terms of trade. After the collapse of the Korean boom, food and raw material prices fell so much that in 1953 Britain could buy 13 per cent more imports for the same amount of exports as in 1951. The 1957–8 world recession triggered off another and slower slide in commodity prices, which eventually improved Britain's terms of trade by another 14 per cent, making 29 per cent altogether. These two movements together represented a gain of well over £2,000m. a year to the British public, measured at the price levels and import volumes of the early 1970s. An improvement in the terms of trade due to a fall in the price of raw materials is sustainable because British demand for such goods is very inelastic, and an improvement in price does not therefore encourage an import-buying spree.

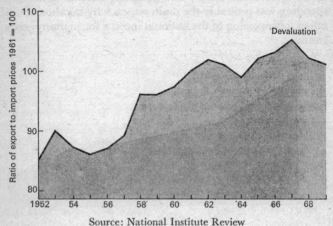

Source: National Institute Review

Figure 6. UK terms of trade

After 1959 there was little more to gain from both these trends and prosperity was limited by the growth of output. There was, it is true, another deceptive improvement in the terms of trade in the mid 1960s; but this was due mainly to rising British export prices. As British exports are mostly manufactured goods for which international demand is fairly elastic, this improvement had to be cancelled out by the 1967 devaluation.

While in the 1950s personal consumption rose more quickly than the underlying growth in output per head, in the five years 1964–9 it actually grew much more slowly. The increase per head of population averaged only about 1·1 per cent per annum,[2] compared with an average of nearly 3 per cent in the previous twelve years. There were

2. Hansard. Written Answer, 3 February 1970.

several factors behind this drastic slowdown. The growth of output was below trend as a result of the government's efforts to reduce the pressure of demand at which the economy was working; there was an unusually large spurt in public-sector spending; resources were being shifted from the home market to exports and import-saving; and devaluation brought about a deterioration in the terms of trade. Many of these depressing influences were by their nature temporary.

'UNDERLYING' PERFORMANCE

So much for the bare record of the 1950s and 1960s. To understand the forces which shaped policy it is essential to distinguish between underlying movements and temporary fluctuations, both in output and in the balance of payments. Several synonyms are often used for the underlying rate of growth, such as 'growth of productive capacity', 'growth of productive potential', or, more tendentiously, 'maximum rate of sustainable growth'.

The main point can be illustrated by imagining that output rises by 6 per cent in the course of a particular year. At the end of that year unemployment has gone down, overtime working has increased and industrialists report that they are working nearer their potential limits. It is then useful to divide the 6 per cent increase into two parts. One part represents simply the absorption of slack and cannot go on once the economy is working at capacity. The other part represents the increase in productive potential or capacity – due to increased efficiency, better machinery, the increase in the labour force (if there is one) and countless other factors.

The rate of growth of productive capacity can thus best be defined as the rate of growth of national output that could be maintained without any change in the pressure of demand as measured by unemployment and related indicators. If, in the year of our example, output had risen by only 3 per cent, if the unemployment percentage had been the same at the beginning and at the end, and there were no reason to attribute this to a time-lag in recruiting or dismissing workers, then productive capacity could be said to have been growing at 3 per cent. Output would have been growing at a normal rate and the pressure of demand would have been constant.

It is convenient to divide the growth of productive potential itself into the underlying growth of output per man-year ('underlying productivity') and the underlying growth of the labour force. For example, in the period 1961–5 the official estimate for the growth of productive capacity was an average of 3·3 per cent per annum, of which about 2·6 represented the underlying increase in productivity and 0·7 the growth of the labour force.[3] In subsequent years little or no growth was expected in the labour force and an actual dip was expected in the early 1970s.

There are many complications about measuring both productive capacity and underlying productivity in practice. An allowance must be made for the time-lag between changes in business conditions and the ensuing changes in employment. Other adjustments have to be made for temporary factors, such as a move to a 40-hour week or a school-leaving bulge, which may affect the growth of productive capacity in any particular year.

It is not surprising, therefore, that estimates of their growth for particular periods have proved volatile and even controversial. But, as they have been much less volatile than year-to-year changes in the growth of output, the distinction is well worth making. Moreover, despite all disagreements, it is pretty well established that in developed Western countries the underlying growth of productivity changes fairly slowly – a move from 3 to 4 per cent growth over five years would almost qualify for the term 'miracle'.

The tendency for underlying British growth rates to lag behind that of other industrial countries goes back into the

3. DEA Progress Report, June 1967.

nineteenth century, as Dr John Knapp and Professor Lomax have shown.[4] A reversal of this pattern would thus involve a break with a very long period of history. There is no lack of hypotheses on why British growth rates lagged for so long, but very little that is solidly established. Indeed, it is doubtful if it is meaningful to seek a single cause for the total behaviour of an economic system determined by a large number of interacting variables, a difference in any one of which could have affected the end result.

The most ambitious attempt to assign weights to the different sources of economic growth is that by E. F. Denison in *Why Growth Rates Differ*.[5] Although some economists would disagree with some of his procedures, and in particular the use of the share of profits in the national income to measure the marginal productivity of capital, his results are interesting, and the comparisons he makes between Britain and other countries point in the same direction as other investigations.[6]

Table 17 is a summary rearrangement of the factors, isolated by Mr Denison, responsible for Germany and France having faster growth rates than Britain in 1955–62. This is roughly the middle part of the period with which this chapter is concerned, and should thus be broadly representative. The fifth line of the table represents Mr Denison's attempt to move from crude growth rates to the underlying growth of output per head, by adjusting for variations in the pressure of demand. (The American growth rate was, allowing for pressure of demand effects, almost identical with Britain's during these years.)

Many of the reasons for faster French and German growth shown in the table were outside British control. The existence

4. 'Britain's Growth Performance', *Lloyds Bank Review*, October 1964.
5. Allen & Unwin, 1967. The implications for the UK are brought out by Mr Denison in his chapter of the Brookings Report, *Britain's Economic Prospects*, Allen & Unwin, 1968.
6. See especially Angus Maddison, *Economic Growth in the West*, Allen & Unwin, 1964, and N. Kaldor, *The Causes of the Slow Rate of Economic Growth of the United Kingdom*, Cambridge University Press, 1966.

of much larger pools of agricultural and self-employed labour would have given the two Continental countries a productivity advantage, even had British progress been equally rapid in every other respect. These special advantages were

TABLE 17

REASONS FOR EXCESS OVER UK GROWTH RATES
1955–62

	% points per annum	
	France	Germany
Total excess	2·76	3·12
Faster increase in employment	−0·28	0·76
Excess in growth of output per head	3·04	2·36
Effects of changes in demand pressure	0·29	0·29
Corrected excess of growth of output per head	2·75	2·07
Effects of contraction of agriculture and self-employment	0·82	0·57
Remaining excess in growth of output per head	1·95	1·50
Economies of scale	0·57	0·82
Capital investment	0·04	0·77
Residual efficiency	0·69	0·00
Reduction of international trade barriers	0·05	0·08
All other influences	0·60*	−0·17

* 0·38 of this is accounted for by a slower drop in hours of work and an improved age–sex composition.

Source: Denison, *Britain's Economic Prospects*, Table 6.5

even greater before 1955, but declined in the 1960s, and will decline even further in the 1970s. Economies of scale, as measured by Denison, were not an independent source of growth but a function of the growth of national output and markets. They thus acted as a booster, magnifying the differences in growth rates due to other factors. The booster was particularly great in Germany in the 1950s as a result of the inflow of refugees from the East.

If one isolates the factor over which the UK might in some sense have had control, the reasons why this country lagged behind France are different from the reasons why it lagged behind Germany. France grew faster as a result of what Mr Denison labels 'residual productivity'. This represents the element in growth rates that could not be attributed to any of the measured influences. Mr Denison identifies this residual with the rate at which different European countries were catching up with superior American techniques and practices. Germany on the other hand showed no signs of faster gains in efficiency from this source, but instead benefited from a much higher rate of capital investment than Britain experienced. In all these respects Britain's lag was probably even greater before 1955 and diminished in the 1960s.

MISPLACED FUNDAMENTALISM

To isolate a poor rate of improvement of general efficiency and a low rate of capital investment does not explain why they occurred. One plausible guess is that in the early post-war period productivity suffered from the low priority given to industrial investment, because pride of place was given first to social expenditure and then to Korean rearmament. The British economy also suffered from a relatively un-competitive business climate, which did not begin to change until the very late 1950s; and it was not until around 1960 that governments began to take a serious interest in struc-tural reforms such as technical education, industrial training, or encouragement to labour mobility, which influence the performance of a market economy. Thus, for a period in the 1950s, the British economy had the worst of both worlds, with little governmental prodding, but little genuine competition.

Guesswork about such fundamentals matters much less for economic management than is popularly supposed.

Macro-economic policy, for which the Treasury is responsible, deals with variables such as demand, exchange rates (and perhaps prices and wages) over which governments can exercise some degree of control. This branch of policy is concerned with how to make the best of the institutions, working habits and managerial skills of the population as they actually exist, rather than as they ought to be.

Some of the more enthusiastic members of the structural school occasionally give the impression that industrial reform can be an alternative to the Treasury's economic management. This is doubly misleading. First of all, the government's influence on industrial attitudes and habits is, at best, indirect and takes many years to produce an effect. Secondly, all good things do not necessarily go together. Structural reform would not necessarily have solved the major problems of economic management. A better system of industrial relations would not necessarily have reduced the rate of inflation; and better technological or business education – well worth pursuing though they are – cannot be regarded as recipes for eliminating a balance-of-payments deficit.

In some ways a misplaced fundamentalism may have actually held back progress. For it led many people in authority to over-estimate the ability of governments to bring about quick changes in deep-seated industrial habits and assumed too quickly that such changes would solve all other problems. This climate of opinion encouraged governments to neglect or postpone their primary task of maintaining external and internal equilibrium, where they would have had a definite and indisputable influence. The panics, uncertainties and abrupt changes of general economic direction, which followed from this neglect, could well have counteracted some of the beneficial effects of the structural reforms themselves.

Gloom on all these subjects can, however, be overdone. The mistakes of economic management did not prevent a gradual improvement in underlying productivity over the period up to 1967. A careful examination of Table 16 at the beginning of this chapter shows an acceleration in the growth of output per head between the early 1950s and the later 1960s. The acceleration was larger in Britain than in other countries, so that the gap, although still large, was narrower by 1962–7. Unfortunately there was little, if any, subsequent improvement in the underlying increase in output per head which remained stuck at barely 3 per cent up to 1970.

THE BALANCE OF PAYMENTS

In the case of the balance of payments it is even more important than when discussing the growth of output to try to separate year-to-year vagaries from the underlying state of affairs. The object is to remove from a particular year's figures, as far as possible, abnormal elements, due to, say, an unusually large increase in stockbuilding, a once-for-all long-term loan, or a Middle Eastern war. This should provide some idea of what the balance of payments would have been if the economy were growing at a normal rate, as defined above, and there were no special factors.

However imperfect and full of conceptual difficulties, estimates of this kind are a less unreliable guide to policy than the balance of payments in a particular year (although the latter cannot be neglected by a country without reserves). In view of the extreme difficulty of calculating the underlying balance of payments, a crude approximation may be obtained by taking the average over a period, in the hope that the special factors will cancel out. The snag about this method is that it conceals changes which have been taking place within the period in question, and for which it is essential to make at least an impressionistic allowance.

No assessment of the underlying balance of payments is strictly meaningful without some assumption about the pressure of demand at which the economy is being run. Quite apart from any more controversial considerations, the lower the pressure of demand in any particular year, the lower is the level of output and real incomes, and, therefore, the lower is the level of imports.

TABLE 18

UNITED KINGDOM: BALANCE OF PAYMENTS

Items	1952–9	1960–67
	annual averages, in millions of £ sterling	
Trade deficit	—140	—295
Government invisibles (net)	—145	—395
of which: Military	—70	—235
Private invisibles (net)	+435	+555
Current account	+150	—135
Long-term capital (net)	—175	—140
Basic balance	— 25	—275
Balancing item*	+ 55	+ 75
Overall balance	+ 30	—200

* The inclusion of the 'balancing item' amply takes care of 'unrecorded exports' in 1960–67.

Source: Bank for International Settlements, *38th Annual Report, 1967–8*, Basle, June 1968

The dominating feature of the period covered by this chapter was the deterioration in the underlying balance of payments up to the time of devaluation. This is dramatically brought out in Table 18, which shows that Britain was in rough overall balance in the period 1952–9, and in severe deficit in 1960–67. Yet the table if anything understates the balance-of-payments weakness. Even in the 1950s the situation was not as satisfactory as it seemed. The balance of payments was only kept in bare surplus by the exceptionally rapid downward drift in world commodity prices. Unlike

434

her Continental competitors Britain did not manage to build up her reserves during the period, and the net outflow of gold and dollars from the USA to Western Europe passed her by.

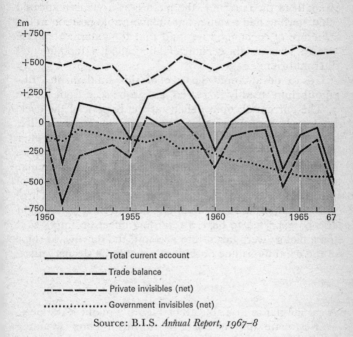

Total current account
— · — · — · Trade balance
— — — — — Private invisibles (net)
················ Government invisibles (net)

Source: B.I.S. *Annual Report, 1967–8*

Figure 7. UK balance of payments on current account

The high current account surplus of £350m. achieved in 1958 was deceptive. This was a year in which import prices dropped by 8 per cent, while output was hardly higher than the three years previously. Even if one allows for the recession in other industrial countries, the underlying surplus in that year was, in the view of the Bank for International Settlements, insufficient to 'support the normal outflow of long-term capital'.[7] The swing into deficit in 1960 is partly attributed by the BIS to the excessive stimulus provided in the 1959 Budget. But in view of what happened in other countries where expansion had not impaired the external strength of the currency, the picture as a whole indicated 'that sterling had a somewhat unfavourable position in the structure of exchange rates and that the external balance was in what might technically be called a fundamental disequilibrium'.

Up to devaluation the size of this fundamental disequilibrium steadily increased, as can be seen from Figure 7. The current account deficits at the bottom of the cycle became larger, the surpluses at the top became smaller, and eventually ceased to appear altogether. Moreover, after 1964 the deficit would have been higher still without a series of artificial restraints on trade and payments, in particular the import surcharge imposed for two years up to the end of 1966 and severe restraints on overseas investment. Three years of abnormally low domestic growth after 1964 might also be expected to have a retarding effect on imports. If these factors were taken into account, the downward slope of the continuous line on Figure 7 would be steeper still.

OVERSEAS SPENDING

A casual glance at Table 18 or Figure 7 might lead one to over-estimate the role of government military spending overseas in the deterioration. The increases in official spending abroad made the balance-of-payments problem worse, but it was by no means the sole element. The crude figures are in fact somewhat misleading. Table 19 shows that there was a large reduction in overseas receipts between the 1950s and 1967; the government's own expenditure, therefore, did not rise nearly as fast as the net figures suggest. In 1952 Britain received large sums of

7. *38th Annual Report, 1967–8*, Basle, June 1968, p. 11. This contains an excellent summary of the background to devaluation.

defence aid from the US; by 1957 defence aid had dwindled, but North American Forces' expenditure in Britain was at peak levels and 'support costs' were being paid by Germany for BAOR. Ten years later, in 1967, Germany was endeavouring to offset BAOR by specially arranged purchases, which appeared in the balance of payments as normal commercial exports. Of a deterioration in government invisibles of about £390m. per annum between 1952

TABLE 19

CURRENT GOVERNMENT OVERSEAS EXPENDITURE (£M.)

	1952	1957	1967	*Change* 1952–67
Expenditure	226	250	485	+259
Receipts	165	106	36	−129
Net expenditure	61	144	449	+388

Source: UK Balance of Payments

and 1967, some £130m. is accounted for by the fall in receipts, leaving £260m. as the increase in the government's own spending. Some £150m. of the latter figure is accounted for by military spending.[8] A certain proportion of this foreign exchange expenditure – perhaps a fifth – would have come back to the UK in the form of British exports to countries where bases were maintained.

It will be seen that non-military forms of gross overseas spending rose by about £110m. – not all that much less. The largest single component here was aid, on which very little was spent in the early 1950s. A high proportion of this was effectively tied in one way or another and therefore came back in export earnings. If the aid programme had gone forward, but gross overseas military spending had been

8. Including military grants and subscriptions to NATO, SEATO, etc.

frozen at its 1952 level in money terms (involving an enormous cutback in real commitments), the balance of payments would, allowing for feedback effects, have been about £50m. per annum better in 1960, and a little more than £100m. better in 1967. There would still have been an average overall payments deficit of about £300m. per annum in 1964–7.

This is a field in which the concept of cause-and-effect is very tricky. The increase in gross current overseas official spending was almost exactly in line with the growth of the money national income. In fact military commitments became so much more expensive in foreign exchange terms that, although gross overseas military expenditure rose by nearly two-thirds between 1957 and 1967, the number of men overseas or afloat fell from 320,000 to 160,000.[9] All one can say is that unwillingness to cut commitments faster made the payments problem worse.

Private invisible earnings were the one part of the balance of payments to show a marked improvement. This was the net outcome of a number of forces working in different directions. A big drop in the surplus on certain traditional items, such as shipping, and a deterioration in the travel balance were more than offset by a gain in net receipts on profits, interest and dividends. Overseas investment earnings were in fact far and away the most buoyant item in the British balance of payments. Unfortunately the resulting improvement in the invisible balance was not enough to outweigh the deterioration in the balance on goods and services.

BRITAIN'S COMPETITIVE POSITION

Sooner or later any examination of the 1950s and 1960s comes back therefore to trade performance. This had two aspects: the large rise in imports of manufactured goods and the rapid fall in the British share of world exports of manufactured goods shown in Figure 8. Both can be regarded as

9. Richard Fry, 'Government Overseas Spending', *Banker*, May 1968.

a decline in the competitiveness of British goods. But it was the behaviour of exports rather than imports that was abnormal by international standards. The ratio of imports of manufactured goods to the Gross Domestic Product rose from 4·1 per cent in 1956 to 7·9 per cent in 1966. The export ratio on the other hand remained obstinately stuck at around 14 per cent. Other countries experienced similar or greater increase in the appetite for imports, which were offset by a rising export ratio.[10]

Figure 8 illustrates the fall in the British share of world exports of manufactured goods, which averaged 0·6 per cent

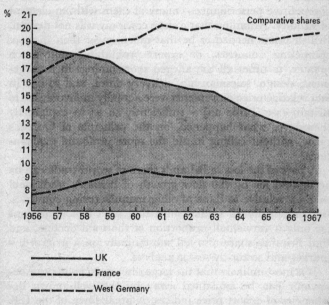

Source: *National Institute Economic Review*

Figure 8. Manufacturing exports of the main industrial countries

10. This point is discussed in detail by Lawrence B. Krause in the Brookings volume.

per annum. This does not, of course, imply that a constant share would have been either desirable or possible. But the rate of decline was too rapid to keep Britain's overseas payments in balance at the growth rate actually achieved, let alone to permit anything faster. The decline was not just part of a general drop in the shares of older countries at the expense of newcomers. The share of both Germany and France measured in the same way remained comparatively stable.

It is at this stage in the discussion that the danger of spurious profundity is greatest. A thousand different explanations are possible of what was really wrong with competitive performance – many of them with an element of validity. Assuming that a siege economy was not desired, British prices needed to be that much lower than those of competing countries, or export profitability that much greater, to offset all the alleged shortcomings in management, design, salesmanship, delivery dates, and so on. In fact relative price movements were actually unfavourable to Britain (see Table 20) – sufficiently so as to explain by themselves what happened, on the principle of Occam's razor, without calling in aid the more profound explanations.

A part of the loss in Britain's share of world trade can be accounted for by the slow growth of Britain's traditional markets relative to those of other manufacturing countries. But practically all studies show that such factors account for only a very small proportion of the total decline, and that Britain's share also fell substantially on a market-by-market and sector-by-sector analysis.

It is most unlikely that the large discrepancies in price behaviour can be explained away by the well-known deficiencies of export price indices. A breakdown of the UK and German price indices by the Board of Trade shows that British prices increased more rapidly than Germany's on a sector-by-sector basis.[11] Differences in the commodity com-

11. 'International Comparison of Costs and Prices', *Economic Trends*, May 1967.

TABLE 20

COMPARATIVE PRICES AND COSTS

	UK*	All Main Countries†	West Germany	France	Japan
% change in prices of exports of manufacture					
(a) 1954–60	+13	+7½	+6	0	−2
(b) 1960–67	+17	+8	+12	+9	+12
% change in wage costs per unit of output ‡					
(a) 1954–60	+24	n.a.	0	+10	0
(b) 1960–67	+19	n.a.	+24	+13	+15

Source: *National Institute Review*

* Up to devaluation.
† UN Index for US, UK, West Germany, Italy, France, Japan, Belgium, Canada, and Netherlands.
‡ Allowing for changes in exchange rates.

position or weighting of the two indices thus do not seem to explain away the discrepancies. Some of the data are reproduced in Table 21.

British money wages rose in fact a great deal less than those of most Continental countries for the greater part of the period. Even in Germany in the 1950s, when the labour market was slack because of the inflow of refugees from the East, wages rose as fast as in Britain and in 1960–67 they rose much faster. Such cost gains as the EEC countries enjoyed were entirely due to more rapidly rising productivity.

The available cost data do not in fact provide a complete explanation of the behaviour of relative export prices. One paradox, still to be resolved, is that in the second half of the period, from 1960 to 1967, British wage costs per unit of output were rising more slowly than those of some competitors, including Germany, yet export prices rose faster. The discrepancy cannot be explained by raw material prices. Moreover, the figures given in Table 20 probably understate the rise in Continental labour costs, as they leave out the social benefits financed directly by payroll taxes. Allowing for this, the Board of Trade suggests that the whole of the advantage gained by the EEC from 1954 onwards from a slower rate of growth of total labour costs per unit of output had been lost by the mid 1960s. British labour costs over the whole period nevertheless rose more rapidly than those of all her competitors taken together, mainly because of the slow rise in American and Japanese costs.

TABLE 21

INDEX NUMBERS OF THE UNIT VALUES OF EXPORT

	Percentage of Exports of Manufactures		Export Unit Value Index 1961 = 100	
	United Kingdom	West Germany	United Kingdom	West Germany
	1961	1961	1965	1965
S.I.T.C. Section				
5 Chemicals	10	13	104	87
6 Manufactures classified chiefly by material	32	25	110	99
7 Machinery and transport equipment	51	52	110	109
8 Other manufactures	7	10	110	106
5–8 Total manufactures	100	100	109	103

Source: Board of Trade

The reason why EEC countries were able to hold down their export prices so much better than Britain up to the 1967 devaluation is a matter of guesswork. A plausible explanation is that EEC manufacturers started out in the previous decade with much more fat in their export profit margins than did British industrialists, and were thus better able to absorb higher labour costs. Another contributory factor may have been that the decisive international cost advantage enjoyed by Continental countries in the 1950s led to a great expansion of export sales effort, involving the setting up of good dealer networks and service facilities, and the gearing of business activity to the requirements of foreign markets. These facilities and attitudes of mind did not disappear when costs rose and profit margins narrowed. The result was that Continental manufacturers occupied an entrenched position in world markets, which Britain found very difficult to erode.

Speculation about the causes of the relative decline in British competitive power, although interesting, was much less important for economic management than the fact that it occurred and was fully documented year by year by the comparative movement of export shares and export prices. As governments did not possess a quick method of increasing the growth of productivity relative to that of money wages there were only two ways of preserving a price and profitability advantage for British exports. One was to allow the exchange rate to depreciate; the other was to keep the pressure of demand consistently low enough to secure an even slower rise in British money wages, relative to competitors, than actually occurred. Neither alternative was adopted and, despite warnings in the government's own *Economic Surveys*, the situation was allowed to drift throughout the 1950s. Even in the 1960s action was for the greater part of the decade concentrated on incomes policy – the weakest of all the remedial instruments.

There is little evidence that incomes policy had any real impact on British costs from its revival by Mr Selwyn Lloyd in 1961 up to the 1967 devaluation. The economic object of an incomes policy is to bring about a change for the better in the unemployment–wage relationship so that a given rate of unemployment will produce less inflation. In fact the relationship, as will be shown below, has deteriorated. The most that can be argued is that without the efforts to regulate incomes directly, it would have deteriorated even faster. The experience of Cripps in 1948–50, Lloyd in 1961–2 and Wilson in 1966–7 suggests that an occasional freeze in an emergency stands a better chance of success than attempts at a long-term permanent policy for incomes. Even in these cases one cannot be sure that the freeze did more than affect the timing of wage increases between one year and another. My own guess, for what it is worth, is that there was a small enduring net effect from both freezes of the 1960s, but not more than 1–2 per cent at most on each occasion.

STERLING'S INTERNATIONAL ROLE

No mention has yet been made of the international role of sterling, to which Britain's difficulties were often attributed. This international role had three different aspects: (a) the use of sterling as a reserve currency by members of the sterling area; (b) the policy of encouraging banks, financial institutions and commercial firms to hold large trading and working balances in London; and (c) the fostering of the City as an international financial centre with gold, foreign exchange and commodity markets, where world trade that did not touch Britain's shores could be financed and loans arranged for overseas borrowers.

Although the three aspects are connected historically, they are to some degree separable. The pound's position as a reserve currency is best seen in the movement of the sterling area's own balances in London. There was no doubt that, in the words of the BIS 1967–8 report, 'the persistent disproportion between reserves and sterling liabilities could be an independent source of pressure on the exchange rate'. The knowledge that the liabilities were hanging over Britain like a Sword of Damocles undoubtedly inhibited the country's freedom of action. The fact remains that the threat was hardly ever realized before 1967. Figure

9 shows how stable the total sterling-area balances in London were for the two post-war decades. The running down of the sterling area's balances contributed in a major way to only one British currency crisis, that of 1957, and even here it was not the decisive factor.

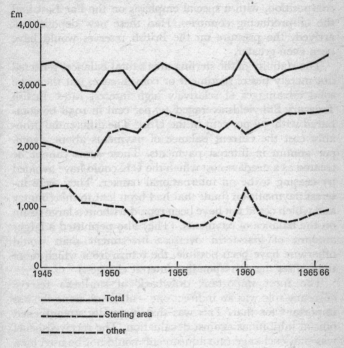

£m

4,000

3,000

2,000

1,000

0

1945   1950   1955   1960   1965 66

——————— Total

– – – – – Sterling area

– · – · – · – other

Source: Bank of England – figures adjusted to give a constant historical series

Figure 9. Net sterling liabilities to countries

The failure to fund the sterling balance in the post-war period, out of misplaced pride, added to Britain's difficulties for a considerable period. But as the balances which accumulated up to 1945 were drawn down, new balances arrived in London. The result was that by the 1960s Britain's liabilities to the sterling area had changed considerably in composition, and were by then no longer postwar debts, but normal reserves and working balances. They had acquired an entirely different geographical composition, with a special emphasis on the Far East and the oil-producing countries. Had these new deposits not arrived, the pressure on the British reserves would have been even greater.

The stability of the sterling area's total balances reflected not merely ties of sentiment or convenience, but the more solid advantages of relatively high interest rates. British Treasury Bill yields averaged 4·7 per cent in 1958–66 compared with 3·2 per cent in the US.[12] The differential probably cost the current balance of payments about £30m. per annum in interest payments. These sums cannot be treated as a needless cost which the UK could have avoided by ceasing to be an international banker. They were interest payments on funds that had been lent to this country and which could not have been repaid without a large strain on the balance of payments. (They also permitted a larger amount of long-term overseas investment than would otherwise have been possible, the return from which more than offset the corresponding interest charges.)

The most important drawback of sterling's reserve currency role was an indirect one – although none the less important for that. This was that it greatly strengthened official inhibitions against devaluation. The received belief was that exchange rate adjustments could not be used by a reserve currency country without catastrophic results. Whether this belief was justified is still controversial. The time for a prudent sterling-area country to move balances out of London is before, rather than after, a devaluation. The adverse reaction after 1967 reflected the desire to insure against a second devaluation, which was widely feared at

12. This is Professor Cooper's calculation in the Brookings study, p. 194.

the time. The same considerations might not have applied if action had been taken before the erosion of confidence had gone so far, and sterling had been left to float to a level from which it was equally likely to move in either direction. In addition the trigger effect of sterling devaluation in starting a wave of speculation against the dollar was probably due more to the fact that the dollar was itself suspect than to the fact that sterling was a reserve currency. But, rightly or wrongly, the reserve currency functions of the pound were regarded for a long time as a decisive argument against adjusting the sterling rate; and in this sense the insistence over two decades on clinging to these functions aggravated Britain's difficulties.

The balances held by non-sterling countries reflected the use of the pound as a trading (or private deposit) rather than as a reserve currency. Figure 7 shows that these 'other' balances were more volatile than those of the sterling area. (From 1961 onwards the chart figures conceal the true extent of this volatility as they include short-term central bank assistance to Britain.) London's highly developed ability to attract such funds indeed had a damaging effect on policy, but in a way opposite to that often alleged. These short-term funds provided a cushion of 'hot' money during periods of payments deficit which enabled governments to postpone remedial action until a very late stage, thereby ensuring that the action was harsher than would otherwise have been necessary and was taken when the economy was already about to turn down. The 'hot' money could have been kept out of the country in the first place by the simple expedient of maintaining lower interest rates. But at no time were British reserves strong enough either to repel short-term private funds or to face with equanimity a net withdrawal of the official balances. The alternative to relying on borrowed funds was to have replaced them by reserves earned from a balance-of-payments surplus – an issue which was never faced by those who railed against 'gnomes', 'speculators' and 'international bankers'.

447

The third aspect of sterling's role, the international financial business of the City of London, provided Britain with useful foreign exchange earnings of moderate dimension, and was on balance beneficial. The great bulk of short- and long-term overseas loans raised during this period were not financed from Britain (with the exception of those for the sterling area[13]). The City acted as an *entrepôt* centre. Control over capital movements was much stricter in Britain than in most other Western countries and a growing proportion of the business was not transacted in sterling at all but in other currencies, especially dollars. The Bank of England was never really content with these strictly *entrepôt* activities and often campaigned very vigorously for the freeing of capital movements into and out of Britain, for residents as well as foreigners. Nevertheless, the City's foreign exchange earnings are not at all dependent on sterling being a reserve currency and only partly dependent on it being held extensively for trading purposes, points which were at last admitted in the semi-official Clarke Report.[14] Amsterdam and Zurich do considerable international business, although the florin and Swiss franc are not international currencies in any sense, and the Swiss authorities have done all they can to discourage any net inflow of short-term funds into their country.

WAS POLICY DESTABILIZING?

After this digression it is necessary to turn to the domestic scene during the 1950s and 1960s. The notable feature here was the perverse nature of government stabilization policy, illustrated in Figure 10.[15]

13. This was regarded as part of the implicit bargain under which the sterling balances were retained in London.

14. W. M. Clarke, *Britain's Invisible Earnings*, British National Exports Council (BNEC), 1967, distributed by Thom. Skinner & Co.

15. Those who prefer to go by monetary indicators might note how well the arrows on the chart coincide with pronounced accelerations or decelerations of Domestic Credit Expansion. (A historical series is given

The expression 'stop–go' does not, when sensibly employed, refer to the use of those two indispensable instruments, the accelerator and the brake, but to the manner of their employment. This produced in this period not steady growth, but a characteristic alternation of steep

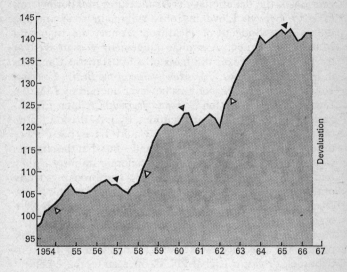

▽ Tax-relief budget

▲ Major deflationary package

Figure 10. Industrial production index

upward phases followed by periods of near-stagnation. The jerky pattern of growth was, as will be argued below, a consequence of the balance-of-payments weakness, but itself had a feedback effect, aggravating the severity of the underlying deficit.

_____

in the Bank of England *Bulletin* for September 1969.) The main exception appears to be 1955.

In the first edition of this book it was claimed that official economic management was actually destabilizing and thus aggravated the fluctuations it was meant to correct. This is indeed suggested both by the general history of the period and from the timing of the most notable government interventions – the deflationary crisis measures of Thorneycroft in 1957, Selwyn Lloyd in 1961, Wilson in 1966 and the reflationary Budgets of Heathcoat Amory in 1959 and Maudling in 1963. A similar judgement was arrived at by J. C. R. Dow, on the basis of a full statistical analysis in his standard work, *The Management of the British Economy, 1945–60*.[16] His conclusion was however queried by I. M. D. Little in a review in the *Economic Journal*.[17] A later investigation of the purely tax interventions, by J. A. Bristow, came to the conclusion that growth would have been more unstable had no tax changes been made, but that the changes would have contributed more to economic stability if they had all been made one year earlier.[18] The Brookings study of the British economy is not entirely clear-cut on this point. Its main findings seem to be that tax changes as such were on balance in the right direction at least, but that, when put together with changes in public expenditure and monetary policy, the net effect was destabilizing. One of the contributors, Professor Richard N. Cooper, states more boldly: 'Both the brake and the accelerator were applied at the wrong time.'

The main reason for these disagreements and uncertainties, as both Dr Little and Professor R. C. O. Matthews have pointed out, is the extreme difficulty of defining a neutral policy, let alone calculating what its hypothetical effects would have been. Official intervention (which was, of course, taking place in other countries as well as Britain) did probably help both to eliminate the long cycles ranging from 6–7 to 11 years, which characterized the 70 years before

16. Cambridge University Press, 1964.
17. December 1964.
18. 'Taxation and Income Stabilization', *Economic Journal*, June 1968.

the Second World War, and to reduce the total drop in levels of activity between boom and slump years. On the other hand, post-war interventions may well have increased the sharpness of year-to-year movements. The common conclusion to all the studies has been well expressed by Professor Matthews, who remarks that, whether the overall effect of official intervention was on balance stabilizing or not, 'it cannot be denied that Government policy did differ considerably from what it ought to have been if the object had been to maintain activity at a stable and consistent level'. Moreover, as the years wore on, fluctuations became more severe.[19]

Britain has certainly not been the only country to have experienced mistimed and even perverse official stabilization policies. Reviewing the experience of the Federal Reserve, Professor Milton Friedman comes to the conclusion that 'too late and too much' has been the general practice. The reason for this has been 'the failure of the monetary authorities to allow for the delay between their actions and the subsequent effect'. They 'tend to determine their actions by today's conditions – but their action will affect the economy only six or nine or twelve or fifteen months later'. Both the length of the lag and the impact of any specific change will vary unpredictably.[20]

Another factor common to most countries is that the indicators which the authorities watch themselves lag behind underlying economic conditions. It takes several months, for example, for a change in the trend of production to be fully reflected in the movement of unemployment. There is also a lag between the onset of domestic overheating, however defined, and its reflection in a payments deficit.

One interesting result of the cumulation of lags is that

19. See R. C. O. Matthews: 'Postwar Business Cycles in the United Kingdom', in *Is the Business Cycle Obsolete?*, 1968. This is in my view much the most illuminating of the studies of the post-war policy cycle.

20. 'The Role of Monetary Policy', *American Economic Review*, March 1968.

prices have actually risen much faster in Britain in years of 'stop' than in years of upswing. (4·9 per cent against 2·2 per cent at factor cost over the period 1952–65.) This is not, however, a strong ground on which to advocate expansionist policies. For the paradox can best be explained in terms of lags. There is a lag before changes in the growth of output affect unemployment, a further lag before labour market changes are reflected in wages, and yet another before wage costs are reflected in prices. If, as is likely, there are similar delays in Continental countries, where policy is very sensitive to the behaviour of prices, this would help to account for their tendency, too, to react too much too late – one of the most notorious examples was the delay of the German authorities in adjusting to the change from boom to recession in 1966–7, so severely condemned in the 1968 annual OECD Report on that country.

There has been a certain amount of argument about whether growth really was more unstable in Britain than in other countries. Professor Thomas Wilson has indeed demonstrated that there were greater absolute deviations in growth rates round the long-run average in many Continental countries (as well as the USA) than in Britain.[21] But, as Professor Wilson shows himself well aware, a variation of, say, 2 per cent around the average growth rate means less for a rapidly growing economy than for a slowly growing one. The argument turns partly on the exact meaning to be attached to words such as 'stable' or 'unstable'. One purely arithmetical consequence of Britain's low average growth rate was that growth was more frequently brought to a near standstill during British recession phases than in those of other countries.

21. 'Instability and the Rate of Growth', *Lloyds Bank Review*, July 1966.

THE PATTERN OF STOP—GO

Whether or not it was worse than other countries', Britain's policy cycle requires special attention for two reasons. First, far more effort was devoted to stabilization policies in Britain than almost anywhere else and the British authorities acquired many tools such as the regulator, non-Budget variations in purchase tax and HP restrictions, and the ability to get Budgets automatically through Parliament which would have been the envy of their counterparts in other countries. Secondly, because of the razor-edge position of the balance of payments and the reserves, successful stabilization policies were more important to Britain. The rate of inflation of wages and prices depends not only on the average pressure of demand over the cycle but on the pressure at peak periods. A ratchet effect is at work and steep increases in costs and prices induced at the top of the cycle are not reversed at the bottom. (It has also been argued that sharp expansionary bursts lead to a higher level of imports for final consumption than would have occurred if the same level of output had been reached more gradually and British supplies given more time to adjust.)[22] The underlying balance-of-payments deficit would thus have been less severe if the peaks and troughs in the cycle could have been ironed out, even if the same average of pressure of demand had been maintained.

But although better cyclical management might have helped, it is doubtful if it alone could have eliminated the underlying deficit. Indeed the causal connection was probably the other way. For the vulnerability of the balance of payments and the reserves was one of the main forces making for perverse policy timing, over and above those operating in other countries. The absence of an external balance-of-payments regulator (other than domestic deflation) ruled

22. See for example Frank Brechling and J. N. Wolfe, 'The End of Stop-Go', *Lloyds Bank Review*, January 1965.

out in this country any policy primarily directed towards domestic stability. When exchange rate variations, export subsidies and import controls were all excluded as economic weapons (or could not be used to the extent required), the timing of changes in home financial policy was inevitably geared to the balance of payments and the state of sterling. As sterling crises or recoveries lagged a good many months behind changes in the balance of payments, and these in turn lagged behind changes in domestic business conditions, the government was forced to hit the economy when it was already moving downwards. The subsequent reflation had also to come too late for fear that earlier action might have upset either the balance of payments or overseas confidence in sterling. But because re-expansion was delayed until unemployment had reached politically alarming levels the government needed quick results and could not afford to take any further risks, and therefore reflated too much.

The balance-of-payments problem has also contributed not only to perverse timing, but also to frequent vacillation among policy-makers about the average pressure of demand they were ultimately trying to achieve. As both the nature and extent of the underlying deficit were very uncertain, official opinion about the maximum long-run pressure of demand consistent with restoring equilibrium was subject to waves of fashion, which Professor Matthews has aptly likened to the 'waves of optimism and pessimism' among businessmen in old-fashioned trade-cycle theory. Professor Matthews is surely right to suppose that this infirmity of purpose offset the potentially good effects of better techniques for forecasting and controlling demand.[23]

As already mentioned, sterling's international role also contributed to the 'too much too late' pattern of official intervention by first masking and then magnifying deficits. Although there was no net build-up of sterling balances in London in the twenty years up to 1966, temporary inflows

23. 'Postwar Business Cycles in the United Kingdom', in M. Bronfenbrenner, *Is the Business Cycle Obsolete?*, Wiley, 1968.

of short-term funds did frequently cover over quite large deficits for considerable periods. In both 1960 and 1964 the authorities were puzzled by the contrast between the alarming balance-of-payments figures and the reassuring behaviour of the reserves; and on both occasions the false reassurance postponed remedial action. On the other hand, once confidence snapped and the exodus of reserves began, corrective action was imperative irrespective of the trend of the domestic economy, or even the balance of payments itself; and the need to restore confidence postponed re-expansion until too late in the cycle.

During most of the period under consideration Chancellors behaved like simple Pavlovian dogs responding to two main stimuli: one was 'a run on the reserves' and the other was '500,000 unemployed' – a figure which was later increased to above 600,000. On the whole (although not invariably), it was officials who became alarmed on the first stimulus, and ministers on the second, although each side usually managed to communicate its alarm to the other.

A response system as crude as this was pretty well bound to generate instability. But from a political point of view it was perfectly rational. During the period there was a strong relationship between unemployment and political popularity. Equally, however, exchange rate variations were not free of both economic and political costs. The idea was unpopular and the effects were regarded as highly uncertain and possibly dangerous. Therefore it seemed rational to governments (a) to keep unemployment as low as possible for as long as possible but (b) to deflate, whenever necessary to preserve the sterling exchange rate, *provided that there seemed a good chance of being able to bring unemployment down again early enough before the next election.*

Quite apart from any other difficulties, this motivation prevented any sustained experiment either in running the economy at a lower pressure of demand, or at a more constant pressure free of the ratchet effects of election booms. But the very pattern of the electoral policy cycle, with its inflationary legacies, was itself highly likely to lead to an increase over the years in the size of the underlying deficit; and thus ultimately bring about a situation in which the risk that the government might not be able to bring down unemployment sufficiently by election day at the existing exchange rate, clearly and obviously outweighed the political risks and disadvantages of devaluation. This point came in November 1967 (although some members of the Cabinet believed that it had already arrived soon after the March 1966 election).

A CONSTRAINT ON GROWTH?

Seen in this way the story has the apparent inevitability of a Greek tragedy; and it would be possible to leave it with a sigh for the vanity of men who imagine they can control their destiny. Yet there are questions in the realm of the might-have-been which are interesting for their own sake and because the issues they raise are of relevance to the future. The first is whether the balance-of-payments weakness actually held back the underlying growth rate, and the second is whether the whole sad story could have been avoided if political circumstances had allowed governments to run the economy at a lower pressure of demand.

The underlying payments deficit of the 1960s had a debilitating effect in many ways: the never-ending crises, the continual recourse to international borrowing, the accumulated debt repayment obligations and the sense of chronic national weakness were all too evident. But did it, and the earlier sterling troubles of the 1950s, actually reduce the underlying growth rate? In other words, what would the underlying growth rate have been if governments had been prepared to let the exchange rate go earlier or had in some other way succeeded in removing the balance-of-payments constraint?

Any answer must be a matter of guesswork. Calculations about the growth of productive potential when output was

frequently being held back for balance-of-payments reasons – and when this experience affected the whole climate
of business expectations – are of little guide to what would
have happened in the absence of this constraint. If the 1967
devaluation, or later world currency developments, succeed
in transforming the underlying balance of payments, it
will be possible to observe a practical experiment. All one
can do for the earlier period is to search out a few clues.

It is unlikely that the balance-of-payments constraint held
down British performance because the *average* pressure of
demand was too low. A higher pressure of demand might
have encouraged innovation and labour-saving investment,
while a lower one might have led to a more competitive
business atmosphere and imposed greater pressures on inefficient and high-cost producers. The Brookings conclusion
was that, taking everything together, neither a higher nor a
lower average pressure of demand would on balance have
helped productivity; and this seems about right.

But while the average pressure of demand over the period
up to 1967 was not too low, the policy cycle described above
almost certainly did have an adverse effect, aggravating all
the other factors making for slower growth. It would be a
mistake to treat the balance-of-payments brake in Britain as a
simple case of cyclical instability to be compared with cyclical
instability in other countries. There are numerous ways
in which Britain's peculiar pattern of instability may have
held growth back which do not emerge from an international comparison of cyclical deviations. Years of virtually
zero growth were more frequent in Britain than in other
countries and it is also probable that booms terminated
more quickly in the UK (which is not to deny that they could
have profitably *moderated* at an earlier stage). But over and
above any such mechanistic distinctions was the difference
between the long-term effects of Continental squeezes –
imposed mainly to combat inflation – and British squeezes
that were known to be caused by a chronic payments deficit,
which itself always cast a doubt on when and to what extent

expansion could be resumed. Indeed memories of these payments crises exerted a pessimistic influence on expectations even in the upward phases. For in laying down new plant businessmen were very well aware that, whatever politicians said, the growth of the British market was likely to be slow; and the alternative of going ahead faster for the sake of the export market was in too many cases regarded as too unprofitable to contemplate. This was in sharp contrast to countries where growth was export-led, and firms had every reason to be confident that, despite occasional checks, there would be no long-term constraints on expansion.[24]

Although the impact on the quality of business investment was not easily measurable, some of the effects on quantity were in fact visible. Figure 11 shows that, in the economic cycle following the Selwyn Lloyd measures of 1961, manufacturing investment only just exceeded its earlier peak, and as a proportion of GDP it had fallen sharply. In one particularly important sector, capital goods subject to import competition, an NEDC study came to the conclusion that industry's willingness to undertake investment sufficient to avoid recurrent capacity shortages would depend heavily on confidence being established that future growth would be a reasonably steady process.[25]

The adverse effects on Britain's growth rate of the balance-of-payments constraint were by no means confined to demand management. One of the most serious was the impediment it imposed to any unilateral move to reduce the protectionist barriers surrounding the economy. Although tariffs were reduced in return for concessions from other countries in the course of the various GATT nego-

---

24. Doubts are expressed in the Introduction, and developed at the end of this and the final chapter, about whether the authorities can really determine the 'pressure of demand' in the longer run. But they certainly have this power for a few years at a time in a period when inflationary expectations are stable.

25. *Imported Manufactures*, HMSO, 1965.

tiations, the average level of protection remained higher than in the US or the EEC (in which, of course, internal barriers were dismantled). The weakness of Britain's overseas payments made it difficult to contemplate any unilateral tariff reduction, and strengthened the lobbies at

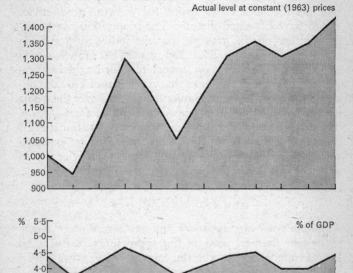

Figure 11. Gross fixed investment in British manufacturing

work to protect declining British industries such as coal and cotton textiles – by a fuel-oil tax in one case and quotas in the other. Even the general dismantling of post-war quota restrictions in the 1950s was criticized by economists such as Sir Roy Harrod and Professor Austin Robinson, who believed – with justice, given the prevailing exchange rate – that it was more than the balance of payments could afford.

After 1964 it became official policy to give concealed favour to import-competing projects wherever this could be done without appearing too blatant. The losses from not being able to open the gates to overseas competition were none the less real because of the difficulty in quantifying them.

It is also possible that if the structure of costs and prices had been conducive to export-led growth, productivity would have benefited directly. The proposition can be argued either on the grounds that the industries and firms that would have benefited from export-led growth would have been those with most opportunity for increasing productivity, or on the ground that a pattern of growth concentrated on a few sectors rather than spread over the whole home market would have helped secure economies of scale. The whole subject is admittedly controversial; but it is for reasons of this kind that the Brookings Institution expected the 1967 devaluation to be beneficial to productivity as well as to the balance of payments.

DEMAND AND WAGES

Although wages in the 1950s and 1960s rose more slowly in Britain than in most of her competitors, there is no logical connection between the causes of a country's deficit and its appropriate cure. An even slower increase of *money* wages than actually occurred would – through its effects on the costs and profitability of exports and import-substitutes – have prevented the British competitive position from deteriorating so rapidly, and thus eventually have been beneficial to *real* wages. What then is there to be said about the view that money incomes would have risen more slowly, and the country's difficulties been avoided, if it had been politically possible to run the economy at a lower pressure of demand with a large margin of unemployed?

Many of those who put forward this proposition merely mean that the pressure of demand on capacity was too high in peak periods such as 1960–61 and 1964–6. Expressed in this way the proposition is simply the familiar one that the country would have benefited from better contracyclical policies and a smoother growth of demand, although it does not explain how such better management could have been achieved in the face of the difficulties outlined above. The more interesting version of the 'margin of slack' concept, of which Professor Paish is the best-known exponent, is that Britain's troubles would not have arisen if the economy had been run at a lower *average* pressure of demand over the cycle as a whole. The recommended targets generally involved up to 1967 unemployment percentages in the $2-2\frac{1}{2}$ per cent range. This would, of course, have meant higher rates both at cyclical peaks and in the heavy unemployment areas; and it must in fairness be said that writers such as Professor Paish were strong advocates of measures to even out regional unemployment variations, without being starry-eyed about the practical possibilities.

If the average pressure of demand had been kept at a lower level from the early 1950s onwards, Britain's competitive position would probably have been a good deal easier. But protagonists of these 'margin of slack' theories did not always follow the implications of their own ideas. For the failure to take their advice must surely have had, in their view, some effect on British money costs and prices. By the 1960s the balance of payments was in a state of fundamental disequilibrium, which could only have been remedied by actually reducing British money costs and prices relative to those of other countries. To have accomplished this without devaluation would have required, as suggested in Chapter 9, a much higher unemployment ratio than anything like the 'Paish' margin. The larger 'margin of slack' theory is best regarded as one that should have been adopted many years before the 1967 devaluation. It is not nearly as neat and simple to operate as those who have merely picked up the slogan imagine.

One advantage sometimes claimed for running the economy at a lower demand pressure is that exports and

import substitutes would gain because of better delivery
dates and an improved competitive atmosphere. An investigation commissioned by the Board of Trade showed
that the position varied from industry to industry. Machine-
tool orders were sensitive to relative variations in British
and German delivery dates. UK car exports, on the other
hand, were not sensitive in the short run in either direction
to the state of the home market. It was claimed that UK
exports as a whole did better when the pressure of demand
was low. This was largely based on the indirect evidence
that the rate of decline in Britain's share of world exports
was least in years such as 1959 or 1963 when the pressure of
demand was unusually low (and usually, too, in the second
year of such periods of slack). It was claimed that exports
might have been nearly £200m. higher in 1965 if domestic
demand had been held back by maintaining a $2\frac{1}{2}$ per cent
unemployment rate.[26]

These conclusions can be disputed. Sceptics would say
that far too much is read into two or three points of in-
flexion on a downward curve of trade shares. They suspect
that world demand for British exports is relatively stable
throughout the cycle compared to that for competitors'
goods. As the British cycle is linked to the international
cycle, British exports can be expected to do relatively well
in slack periods and relatively badly in booms. (In other
words the elasticity of demand for British exports with
respect to fluctuations in the trend of world trade is less
than unity.)

The main snag, however, about using these calculations
for long-term policy is that they refer to cyclical variations in
the pressure of demand, and not to the effects of a long-term
policy of running the economy at a higher unemployment

26. J. R. Ball, J. R. Eaton and M. D. Steuer, 'The Relationship
between UK Export Performance in Manufactures and the Internal
Pressure of Demand', *Economic Journal*, September 1966, and 'The Effect
of Waiting Time on Foreign Orders for Machine Tools', *Economica*,
November 1966.

percentage. If such a policy were adopted, physical capacity would surely be adapted to lower average demand levels, and a sudden upsurge of demand in times of booms would still lead to a lengthening of delivery dates.

Much the most important part of the argument relates, therefore, not to delivery dates, but to the continuing impact a higher average margin of unemployment would have had on the movement of British costs and prices; and it is on this that the advocates of a lower pressure of demand rightly rest their case. Figure 12 shows a pronounced inverse relationship between unemployment and wage increases, certainly up to 1967. The relationship in question is usually expressed by means of a 'Phillips curve' showing a trade-off between unemployment and the growth of money earnings; and the implication is usually drawn that a fairly moderate increase in the unemployment percentage compared with the post-war average could have had a striking effect in curbing wage inflation. Professor Paish believed that if unemployment could be held steady in the 2–2½ per cent region,[27] the rate of increase in earnings could actually be held down to the increase in productivity. Other studies have pointed to even more favourable relationships.

The snag, frequently pointed out, is that it is dangerous to argue from the experience of short post-war recessions to a situation in which a given unemployment rate is maintained as a permanent policy. In the second situation unemployment would be steady rather than rising and – in contrast to recession situations – the background would be one of steadily rising output and profits. Although a higher unemployment percentage would undoubtedly have slowed down the growth of money incomes, the Paish–Phillips school was probably too optimistic about the quantitative impact of an increase in the unemployment rate confined to ½ per cent over the post-war average.

The graph in Figure 12 nevertheless confirms the com-

27. See, for example, *Lloyds Bank Review*, April 1968, and *Studies in an Inflationary Economy*, Macmillan, 1962.

mon-sense conclusion that the tighter the labour market, the faster will money wages rise. If an attempt were made to fit one curve to all the points, the fit would be a very bad one.

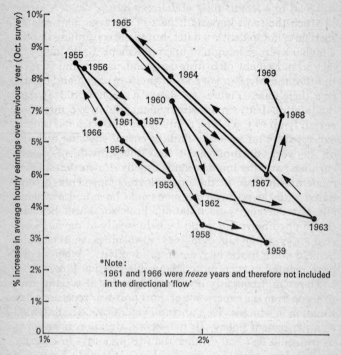

Source: Dept of Employment and Productivity

Figure 12. Unemployment and wages

Joining the years in chronological order shows that there was indeed a 'Phillips curve', but that it was shifting its position in an unfavourable direction. In other words a given rate of unemployment was associated with more rapid wage increases, and a given rate of wage increase

464

with higher unemployment as the years passed. The two freeze years, 1961 and 1966, are left off the directional lines on the grounds that the freezes of that year at least succeeded in postponing some of the wage increases which would otherwise have been brought about by market forces.

In interpreting the chart one must bear in mind the change in the meaning of the unemployment figures near the end of the period. By 1968 an unemployment percentage of $2\frac{1}{2}$ was associated with a much smaller degree of slack in the labour market than had accompanied such a figure up to the middle 1960s. Judging by the vacancy figures, it was equivalent to about $1\frac{3}{4}$ per cent unemployment in earlier years. This change was probably a delayed response to the redundancy payments scheme which began at the end of 1965 and earnings-related unemployment benefit, which began in October 1966. Both changes had the effect of giving workers a little longer to decide on the right new job. There may also have been more 'structural unemployment', in other words a greater discrepancy between the unfilled vacancies and the skills or geographical location of the unemployed. The changes in the composition of demand following devaluation, as well as specific influences, such as the pit closures, would have had this effect. Such changes would help to explain the sharp shift shown in the chart for 1968 and 1969.

It is doubtful, however, if they explain the whole of it. Nor can they explain the upward drift of the Phillips curve in earlier years, which emerges so clearly from the diagram. This is fundamentally due, as Professor Milton Friedman has suggested,[28] to the gradual adjustment to the facts of inflation. As time goes on, both workers and employers begin to take rising prices more and more into account in their bargaining; and an unemployment percentage which might have led to a 5 per cent annual rise in money wages in conditions of price stability eventually leads to an 8 per cent rise when prices are rising by 3 per cent.

28. Op. cit.

But the process does not, of course, end there. An 8 per cent increase in money wages is more inflationary than a 5 per cent increase, and thus expectations of a still more rapid rise become built into the system, and money wage settlements become higher still. The logical conclusion, which Professor Friedman does not hesitate to draw, is that if unemployment is pegged at anything less than a rate consistent with price stability, the result will be a gradually accelerating rate of growth of money incomes (which could lead to the rate of inflation becoming explosive in the very long term) unless there is a most unlikely offsetting increase in productivity. There is thus one natural rate of unemployment consistent not merely with stable prices, but any constant degree of inflation. If expectations of, say, 5 per cent per annum inflation have become built into the system, unemployment will have to rise for some years above the 'natural' rate, simply to reduce inflation to 3 per cent. At the other extreme the authorities can temporarily reduce unemployment below its natural level by pushing up monetary demand. But it will return to it once the authorities decide merely to peg the rate of inflation and prevent any further increase.

Devaluation and the associated increases in indirect tax led to a sharp and abnormal jump in the rate of price increase, from an average of just under 3 per cent in the previous decade to nearly $5\frac{1}{2}$ per cent per annum in 1968–9. This led to an increase in inflationary expectations (which also showed themselves in high interest rates on both sides of the Atlantic). Just as people had previously been very slow in adjusting their behaviour to rising prices, they now tended to project the post-devaluation rate of increases indefinitely into the future; and this probably accounted for the extremely unfavourable trade-off between unemployment and money wages that prevailed in those years. Unfortunately, just as the rate of price increase was beginning to decline and an opportunity was dawning to bring about a gradual reduction in inflationary expectations, the pre-election phase began; and the government adopted an anti-incomes policy of buying off industrial troubles especially in the public sector, and this led to larger wage awards than would have otherwise occurred in the prevailing market conditions.

This last example shows that the natural rate of unemployment is not given in heaven. It can be increased by a more militant use of the unions' monopoly power, or by the unwise use of the government's influence over the labour market. It can be reduced by retraining of workers in appropriate skills, or by a better regional distribution of the demand for labour.

Too much comfort should not be drawn from these qualifications. The real threat to full employment in this country will come if the rate of inflation has to be brought down quickly from an established high or accelerating level, either for international reasons, or because of a threat to internal confidence in the currency. To reverse and adapt the old Roman adage: if you are interested in full employment go for reasonable price stability – but if you have erred from the path of virtue, make sure that your return is gradual and slow.

11

CONCLUDING THOUGHTS

The machinery of government: unemployment and inflation: automatic pilots: taxation: the EEC: a misguided orientation

THIS final chapter is in no sense a summary. The conclusions which might be drawn from the various events and episodes are to be found in the chapters dealing with them; and to repeat them would be to overload an already long book.

THE MACHINERY OF GOVERNMENT

It seems as necessary now as in both previous editions to warn against supposing that any institutional device can be an adequate substitute for wise policy decisions. This was the chimera that beguiled both the Labour leadership in 1964 and the Conservatives in 1970.

The cost in confusion, and time-wasting of each organization of government machinery, is enormous. After each 'dynamic' reshuffle, ministers and officials have to spend months getting used to their new environment – which means everything from office arrangements to jockeying for position in the new hierarchies. The result is that high-level time, which should be devoted to analysis and policy, has to be devoted to demarcation and personnel problems. Many in Whitehall over the last decade would have preferred an imperfect structure to one that changed with such disconcerting and unnecessary rapidity.

A good generalization is that the fewer ministries there are the better. Decisions are likely to be both quicker and better if the people who have to coordinate their activities are working in different parts of one ministry than if they are separated by interdepartmental barriers. As departmental ministers cannot give each other instructions, the division of aspects of a subject among several departments makes it difficult to assign individual responsibility, and decisions are especially likely to become bogged down in the committee network. Even worse, officials and specialists spend a great deal of their time, not tackling problems at first hand, but taking positions on the proposals put forward by their opposite numbers in other departments. The temptation to go for a weak compromise and avoid a positive lead is then strong. Otherwise the most trivial disputes waste the time of Cabinet committees; and no one has time for thought and reflection.

Large 'federal' ministries do of course raise many problems of their own. The larger the span of control, the more unfamiliar the minister and his most senior officials are likely to be with the substance of policy; and the more they are likely to be engaged on administering and 'processing' policy papers from below. But the lower the level at which policy is made, the more difficult it is for the person concerned to take more than minor initiatives, or to change the framework in which advice is given. The best practical compromise might be to retain, at the cost of administrative untidiness, areas or policies which are run directly from the top without a long chain of command; the location of this area could shift as different problems come to the fore and as personalities change. This is even more important than 'hiving off' subordinate urgencies.

Most of my specific ideas on the departments and their structure are to be found in the appropriate place in Part I of this book. The most important innovation after the 1970 election was the establishment under Lord Rothschild of a central unit which aimed, not so much to interfere with Treasury control over public expenditure, as to help the Cabinet in choosing between alternative options both in public expenditure and in other policy areas.

The lack of such a staff, unattached to departmental

interests, was a great weakness. The problem of the new body will be to combine quality, independence and effectiveness. It was absurd that the Prime Minister should for so long have been the one minister without adequate staff briefing. But one cannot entirely welcome an increase in the presidential role of the Prime Minister, in the absence of all the checks and balances which make the President's power just about tolerable in the USA. As a *quid pro quo*, there should be a much more serious development of the Commons committee system and – even more important – some check on the inordinate power of personal patronage exercised by the Prime Minister of the day which has increased, is increasing and ought to be diminished.[1]

A particluar feature of Whitehall hampering British economic policy has been the existence of what Mr Roger Opie has christened the 'overseas lobby'. One does not need to have any truck with the more chauvinistic forms of patriotism to be mildly disturbed by the number of departments which approach economic problems primarily from the point of view of international negotiation, and how few are professionally concerned to put forward the interests of this country, 'let alone of something as materialistic and crude as the standard of living'.[2]

The Treasury has not been the centre of this lobby, although it joined it on some issues, such as the sterling area or debt repayment, and did not oppose it vigorously enough on others. Mr Opie's main example was the way in which the entire 'overseas lobby' worked singlemindedly in early 1966 to ensure that the Temporary Import Charge was neither extended nor replaced by any other direct import restraint, despite the abysmal balance-of-payments outlook. The principal example at the time of writing is the

1. The case for a Select Committee on Economic Affairs is explained in detail in the Memorandum of Evidence, by P. Jay and S. Brittan, published in the 1970 Report of the Select Committee on Procedure.

2. 'The Making of Economic Policy', in *Crisis in the Civil Service*, edited by Hugh Thomas, Anthony Blond, 1968, p. 62.

'entry at any price' approach to the EEC; and this attaches to itself a whole array of 'European' technological and aerospace projects, not viable commercially and destructive of amenity, but supposed to be necessary to show our European good faith.

A general assessment of the Treasury itself has already been given in Part I, especially pp. 46–52 and 67–98, and there is no point in repeating it here. Members of a closely knit group such as the Treasury will inevitably tend to become set in given procedures and frameworks of thought. Many of the individuals who came together in the re-united Treasury in 1969 have learned to react with almost Jamesian sensitivity to each other's every unspoken nuance. They know what not to put forward and have an instinct for the movement of fashion at the highest levels of the Treasury and Bank.

If fresh air is to be let in, there is a strong case for restoring and for developing into a full council of economic advisers the embryonic group described on pp. 97–8. This would supplement the new central-policy unit, which will not be enough on its own. The case for such a council rests on the need for a focus of explicitly professional economic expertise within Whitehall, independent of the regular departmental hierarchies, and supplementary to the economists now diffused through the operational branches of government. A council of economic advisers would be a healthy middle way between the unfettered sway of departmental expertise and the unsatisfactory institutionalized conflict of the former Treasury-DEA division.

The council should contain both a couple of the top departmental economic advisers and independent academics on full- or part-time assignment, served by a small staff closely linked with the new central unit. If the council's range of interest is wider than that of macro-economic management there will be less danger of its becoming an anti-Treasury. It should certainly have better things to do than duplicate the Treasury's short- or medium-term forecasting. The more the advisers concentrated on building up a reputation for independence and integrity, and the less they worried about day-to-day influence in Whitehall, the more successful they be likely to be. But for the experiment to develop in this way the government would have to allow them occasionally to speak in public without necessarily committing ministers to every word.

UNEMPLOYMENT AND INFLATION

The case for such machinery is particularly strong now that the official British variant of 'Keynesianism' has been subject to greater theoretical and practical challenge than ever before. (The quotation marks are very necessary to leave open the question how far Lord Keynes would have himself endorsed the post-war orthodoxies.)

The basic assumption behind most post-war writing on economic policy was that the authorities can, whether by fiscal or monetary policy or both, determine the 'pressure of demand' – in other words the unemployment percentage and the degree of utilization of capacity. A high pressure of demand was associated with more rapidly rising prices than a low one (and under a fixed exchange rate with a worse balance of payments). There was therefore a trade-off between employment and price stability, and the authorities had to choose their own compromise.

This view has been severely challenged, for the reasons explained at the end of the last chapter. I must ask the reader at this point to re-read pages 463–7 of that chapter; as the whole of the present section is a direct continuation and may otherwise be unintelligible. It is there suggested that because people eventually see through 'money illusion', and start to bargain in real terms, there is a natural rate of unemployment consistent either with broadly stable prices or any constant degree of inflation. It is therefore not possible to secure a permanent increase in employment above that level by boosting demand, for this would require not merely a rapid, but an accelerating, degree of inflation. The social strains of accelerating inflation, as well as the need for usable money, are such that no society could allow this to continue indefinitely.

The above view is sometimes known as the theory of 'adaptive expectations'. In other words price expectations are adjusted to past experience. This, however, is a somewhat oversimplified view of the reaction mechanism. After the onset of a moderate inflation there may be a period of years, or even a decade or two, in which 'money illusion' persists – i.e. wage bargains, interest rates, salary arrangements, the 'reverse-yield gap' and similar phenomena are not adapted to the facts of inflation. Adaptation when it comes may be sudden; and for a time people may actually over-react on the basis of excessively pessimistic inflationary expectations which then prove self-justifying. (For reasons of this kind econometric verification or falsification is extremely difficult.)

The argument so far has had fairly conservative implications. But a modification with more radical overtones is required. For it is not strictly true that the 'natural' rate of unemployment is consistent with *any* constant degree of inflation, or with price stability. In a given historical situation the 'natural' rate of unemployment may be inconsistent with price stability, or rates of inflation below a certain minimum. *This is because the economic system is highly resistant to downward changes, not only in the general level of wages and prices, but even in their rate of increase, once a given degree of inflation has come to influence behaviour and expectations.* It is in emphasizing this aspect that the 'monetarist' or 'new old' economists differ from the traditional 'tough-money' school.

Because of the inertia of wages and prices, sudden and severe attempts to halt the expansion of monetary demand will lead to stagnation of output and unemployment, while the beneficial effects on prices will come through slowly and very much later. (This is the origin of 'inflationary recessions'.) As Professor Milton Friedman once remarked, 'The only way to stop inflation in short order would be to engineer a real monetary collapse'.

The case for flexible exchanges arises basically from the difficulty of making large and rapid downward changes in domestic costs and prices or in their rate of increase; and this is why attempts to secure an underlying payments deficit by deflation *alone* will, as explained with arithmetical illustrations at the beginning of Chapter 9, lead to unnecessary unemployment and stagnation. The dilemmas inherent in this situation are a strong argument against indulging in inflationary policies in the first place. But, once this error has been committed, the best hope is by means of what has been called 'gradualism'. In other words there should be a gradual slowing down in the growth of monetary demand. Output would grow, but by less than the underlying growth of capacity; and the increasing margin of slack would by degrees affect the labour and goods markets. Gradualism, one must warn, is a matter of several years, not months.

Nor should one minimize the costs in output and employment that are probably unavoidable once inflationary psychology has taken root and price rises are accelerating. It may well be necessary to allow unemployment to rise *above* its natural level to affect expectations and stop the acceleration of wages and prices. After this, unemployment can fall back – but only to its natural rate, if the whole process is to be prevented from starting again.

A further modification is needed. This is that there may be a minimum rate of steady inflation, which cannot be reduced, however gradually, without pushing up unemployment well above its 'natural' level. This can reflect trade-union psychology, or the fact that employers who are short of labour bid wages up, while those in surplus industries do not reduce them; and for this reason a dynamic economy may have an inflationary bias. *In other words the natural rate of unemployment is that consistent with any consistent rate of inflation above a certain minimum determined by institutional forces.*

Figure 13 is an attempt to make the above argument comprehensible in a rough schematic way. It is a 'long-term Phillips curve' showing the relation between wages and unemployment after people's behaviour has become fully adjusted to the prevailing movement of prices. Point X is the natural unemployment rate. The left-hand segment of the curve is extremely steep – unemployment cannot be permanently reduced much below X without runaway rises in money wages. The section to the right is nearly flat. For wage increases are near their institutional minimum; and attempts to push them down further will lead to large-scale unemployment with very small gains in wage and price stability. The moral is that there are certain minimum levels of *both* inflation and unemployment which demand managers must accept as given. They can do very little by their own action to improve these levels, but they can very easily make them worse by inept policies.

Unfortunately for system builders, the natural level of unemployment and the minimum rate of inflation can themselves change, and sometimes quite quickly. Wages are determined by other forces apart from the demand for labour and price expectations. No formal economic model, or informal economic commentary, could or did predict the wage explosion that began in the winter of 1969–70.

The state of the labour market and price expectations are not the only influences on money wages. A third factor is that workers, like other groups, are resistant not only to reductions in their absolute standard of living, but to reductions in the rate of increase to which they have become accustomed. If real incomes have been squeezed in the recent past, wage demands will be more aggressive than would otherwise have been expected in the same economic climate. Here is probably one of the main explanations of the 1969–70 experience. This came at the end of a five-year period in which personal disposable incomes had risen by a

475

third of their long-run average – and in the last year and a half of the period they had ceased to rise at all.

The need for such a brake on the growth of living standards arose from the need to make sudden large shifts in resources for the home market to exports or import-

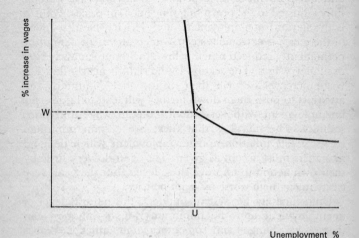

Figure 13. Unemployment and money wages: the long-term tradeoff.

savings in a short space of time. Such episodes are endemic to a country on a supposedly fixed-exchange-rate system, which also enjoys access to ample supplies of international credit, both official and private, for a *temporary* period. This allows a large underlying deficit to accumulate, which has then suddenly to be shifted into surplus in a short space of time, with or without a devaluation. If exchange rates could move gradually over time, the need for such dramatic shifts need never arise; and, even if the long-term drift of the rate is downwards, the effect on import prices and living standards in any one year would be moderate.

The international movement of costs and prices is a fourth factor which influences how much employers will concede. The exact form of the relationship is complex and would repay further study. It is clearly not a very fortunate one. For it appears to be an aggravating factor at a time of rapid world inflation but is not close enough to prevent payments disequilibrium from arising at a fixed rate of exchange.

It would be other-worldly to ignore a fifth set of influences, coming from the general social climate, trade-union attitudes and government policies. Some of these influences can be put into economic jargon by talking, for example, about increases in the degree of monopoly power exercised by unions; but, without a theory about when such increases will take place, one is just playing with words.

The above remarks obviously do not provide a complete model of wage determination, or of the interaction of economic, psychological and institutional forces. But I believe that a schematic picture, such as that summarized in Figure 13, is, for all its defects, essential to thinking and policy. Knowledge of the existence of point X – even though it shifts around – is a check on the hubris of the country's monetary managers and provides some guarantee against disastrous policy errors.

Monetarist economists can reasonably claim that if the money supply were controlled there would be a limit to the extent that nominal (or money) national income could rise. But there is nothing in their findings to prevent this result from being achieved through a higher level of incomes being spread among a smaller number of jobs. In practice a wage-push can go a certain distance with the aid of an increase in the velocity of circulation. After that, once the inflation has developed momentum the authorities face the unenviable choice of either maintaining their money supply limits at the cost of recession and unemployment or of 'financing inflation'. They are likely in fact to go for an unsatisfactory compromise, involving both a breach of the established monetary guidelines and more unemployment. The same dilemma would apply if the level of money demand and incomes were successfully regulated by fiscal policy instead. No form of demand management provides ministers with a magic wand, which would enable them to escape the consequences of misguided policies in other spheres. There is no escape from actually looking at the grassroots forces affecting money wages.

It is the task of economic policy *other than demand management* to attempt to shift X so that the minimum sustainable levels of unemployment and inflation are as low as possible. Formal incomes policy has had disappointing results, and periods of restraint have always been followed by subsequent bursts of wage increase. But the crucial argument concerns the adverse side effects of incomes policy in too many directions. The medieval myth that there is a 'just price' for people's services different from the market level, known to men of goodwill, is perpetuated. The inevitable result is that everyone's 'just reward' adds up to more than the total available; and the more that people, whether farmers or teachers or dockers, come to look to the state to secure their reward, the worse inflation threatens to be in the longer run. For it is the nature of the political process to buy off each piece of trouble when it arrives, irrespective of the total coherence of the actions taken. In addition, incomes policy tends to be 'backed' by a whole series of actions – from pressures on the nationalized industries to keep their prices artificially low, to dividend and price control, and penal taxation of higher incomes and profits – which are inimical to the efficient working of a market economy and which, pushed too far, are also a threat to personal liberty.

But while a formal 'incomes policy' is a snare and delusion, ministers do inevitably have to have a policy towards incomes. The public sector, especially when elections are approaching, has been all too inclined to give an inflationary lead. This is abetted by the absence of market disciplines over many areas, and the convention of measuring public expenditure in 'real terms' so that (despite one or two recent attempts at refinement) large wage increases do not disturb the announced ceilings. The conciliation and industrial relations of branches of government have an influence which can be used in various directions; and employers are very conscious of any hints that the government will intervene to buy off trouble if this attempt to make a stand fails.

Statutory control over wages paid in individual establishments, as a permanent system, is both incompatible with a free society and in the longer run threatens to ossify the industrial structure. Some reserve powers may in the end prove inescapable. But the right context in which to exercise them is that of anti-monopoly policy. Industry-wide wage bargains are struck between monopolistic sellers of labour and monopsonistic buyers. There would be no threat to either liberty or economic efficiency if the state or a public body had statutory powers over such bargains, *provided that individual employers were still free to make their own bargains with employees*. The result of such controls would probably be to accelerate the shift of bargaining from national to local level. This would not be a panacea; but it might make the whole labour market more sensitive to economic conditions. A more important instrument is the very occasional complete wage freeze in times of crisis. This is both more effective, and less damaging in its side effects, than a continuing attempt at a long-run incomes policy.

AUTOMATIC PILOTS

Although demand management cannot perform many of the tasks commonly expected of it, it still has a vital role. It can determine how far above the minimum the actual rate of inflation is to be. It can avoid the blunders that lead to needlessly high unemployment above the 'natural' rate; and it can attempt to avoid unnecessary fluctuations in employment, prices and activity – or at least refrain from adding to instability.[3]

A recurrent theme in the historical chapters is that the authorities reflated or deflated by the wrong amounts at the wrong time – usually too much too late. The conventional succession of hard and soft Budgets, of changes in hire-purchase regulations, credit directives and all the rest, presupposes an ability to forecast short-term economic movements and the effects of policy changes, as well as a speed of political and administrative reaction, which is belied by the experience of nearly all major countries. In the British case, the sudden lurches in financial policy have not even been intended to smooth out fluctuations in output, but have been taken in response to the ebb and flow of overseas payments. But as the previous chapter has shown, the time lags involved are such that 'discretionary' intervention has increased the almost comic amplitude of the British payments cycle and aggravated the underlying difficulties.

The alternative to the discretionary intervention, so beloved by authority figures of right and left, would be to have announced guidelines for fiscal and monetary policy. These would involve setting a *long-term target balance for the British Budget (or preferably the whole public sector) at a hypothetical 'high-employment' level of activity, and a steady annual target for the growth of the money supply*. (See pp. 147–54 and pp. 156–63). The exact figures of these targets would be less important than avoiding abrupt changes in them. Such a policy would have a strong built-in stabilizing effect. In a recession there would be an automatic increase in the Budget deficit and in the ratio of the money supply to output; in a

3. More ambitious 'expansionist' experiments may be attempted for a temporary period of a few years, if there has previously been moderate price stability – or reasonably stable inflation and people are slow to adjust their price expectations. Such experiments require a safety valve for the balance of payments. An opportunity in this direction was lost in the early 1960s, and will not quickly recur.

boom the Budget would move towards surplus and money would become tighter. This stabilizing effect might be frustrated if the velocity of circulation fell sufficiently in a recession and rose sufficiently in a boom; but even then the suggested rule would be less destabilizing than either tying monetary growth to actual output (instead of its trend rate) or than discretionary policy as operated in practice. The major advantage of a fixed rule is that it would prevent official policy from contributing to instability,[4] which would itself be an economic gain.

There are no rules without exceptions. Faced with a severe or prolonged recession it would be right to allow the money supply and the Budget deficit to increase more than could be expected automatically. But in most circumstances these long-term guidelines hold promise of a steadier growth of demand, both real and monetary, and a better climate for investment and corporate planning than we have had in this country since the war.

The obstacles to the rational conduct of economic policy imposed by a 'fixed' exchange rate have been a recurrent theme of this book in all editions. A flexible rate is of course no magic wand. Anyone who believes that home demand could then be allowed to rip without disastrous consequences is making a great mistake. Those who labour under any such misapprehension will discover the truth if and when a British government takes the plunge. A flexible rate can, however, correct international imbalances without forcing a deficit country into attempting a sudden reduction of its costs and prices or their rate of increase. Equally a surplus country would not be forced by international pressure, or the inflow of funds, to push up its rate of inflation (and thereby increase the world average).

Under a floating rate, an incipient deficit would be reflected at an early stage by downward movement in the exchange rate, which would encourage foreign demand for

4. See Friedman, *The Optimum Quantity of Money*, Macmillan, 1969, especially pp. 153-4.

British goods and discourage British demand for foreign goods. Conversely an above-target surplus would lead to an appreciation of sterling which would set opposite forces in motion. Contrary to popular superstition, exchange-rate changes would also be very likely to have an equilibriating effect on capital movements, both short-term and long-term. This is a general conclusion about international adjustment, not confined to Britain. But it is a system which this country can adopt on its own, without waiting for others.

The alternative of 'temporary' import controls is subject to grave objections. They are not only an inducement to domestic inefficiency. They create a false sense of security and do nothing to prevent a resumption of the deficit when they are removed. If a country that is short of reserves is facing a deficit which it really thinks is temporary, the appropriate course is to borrow from the IMF, which exists precisely for this purpose.

As a short book of mine on flexible and floating rates has just been published,[5] I can be brief about most of the supposed objections. The most popular one is that the resulting instability would be disturbing to trade. This objection is based on an implicit comparison with a dream world of perfect stability and on the false assumption that floating rates must be violently unstable.

Of more particular relevance at this point of the argument is the impact of a 'fixed' pegged exchange rate on internal policy. Lacking an external regulator the management of home demand has inevitably been mishandled. For, as explained *ad nauseum* in previous chapters, in the face of a run on the pound governments had to take deflationary action irrespective of whether the economy was already on the downturn or not; and the subsequent reflation came too late (and was therefore often excessive) for fear that earlier action might have upset either the balance of payments or overseas confidence in sterling. This was the origin of 'too much too late'. There is not the slightest

5. *The Price of Economic Freedom*, Macmillan, 1970.

chance of achieving the more stable long-term fiscal and monetary guidelines advocated above so long as we lack an external payments regulator. Mr Churchill's Conservative government missed its chance to free the British economy from its straitjacket in the early 1950s when it rejected the Robot Plan for putting the country on a floating rate of exchange (pp. 195–200).

Inside the UK the fixation of government policy with the balance of payments under a fixed exchange rate, so far from being the constraint that traditionalists suppose, has been an active agent of inflation. For it has the effect of drawing attention away from the real arguments against inflation, which are internal, and of suppressing all discussion on the merits of the issue. For long periods at a time governments allow inflation to gather momentum – either because the rest of the world is inflating or because there is a long lag between inflationary policies and subsequent payments difficulties. By the time 'tough measures' are applied, it is too late, as the currency is already overvalued, and there is no real alternative to a major devaluation, which itself gives the inflationary screw a further turn, as well as providing the authorities with a few more years of freedom from currency worries.

Equally important, every aspect of economic and foreign policy has been distorted by balance-of-payments fears, artificially created by a rigid exchange rate. Monopoly and merger policy, attitudes to tariffs and trade agreements, the degree of agricultural protection, the case for payroll taxes and many other issues were not decided on the basis of how best to use our domestic resources. Instead they were heavily influenced by the desire to make a marginal improvement in the balance of payments at an arbitrary exchange rate. Similarly the economic argument about the EEC at the time of writing is being conducted by all sides, not in terms of the likely effects on real incomes, but on an utterly misleading balance-of-payments basis.

TAXATION

Apart from balance of payments, demand management and incomes, the aspect of policy of closest concern to Chancellors has been the tax structure. Every politician would like to find tax reforms which would make many people better off and no one worse off. In opposition, or in the early stages of government, they hope to do this by major changes in the whole tax and public expenditure system. Chancellors of established governments hope to do the same by ingenious manipulation of individual tax rates.

Unfortunately the philosopher's stone for which they are looking does not exist. Tax handouts may be given in some years in the supposed interest of demand managements, just as taxes may be increased in other years for this reason. But it is an elementary error to confuse short-term cyclical variations with a long-term tax strategy. The tax burden must depend in the main on the movement of public expenditure. If revenue is very buoyant, rates may occasionally be reduced without upsetting the fiscal balance; this is simply a way of preventing the effective burden from increasing, and the apparent reduction is an optical illusion.

A magic word often used in this context is 'savings'. More savings can mean less taxes. But overwhelmingly the most important influence on the savings ratio is the growth of personal disposable incomes in relation to trend. This was exceptionally depressed in the five years up to 1969. If output and real incomes can resume a normal rate of growth the savings ratio will automatically benefit. But this will happen without any 'tax reforms'. All 'savings incentives' amount to an increase in the effective interest rates paid to lenders – although this may be disguised from the rest of the public by making them pay through the tax system rather than as borrowers. Yet it is just those politicians who talk most about savings incentives who complain most bitterly about high interest rates.

The present differentiation against investment income

amounts, together with the capital gains tax, to a considerable tax on the yield of savings. Taxing 'savings income' is very unpopular; taxing 'unearned' income more severely than earned income is very popular – an interesting example of the persuasive use of language. The worst socially regressive effects of abolishing the unearned income differential could be offset by a moderate wealth tax, starting at a fairly high level of capital ownership and/or an effective (but probably lower) system of death duties involving a gifts tax and the shift to a legacy basis.

Most of the politically influential plans for reducing taxes depend on reductions not of public expenditure on goods and services, but of transfer payments (see pp. 111–17). These reductions may or may not make good sense; but they do not create resources out of thin air. Let us take three examples: agricultural support, social-service payments and investment grants.

The 'savings' arising from switching from deficiency payments to levies are entirely spurious. The citizen pays less as taxpayer, and instead pays more for food in the shops. So long as farm support is a charge on the Budget there is at least some check on its size. Once it becomes just one of many items determining the cost of living, it is much more difficult to keep under control. While a change to levies may be a necessary evil as part of the bargain for EEC entry, to argue for the change on its own merits is an example of the triumph of naïve Budgetary arithmetic over the most elementary economics.

By contrast, a move from universal social benefits to selective payments to those whose incomes require supplementation would make excellent sense, especially if carried to its logical conclusion in a negative income tax. It would not do anything to increase taxpayers' real disposable incomes as is commonly understood. Tax might be cut; but so would, for example, family allowances and housing subsidies; any net gains by some would be at the expense of net losses by others.

Some of these changes should be warmly supported, as

they would increase the citizens' freedom of choice. But it is naïve in the extreme to equate real income gains with the crude tax savings. Let us take a skilled worker, who is deprived of a subsidy on a council house for which he now has to pay an economic rent and receives a tax cut in return, the whole transaction amounting to £100. He is in a real sense better off, as he can now choose whether to spend the £100 to stay in the same house, to help finance alternative accommodation, or for some entirely different purpose. Equally, however, it is absurd to regard the gain in his real income as anything approaching £100.

The switch from investment grants to tax allowances will be a trivial accountancy change. More interesting would be a reduction in the amount given. Companies could respond in some combination of the following three ways: they might reduce investment, raise prices, or borrow more in the market. Only a reduction in investment would make anything available for personal spending. To the extent that the other two routes are chosen, personal spending would be squeezed by a rise either in prices or in interest rates. Indeed it is these alternative consumer levies which would make the tax cuts possible.

The hard fact is that it is only at the top and at the bottom of the income range that improvements can readily be made in real disposable incomes, because of the small numbers involved. The decisive argument against the top rates of surtax on the upper ranges of incomes which prevailed up to the beginning of the 1970s was the trivial economic cost to the Exchequer of concessions in this direction. There was nothing to be lost by cutting drastically the more penal marginal rates, except from the point of view of those who derived a positive utility from the discomfiture of the better paid. There was in any case no justification for singling out *income* for specially severe treatment, when – despite nominally high rates of estate duty – large property owners were much more lightly treated; and it is in the distribution of property, rather than earned income, that the most glaring inequalities are to be found. The main impact of government policy on managers, executives and professional people in British business is through the taxes they pay. Other policies are less effective than they might be if personal financial success in these classes is pilloried as unworthy. The difficulty of demonstrating this contention at all rigorously does not absolve one from making a judgement.

More help to the poor would also be perfectly feasible, because they too are now a minority, although one cannot pretend it would be costless. But for the vast majority of the taxpayers who provide most of the revenue, nothing much can be done except through optical illusion. The discussion of fiscal questions would be enormously illuminated by treating taxation together with transfer payments and policies affecting prices and interest rates, as a single subject. The calculation of the public expenditure/tax burden given on p. 117 is an improvement on the conventional presentation; but it still does not get to the heart of the matter. What matters to people's living standards is real personal disposable income after tax, and the real value of public services received in kind. It is all too easy to think up vast switches in the tax system, involving hundreds or thousands of millions of pounds of nominal reductions, which after vast administrative upheaval and bitter political wrangles leave these key variables unaffected, or lead to small net changes in the distribution of incomes which could more easily be made directly.

Admittedly a given tax burden appears to be less resented if it is paid indirectly through higher prices in the shops than if it is levied directly on incomes. There would in normal circumstances be something to be said for respecting this ' tax illusion' of the public and making a net shift from direct to indirect taxes. Great caution should, however, be exercised about making such a shift in the early 1970s, when the problem of inflationary expectations looms so large. The decade has started with rapidly rising wages and prices;

and there are innumerable forces on the horizon which would give costs and prices a further upward twist. There are decimalization, equal pay for women and the possible effect on food prices of the Common Agricultural Policy, to name only a few instances. To add to these gratuitously by pushing up indirect taxes would be a dangerous exercise.

The above extremely sketchy outline of a few general principles of economic management is designed to provide a favourable environment for economic growth in a free society. These are, of course, only part of economic policy. Measures on the 'supply' or 'micro' side such as industrial training, policies to promote competition, tariff policy, company law and trade-union law, as well of course as the better management of the public sector, may in total be more important, even though they fall outside the scope of this book. Such measures can be presented either as sensible economic planning or as policies to secure a healthy market economy. Having had some experience in presenting the same wine in different bottles, this is one thing of which I am reasonably confident.

The question 'Are you in favour of government intervention in industry?' is one that a reasonable man should refuse to answer. It is the kind of intervention that is all-important. Economic liberalism is still a valid philosophy; *laissez faire* is not. The real distinction is between those who regard consumer demand as the main criterion of what should be produced and those who would like to substitute a more paternalistic system. Market imperfections, and the well-known discrepancies between private and social costs and benefits, are such that some intervention is required if consumer wants are to be correctly reflected and efficiently served by business enterprise. An economic liberal will prefer such intervention to take the form of removing obstacles to competition and using the price mechanism as a policy instrument (for example, to charge for scarce road or parking space) and he will dislike administrative forms of control for both practical and philosophical reasons. But the idea that the state can leave the ring altogether is merely fanciful. The interesting question concerns the nature rather than the extent of government intervention.[6]

THE EEC

The most agonizing contemporary issue for the economic liberal is undoubtedly that of British membership of the EEC. A more competitive business environment could probably do more for the British growth rate than any amount of committees, government grants or 'dynamic' industrial intervention. A change is needed in the market environment which will enable the efficient firm to go ahead more rapidly and speed the demise of the 'sleepers'. A reduction of barriers to international trade is much the most promising way of promoting such pressures. With vigorous international competition there would also be less need to worry about mergers and larger units at home.

The Kennedy Round tariff cuts which should be in full force by the early 1970s should indeed help here. Yet even then, effective tariff rates, reckoned as a percentage on value added, will still be sizeable. Added to these are 'non-tariff barriers', resulting from customs regulations, concealed subsidies, or government purchasing policies and other restrictive devices. Membership of a large trading area would combine the stimulus of more competition at home with more favourable market opportunities.

Viewed in purely economic terms a North Atlantic Free Trade Area would be an attractive way of achieving this result. But not only are there doubts about the political feasibility of NAFTA for some years to come; such an area, if formed, would be politically top-heavy in view of the inevitable American preponderance. So many British policy mistakes since the war, both of the kind discussed in

6. The political background is discussed in my book, *Left or Right: the Bogus Dilemma*, Secker & Warburg, 1968.

this book and in other areas, have been intimately associated with the idea of a 'special relationship' with the USA that one hesitates to recommend anything which would give such notions a new lease of life.

The main tangible benefit of membership of the EEC alternative would in fact lie in the reduction of the average level of tariff protection around British industry – a benefit which appears as a cost in the normal superficial balance-of-payments type of analysis. The much canvassed 'mass market' is more difficult to discover. The removal of the tariff barrier separating us from the Six would just about compensate for the loss of Commonwealth preference and the opening of the EFTA markets to the Six.

This way of putting it may slightly understate the longer-term opportunities if EEC markets continue to grow more rapidly than Commonwealth ones. More important, industrialists seem to find advantages in a geographically compact market compared with an equivalent but more scattered one. The political institutions of an enlarged EEC may also provide some insurance against a sudden imposition of government restrictions. They may even in time lead to a lessening of non-tariff barriers, a unification of capital markets and a common system of company law – although these goals are alas distant ones, thanks to the misguided order of priorities emanating from Brussels.

A zero or negative weight should be attached, however, to the fashionable arguments about advanced technological industries, such as aerospace or computers, in which Europe 'needs to unite' if it is to compete with the USA. Whenever he hears of 'advanced technology', the European taxpayer ought to be on his guard, as it is normally a pretext for making him subsidize high-cost prestige industries which do not pay commercially and which, as in the case of the Concorde, may have hideous social and economic side-effects, which do not appear in the books of the Departments or companies involved. The fact is that, owing to their large defence overheads, the Americans do have a comparative advantage in certain high-technology products; and it is entirely rational to purchase these products from the US or make them under licence, rather than develop them on this side of the Atlantic.

The strongest arguments for EEC membership are political ones. But to say this does not dispose of the issue or justify accepting any terms, however detrimental to the British standard of living. Nor does it justify an uncritical acceptance of the Brussels philosophy, which has no copyright on the name of 'European', and which indeed is more concerned with bureaucratic aggrandisement than with establishing a European voice on the world scene.

The two big issues which have to be resolved before British membership can be recommended are the agricultural and monetary ones. The true burden of the Common Agricultural Policy is measured, not by the balance-of-payments cost, but by the net payments to Brussels in levies and direct contributions and by the switch to high-cost European food from low-cost supplies further afield. The expansion of British agriculture, so far as it displaces Commonwealth or other cheap overseas foodstuffs, means a less efficient allocation of British resources and would be a burden rather than a benefit. The eventual cost of the Common Agricultural Policy, assuming equilibrium exchange rates, is likely to be in the region of 1–2 per cent of the GNP. This is far from negligible in relation to the probable benefits. We need not only a transitional period, but a clear limit to the size of the British contribution.

More important even than agriculture is the need to retain the ability to vary our exchange rate. The Brussels Commission's insistence on fixed exchange rates in a wider EEC and early monetary union are a classic confusion of ends and means. There is no chance of ruling out exchange-rate changes between countries with such different traditions of cost and price behaviour, and such different trade-union and management psychologies, as those of the proposed Community of Ten or even of the present Six. All that projects for 'monetary union' can do is to substitute acrimonious and disruptive revaluations or devaluations for the gradual exchange-rate changes favoured by more liberal economists.

In Britain's case nothing could be a greater mistake than to concentrate entirely on agriculture in the forthcoming negotiations and pay lip service to EEC ideas of monetary union. This attitude is equally disastrous if it is expressed in bad faith for diplomatic reasons, or in good faith by central bankers who fondly imagine that the exchange rate of the day can be maintained for all time – or that they can use the EEC to whip British governments into financial discipline.

There is a strong possibility of the transitional period of EEC membership beginning at a time when the competitive advantage of the 1967 devaluation has been eroded and we are once more on the verge of fundamental disequilibrium. We would then have to face large but uncertain transfer payments across the exchanges, and have therefore to choose between another substantial fixed-rate devaluation, severe domestic deflation or further international borrowing. The consequences of having to make such a choice would be disastrous, psychologically as well as politically – and the end result might be to embitter British relations with Europe for decades to come.[7]

A MISGUIDED ORIENTATION

Of the various conclusions in the original *Treasury Under the Tories*, the one I would now emphasize most concerns the excessive 'overseas' orientation among the upper reaches of British policy-makers, which gave priority to the maintenance of a world role the country could no longer carry. Although parts of the Treasury shared too much of this orientation for too long, the basic weaknesses of policy reflected deep-seated attitudes among a much wider circle.

7. The issue is discussed further, and certain British policy objectives for the EEC negotiations advanced, in my book *The Price of Economic Freedom*, Macmillan, 1970.

Here, in my view, is to be found the common factor behind our failure to join the European movement when we could have got in on our own terms, the crippling of the economy in the Korean armament drive, the failure to fund the sterling balances after the war, the long delay in re-thinking both the international role of sterling and its exchange parity, the investment of large resources in a series of military and aerospace projects, many of which had to be cancelled before completion, and the growth of over-seas defence commitments (the scaling down of which is still a subject of controversy). The thinking concerned was for a long time intimately connected with the idea of a special relationship with the United States; and similar 'top-table' attitudes are now reflected by some of the more enthusiastic Common Marketeers.

The view presented here may sound insular. But those who think so might ponder how low Britain's real influence in the world eventually sank as a result of the orthodox, outward-looking overseas and financial policies of the post-war period. While British leaders rushed from capital to capital on self-appointed international peace-making missions, the rest of the world was more conscious of the rustle of their begging bowl, their utter dependence on the USA, their repeated humiliation by de Gaulle on the Common Market issue and their inability to impose their will on the breakaway Rhodesian régime, still less to affect the course of events in the Middle or Far East. The climax came in November 1967, with a devaluation which in all but the technical sense was forced, and which it had been the main object of policy of both parties to avoid. None but the incurably blinkered can seriously believe that all would have been well if there had not been a Conserva-tive government in power up to 1964, or a Labour govern-ment in 1964–70.

The best that governments can do to help people recover a healthy patriotism and sense of national pride is to con-centrate on the welfare of the inhabitants of these isles. This may seem a prosaic form of patriotism, but it is the main alternative both to outmoded ideas of Britain's international position and to the narrow-minded xenophobia into which this country seems at times inclined to sink. Britain will eventually find a new and worthy role among nations, but the sooner the present preoccupation with the subject ceases, the sooner this role will be found.

INDEX

Action Committee for a United States of Europe, 238
Allen, Sir Douglas, 71–2, 388, 396
Amory, Derek Heathcoat (Viscount Amory), 143n., 193, 202, 219, 235, 241
Chancellor, 219–26, 228–30
Anderson, Sir John (Viscount Waverly), 188
Arab–Israeli War, 348, 367, 493
Armstrong, Robert, 81
Armstrong, Sir William, 71, 157, 271–2, 335, 345
Artis, M. J., 160
Aswan Dam, 206, 207
Atkinson, F. J., 96
Automatic Pilots, 479–83
See also Regulators

Balance of Payments,
forecasts, 148
1964 deficit, 284–5
1965 deficit, 321
1967 forecast, 342
1967 deficit, 348
1968 deficit, 387–92
'Pink Book', 390
1964–8 deficit, 389–92
1969 visible deficit, 395, 397–8
'missing exports', 397–8
July 1969 visible deficit, 400
August 1969 visible surplus, 400
recovery, 407, 408
1970 prospects, 413–15
underlying trends, 433–6
and stop–go, 448–50, 453–6
and growth rate, 456–60

and exchange-rate changes, 368–73
Ball, J. R., 462n.
Balogh, Thomas (Lord Balogh), 98
Bank of England, 99, 308, 344, 388, 393, 400, 405
relationship with Treasury, 54–5, 69
and sterling management, 77–83
role of, 83–7
and 1949 devaluation, 186
and floating exchange rate, 196–200
and 1957 sterling crisis, 213–14
and 1964 sterling crisis, 302–4
and 1967 devaluation, 356, 357, 358–9, 362–3
and money supply, 157, 163
and fiscal balance, 153
Bank for International Settlements (BIS), 89, 291, 359, 384, 434–6
Bank-Rate Changes, 79, 201–2, 211, 213–14, 255, 302–3, 308, 329, 330, 332, 348, 355, 358, 363, 392
Barber, Anthony,
Chancellor, 411, 412
Barry, Brian, 121
Basle Agreement, 1968, 386–9, 392
Beaver, Sir Hugh, 240
Beckerman, Wilfred, 98
Bell, Geoffrey, 81
Berman, L., 81
Berrill, Kenneth, 98

Betting Tax, 323

Bevan, Aneurin, 184

Birch, Nigel, 213

Bonn Conference, 1968, 391

Borrowing Requirements, and Budget, *see* Fiscal Balance

Brandon, Henry, 292n., 298–9, 302

Brechling, Fred, 453n.

Bretton Woods System, 403, 404, 481–3

Bridges, Sir Edward (Lord Bridges), 42, 43, 68–9

Bristow, J. A., 450

Brittan, Samuel, 66n., 470n., 489n., 492n.

Brook, Sir Norman (Lord Normanbrook), 71

Brookings Institution, *Report on UK*, 371–2, 374, 460

Brown, George (Lord George-Brown), 55–60, 242, 287, 289, 330–31, 338

First Secretary of State for Economic Affairs, 311–20

Brussels Commission, 491

Budget,

1952, 191

1953, 191

1954, 191–4

April 1955, 194, 200–203

October 1955, 194, 203, 214

1956, 205, 214

1957, 210

1958, 220–21, 223–6

1959, 223–4

1960, 228–9

April 1961, 258–9

1962, 265

1963, 280–82

April 1964, 258–9

November 1964, 300–301

1965, 305–7

1966, 324–8

1967, 319, 341–7

1968, 137, 138, 380–83, 408

1969, 149–51, 392–5, 407–8

1970 pre-election Budget, 405–12

1970 Barber 'Mini-Budget', 412

'judgement', 143, 147–8, 393

planning, 128–43

and concepts of economic management, 128–68

fiscal balance, 147–56

'high employment balance', 148–56, 167

and money supply, 63–8

Butler, R. A., 206, 214

Chancellor, 188–203

'Butskellism', 181, 187–90

Cabinet

and economic policy, 74–5

and responsibility, 65–6

Cairncross, Sir Alec, 38, 92, 95, 254

Callaghan, James, 49, 86–7, 88, 98, 202, 282, 289, 377, 383n.

Chancellor, 291–363, 373n.

and November 1964 Budget, 300–4

1965 Budget, 304–7

and 1965 sterling crisis, 308–10

and DEA, 313

and SET, 324–8

and July 1966 measures, 329–40

1967 Budget, 340–47

and REP, 345–6

and devaluation, 351–63

Capital Gains Tax, 206, 301, 305, 381

Capital Issues Committee, 211

Cassell, Frank, 81

Castle, Mrs Barbara, 38, 99, 406–7

Catherwood, Fred, 318

Central Economic Planning Staff (CEPS), 75

'Central Policy Review Staff', 102
Central Statistical Office (CSO), 73, 81
Centre for Administrative Studies, 32–3
Chapman, Brian, 34n., 35
Chapman, Richard, 28
Cheap Money, 159–60, 179–80
Cherwell, Lord, 96
Chester, D. N., 49
Chicago 'Monetarist' School, 157–8, 162
Churchill, Sir Winston, 188n., 189–90, 193, 196, 205, 483
and Operation Robot, 195–200
City Liaison Committee, 83
Civil Defence College, Sunningdale, 33
Civil Service, British,
policy-making and managerial functions, 23–7, 120
and Overseas Civil Service, 26–7
training and recruitment, 27–9, 30–36
pay, 31
career structure, 30, 32–6
specialization in, 36–7
economists, 38–40
characteristic attitudes, 41–4
and temporary Civil Servants, 55–60
secrecy, 60–66
numbers, 42
and economic policy, 470–72
Civil Service College, 33
Civil Service Commissioners, 28–9
Civil Service Department, 40–41, 48, 61, 120
Civil Service, French, 34. 59
Civil Service. Swedish, 44, 61
Civil Service, US, 34n.
Clarke Report, 448
Cobbold, Cameron (Lord Cobbold). 84, 188, 252

Committee on Expenditure, 103
Common Agricultural Policy, 491
Community of Ten (proposed), 491
Comptroller and Auditor General, 102–3
Concorde, 297, 490
Confederation of British Industries, 377
Consolidated Fund, 154
Contractual Savings Scheme (Save-As-You-Earn (SAYE), 394
Cooper, Richard N., 446n., 450
Corporation Tax, 258, 301, 306
Council on Prices, Productivity and Income, 210, 215
Cripps, Sir Stafford, 69–70, 92, 180, 182, 234, 242–3, 444
Cromer, Earl of, 84–5, 255, 302
Crosland, Anthony, 98
Customs and Excise Board, 143–6

Dalton, Hugh, 69, 159–60, 179–80, 199
Dayan, General Moshe, 367
Defence Expenditure, 108, 379, 414, 436–8, 493
Deming, Fred, 89
Denison, E. F., 429, 430–31
Department of Economic Affairs (DEA), 45, 73, 75, 96, 98, 130
forecasts, 94–5
role of, 98–9
relationship to other departments, 45, 310–13
and the Statement of Intent, 314–17
work of, 318–20
Department of Employment and Productivity, 75, 98–9
Devaluation
and Bank of England, 85–7
1949, 185–6

opposed by Wilson, 291–4, 334–7
1967, 353–66, 367–74
and international role of sterling, 446–8
Development Areas, 288
Devons, Ely, 24n.
Domestic Credit Expansion (DCE), 164–7, 388, 396, 401, 409
Durbin, Evan, 180

East of Suez policy, 379, 414, 493
Eaton, J. R., 272n.
Eccles, Sir David (Lord Eccles), 105, 265
Economic Advisers, 95–8
Economic Development Councils (EDCs or Little Neddies), 99, 318
Economic forecasts, 91–5
and Budget, 148, 156
and public expenditure, 115
Economic Management, concepts of, 128–58
Economic Planning Board, 243
Economic Situation, The, 296
Economic Survey, 190
1947, 181
1950, 181
1954, 193–4
1956, 206
1958, 212, 221
Edwards, Andrew, 81
Emminger, Otmar, 358, 405
Estimates, 110–11, 119
European Economic Community (EEC), 208, 222–3, 343, 355, 403–4, 413, 414, 471, 489–92
Britain's negotiations for membership, 236–8, 265
Britain's second negotiations for membership, 330, 348–9, 365
trading performance, 440–43

European Free Trade Association (EFTA), 298–300, 302–3, 490
European Monetary Agreement, 198–9
Exchange Rate, 216–17
floating, 195–200, 375, 402–3, 405
and welfare benefits, 423
argument about, 367–73
reform, 403–5
See also Devaluation
Expenditure (Public),
allocation, 107–8, 117–20
measurement, 111–17
definitions, 113–17
control, 101–9
and income distribution, 121–2
Export Rebate, 296
Exports, comparative figures, 440–44
See also Balance of Payments

Feather, Victor, 262
Federal Reserve, US, 384, 403, 406
Federal Reserve Bank of St Louis, 157
Federation of British Industries (FBI), 241–2
Brighton Conference, 239–40, 246
and the Statement of Intent, 314–17
Finance Act, 1965, 211
Finance Group, see Treasury
Financial and Economic Obligations of the Nationalized Industries, 122, 245–6
Fiscal Balance, 147–56, 408–9
Fisher, Sir Warren, 67–8
Five-Year Programmes, 104–9, 119
Flanders, June, 185n.
Fowler, Henry, 391

France,
Civil Service, 34, 59
departure from 'Gold Pool',
383
devaluation of franc, 211, 391,
400
Four-Year Plan, 238
growth rate, 429–31
Friedman, Milton, 157, 161, 451,
465, 474, 481n.
Fry, Richard, 438n.
Fulton Committee Report, 23, 24,
26, 27, 29, 32, 34, 35, 36, 37,
39–40, 44, 45, 50, 55–7, 61,
66, 120
Managerial   Consultancy
Group's Report, 37, 41

Gaitskell, Hugh, 180, 184, 226,
237
de Gaulle, Charles, 222, 237, 365,
383, 391, 493
Geddes, Sir Reay, 240
General Agreement to Borrow
(GAB), 88
General Agreement on Tariffs and
Trade (GATT), 299–300,
458–9
Germany,
German mark, 211, 252–3, 397
revaluation, 393, 395, 402–3
balance-of-payments surplus,
390–91
growth rate, 238, 420, 429–31
export performance, 439–40
Godley, W. A. H., 96–7, 149,
231n.
'Gold Pool', 383–4
Gold Speculation, 383
Goode, Richard, 377
Gordon-Walker, Patrick, 303
Grebenik, Eugene, 33
Group of Ten, 87–8, 404
Growth in the British Economy,
241

Growth Rate
under Selwyn Lloyd, 262–4
UK, compared with other
countries, 419–22
underlying, 427–31
and industrial reform, 431–3
and balance of payments, 456–
60

Hall, Sir Robert (Lord Robert-
hall), 48, 95–6, 180, 185, 194,
195–6, 210, 214, 224, 229,
248
Hamilton, Sir Horace, 68
Hare, John (Lord Blakenham),
243, 260, 267
Harrod, Sir Roy, 68, 459
Heath, Edward, 49, 85, 259, 410
President of the Board of Trade,
288–90
Helsby, Sir Lawrence, 260, 262
'High Employment' Balance,
148–56
Hire-Purchase Controls, 229, 231,
241, 323, 352, 388, 391
Hogg, Quintin (Lord Hailsham),
243, 265–6
Hopkin, Bryan, 96
Hopkins, Sir Richard, 68
House of Commons Standing
Order, 78, 102

Imports,
control of, 284, 375
Surcharge, 78, 296, 299, 302, 304
Income Tax, 280, 408
Income Distribution, 121–2
'Income-Velocity of Circulation',
159–60
Incomes Policy, 99
Thorneycroft's, 210
Maudling's, 287
Jenkins's 382–3, 406
voluntary, 322–3
and costs, 443–4

assessment of, 472–89
  See also Pay Pause, Wage Freeze
India, devaluation of rupee, 329
Industrial Organization Corporation (IRC), 319–20
Inland Revenue Board of, 139, 143–7
International Bank for Reconstruction and Development (IRBD), 90
International Development Association (IDA), 90
International Monetary Fund (IMF), 81, 82 87–8, 149, 157, 164, 165, 198, 210, 215, 304, 308, 329, 348, 371, 376, 377, 378, 385, 387, 389, 395–6, 397, 402, 403–5, 423
Investment Levels, 209–10, 458
Irregulars, *see* Civil Service

Jacobsson, Per, 255–6
Jay, Douglas, 303, 313
Jay, Peter, 119, 470n.
Jenkins, Peter, 63
Jenkins, Roy, 51, 60, 138, 142, 146, 339, 383, 399
  Chancellor, 378–409
Johnson, Harry, 365
Johnson, Lyndon B., 247, 362
Joint Statement of Intent on Productivity, Prices and Incomes, 314–17
Jones, Aubrey, 320

Kaldor, Nicholas, 98, 282, 325n., 345, 429n.
Keith, Kenneth, 83
Kennedy, John F., 238
Kennedy Round, 489
Kent, William, 46
Keynes, John Maynard (Lord Keynes), 68, 70, 82, 187, 472
'Keynesian' Economics, 147, 151, 153, 156, 159, 160, 162, 472

King, Cecil, 400, 401
Kipping, Sir Norman, 286–7
Knapp, John, 428–9
Korean War, 181, 183–5, 493
Krause, Lawrence B., 439n.
Kristensen, Thorkil, 292
Kuwait Gap, 211

Larre, M., 360
Lawson, Nigel, 267n.
Lee, Sir Frank, 71, 209, 229, 233–8, 242, 245, 246, 247, 259, 271–2
Letter of Intent, 395–7, 398
Lever, Harold, 396, 398, 399
Liquidity, 203
Little, I. M. D., 450
Lloyd, Selwyn, 105, 202, 207–8, 210, 270, 271, 273, 274, 291, 327, 338, 443–4, 458
  Chancellor, 232–67
  appraisal, 232–5
  and application to join EEC, 236–8
  and NEDC, 238–45
  and 1961 sterling crisis, 251–6
  and the pay pause, 257–61
  1962 Budget, 264–6
  dismissed, 266–9
Lomax, David, 387n.
Lovell, A. H., 81
Low, Sir Toby (Lord Aldington), 126–7
Lyttleton, Oliver (Lord Chandos), 197

MacArthur, General, 183
MacDougall, Sir Donald, 49, 95, 96, 98, 196, 345
Machinery of government, 468–72
Macleod, Iain, 147, 259, 265–6, 410
Macmillan, Harold, 128, 188, 194, 270, 272, 299
  Chancellor, 203–7

Prime Minister, 207 ff.
and his Chancellors, 217–19
and the EEC, 236–8
and Selwyn Lloyd's pay pause, 260–62
and Lloyd's dismissal, 268
Maddison, Angus, 429n.
Makins, Sir Roger (Lord Sherfield), 71, 208–9, 212, 214, 224n., 229
Marples, Ernest, 265
Marshall Aid, 182
Marshall, Alfred, 278
McChesney Martin, William, 397
Matthews, R. C. O., 450, 454
Maudling, Reginald, 49, 85, 142, 242, 244, 259, 296, 315
Chancellor, 270–90
Middle Eastern War, 348, 367, 493
Mill, John Stuart, 113–14
Mills, Lord, 265
Ministers, and Civil Servants, 41–2, 43, 52–5
Mitchell, Jean, 184n.
Monckton, Sir Walter, 193
Money Supply, 156–67, 388, 401
Monnet, Jean, 238
Morrison, Herbert, 69
Mortgage, option, 323

Nasser, President, 367
National Board for Prices and Incomes (NBPI or PIB), 99, 320, 382
National Economic Development Council (NEDC), 50, 75, 96, 99, 235, 278–80, 286
formation of, 242–5
and growth rate, 262–4
National Economic Development Office, forecasts, 94
National Incomes Commission, 262

National Income Forecast (NIF), 93
National Institute of Economic and Social Research, 48–9, 234, 281, 309
National Insurance, 149, 275
and the regulator, 249–50
National Loans Fund, 154–6
National Plan, 94, 106, 109, 290, 305, 309, 315
Nationalized Industries, control of expenditure, 122–7
Nationalized Industries: Review of Economic and Financial Objectives, 1967, 124, 126, 235, 245–6
Neild, Robert, 98
Nobay, A. R., 160
Norman, Montagu, 84, 188
North Atlantic Free Trade Area (NAFTA), 489
Nuffield College, Oxford, 49

O'Brien, Sir Leslie, 85, 337, 357, 359, 399
Official Secrets Act, 60, 62
Opie, Roger, 470
Organization for Economic Cooperation and Development (OECD), 87, 281, 359, 388, 389n., 412
Organization for European Economic Co-ordination (OEEC), 259
Ossola, R., 358
Overseas Development Ministry, 90

Page, Robin, 62n.
Paish, Professor F., 337
Pay Pause, Selwyn Lloyd's, 257–61
Payroll Tax, 248–9
Personal Tax, 408
Phillips, Sir Frederick, 80

Planning Board, 242–3
Planning, Programming and Budgeting (PPB), 117–18
Playfair, Sir Edward, 103
Plowden, Sir Edwin (Lord Plowden), 95–6, 105, 196, 274
Plowden Report, 104–5, 107, 109, 118–19, 120, 235
Polak, J. J., 165
Political Economy Club, 48
Pompidou, Georges, 331, 391
Posner, Michael, 98
Pound sterling, *see* Sterling
Powell, Enoch, 213
Premium Bonds, 206
Prices and Incomes Act, 344–5, 382
Priestley Royal Commission, 1955, 26
Profits Tax, 229, 258
Public Accounts Committee, 41, 103
Public Expenditure Surveys, 105–11
Public Loans Works Board, 308
Purchase Tax, 274–5, 381, 393
Purchase Tax, regulator, 247–8, 274

Radcliffe Report on the Monetary System, 83, 84–5, 156–7, 208, 222, 224n., 229, 332–3
Reading, Brian, 387n.
Reddaway Report, 306
'Redeployment', 337–8
Rees, Graham L., 196n.
Rees-Mogg, William, 324
Regional Boards of Government, 318
Regional Councils, 318
Regional developments, 288
Regional Employment Premium (REP), 345–7
Regulators, 246–51, 273, 335–6, 391, 479–83

Resale Price Maintenance, 290
Reserves, UK, 422–3
Restrictive Practices Act, 232
'Revenue Departments', 130
Rhodesia, 51, 342, 493
Richardson Committee, 147
Robbins, Lord, 213
Robbins Report on Higher Education, 288
Robertson, Sir Dennis, 210
Robinson, Austin, 459
Robot, Operation, 195–200, 483
Rogow, A. A., 181
Roll, Sir Eric, 298–9, 335
Roseveare, Henry, 67
Rothschild, Lord, 102
Rowan, Sir Leslie, 212, 237n.
Royal Commission on the Civil Service, 1955, 26

Sales Tax, 247
Salter, Sir Arthur (Lord Salter), 196, 200
Samuelson, Paul, 31, 52
Schiller, Karl, 395
Schultze, Charles L., 112n.
Schweitzer, Pierre-Paul, 358, 359, 360, 362, 404
Select Committee on Estimates, 103–4
Select Committee on the Nationalized Industries, 104, 126–7
Seamen's Strike, 329, 342
Selective Employment Tax (SET), 141, 249, 307, 346, 381, 393
   introduction of, 324–8
'September Measures', 1957, 211–17, 219
Sheldon, Robert, 360–61
Shepherd, J. R., 231n.
Shone, Sir Robert, 244, 249
Shonfield, Andrew, 184n.
Shore, Peter, 181n., 351–2

South Africa, and gold market, 384, 385
Special Deposits, 164, 229, 307, 332, 412
Special Drawing Rights (SDRs), 87, 351, 385, 404, 413
Steering Committee on Economic Policy (SEP), 74
Sterling,
  management, 77–83
  1957 crisis, 211–14
  1961 crisis, 251–62
  1964 crisis, 298–304
  1965 crisis, 308–10
  1966 crisis, 329–40
  1967 crisis, 347–66, 367, 368
  persistent weakness of, 1969, 397
  international role of, 447–8, 454–5
Sterling Area, 222, 378, 386, 392
Steuer, M. D., 462n.
Stevenson, Mark, 259
Stewart, Michael, 338, 344–5
'Stop-go',
  analysis of, 448–56
Strauss, Franz Josef, 395
Suez Affair, 206–7
Surtax, 235, 258
Sweden,
  Civil Service, 44, 61
  policy-making ministries, 146
Swinton, Lord, 189–90

Taxation, 14, 484–9
  tax structure, 143–7
  and Budget, 133–41, 147
  reform, 143–7, 410
  proposed regulator under Selwyn Lloyd, 246–51
  and income distribution, 121–2
  See also Income Tax, Purchase Tax, etc.
Terms of Trade, UK, 425–6
Thomas, Hugh, 470n.

Thorneycroft, Peter, 219, 230, 253
  Chancellor, 207–19
Trade Performance, UK, 401–2, 438–44
Trades Union Congress (TUC), 50, 310
  and Cripps's wage freeze, 182
  and formation of NEDC, 242, 244–5
  and Selwyn Lloyd's pay pause, 260–62
  and 1964 incomes policy, 286
  and Statement of Intent, 314–17
Travel Allowance, 336, 350
Treasury, 24, 120
  characteristics, 46–52
  Economic Section, 91–100
  Finance Group, 77–83
  officials, 75–6
  organization, 72–7
  Permanent Secretaries, 67–72
  and 1970 new appointees, 98
Treasury Advisory Committee, 189–90
Treasury Bills, 164, 165, 446
Treasury Buildings, 46–7
Trend, Sir Burke, 43, 52, 335
Tuesday Club, 48

Unemployment, 223, 228, 275–7, 292, 321–2, 324, 333–4, 336–8, 350, 407, 455–6
  and Budget planning, 131–6
  and development areas, 276–7
  and wages, 463–7
  and inflation, 472–83

Value-Added Tax (VAT), 247, 414
Van Lennep, Emile, 291–2, 358
Vietnam War, 376, 383
Vote on Account, 379

Wages
  and demand, 460–67

Cripps freeze, 182–3
under Butler, 193–5
and unemployment, 463–83
See also Incomes Policy, Pay Pause
Waley, Sir David, 80
Walter, Alan, 160
Washington Gold Agreement, 1968, 383–5
Wheeler-Bennett, Sir John, 188n.
Wilson, Harold, 47–8, 73, 75, 103, 184, 227, 236, 253, 259, 279, 285, 290, 444
opposition to devaluation, 292–4
economic philosophy of, 294–5
and 1964 sterling crisis, 298–304
and 1966 sterling crisis, 329–39
optimism in 1967, 339–43, 377

and physical intervention in the economy, 351–3, 370
and 1967 devaluation, 353–6
post-devaluation strategy, 367–409
Wilson, Sir Horace, 68
Wilson, Thomas, 452
Winnifrith, A. J. D., 46n.
Wolfe, J. N., 453n.
Wood, Sir Kingsley, 128, 189
Wood, Richard, 260
Woodcock, George, 262
Woolton, Lord, 52–3, 190, 190n., 193
Working Party Three (WP$_3$), 87–8, 359
World trade forecasts, 93
Worswick, G. D. N., 211n.

MORE ABOUT PENGUINS
AND PELICANS

Penguinews, which appears every month, contains details of all the new books issued by Penguins as they are published. From time to time it is supplemented by *Penguins in Print*, which is a complete list of all books published by Penguins which are in print. (There are well over three thousand of these.)

A specimen copy of *Penguinews* will be sent to you free on request, and you can become a subscriber for the price of the postage. For a year's issues (including the complete lists) please send 30p if you live in the United Kingdom, or 60p if you live elsewhere. Just write to Dept EP, Penguin Books Ltd, Harmondsworth, Middlesex, enclosing a cheque or postal order, and your name will be added to the mailing list.

Some other books published by Penguins are described on the following pages.

Note: *Penguinews* and *Penguins in Print* are not available in the U.S.A. or Canada

A Penguin Special

THE LABOUR GOVERNMENT
1964–70

Brian Lapping

This book describes the six years of Wilson's parliament and examines the area of manoeuvre available to the government. It discusses the kinds of choice the government actually made and where, if at all, Tory policy differed.

The author, a committed Labour party man, believes both Wilson and Heath to be men of the centre, and that therefore their policies are virtually indistinguishable. His analysis is one of six years of consensus government – but consensus precisely because the range of activity open to parliament is severely limited by the logic of the choices made by governmental apparatus. One of the problems that became clear during these six years was the growing need to restore the power of government to parliament.

Lapping develops the history of governmental activity, illustrating this struggle and illustrating, too, the struggle of the Labour Party to reconcile its principles with the limitations placed on its choice of action.

A Pelican Original

BRITAIN IN FIGURES
A Handbook of Social Statistics

Alan F. Sillitoe

How many tourists do we have each year? How much tax do we pay compared to other countries? What exactly is our balance of payments position, and how much time do we spend on gardening and knitting?

This extraordinarily graphic account of what we in Britain are and do now, and have been and did recently, has been drawn up by Alan F. Sillitoe, Senior Lecturer in Sociology at the University of London Goldsmiths' College. It is a venture of great competence and originality which, in the interest of solving arguments quickly, no home can afford to be without.

21 POPULAR ECONOMIC FALLACIES

E. J. Mishan

Increased taxation must lead to inflation.
Prices should cover costs.
A large home market helps exports.
The country needs immigrants to meet labour shortage.
Economic growth enriches society.

Such are some of the axioms from which people start their economic thinking today. Dr Mishan of the London School of Economics, who wrote *The Costs of Economic Growth*, examines twenty-one such elementary fallacies in this entertaining and instructive book. 'It is important', he writes, 'that official complacency be ruffled a little and that post-war orthodoxies be exposed for the humbug they are.'

'The perfect book for anyone wishing to start the study of economics' – *Economist*

'Can be recommended as a course of shock treatment not only for our bewildered citizenry but also for the political and other creators of that bewilderment' – George Schwartz in the *Sunday Times*

Not for sale in the U.S.A.

ECONOMIC PLANNING AND DEMOCRACY

Firmin Oulès

The currents of economic planning and democratic freedom run counter. Hence one of our acutest dilemmas.

Professor Oulès, leader of 'The New Lausanne School' of economists, faces this difficulty squarely in a new Pelican in which he effectively 'demystifies' the economic complex of Western Europe, laying bare the forces which determine the array of facts and figures we call economics. His examination is both honest and intelligent, and he comments forcefully on the anti-democratic trend of 'indicative planning', as practised notably in France.

As an alternative Professor Oulès makes his own recommendation. It is for 'planning by enlightenment' – a concept which combines budgetary coordination, at the national level, with the systematic provision of enough data for industry, finance, commerce, and labour to act rationally yet freely.

Economic Planning and Democracy is at once a brilliantly clear exposition of the material realities of trade and industry and a constructive solution of a problem which is today admitted by most politicians and economists.

A Pelican Original

BRITAIN AND THE WORLD ECONOMY

J. M. Livingstone

In the world's market-place every country keeps a stall and every country goes shopping. The result – in currency, credit, and kind – is a network of transactions as intricate and alive as a printed circuit.

Britain and the World Economy is a short, readable survey of the part played by one country in this world network. Britain, partly by necessity, partly by choice, plays a variety of economic roles in the world and J. M. Livingstone emphasizes the country's growing dependence on events abroad in this examination of her contributions as an international banker operating the sterling system; as the leader of a still powerful Commonwealth; as a force in a revitalized Europe; as a world trader; and as a 'have' with responsibilities towards the 'have-nots'.

ECONOMIC PHILOSOPHY

Joan Robinson

This exceptionally stimulating book begins by showing how the basic human need for a morality on which the conscience can work has led to the necessity for a philosophy of economics in any society. It is stressed that economic values and money values are not identical and it is the task of the economist to justify the image of Mammon to man 'not to tell us what to do, but show why what we are doing anyway is in accord with proper principles'. The relations between science and ideology over the last two hundred years are traced from Adam Smith, through Marx and Keynes, to the dichotomy that exists in current economic thinking and the pressing fundamental problems which must now be faced.

'It would be difficult to think of a better book than this to place in the hands of the reader who thinks that economics is simply a matter of statistics, and who needs to be convinced of its intellectual interest and excitement' – Samuel Brittan in the *Observer*

Not for sale in the U.S.A.